John M. Baugh
2-25-01

Greenhill Books

1815
THE
WATERLOO
CAMPAIGN

"It is on account of these little stories, which must come out, that I object to all the propositions to write what is called a history of the battle of Waterloo. If it is to be a history, it must be the truth, and the whole truth, or it will do more harm than good and will give as many false notions of what a battle is, as other romances of the same description have. But if a true history is written, what will become of the reputation of half of those who have acquired reputation, and who deserve it for their gallantry, but who, if their mistakes and casual misconduct were made public, would not be so well thought of? I am certain that if I were to enter into a critical discussion of everything that occurred from the 14th to the 19th June, I could show ample reason for not entering deeply into these subjects. "

From a letter from the Duke of Wellington to the Earl of Mulgrave, written in Paris on 21 December 1815. WSD, vol XIV, pp 619–20.

1815
THE
WATERLOO CAMPAIGN

Wellington, his German Allies and the
Battles of Ligny and Quatre Bras

PETER HOFSCHRÖER

GREENHILL BOOKS, LONDON
STACKPOLE BOOKS, PENNSYLVANIA

1815: The Waterloo Campaign
first published 1998 by

Greenhill Books, Lionel Leventhal Limited,
Park House, 1 Russell Gardens, London NW11 9NN

and

Stackpole Books,
5067 Ritter Road, Mechanicsburg, PA 17055, USA

British Library Cataloguing in Publication Data
Hofschröer, Peter
1815 : the Waterloo campaign
Wellington and his German allies to 16 June 1815
1.Waterloo, Battle of, 1815
I.Title II.Eighteen fifteen
940.2'7

ISBN 1-85367-304-8

Library of Congress Cataloging-in-Publication Data
Hofschröer, Peter
1815 : the Waterloo campaign / Peter Hofschröer
p.   cm.
Includes bibliographical references and index.
Contents: v. 1. Wellington and his German allies to 16 June 1815.
ISBN 1-85367-304-8
1. Waterloo, Battle of, 1815--Foreign public opinion, German--Sources.
2. Public opinion--Germany--Sources. 3. Napoleon I, Emperor of the French,
1769-1821--Military leadership--Sources. 4. Wellington, Arthur Wellesley,
Duke of, 1769-1852--Military leadership-- Sources.   I. Title
DF241.5.H64 1998
940.2'742--dc21   97-31647
                                                   CIP

Edited and designed by Donald Sommerville
Maps drawn by John Richards
Printed and bound in Great Britain by
Creative Print and Design (Wales), Ebbw Vale

Contents

List of Tables and Appendices   6
List of Illustrations   7
List of Maps   8
Acknowledgements   9
Quotations and Sources   12
Abbreviations and Conventions   13

     Preface   15
     The Leading Allied Personalities   19
1   Europe before Waterloo   27
2   Wellington and the Germans   39
3   The Prussian Army of 1815   59
4   Wellington's German Contingents   70
5   Plans to Defend the Netherlands   84
6   Preparations for War   103
7   The Outposts   124
8   Intelligence and Communications   136
9   The Advance on Charleroi   161
10   The Breakthrough to Frasnes   192
11   The Night of 15 June   209
12   The Morning of 16 June   223
13   The Battle of Ligny-Quatre Bras   248
14   'Mine Enemy' the Prussians   331

Appendices   352
Orders of Battle   370
Bibliography   383
Index   391

List of Tables and Appendices

Organisation of the King's German Legion   72
Organisation of the Hanoverian Infantry   76
Hanoverian Forces in 1815   76
Organisation of the Brunswick Corps   78
Organisation of the Nassau Contingent   81
Forces around Frasnes on the Afternoon of 15 June 1815   202
The Frasnes Letter   337
The Frasnes Letter and de Lancey 'Disposition'   338
The de Lancey 'Disposition' and the   339
    'Memorandum on the Battle of Waterloo'
Casualty charts, 15 and 16 June 1815:   348
    Prussian Army of the Lower Rhine
Casualty charts, 15 and 16 June 1815:   349
    The Anglo-Dutch-German Army
Timetable of events on 15 June 1815   352
Messages 15–16 June 1815   354
Wellington's Headquarters Papers   356
A comparison of the de Lancey 'Disposition'   357
    with the actual situation
Where the Anglo-Dutch-German forces really were   360
The 'Missing Letters'   366
Timetable of events on 16 June 1815   368
Speeds at which bodies of troops marched   369

    Orders of Battle

Prussian Army, 15 and 16 June 1815   370
French Army, Ligny, 16 June 1815   374
French Army, Quatre Bras, 16 June 1815   378
Anglo-Dutch-German Army, Quatre Bras, 16 June 1815   380

List of Illustrations

Between pages 160 and 161

1. Arthur Wellesley, first Duke of Wellington
2. Napoleon Bonaparte
3. Napoleon on the road from Grenoble
4. Gebhard Lebrecht von Blücher
5. Neidhardt von Gneisenau
6. Hans Joachim von Zieten
7. Friedrich Graf Kleist von Nollendorf
8. News of the breakthrough to Quatre Bras
9. Johann Adolph Freiherr von Thielemann
10. Karl von Borstell
11. The British attacking at Quatre Bras
12. The Battle of Ligny
13. Jean Victor de Constant Rebeque
14. The Earl of Uxbridge
15. Blücher's fall at Ligny
16. Friedrich Wilhelm III of Prussia
17. Carl von Clausewitz
18. Jean Baptiste van Merlen
19. Carl von Müffling
20. Prinz August von Thurn und Taxis
21. Sir Thomas Picton
22. Friedrich August of Saxony
23. Henckel von Donnersmark
24. Friedrich Bülow von Dennewitz
25. Prinz Wilhelm, later Emperor of Germany

List of Maps

1. Prussia's expansion plans 34
2. The Theatre of War 110
3. Cantonments of the Prussian 1st Brigade 128
4. Part of Belgium showing the Theatre of War 144
5. Positions of the French Army, evening of 14 June 158
6. Positions of the three armies, on the night of 14–15 June 162
7. Positions of the three armies, at 2.30 a.m. 15 June 166
8. Charleroi and environs 175
9. The region of Gilly and Gosselies 180
10. The French Army, evening of 15 June 204
11. Positions of the Anglo-Dutch-German Army, 6–7 p.m. 15 June 210
12. Positions of the Anglo-Dutch-German Army, 10 p.m. 15 June 214
13. Actual positions of Wellington's army, 7 a.m. 16 June, 226
    and of the French and Prussians
14. Positions of Wellington's army, 7 a.m. 16 June, as given in the 230
    de Lancey 'Disposition', and of the French and Prussians
15. Positions of the three armies, 2 p.m. 16 June 240
16. Quatre Bras and Ligny, 2.00 to 2.30 p.m. 16 June 246
17. The Battlefield of Ligny 250
18. Ligny: Movements of the Prussian I. Armeekorps 252
    prior to 10 a.m.
19. Ligny: arrival of the Prussian II. and III. Armeekorps, 254
    and the first French positions
20. Ligny: French dispositions, 2.30 p.m. 256
21. Ligny: Prussian dispositions, 2.30 p.m. 258
22. The Battle of Ligny, 2.30 p.m. 266
23. Ligny: French assaults on St Amand, 3.00 to 3.45 p.m. 268
24. Ligny: Prussian counter-attacks, 4–5 p.m. 272
25. Positions of the three armies, 5 p.m. 276
26. Ligny: Pêcheaux's, Hanbert's and Domon's attacks 280
27. Ligny: 6–7 p.m. 282
28. Ligny: Prussian counter-attack, 6–7.30 p.m. 284
29. The Battle of Quatre Bras, 2 p.m. 290
30. The Battle of Quatre Bras, 3.15 p.m. 296
31. Ligny: Vichery, Vandamme and Girard 310
32. Ligny: Preparations for the French general assault, 6 p.m. 314
33. Ligny: Appearance of an unidentified Corps, 6 p.m. 316
34. Ligny: Final French assault, 7–9.30 p.m. 320
35. Ligny: Retreat of the Prussians, 9.30 p.m. 322
36. Ligny: Final positions, 10 p.m. 324

Acknowledgements

My thanks go firstly to Dr David Chandler for his consistent support and encouragement over the many years I have enjoyed his friendship, as well as for his assistance in obtaining access to some of the sources used in the preparation of this work. Thanks to his ability constantly to engender interest in the period, the current generation of Napoleonic enthusiasts probably owes more to this man than to any other. I am also much obliged to Colonel John R. Elting, with whom I much appreciated exchanging correspondence; his razor sharp mind caused me to tidy up many a point and helped shape the final result; also to John Houlding for his advice on the English-language sources and his encouragement to persist, as well as his numerous suggestions on improvements to the text. These two kind people played an important role in making this work what it is.

My thanks also go to George Nafziger, ever helpful, for providing part of the source material; to Jim Bambra, one time games designer at MicroProse Software for drawing my attention to the Waterloo Campaign and getting me finally to do some serious research on the subject; and to Phil Lawrence of Alma Miniatures for making me realise that it was even interesting and worth my attention.

I am also grateful to Dr Charles Esdaile for providing me with a list of published sources on the British political history of the time. The encouragement and practical assistance of my father, Heinrich Paul Hofschröer, should also be acknowledged. Dr Michael Occleshaw and John Cook also deserve mention for their responses to many of my ideas during the conception of this work. Their considered opinions were always taken into account. To David Hollins, I owe a special word of thanks, not only for his assistance in obtaining certain of the sources used here, but also for his expert advice as a lawyer of great merit on aspects of the text. I am particularly indebted to Derek S. Mill for his constant help in using the 'Waterloo Correspondence', and for allowing me to benefit from his great knowledge of Waterloo source material. I should also thank Robert Hornby and Rod MacArthur for their responses to my requests for assistance. The specialist knowledge on manuscript sources which Professor Spiers of the University of Leeds shared with me was of great assistance. Geert van Uythoven kindly helped me obtain several important Dutch works. Pierre de Wit and Patrick Maes were kind enough to provide me with assistance in obtaining several sources. The latter also shared with me his expert knowledge on the battlefield of Ligny. David Stewart was kind enough to obtain copies of important documents for me from the Public Record Office of Northern Ireland in Belfast.

My thanks also go to John White of the Waterloo Committee for his help, as well as to Dr M.R. Howard, Claude Whistler and Jacques Logie. I also greatly appreciated Glenn A. Steppler's guidance on British regimental archives. I am also grateful to Hans-Joachim Boschen for all the encouragement he gave me during the writing of this work, as well as for the doors he opened for me. R.J. Wyatt was kind enough to share with me his expertise on material referring to the Duke of Wellington. My thanks go also to Georg Ortenburg for his assistance in obtaining access to and using material from various archives. A special thought goes to both Stephen Petty and Frederick White, both admirers of the first Duke of Wellington. Despite their personal views on the subject, and their great sadness, they did not stop selflessly supporting and encouraging my researches. My thanks also go to Arthur Harman for his expert advice and assistance in obtaining part of the source material used, as well as for sharing his knowledge of the period with me.

Not to be forgotten are Mike Taylor and his companion Lynne who were kind enough to offer me shelter during most of my many visits to London when researching this work. Mike had to listen to my progress reports every evening. His interest in the subject matter was such that he often left me talking to his cats, no doubt now among the best informed creatures on this subject.

Private Archives & Collections

Lord Raglan was most helpful, responding to all my questions on his ancestor, Fitzroy Somerset, and indicating the whereabouts of his papers. The Earl of Cathcart and Marquess of Anglesey kindly allowed me access to their family papers, and the latter engaged in a long correspondence with me. Viscount Colville went to great lengths to provide me with copies of documents from his archives for which I am most grateful. Virginia Murray of John Murray (Publishers) Ltd kindly provided me with information from that company's records.

Institutions

On several occasions, Dr Peter Boyden of the National Army Museum kindly assisted my searches for manuscript materials. The staff and students of the Hartley Library at the University of Southampton also helped with my researches into the Wellington Papers, and I am particularly grateful to Karen Robinson, Mark Romans and to Dr Christopher Woolgar. The latter was kind enough to respond to my constant enquiries about the Papers, and I only hope I was not too tedious. Special thanks must go the Susan Corrigall of the National Register of Archives (Scotland) who went to considerable pains to assist me in obtaining copies of various documents. David Rimmer of the Gwent County Archives did much to help me, as did Una O'Sullivan of the Royal Commission on Historical Manuscripts. Major P.A. Lewis, Regimental Archivist of the Grenadier Guards, provided me with every possible assistance, as did John Westmancote, to name but one of many British Library staff who contributed their man-hours to my efforts.

My gratitude is due to the following archives, museums and libraries that assisted me with my researches: County Archives Service, Dorset; Southwark Local Studies Library, London; Niedersächsisches Hauptstaatsarchiv, Hanover; Department of Manuscripts & Special Collections, University of Nottingham; Kriegsarchiv, Vienna; Geheimes Staatsarchiv Preussischer

Kulturbesitz, Berlin; British Library, London; Bodleian Library, Oxford; Manuscripts Department, Trinity College, Dublin; Militärbibliothek, Potsdam; Militärgeschichtliches Forschungsamt, Freiburg; the Bundesarchiv – Militärarchiv, Freiburg; Royal Engineers Museum and Library, Chatham; RAMC Historical Museum, Aldershot; Wellcome Medical Museum, London; Algemeen Rijksarchief, the Hague; National Army Museum, London; Public Record Office, London; Public Record Office of Northern Ireland, Belfast; Deutsches Adelsarchiv, Marburg; Museum of the King's Royal Hussars, Winchester; Hessisches Hauptstaatsarchiv, Wiesbaden; Manuscripts Division, National Library of Scotland; the Royal Commission on Historical Manuscripts; the National Register of Archives (Scotland), Edinburgh; the British Embassy in the Hague; the Bibliothèque Nationale de France, Paris; the Koninklijke Landmacht, Sectie Militaire Geschiedenis, the Hague; Landesbibliothek, Koblenz; Stadtbibliothek, Gütersloh; and any other archive, library or museum whose kind assistance I may have inadvertently omitted.

Without the help of all those people mentioned above, this project would have been much more difficult to complete. Having said that, the responsibility for all errors in this work is mine.

Finally I would like to thank my publisher, Lionel Leventhal, his colleagues Kate Ryle and Jonathan North, my editor, Donald Sommerville, and John Richards, who drew all the maps.

I am sure that this will not be the last word on the subject; if anything, only the beginning of the end, though now that most archive sources available on this matter are available for inspection, surely not much more can be said?

Quotations and Sources

I have reproduced many quotations in this book from sources not in the English language. I have translated each of these into English myself and am therefore entirely responsible for any possible mistranslation. As all the sources used for the quotations are given, the reader is welcome to examine the originals and make his own mind up as to how accurate the translations are. Where sources not originally in the English language have already been translated into English, I have still tried to refer to the original work and translate the parts used into English myself. This may explain any minor differences between the wording of quotations appearing in this work and the versions used in other works.

In the interests of saving, space footnote references have been abbreviated as follows:

BL	British Library, London
DNB	Dictionary of National Biography, Oxford (1921–22 edn.)
GGS	Grosser Generalstab (German General Staff), Berlin
GStA	Geheimes Staatsarchiv Preussischer Kulturbesitz, Berlin
JSAHR	*Journal of the Society of Army Historical Research*, London
MWBl	*Militair-Wochenblatt*, later *Militär-Wochenblatt*, Berlin
NAM	National Army Museum, London
NLS	National Library of Scotland, Manuscripts Division
PRO	Public Record Office, London
USJ	*United Services Journal*, London
WD	Gurwood, *Dispatches of Field Marshal The Duke of Wellington*
WP	Wellington Papers, University of Southampton
WSD	Wellington, 2nd Duke of, *Supplementary Despatches, Correspondence, and Memoranda of Field Marshal Arthur Duke of Wellington*

The accounts of the combats consist largely of extracts from official reports and eye-witness accounts of the German participants. As such, these accounts are one-sided, and not necessarily the whole story. To endeavour to obtain a more balanced view of those events, readers should refer to the many accounts available that are written from a British or French point of view.

Abbreviations and Conventions

Army corps and divisions in all armies have been designated following the usual style of roman numerals for corps and arabic ordinal numbers for divisions (III Corps, 3rd Division etc). Brigades in all armies, and regiments in the Anglo-Dutch and Prussian armies, have also been designated with arabic numerals (3rd Brigade, 42nd Foot etc). French regiments have been designated partly in the French style (2e Line etc) with battalions and any other sub-units as 2/1er Chasseurs etc. Battalions in the Prussian Army or in other German units have been designated in roman numbers for the musketeer or line battalions (I., II.), and with F. for the fusilier battalion (e.g. I./3rd Westphalian Landwehr). Prussian cavalry squadrons have been shown with Arabic numbers, such as 2./1st Silesian Hussar Regiment. It is hoped that these conventions will avoid all confusion.

Seniority between two officers of the same name in the Prussian Army was usually indicated by a Roman numeral after the name. Thus Major-General von Pirch I, commander of the II Army Corps, should not be confused with his junior Major-General von Pirch II, commander of the 2nd Brigade in the I Army Corps.

Preface

Histories written in English tend to regard the campaign and battle of Waterloo as principally an affair between the French Empire and the forces of the British Crown. French-language works tend not to want to concede that their Emperor was defeated at all, but if this concession has to be made, then defeat was partly at the hands of incompetent and treacherous subordinates, and partly at the hands of an English aristocrat; the Emperor himself, of course, was entirely blameless. That an uncouth Prussian had played a role in this affair at all is only grudgingly admitted. The English-language sources usually play down the role of any troops except those who had sworn an oath of loyalty to the British Crown. That the troops of Wellington's army were in the main of nationalities other than British is forgotten, except, of course, where blame is imparted.

Every historian has an axe to grind and I am no exception. My contention is that the accepted view in the English-speaking world of this campaign and battle needs challenging and revising. Moreover, other than a few short chapters by a Bundeswehr officer in a work edited by Lord Chalfont and published over 15 years ago, *Waterloo – Battle of Three Armies*, there has been no serious attempt to present the German view of this campaign in English. This work is the first comprehensive effort in the English language to explain the German perspective. Drawing mainly on German archives, published and unpublished sources, this work presents, supports, explains and justifies the point of view of the overwhelming majority of the Allied participants in this campaign, the Germans.

The research I conducted into this campaign was an interesting exercise in itself. A good deal has been written on this subject over the years and it was fascinating to observe how the way in which it has been treated has varied according to fashion and the contemporary political circumstances. French historians right from the day after the battle have tended to want to make excuses for their Emperor. French participants, particularly those at the higher levels of command, engaged in a considerable degree of back-covering, self-justification and excuse-making. Their memoirs, and the various and differing accounts produced directly or indirectly by Napoleon, have only limited value to the genuine historian.

Broadly speaking, British accounts can be placed in one of three categories. Firstly, those serious histories written up to the middle of the nine-teenth century, which are mostly balanced, well-written and thoroughly researched, and are of considerable merit in the study of the campaign.[1] Later the fashion of writing nationalist history by 'my country right or wrong' historians came to the fore. This was particularly because of the deterioration

---

[1] Particularly the great classics written by Siborne and the penetrating analysis produced by Chesney. For full details, see the bibliography.

of the relationship between Britain and the newly founded German Empire at the end of the last century. It was here that the myth of the campaign being a British as opposed to an Allied victory became most apparent. In a Europe deeply divided along national lines, Britain made the most of its great heroes, particularly the Duke of Wellington. Finally, there are those modern accounts in the English language that tend to be shallow, superficial works that repeat and embellish selected myths without bothering to refer to the better accounts of the campaign.

In his own lifetime, the Duke of Wellington very carefully nurtured his reputation. The whole truth was, at times, a casualty in this process.[2] His supporters continued to embellish these legends during and particularly after their hero's lifetime, publishing their memoirs of conversations with him. A myth-making industry grew up, with those myths gaining credence by their repetition over the years. Even today, historians constantly repeat them. The response of certain German historians of that period was to play on the point of Wellington's unreliability and to attempt to read a sinister plot into his human weaknesses.[3]

Although my writings on the Napoleonic Wars are already known, I have, until recent years, avoided looking seriously at the campaign of 1815. Until my attention was drawn to the matter, I always considered that so much had already been written on the subject, there was little point in writing any more. Furthermore, I hold the general opinion that this side of the First World War, comparatively little of note has been written on the Napoleonic Wars, while the best material available tends to be in the German language, particularly those works published by the Austrian and German General Staffs.

The only recent account in English of the Waterloo campaign worthy of interest is *Waterloo – Battle of Three Armies*, which I have already mentioned. This took the approach of using contributions by three historians, each viewing events from the perspective of one of the participating armies, but only one of these accounts was of any real merit in my view. The German historian, Oberst Eberhard Kaulbach, then a teacher at the Bundeswehr University, explained and analysed the events with the keen mind of a trained staff officer. What remained firmly fixed in my mind after reading that work was that certainly from the German point of view there was still much to be said on the subject to the English-speaking world.

A few years ago now, Phil Lawrence, then of Alma Miniatures, approached me and told me that he was planning a battlefield tour of Ligny, and also a demonstration wargame of the engagement. He asked me to be the guide of the tour. Foolishly, I agreed. My professional commitments being what they are, I was really promising something I would probably not have the time to complete. However, many a late night and burnt candle later, fuelled by the odd bottle of good vintage, the research was ended with a 10,000 word essay written on the battle. My then employer, MicroProse Software, was in the

---

[2] See, for instance, Wellington's 'Memorandum on the Battle of Waterloo' of 1842.
[3] Lettow-Vorbeck's account is a particularly good example of this.

process of programming a revolutionary computer game based on the Waterloo Campaign. Jim Bambra, the designer, knowing my interest in the period, asked me to cast an eye over the database on the Prussian Army that their researcher had written. As with so much material on the subject produced in the English language, any resemblance to fact was merely coincidence. More late nights were spent correcting that misinformation.

My researches led me to challenge much of what is often accepted as fact in the English speaking world. My reading started with a work entitled *Napoleons Untergang 1815* ('Napoleon's Downfall 1815'), the German General Staff history of the campaign, this particular volume being written by Lettow-Vorbeck and published in 1904. In the bibliography in this book was a reference to a work entitled *Waterloo Lectures*, by Colonel Charles C. Chesney, R.E., first published in 1868. Lettow-Vorbeck described it, perhaps a little unfairly, as being 'the first unbiased account in English'. My curiosity being aroused, I set about obtaining a copy. Chesney was at one time Professor of Military Art and History in the Staff College of the British army. His work ran to four editions, the last being published in 1907, and was used as teaching material for British army officers. Since it had been translated into French and German, there had been ample opportunity for French and German historians to make comments on these lectures, and all final amendments were incorporated into the fourth edition. The fourth edition was the last to be published for many years (although Greenhill Books has recently made this account available again).

The third great classic of Waterloo literature in the English language is that written by John Codman Ropes. His *Campaign of Waterloo* was first published in 1892 in New York. As an American, he was also able to take a dispassionate view of those events.

I mentioned in passing to an old friend, George Nafziger, what my current project was. His response was to mail me a photocopy of a work entitled *Belle Alliance* by Julius von Pflugk-Harttung. This historian was already known to me as the author of several popular picture books published in Germany, for the centenary of the Wars of Liberation of 1813–15 among others, but I had never seriously considered him as an historian of note. I had not even read the text of these works as I had foolishly already decided that they would be of little value to the serious researcher. However, *Belle Alliance* was very impressive indeed. This work was in fact the German equivalent of the *Waterloo Letters* from the Siborne stable. My interest aroused, I then referred to Kaulbach's bibliography for his section of *Waterloo – Battle of Three Armies*. Most of Pflugk-Harttung's other works were listed here. It became clear that this historian had written the most thoroughly researched works on the campaign of 1815, and its political background. Without the information provided by Pflugk-Harttung, particularly as to source material, then this book would not have been anywhere near as informative as I hope it is.

Julius von Pflugk-Harttung was born on 8 November 1848 in Warnekow, near Potsdam, in the Province of Brandenburg. At the age of 14, he went to America, spending time in New York, Boston and Providence before returning to Hamburg, where he took over his stepfather's business. Later, he decided to pursue his artistic and academic leanings, enrolling at the University of Bonn. Persuaded to study history instead of art, he moved on to Berlin and Göttingen before returning to Bonn to complete his doctorate. Before qualifying as a university lecturer in 1877, he had various works on medieval history published. Shortly thereafter, he received his chair. In 1886, he went to Basle to teach but stayed there only three years. His main publications at this time were on the history of the Papacy. An acclaimed historian, he was a member of academies and historical societies throughout Europe, receiving many awards. In 1906, along with the noted British Napoleonic scholar Sir Charles Oman, he contributed a chapter to the new edition of the relevant volume of the Cambridge Modern History. He died in 1919 in Berlin. Clearly a most capable and internationally respected historian, Pflugk-Harttung was indeed cosmopolitan, so there are few grounds to accuse him of nationalistic bias in his writings, particularly as he wrote before the bitter fighting in the Great War. Much of my current work is based on the research carried out by Pflugk-Harttung. It can, in part, be regarded as an extension of the research he conducted, using archive materials to which he did not have access.

Since it has been my intention from the start to approach this campaign from a judicial point of view, relying on the testimony of witnesses who are shown to be credible, and exposing those who are not, it would now be appropriate to describe some of the investigations I carried out. To establish the credibility or indeed to refute the testimony of certain witnesses, much detective work was undertaken. Footnotes in published sources were followed back to their original sources and checked. Translated quotations were traced back to their original publications and checked, and numerous archive documents were examined. All leads were followed, and at each stage of the investigation, the questions raised were examined further. Several crucial documents were found to be unavailable in Wellington's records. Statements made by certain parties in support of the Duke's actions were established as being simply not credible. It became clear that, from 18 June 1815 onwards if not earlier, there has been a deliberate effort by certain participants to deny their own mistakes, and for reasons of national pride and political interests to falsify the record. I believe I have scored a first in that I have endeavoured to examine all the available primary evidence of this series of events before coming to conclusions that reappraise the current popular view of the campaign.

Peter Hofschröer, 1998.

The Leading Allied Personalities

The British

Robert Stewart, Viscount Castlereagh, (1769–1822)[1]

The second, but eldest surviving son of Robert Stewart, the first Marquis of Londonderry, Robert junior was an accomplished scholar. He entered politics in 1790, winning a seat in the Irish Parliament before going on to become a member of the British House of Commons. Appointed Secretary of State for the War and Colonial department in July 1805, Castlereagh directed much of Britain's war effort against the Napoleonic Empire until 1809. He was then out of office for a time but became foreign secretary in 1812 and would hold that post until his death by suicide in 1822. Along with his half-brother, Charles Stewart, Castlereagh represented Britain at the Congress of Vienna from September 1814. Here, he made considerable efforts to obtain a balance of power in post-Napoleonic Europe that was favourable to Britain, instigating a secret treaty between Britain, France and Austria that was designed to act against Russian and Prussian ambitions. Castlereagh returned to London in February 1815 to deal with a political crisis there, being replaced by the Duke of Wellington, who pursued the same objectives.

Colonel Sir William Howe de Lancey, (d. 1815)[2]

De Lancey came from a family of New York loyalists of Huguenot descent. In 1792, he obtained a cornetcy in the 16th Light Dragoons. Serving partly in the East Indies and partly in Britain, he worked his way up the ranks, becoming a major in the 45th Foot by 1799. In the Peninsular War, he served on the staff of various divisions, at first as an assistant quartermaster general, and later as a deputy quartermaster general, the position he held in the 1815 campaign. Mortally wounded at Waterloo, he died a week later tended by his wife.

Lieutenant-Colonel Sir Henry Hardinge, (1785–1856)[3]

Starting his military career in 1799 as an ensign in the Queen's Rangers in Upper Canada, Hardinge purchased his way up the ranks to captain in the 57th Foot in 1804. In 1806 he joined the Senior Department of the Royal Military College, passing out in 1807. As a deputy assistant quartermaster-general, he joined the forces fighting in the Iberian Peninsula in 1808, where he caught Wellington's eye. Described by Wellington as a 'staff-officer who has intelligence',[4] in April 1815, he was appointed by the Duke to the post of British military commissioner in the Prussian headquarters in Liège. At the

---

[1] DNB, vol XVIII, pp 1233–45.
[2] DNB, vol V, pp 754–5.
[3] DNB, vol VIII, pp 1226–9.
[4] DNB, vol VIII, p 1227.

Battle of Ligny on 16 June, his left hand was shattered by a stone thrown up by a cannon ball, making its amputation necessary. He recovered to have a distinguished political and military career in later life, eventually becoming Field Marshal Viscount Hardinge of Lahore.

Field Marshal Arthur Wellesley, 1st Duke of Wellington (1769–1852)[5]

Born into a long established English family of landowners in Ireland, Wellesley bore the characteristics of his caste. Although he did not have a particularly distinguished school record, he was educated partly in France, learning to write the language fluently. He started his military career in 1787 as an ensign in the 73rd Foot. For a time he combined his military duties with those of a Member of the Irish Parliament, having been elected to represent Trim in 1790. This mixture of soldier and politician was to be characteristic of Wellesley throughout his career.

After a short involvement in the Revolutionary Wars, Wellesley next went to India, where he spent several years, making a reputation for himself as a skilled soldier and astute diplomat. He returned home in 1805 and became a member of the British Parliament. In 1807 he joined the Tory government of the Duke of Portland as Chief Secretary of Ireland. His military career began its climb to its zenith when, now a lieutenant-general, he was placed in temporary command of the expeditionary force to Portugal. In the ensuing years, he made a reputation for himself as one of the most successful great commanders not only of the period, but of history.

With the fall of Napoleon in 1814, now Field Marshal the Duke of Wellington, he returned to a career in politics, being appointed ambassador to France. He participated in the Congress of Vienna for several weeks as British plenipotentiary before being called away to serve as commander of the Anglo-Allied forces being assembled in the Netherlands to oppose the new threat from France. All his skills as a commander of a multinational force were needed to hold his army together, while all his skills as a politician were needed to keep his Prussian allies in check. Despite several quite serious errors of judgement in the campaign of 1815, Wellington came out on top and is generally regarded as the victor of Waterloo.

In later life his political career continued. He was prime minister for two separate periods in the 1820s and 1830s and was also commander-in-chief of the British army from 1842 until his death, but did not see any further active service after Waterloo.

The Netherlanders[6]
Willem I, King of the Netherlands, Grand Duke of Luxembourg (1772–1843)

Born in The Hague, Willem-Frederik, the Hereditary Prince of Nassau-Orange, was the son of Willem V, Prince of Nassau and Orange, the last

---

5 The best *Life* of Wellington is probably that by Maxwell.
6 This section is based mainly on De Bas & T'Serclaes de Wommersom, vol III.

Stadholder of the Republic of the United Provinces of the Netherlands, and of Frederica-Sophie-Wilhelmine, Princess of Prussia.

Willem's military career began on 22 November 1777 as a captain in the grenadiers of the 3rd Regiment of Nassau-Orange. The Prince rose to the rank of general three years later, first serving in wartime in 1793, when he was placed in command of the district of Nijmegen. During the Revolutionary Wars, he participated in several combats, attacks, sieges and bombardments, including the two battles at Fleurus in June 1794. That autumn, he was engaged in the unsuccessful defence of the Dutch Republic against the French invasion. His family fled to Britain in January 1795. The Prince went to Berlin in September that year, and on 1 January 1798 was appointed to the Prussian Army with the rank of lieutenant-general.

In May 1803, as the Prince of Nassau-Orange, he took up the government of his German possessions. In February 1806, he was appointed colonel-in-chief of a Prussian infantry regiment. He commanded a Prussian division at the fateful battle of Auerstedt on 14 October 1806, and found himself directing the negotiations for the capitulation of the fortress of Erfurt two days later. The committee investigating the series of shameful surrenders that followed the catastrophes of Jena and Auerstedt found Willem to be the main culprit for the needless surrender of that important fortress. However, thanks to the intervention of the King of Prussia, his brother-in-law, the Prince escaped the consequences of his actions.

The investigation committee included a newly promoted Lieutenant-Colonel von Gneisenau whose successful defence of the fortress of Kolberg had made him a popular figure in a downcast Prussia. This confrontation was to do little to promote a harmonious relationship between the two men when they were allies in 1815.

Returning to the Netherlands on 30 November 1813 in the wake of the Allied invasion, Willem accepted the sovereignty of the United Provinces of the Netherlands, taking up the reigns of government on 6 December. On 1 August 1814, he became Governor General of Belgium. These acts opened the way for him to be proclaimed King Willem I of the Netherlands (formed from the United Provinces and Belgium) and Grand Duke of Luxembourg on 16 March 1815.

The Prince of Orange, later Willem II, King of the Netherlands, (1792–1849)

Born in the Oude Hof in The Hague on 6 December 1792 as Willem Frederik George Lodewijk, Hereditary Prince of Orange-Nassau, he was the son of Willem II and the Prussian princess Frederica-Wilhelmine-Louise.

He was taken to Britain in 1795, as a small child, when his family fled the Netherlands in the face of the French invasion. He lived with his mother and grandmother in Yarmouth and Colchester. He was commissioned in the Prussian Army on 10 April 1809. He became a lieutenant-colonel in the British army on 20 May 1811.

A month later he embarked on the frigate *Mermaid* at Spithead, bound for

Portugal. He arrived there on 6 July, disembarking at the Duke of Wellington's headquarters at San Vincenti, and accompanied by Lieutenant-Colonel Baron de Constant Rebeque. In the coming two years, he saw a good deal of action in the Peninsular War, before returning to Britain at the end of 1813.

The collapse of the Napoleonic empire in the wake of Napoleon's defeat at Leipzig in October 1813 enabled the Allies to occupy the Netherlands. The Prince arrived in The Hague on 19 December 1813, some 18 years after being forced to leave his place of birth. He was soon appointed as a general of infantry in the army of the Netherlands with the function of Inspector General of all arms and of the national militia. He saw action again in the campaign of 1814.

When his father was proclaimed King of the Netherlands on 16 March 1815, William adopted the title of the Prince of Orange. A week later, he was appointed commander in chief of the Allied troops in the Netherlands. A young man lacking the experience of diplomacy on the stage of the theatre of Europe, the Prince conceded his position to the Duke of Wellington, but retained overall command of the Netherlands troops. He fought at Quatre Bras and Waterloo.

Jean Victor de Constant Rebeque (1773–1850)[7]

Constant Rebeque joined the Dutch Army in 1793 and moved to Prussia in 1795 when his home country was overrun by the French. In 1805 he became military tutor to the young Prince of Orange. From 1811 to 1813 he served with the Prince in Spain with the British forces. He returned to the Netherlands to become chief-of-staff of the royal army.

During the campaign of 1815 he was present in the Prince of Orange's headquarters and he himself made one of the crucial decisions; by disobeying Wellington's orders, he ensured that the Allies maintained their positions holding the vital crossroads at Quatre Bras.

The Prussians
Generalfeldmarschall Gebhard Lebrecht Fürst Blücher von Wahlstatt (1742–1819)[8]

Born in Rostock, a town on the Baltic coast, the young Blücher joined an hussar regiment raised locally for Swedish service in 1758. Two years later, he was captured in a skirmish with Prussian hussars and was persuaded by their commander, Belling, to join that regiment. This was the beginning of a stormy career in Prussian service which, with many trials and tribulations, was to see Blücher become one of the most famed soldiers in history. Blücher was always a passionate man, with strong emotions that at times caused him mental instability. He was a German patriot who suffered the great agony of seeing his country defeated and plundered by a predatory neighbour. He felt the

---

[7] Aa, *Biographisch Woordenboek der Nederlanden*, pp 676–8.
[8] Priesdorff, vol 2, pp 413–27

humiliation of Prussia by Napoleon in 1806 very personally, and devoted much of his considerable energy to righting the wrongs of the following years of foreign domination. Loved by his men, very much a soldier's soldier, he had the ability to inspire all around him, from the lowliest private to the great statesmen of the period.

Blunt, unrefined, honest and honourable, Blücher detested the political machinations of the Congress of Vienna, which he saw as giving away all that had been gained at so much cost on the field of battle. When Napoleon escaped from exile on the isle of Elba, the Field Marshal itched to take up the sword again to right the wrongs of the politicians. As Prussia had been plundered and impoverished by the French occupiers, Blücher was determined to carry the war into France this time and lay waste to whatever was in the path of his army.

Blücher was a rather naïve soldier with no political skills or ambitions. He trusted his ally, the Duke of Wellington, implicitly, which was to be one of his great faults in the coming campaign.

Bruised and battered in the last cavalry charge of the day at Ligny, the Prince came close to being captured by the French. Rescued by Nostitz, his faithful aide-de-camp, he pulled his beaten army together, and with great determination, brought it to the field of Waterloo.

Blücher was one of the major figures of this period, who helped to put an end to the Napoleonic Wars and secure a period of peace and prosperity in Europe.

Generallieutenant August Wilhelm Anton Graf Neidhardt von Gneisenau, (1760–1832)[9]

Gneisenau was of relatively humble origins, not from of one of Prussia's established military families, becoming a career soldier at the age of 18. He tended towards service in the new light infantry formations that were becoming prevalent in late 18th century Europe. He entered Prussian service in 1786, first fighting in Poland nearly a decade later. Known in informed circles as an interesting military theorist, he started to draw attention from the wider public with his distinguished conduct in the 1806 campaign. Fame came to him after he led one of the few successful episodes of the campaign, the defence of the Prussian fortress of Kolberg.

Appointed to the Military Reorganisation Commission in 1807, he greatly influenced the modernisation of the Prussian army. Gneisenau was also involved in more unpleasant tasks, particularly the investigations into the many shameful capitulations of Prussian fortresses, including Erfurt where the the future King Willem was involved.

From 1809 to 1812, Gneisenau was involved in various diplomatic missions. He took up his sword again on the outbreak of the Wars of Liberation in 1813, standing at Blücher's side in a partnership that was to go

---

[9] Priesdorff, vol 4, pp 33–65.

through thick and thin over the coming years. He viewed his allies in 1815 with a somewhat jaundiced eye, not trusting the motives of the Duke of Wellington.

Gneisenau's contribution to the Allied effort in the Napoleonic Wars in general, and in 1815 in particular, should not be underestimated. His decision to try to keep the Prussian Army in contact with its allies after the defeat at Ligny on 16 June 1815 was crucial in turning a tactical defeat into a strategic victory.

Generalmajor Karl Wilhelm Georg von Grolman (1777–1843)[10]

Coming from an influential Prussian family, Grolman started his military career in a typical fashion. Joining a regiment of foot as an adolescent *Gefreiterkorporal* in 1791, he rose through the ranks, fighting as a junior captain at Auerstedt in 1806. A year later, he was appointed to the influential Military Reorganisation Commission. Unable to sit one the sidelines in 1809, he left the Prussian service and joined the Austrian Army. In 1810 he went to the Peninsula and fought in a *Légion extrangera* of the Spanish Army, until he was taken prisoner by the French at the capitulation of Valencia in 1812. He escaped, returning home via Switzerland.

At the beginning of the Wars of Liberation, he was appointed a major in the General Staff of the Prussian Army. Fighting in the Army of Bohemia in the autumn campaign, he came under Blücher's command in 1814.

In December 1814 he was sent to participate in the Congress of Vienna as a military advisor. On Napoleon's return to France, he was sent to Blücher's headquarters as a quartermaster-general. He led the Prussian assault columns on Plancenoit on 18 June.

Generallieutenant Wieprecht Hans Karl Friedrich Ernst Heinrich Graf von Zieten (1770–1848)[11]

Coming from one of Prussia's most famous military families, this particular Zieten joined his father's regiment of hussars as a cadet in 1785. As a young second lieutenant, he gained his first combat experience in the Revolutionary Wars. He fought at Auerstedt in 1806 and remained an active cavalry officer until the end of 1809, when he received his first brigade of all arms. Fighting at several major battles in the Wars of Liberation from Gross-Görschen to Paris, he was decorated on numerous occasions.

In 1815, he commanded the Prussian I. Armeekorps, which fought and marched continuously in the decisive days of the campaign from 15 to 18 June. Zieten's corps did much to delay the French advance on 15 June. It suffered the heaviest casualties of any formation involved in the fighting of 16 June, and Zieten's decision to disobey his orders and use his initiative to support Wellington's crumbling left flank on 18 June was one of the most important decisions of the campaign.

---

[10] Priesdorff, vol 4, pp 238–47.
[11] Priesdorff, vol 4, pp 253–60.

Generalmajor Georg Dubislav Ludwig von Pirch I (1763–1838)[12]

The older of two brothers, both of whom entered their father's 45th Regiment of Foot as *Gefreiterkorporale*, the elder Pirch first fought in the War of the Bavarian Succession (1778–9), and took part in the occupation of Holland in 1787. He later saw action in the siege of Mainz in 1793 before fighting at Jena in 1806. Held as a prisoner of war in France, he returned home in 1808. He rose through the ranks and fought throughout the Wars of Liberation.

Pirch became temporary commander of II. Armeekorps after Borstell was removed because of his complaints about the handling of the Saxon rebellion. Some, notably Blücher's ADC Nostitz, felt that he had been promoted beyond his capabilities. He was, nevertheless, a most capable and brave officer.

Generallieutenant Johann Adolf Freiherr von Thielemann (1765–1824)[13]

The son of a Saxon official, Thielemann joined the Saxon army as a cadet in 1780. He first saw action in the Revolutionary Wars as a young hussar officer. In the campaigns of 1806–7, he fought first against the French at Jena, and then with them at Heilsberg and Friedland. He fought at various battles in the campaign of 1809, and then, commanding a brigade of cavalry, was given an award for his bravery at Borodino in 1812. As governor of the important fortress on Torgau on the river Elbe, he quit Saxon service in protest at being ordered to hand over this vital crossing to the French. Now entering Russian service, he fought throughout the campaigns of 1813 and 1814.

After commanding the III German Federal Corps on the Lower Rhine for several months, he joined the Prussian Army in March 1815. Clausewitz was his chief of staff, and together they organised the defence of Wavre on 18 June.

General der Infanterie Friedrich Wilhelm Graf Bülow von Dennewitz (1755–1816)[14]

A scion of one of the leading families in Prussia, Bülow's route into the army was through the customary cadet scheme, joining a regiment of foot in 1768. He first saw action as a second lieutenant in the War of the Bavarian Succession. As an aide of Prince Louis Ferdinand, he fought in the Revolutionary Wars, rising through the ranks in the following years. Receiving his first brigade in 1808, he commanded a corps in the campaigns of 1813 and 1814. His most famous victory was at Dennewitz on 6 September 1813, for which he was made a count.

The campaign of 1815 started badly for him when vital orders requiring him to move to the front rapidly were delayed in getting to him. On 18 June, it was Bülow's relatively fresh corps that made the decisive flank attack at Plancenoit, giving the Prussian aristocrat the opportunity to make up for his earlier failings.

[12] Priesdorff, vol 3, pp 439–41
[13] Priesdorff, vol 3, pp 458–66.
[14] Priesdorff, vol 3, pp 294–306.

Chapter 1
Europe before Waterloo

Germany during the Napoleonic Wars

When the French Revolution began in 1789 what we now know as 'Germany' was made up of a myriad of states, some large and genuinely independent and others tiny and overlooked by more powerful neighbours. All were nominally part of the Holy Roman Empire of the German Nation, the 'First Reich' which had been in existence for the best part of a thousand years. Austria was supposedly the leading power in the Empire but had been challenged for the past 50 years and more by the expansion of Brandenburg-Prussia.

The French Revolution brought wars in its wake and French armies conquered all the German lands west of the Rhine by 1795. More campaigns followed in which various combinations of German, Austrian and Russian forces were beaten time and again. During these wars an ambitious young general took control of the French government and made himself France's absolute ruler as the Emperor Napoleon I. Further victories from 1805 to 1809 confirmed and consolidated Napoleon's domination of almost the whole of Europe. Germany was ruthlessly plundered to support the French wars of conquest and various of the small German states were formed into a puppet Confederation of the Rhine whose armies fought as Napoleon's allies.

Napoleon's empire began to fall apart when he decided to attack Russia in 1812. His *Grande Armée* was virtually destroyed and, with Russian support, Prussia declared war on France on 17 March 1813. The Wars of Liberation, as they are known in Germany, had begun. Many of the smaller states of northern Germany rose up against France, though the King of Saxony, who looked as if he was going to throw his lot in with the Allies and draw his sword against France, failed to do so in the end. The campaign of 1813 culminated in a devastating defeat for Napoleon at Leipzig in October at the hands of Austrian, Russian, Prussian and Swedish forces. Although there were flashes of the old operational genius from Napoleon when the fighting continued in early 1814, the Allies eventually made their way to Paris and forced him to abdicate. Napoleon was sent into exile on the Mediterranean island of Elba while the Allied leaders pondered how to redraw the map of Europe.

Successful though the Allies may have been, their alliance had been fraught with fundamental differences, conflicts of interest and divergent aims. Napoleon may have been unsuccessful in his gamble that the coalition would break up before it overthrew him, but there was no certainty that, even in victory, the Allies could agree among themselves on a lasting peace settlement. Not only was there friction between Austria, Russia and Prussia, the three main continental powers, on how they were to divide the spoils, there were also at times intense differences of opinion between the politicians and generals of each particular power.

The aims of each of these powers were at variance with those of the others. Austria's leading statesman Prince Metternich[1] feared a strong Russia and Prussia more than what was left of the threat from France. Austria's wish at the start of 1814 was merely to confine Napoleon's empire to the left bank of the Rhine. Russia sought to expand her territory westwards, particularly by annexing much of what is now Poland. This impinged on territory that Prussia also claimed, so Russia offered Prussia compensation in Saxony and northern Germany. Like Austria, Russia might have accepted, as far as her own interests were concerned, a peace with Napoleon based on France's 'natural frontiers' of the Rhine, Alps and Pyrenees, but Prussia, laid waste and impoverished by the years of French occupation, would settle for nothing less than the total overthrow of the Bonaparte dynasty. As Russia's expansion westwards required Prussian co-operation, Prussia could count on Russia's support for this part of her political and military aims.

Britain's aim in this complex pattern of conflicting ambitions was to reach a peace that established a harmonious balance of power in Europe, left her with her colonial conquests and stopped the worst excesses of Russian and Prussian expansion. This generally meant restraining Russia and Prussia, while supporting Austria and assuring that, once Napoleon was overthrown, France would be weakened but not laid prostrate.

The leading personalities in Europe's political concert included Prince Metternich, the Austrian statesman who would play a leading role in shaping Europe for another 30 years. He overshadowed most contemporary politicians and even his own Emperor, Franz I, played second fiddle to him. Prussia's foreign policy was directed by Prince Hardenberg, the Prussian Chancellor. Although he had done much in the recent years to reform and modernise his country, Hardenberg lacked Metternich's stature and authority. The king of Prussia, Friedrich Wilhelm III, stood in the shadow of his protector, the czar of Russia. He was easily swayed to carry out the wishes of others. Prussia's generals, notably Blücher and Gneisenau, took a much harder line than the politicians, but all parties in Prussia pursued a policy of revenge against France, having suffered so much from the French occupation.

Hanover, ruled by British kings, had been occupied by Prussia for a time before the catastrophe of 1806 and then been incorporated in France until after the Battle of Leipzig. Now Hanover was again coveted by Prussia. If Prussia were to lose her former Polish territories and be denied compensation in Saxony, as was Britain's wish, then she would hope to look elsewhere, with the annexation of Hanover one possibility. This issue was a source of conflict between Prussia and Britain. Hanover would be represented in the coming discussions by Graf Münster, who was respected and trusted by the British.

---

[1] For a detailed description of Metternich's role in the reconstruction of Europe, see Kraehe, *Metternich's German Policy*, vol II *The Congress of Vienna 1814–1815*.

Larger German states such as Bavaria, Baden, and Württemberg had gained territory and prestige from the years of French rule in Germany. They now also hoped to profit from the destruction of the Confederation of the Rhine. The smaller German states were mere pawns in power politics.

Partly as a punishment for their collaboration with Napoleon, and partly from necessity, caused by the general exhaustion of available manpower, the German states were required to raise larger contingents and provide more resources for the invasion of France in 1814 than even their former 'protector' had required them to do for his purposes. However, owing to their divided loyalties, the forces of Napoleon's former German allies were in the main deployed in secondary theatres during this campaign. The fate of the new kings and old princes of Germany who had given Napoleon so much support was to be decided once the Bonaparte dynasty was overthrown.

British Foreign Policy under Castlereagh[2]

Lord Castlereagh became Britain's foreign minister in the fateful year of 1812 when Napoleon assembled his greatest army ever for his invasion of Russia. Britain was diplomatically isolated from most of Europe at that time. Napoleon's so-called Continental System and his long years of military success had left Britain with only six diplomatic missions to other European countries in existence – and five of these were to courts whose monarch was either in exile, imprisoned or had lost the greater part of his territory. Britain maintained contact with certain foreign governments, however, through the Hanoverian representatives at these courts. In this way, Austria and Prussia conducted a dialogue with Britain throughout 1812. Once the *Grande Armée* was destroyed, Britain was in a position to set about forming a new coalition against France.

Being physically isolated from Europe and lacking a substantial army, Britain's role in Europe was restricted. Britain's major strength was a dominant navy, backed by the wealth created from a world-wide trading empire and the enormous credit resources engendered by the sophisticated British financial system. This meant that Britain was able to act as paymaster of the coalition.[3] Promises of subsidies were used to create the alliance as well as being a lever to obtain the aims of British foreign policy once the alliance was in being. However, Britain's diplomats were not as strong-minded as certain others, failing to make the most of their country's economic position. Viscount Cathcart, Britain's representative in the Russian headquarters, and Sir Charles Stewart (Castlereagh's half-brother), attached to the Prussian headquarters, both lacked the knowledge, stature and determination to establish a position of real influence in their posts. The Earl of Aberdeen, ambassador to Austria, was a lightweight when compared to Metternich. The credit for any success in Britain's foreign policy can only be given to Castlereagh's own efforts.[4]

Britain's territorial claims in Europe were minimal and the other Allies

[2] For further details, see Webster, *The Foreign Policy of Castlereagh*, vol I.
[3] For details of Britain's subsidies to her allies, see Sherwig, *Guineas and Gunpowder*.
[4] Webster, *The Congress of Vienna 1814–15*, p 11 f.

conversely were little interested in Britain's colonial ambitions. Once the issue of the future of Hanover was settled, and this was done quickly, Britain could concentrate on acting as mediator in the complex territorial disputes between the other allies. By adjudicating between their various objectives Castlereagh would also be advancing the overall British policy of creating a balance of power in Europe.

The Peace of Paris

Discussions on the future of Europe took place in 1814 even while the war in France was continuing. The first written agreement was the Treaty of Chaumont of 9 March 1814 in which the four great powers pledged themselves to continuing the war until certain aims were achieved. Their main objectives were defined as a new German confederation, an independent Switzerland, an Italy consisting of several independent states, Spain ruled by the House of Bourbon, and an enlarged Netherlands under the House of Orange.[5] This treaty established the Quadruple Alliance of Britain, Austria, Russian and Prussia.

Once Napoleon had abdicated, the Allies set about re-shaping the map of Europe in earnest. The first attempt at coming to a settlement was made in the Peace of Paris in May 1814. The major issues of contention became clear; the future of Saxony and Poland. Russia wanted to annex all of Poland while Prussia coveted Saxony. Austria was prepared to agree to the Prussians taking the whole of Saxony, if Prussia's demands elsewhere were limited. This related especially to concerns about the future of the fortress of Mainz, sited on an important crossing point on the Rhine. Austria did not want Mainz to fall into Prussian hands, so insisted that the annexation of Saxony depend on Prussia renouncing this claim. When Prussian troops nevertheless occupied this great fortress, an impasse was reached.

The Peace of Paris accordingly made little reference to German affairs other than to state that the territories on the left bank of the Rhine recently ruled by France should be used to compensate the Netherlands, Prussia and other German states. Final decisions were postponed until a further meeting in London. The discussions that took place there were even less satisfactory than those in Paris, so it was agreed to convene a congress in Vienna, to commence in September 1814.

The Rhineland and The Netherlands

Britain's prime objective with regard to Germany was to establish some sort of order out of the 'German chaos'. Germany had to be made sufficiently strong to withstand any potential French aggression, but any new order in Germany should not result in a state that would be so strong that it would soon pose a potential threat to its neighbours. To establish a balance in power in central Europe, the major German states would have to be strengthened, but only by a sufficient degree to achieve that end. This balance of power had to be

[5] Webster, *Congress*, p 31.

achieved by establishing an equilibrium between Austria and Prussia, while making the medium sized German states sufficiently strong to play a moderating role in Austro-Prussian relationships. Britain regarded Prussia particularly as territorially ambitious and a potential threat to European harmony. Indeed, during the Napoleonic Wars Prussia had, with the occupation of Hanover, encroached on regions important to Britain. Britain's leading soldier, the Duke of Wellington, is also recorded as having expressed his fear of the 'republican military spirit' evident in certain circles in the Prussian hierarchy.[6]

Castlereagh wished to begin by establishing a barrier against France along the Rhine. He considered Prussian help the best way to achieve this at first. By satisfying Prussian territorial demands with gains on the Rhine, he could perhaps draw Prussia away from Russian influence. He had to weigh up this consideration with the demands of the House of Orange for a 'Greater Netherlands', as well as British concerns for the major port of Antwerp, which should not be allowed to fall into the hands of any major power.

The Prince of Orange had visions of joining his family's territories in Germany with those in the Netherlands. He sought Castlereagh's agreement to an annexation of the left bank of the Rhine down as far as the Moselle, as well as of the Duchy of Berg, thus gaining the important cities of Cologne and Düsseldorf.[7] The Prince was quick to point out that, if Prussia were to possess the Rhineland, then she might dominate trade with Switzerland and south-west Germany, which could not be in British interests. Achieving a 'Greater Netherlands' remained British policy for a time, with Castlereagh trying to gain Maastricht, Aachen and Cologne for the House of Orange.

The Prussian minister Prince Hardenberg strove to achieve territorial ambitions in this region also. After all, as far as Prussia was concerned, it was Prussian troops under General von Bülow who had ejected the French from the Netherlands in 1814, so Hardenberg believed that Prussia had a claim there, established by the right of arms. Prussia regarded the Meuse river as being the natural boundary of the Netherlands, although Venlo and Maastricht were seen as Dutch towns. As for the other territories ruled by other branches of the House of Orange, their rights could be accommodated by providing them with domains on either side of the Netherlands–German border. These states would be members of a new German confederation under Prussian military protection.

The talks in Paris at the end of May 1814, in which the Duke of Wellington participated, largely settled this issue between Britain and Prussia. Prussia was to gain territory on the lower Rhine in return for abandoning any claims to the possessions of the House of Orange on the middle Rhine[8] – but the Netherlanders would still remain nervous of Prussian ambitions throughout the Hundred Days.

---

[6] Botzenhart, *Stein*, vol V, p 217, citing Stein's Journal, 24 February 1815.
[7] Colenbrander, *Gedenkstukken*, vol VI, p 1952, memorandum of Willem VI of Orange dated 9 November 1813; vol VII, p 451, memorandum dated 10 January 1814; Vane, *Castlereagh*, vol IX, pp 80 and 248.
[8] Griewank, *Kongress*, p 123.

The talks in May 1814 did not, however, end another dispute, over the Duchy of Luxembourg and its strategic fortress. While it was desirable for British interests to have a Prussian garrison there to check any possible French aggression, the House of Orange also forcefully claimed this territory. Further talks followed in London during June and July 1814. Here, Hardenberg came to a compromise with Castlereagh. While Prussia agreed to acknowledge the claims of the House of Orange, Hardenberg also insisted that both Luxembourg and Mainz should be fortresses of the German federation, preferably with Prussian garrisons.[9] Hardenberg also pressed for the Netherlands, or at least the Belgian part of its territories, to be included in the German confederation as the 'Burgundian District'. He even claimed that the Prince of Orange supported him on this.[10]

The discussion continued in Vienna. Castlereagh now received a proposal from Hardenberg that Luxembourg should become a federal fortress, while the Duchy itself was to be ceded to Bavaria. In return, Prussia was to receive Mainz and Frankfurt, to which Bavaria had claims. Castlereagh did not reject this suggestion immediately. However, Wellington did so later, as he had little trust in Bavaria. British policy remained to establish Prussia as the buffer against France along the Rhine.[11]

Hanover and Prussia

Castlereagh's major concern was with establishing a general framework for the future of Germany. He left the details of the matters of the lesser states to Graf Münster, the long-established Hanoverian representative in London. During the years of French occupation and annexation of northern Germany, Münster became a focal point for Germans in exile in London. The British government made great use of his knowledge of German affairs during the years of their isolation from the mainland of Europe. Münster's major political aim was to increase the standing of the Hanover in Germany. At the Congress of Vienna, he succeeded in establishing Hanover as a kingdom and also sought territorial aggrandisement.

Like many of his compatriots, he opposed Prussia's aims in northern Germany. In 1813 he had tried to have Prussia's territorial extent limited to the right bank of the Elbe. He did not succeed, so he pursued a policy of obtaining territory elsewhere, later gaining East Friesland, formerly ruled by Prussia, for his new king. Prussia was prepared to make concessions to Hanover rather than face conflict with Britain on this issue, as there would hopefully be easier pickings elsewhere.

Münster also favoured a restoration of the old Empire with a Habsburg Emperor. In pursuit of his wish to build a loose German confederation, he

---

[9] Colenbrander, vol VII, p 160, Fagell's letter to Castlereagh, July 1814; Griewank, *Kongress*, p 124, memorandum of Hardenberg and Münster dated 15th July 1814.

[10] Griewank, *Kongress*, p 124. Letter from Hardenberg to Castlereagh dated 27 August 1814.

[11] Vane, *Castlereagh*, vol X, p 166; Colenbrander, vol VII, p 187, Hardenberg to Castlereagh 28 September 1814; p 193 Castlereagh to Wellington 1 October 1814.

collaborated in Vienna with the representatives of the House of Orange, some of whose territories bordered Hanover. In doing so he also restrained certain of their territorial demands.[12] During the Congress, the Count did much else to represent British interests to the lesser German states. His role in shaping the future of Europe should not be underestimated and it is important to note that, though the interests of Hanover and Prussia often diverged, Hanover should not be regarded as merely Britain's junior partner in Germany. The Hanoverian and Prussian troops would, however, fight in different armies in the 1815 campaign.

The Congress of Vienna

The Congress of Vienna began with the disputed territories in the hands of one or other of their claimants. Russia held all of Poland and Saxony, while Prussia held the left bank of the Rhine and Mainz. As such, there was every reason for them to present the other Great Powers with a fait accompli. All that was agreed initially was that each power would maintain at least 75,000 men on a war footing as security against France. However, it is revealing that each country also chose to position these troops so as to be able to intervene easily should the territorial disputes among the Allies worsen; they were not in a position to move against France, should that become necessary.

The British representatives at the Congress included Castlereagh himself, his half-brother Sir Charles Stewart, Lord Cathcart, and Lord Clancarty. In the middle of February 1815 Wellington replaced Castlereagh and, when Wellington left to take up his post as Allied commander in the Netherlands in March, Clancarty was placed in charge of the British mission. Prince Hardenberg, the Prussian Chancellor, and Wilhelm von Humboldt headed Prussia's team throughout. The Prussian General Staff also played a significant role, with Generallieutenant von der Knesebeck advising the Chancellor on military affairs. Czar Alexander's advisors were mainly non-Russians; his foreign minster was the Graf von Nesselrode-Ereshoven, one of many generals and politicians of German origins in the czar's government. Metternich was the leading Austrian delegate and, at home in Vienna, naturally had much say in the running of the congress.

The new French government's representation was led by Talleyrand, Napoleon's former foreign minister, who had deserted his old master early enough to be accepted by the restored king. Britain wanted to establish a friendly relationship with the new regime in France, and tried to involve Talleyrand in the decision-making process. Prussia, on the other hand, was mainly interested in getting retribution for her long sufferings under French occupation.

The Congress dragged on through October 1814 without agreement even on the procedure for discussing the major issues at question, never mind an examination of the issues themselves. Discussion was confined to an informal exchange of memoranda between the affected parties. Talleyrand,

[12] Webster, *Congress*, p 21, Münster to Prince Regent, 19 February 1814.

Map 1
Prussia's Expansion Plans
Hardenberg's Proposal of 29 April 1814

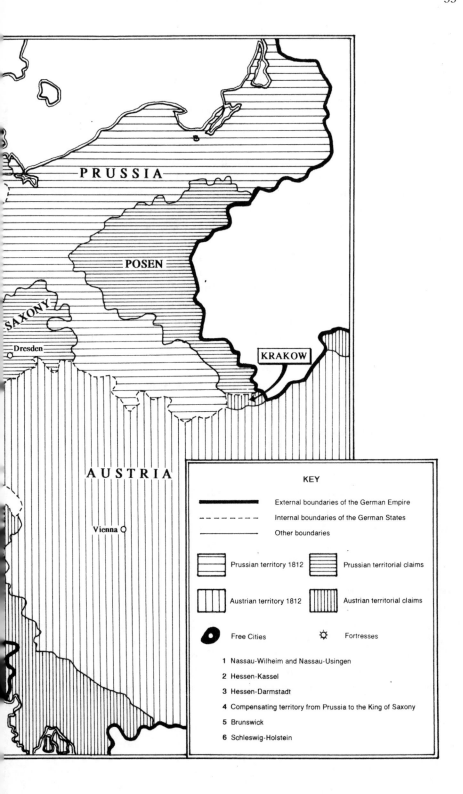

PRUSSIA

POSEN

SAXONY

Dresden

KRAKOW

AUSTRIA

Vienna

KEY

▬▬▬▬▬	External boundaries of the German Empire
– – – – –	Internal boundaries of the German States
─────	Other boundaries

Prussian territory 1812   Prussian territorial claims

Austrian territory 1812   Austrian territorial claims

Free Cities   ☼ Fortresses

1 Nassau-Wilheim and Nassau-Usingen

2 Hessen-Kassel

3 Hessen-Darmstadt

4 Compensating territory from Prussia to the King of Saxony

5 Brunswick

6 Schleswig-Holstein

Castlereagh and Metternich started to form one camp; Prussia and Russia another – but, in effect, the Congress had not properly begun.

The Congress only got going properly when Czar Alexander forced a formal discussion of Polish affairs on 24 December 1814. A Committee of Four was now officially constituted[13] though Castlereagh and Metternich insisted that France be included also. This stance met such vehement opposition from Prussia and Russia that it seemed as if the Allies would go to war amongst themselves.

Hardenberg knew that French participation would end his chances of obtaining all of Saxony, so he even threatened war. The Prussian Army started to mobilise against Britain, Austria and France. The same day, 1 January 1815, news arrived of the end of the so-called War of 1812 between Britain and America. With one war just finished, Britain was clearly in a better position to make credible threats about getting involved in another. Castlereagh, Talleyrand and Metternich drew up a secret treaty of alliance on 3 January 1815. Bavaria, Hanover and the Netherlands indicated their support of this alliance. Britain was the architect of this anti-Prussian coalition, a fact that was certainly not to be forgotten in certain quarters over the coming months.

After they signed their secret treaty, Metternich and Castlereagh refused to allow France to be excluded from the negotiations over Saxony and Poland. The czar, having heard rumours of the treaty, now showed willingness for a settlement and Hardenberg indicated that he was prepared to compromise, too. Metternich sensed the Prussians and Russians were backing down and increased his demands. Castlereagh intervened, spending the next six weeks hammering out a workable compromise, which was far from easy. By 6 February 1815, Castlereagh was able to inform his government at home that: 'the territorial arrangements on this side of the Alps are, in fact, settled in all their essential features.'[14]

The Duke of Wellington and Germany

The Duke of Wellington is best known as a soldier and one of the major figures in the campaign of Waterloo, but he was a soldier with extensive political experience. With the abdication of the 'Corsican Ogre' on 6 April 1814, it appeared that Wellington's career as a field commander was over, so he sought to renew his political career. He went to Paris in the autumn of 1814 as the British ambassador to France. Over the next months he turned down offers of a military command in North America and a role as advisor to Castlereagh at the Congress of Vienna, but early in 1815 he accepted a promotion to be Castlereagh's successor as plenipotentiary in Vienna. He joined the congress on 3 February 1815, only weeks before Napoleon returned to France. Wellington the politician then became very much involved in discussions and arrangements on the constitutional future of Germany, doing much to thwart Prussian territorial and political ambitions.

[13] D'Angeberg, p 1861.
[14] PRO FO 92/11, Castlereagh to Liverpool, 6 February 1815.

Once Napoleon had re-established himself in Paris, Wellington still attempted to reduce Prussia's influence, and ensure that a Prussian-dominated 'German' army did not come into existence. Instead, as Chapter 2 will show, he tried to have the armies of as many German states as he could placed under his own command. Wellington's political involvement was to cause doubts about his sincerity in the minds of certain Prussian officers during the Waterloo campaign. How much this affected decisions made by the various commanders remains to be discussed later.

The German question was a complex of issues involving both constitutional and territorial matters. Prussia wanted to annex the Kingdom of Saxony and to divide the lesser states of Germany into a number of districts supervised by one of the larger states – Austria, Prussia, Hanover, Bavaria and Württemberg. The armed forces of these districts were, of course, to come under the command of their protectors, so in effect, all the military resources in northern Germany, except for Hanover, would come under Prussian control. Austria, quite naturally, opposed this, favouring instead a looser confederation under the control of a collective central authority, with this authority residing in Vienna. The lesser states tended to favour the Austrian model for reasons of self-preservation but would acquiesce willingly only if their territorial demands were met.[15]

Wellington took up his position in Vienna just when these controversies were reaching their climax. Since he was representing the British king, he naturally took most interest in the future of Hanover but he was also approached by representatives of various lesser German states who hoped that British support, moral and, if necessary, financial and military, could be enlisted for their claims to independence. Britain generally favoured the idea of a loose confederation under Austrian supervision, so Wellington's response to these approaches was not particularly favourable, but Prussia's representatives still regarded his activities with suspicion.

The Final Settlement in Germany

Prussia eventually received about half of the Saxon territory, including two-fifths of the population, about 850,000 people, along with the important Elbe fortresses. Most of the disputed territories on the Rhine, but not the fortress of Mainz, also became Prussian, along with the Duchy of Westphalia. A Prussian garrison was placed in the fortress of Luxembourg, although the House of Orange ruled the Duchy. Hanover acquired East Friesland, a former Prussian territory, and was raised to the rank of kingdom. The idea of a greater Hanover as a buffer against the French was dropped in order to provide Prussia with territory in the west. Austria regained the Tyrol from Bavaria, with her claims to former territories in the west being abandoned. Mainz was made a federal fortress and Bavaria received the Palatinate. The treaty finally consisted of 121 articles and was not completed until 26 June 1815, by which

---

15 For a fuller discussion of these issues, see: Kraehe, *Metternich's German Policy*, vol II: *The Congress of Vienna 1814–1815*, pp 327-44.

time a new war was actually in progress. A military conflict between the Allies had indeed been avoided, but the repercussions of their rivalries were to be evident during the course of the Waterloo Campaign.

Chapter 2

Wellington and the Germans

The Struggle for German Manpower

News that Napoleon had escaped from Elba first reached Vienna on the evening of 7 March 1815. Three days later, the Congress heard he had landed on the southern coast of France. From there Napoleon began a triumphant march to Paris while King Louis and his supporters fled into exile once again. What had been a diplomatic contest to control German territory turned into a struggle for German manpower.

The only troops deployed to oppose France at this time were about 22,000 men under British command in the Low Countries, mainly Netherlanders, Hanoverians and Nassauers; a German corps of roughly 30,000 men under the Prussian General Kleist at Koblenz;[1] an Austro-Bavarian formation in the Palatinate; the Austro-Prussian garrison of Mainz;[2] the Saxons around Cologne; and the Austrian army in Italy. The Russians had already withdrawn their forces into Poland and the Swedes had returned home. The Spanish were too involved in their internal affairs to be concerned about events to their north.

On 13 March the Congress declared Napoleon an outlaw. On 25 March, the four Great Powers – Austria, Russia, Britain and Prussia, – formed a new coalition, reviving the terms of the Treaty of Chaumont of 1 March 1814.[3] According to this Treaty, if the balance of power in Europe were disturbed, each of the Great Powers would be required to raise or fund an army of 150,000 men to restore it.

In terms of manpower, the three continental powers would not have much difficulty in achieving this. However, Britain did not have such a large army at her disposal as most of Wellington's veterans from the Peninsular War had been sent to North America to participate in Britain's war with the United States of America, the so-called War of 1812. Although this war had recently ended, there would be a delay before these troops could return Europe. So it was stipulated that Britain was to supply part of her requirement in the form of subsidies to the Allies, while raising additional forces by employing mercenaries from Germany. These additional troops were to come mainly from the smaller German states, quarrels over whose future status had almost brought Prussia, Austria, Britain and France into conflict at the beginning of 1815. The Allies, having made progress in settling their territorial disputes, now found

---

[1] Maxwell, *Life of Wellington*, vol I, p 395.
[2] Neumann, vol II, p 477 f.
[3] Klüber, *Übersicht*, p 63 ff.

themselves reopening a wound that had barely begun to heal. Wellington and the Prussians again found themselves with a conflict of interests.

Austrian, Russian and Prussian representatives first met on 11 March 1815 to discuss how to respond to Napoleon's return to power in France. Knesebeck, the Prussian Generaladjutant, called for the following contingents to be listed for use under Prussian command: Royal Saxon, Saxon Duchies (various small independent states in the province of Thuringia), Hesse-Kassel, Mecklenburg, Nassau, Schwarzburg, Anhalt, Waldeck, Lippe, Reuss, Hamburg, Lübeck and Frankfurt-am-Main. Prince Schwarzenberg, the Austrian representative, objected only to the inclusion of the Frankfurters. Knesebeck required this as certain contingents had already withdrawn from Kleist's command, namely those of Hesse-Kassel, Mecklenburg and certain Saxon Duchies. Furthermore, the contingents of Hanover, Brunswick and Oldenburg were allocated to the British army, so the remaining North German contingents were divided into two groups, the larger being allocated to the Prussians, the smaller to the British.

On 17 March there was a further discussion in Vienna, at which the Duke of Wellington was present. Prussia had the best of these talks. Lacking the economic resources of Britain, she was unable to buy favour. Her strength, however, was her relationship with Russia who was better able to apply pressure on the German princes. Prussia was in fact Russia's tool in the czar's ambitions to expand his territory and influence westwards. At this meeting, and against the wishes of the Duke of Wellington, Prussia was able to establish that all north German contingents, including the Saxon Army but excluding the Hanoverians, were to come under the command of a Prussian general.[4] The Russo-Prussian axis won this round, which was a blow to British interests.

The Russian card may well have been Prussia's best trump, but Britain's economic resources ensured that other cards could be played as well. It was also agreed that the Saxons would be required to supply 14,000 men and the small north German states 8,000 men. As 8,000 men seemed rather few, the requirement was soon more than doubled, while Prussia and Britain very soon started to dispute the details of the arrangements.

Revealing comments on the negotiations were recorded by the Freiherr von Marschall, foreign minister of Nassau, a small duchy on the Rhine ruled by the Dutch House of Orange. Marschall was also the Nassau representative in Vienna. On 21 March 1815 he wrote home to Wiesbaden, the capital of Nassau, that,

> It is the wish of the English that the troops of the North German princes join the Dutch Army under Wellington. The Prussians want to have them join their army. I can reliably report that this has led to disagreements.[5]

On 25 March, Marschall produced a more detailed report, commenting,

> There have been numerous meetings of the military committees. In these, the

---

[4] Pflugk-Harttung, *Gegensätze*, p 130.
[5] Pflugk-Harttung, *Gegensätze*, p 129.

Prussians tended to want all the German troops of the small princes to join their army. This plan met with great resistance from the Duke of Wellington and resulted in great arguments as the latter wanted these German troops to join the Dutch Army.

Wellington was clearly exasperated at this stage of the negotiations. On 26 March 1815, he wrote to Castlereagh,

We shall be very short in our numbers in the Netherlands, and the troops in that quarter are not of the best description; and you will see by my dispatch the difficulty I experienced and shall still experience in getting any reinforcements from Germany.

It seems to me, that it would be advisable to try to get the Portuguese, or some of them at least, there... Of these, we might safely take 12,000 or 14,000 into the Netherlands.[6]

Pondering on the situation a short while, Wellington next made an astute move. The Nassau ambassador related in his report of 28 March 1815 that,

Wellington has yet to leave. He had demanded that a Prussian Army Corps should join him. This had been considered as accepted. However, it is now the case that no Prussians will come under his command. On the other hand, it is all the more likely that he will be joined by those German contingents that the Prussians wanted to have in their army, and which had been the cause of much dispute. All the powers, with the exception of Prussia, are pressing for this agreement.[7]

The Duke's demand had isolated Prussia, leaving her the choice of allowing part of her army to come under his command, which could not be acceptable, or of conceding the control of troops of the German states, which was equally undesirable. Thus, a compromise had to be found. The next day, Wellington left Vienna to join his army in the Low Countries. The compromise agreed was that he would command an Anglo-Dutch army, which would be joined by the Hanoverian and Brunswick contingents as well as those of the remaining smaller German states. An exception to this were the Hesse-Darmstadters who were designated to join the Austrian Army. The Prussian Army under Blücher and Gneisenau was to link up with the Anglo-Dutch army. Although they were not to be directly under the Duke of Wellington's command, the Prussians were nevertheless to come under the Duke's direction and to fall in with his plans.

The next military conference took place on 31 March. Here, it was agreed that the Prussians would raise an army of 153,000 men under Blücher on the lower Rhine, and that Wellington would command a mixed-nationality army of unspecified strength in the Netherlands. The question of who was to receive the contingents from Hesse-Kassel, Mecklenburg, Nassau, Waldeck, Schwarzburg, Reuss, Lippe, Anhalt, the Kingdom of Saxony, the Saxon

6 WD, vol XII, p 281.
7 Pflugk-Harttung, *Gegensätze*, p 130.

Duchies, Oldenburg, Brunswick and the Hanseatic cities was again discussed on the 31st, as both Britain and Prussia still claimed them. The other Allied powers generally favoured allocating them to Wellington, whose forces were likely to be weaker, but Knesebeck managed to avoid conceding this. Thus, the decision on this issue was postponed, the matter being passed on to the politicians.

The subsequent political conference passed control of the contingents of Nassau, the Kingdom of Saxony, Brunswick, Oldenburg and the Hanseatic troops to Wellington, so Prussia definitely lost some ground. The remaining smaller states would come under Prussian command, however, or so it seemed until certain of the smaller states, particularly Weimar and Reuss, objected to this. Other states said that they were only prepared to come under the command of the army of their choice. In this way the entire issue was thrown open to debate again, even though it was now a month after Napoleon's return to France.

Although they had had to make concessions, the British had won this round. The Prussians would now find it more difficult to achieve their objective of obtaining a major share in winning the war, and a major say in the subsequent peace negotiations. Prussia's aim to dominate northern Germany was thwarted, but Britain's hope of commanding the entire military operation in the Low Countries was compromised. As the Anglo-Netherlands army was not to be the sole military force in this theatre, a military victory there might be credited to a commander other than Wellington. This would not further Britain's policy of having the greater say in the establishment of a new European order, so the Duke would have to find a way to ensure that the final victory against Napoleon would be his.

A further meeting on 1 April 1815 was the first real attempt at finding a satisfactory conclusion to these problems.[8] The Allies now planned to form three main armies, one on the upper Rhine, one on the middle Rhine and one in the Netherlands, and the meeting discussed how to share the German contingents between them. It was agreed that Wellington's British army would be joined by certain north German contingents, in addition to German troops already in British service like the King's German Legion (KGL). These formations were to join Wellington as allies, not mercenaries. An appropriate number of troops from the German states were to be placed under Blücher's Prussian army and the Prussians, Austrians and Russians separately undertook to ensure that all German princes who provided troops for the campaign would receive suitable subsidies from Britain.

Cathcart reported the events of this meeting in a letter to Castlereagh that day:

> There were present at this conference his Majesty the Emperor of Russia, the Prince Royal of Wurtemberg [sic], Field Marshals Prince Schwarzenberg and Prince Wrede, myself, Lieutenant-Generals Knesebeck and Prince Volkonsky, and Major-General Langenau to hold the protocol.

8 Pflugk-Harttung, *Gegensätze*, p 127.

After reciting the matters which had been considered at the former military conferences, at which Field Marshal the Duke of Wellington was present, it was stated that the object of the present assembly was to settle, as far as possible, the composition of the several armies, and the garrisons of Mayence [Mainz], and the quarters, marches, and communications, of the several corps.

It was agreed to begin with the left army, which is to assemble on the Upper Rhine. This army is to consist of upwards of 140,000 men, viz.:-

Bavarian force under Field-Marshal Wrede	65,000
Under H.R.H. the Prince Royal of Wurtemberg	
Wurtemberg troops	25,000
Baden troops	8,000
Colloredo's Austrian corps	8,000
Prince of Hohenzollern's corps, all Austrian	40,000
	146,000

Schwarzenberg was accepted as commander-in-chief of this army and Cathcart's letter continued,

Mayence is to be garrisoned by detachments. It was proposed that the detail should be made up by Austrians, 4,000; Prussians, 4,000; Bavarians, 3,000; Prince Nassau, Princes Reuss, and other states, 3,500; and that Hesse-Cassel should be required to make up the remainder of the complement of 21,000 – that the use of this fortress should be given to the several armies in proportion to their emergencies – and that the great road leading to it should be kept unencumbered.

It has been very strongly reported that the Archduke Charles will take the government of Mayence.

…The Prussian general [Knesebeck] vehemently objected to any idea of appropriating the contingents of the northern and centre States of Germany to the Duke of Wellington's army… He did not object to giving up the contingents of Hanover, Brunswick, Oldenburg, and of the Hanseatic towns, but most strenuously deprecated giving that destination to Hesse-Cassel.[9]

Not surprisingly, the British government made no immediate decisions as to which of the minor German states would receive what subsidies. Much depended how compliant these states would be to British desires. Prussia clearly wished to bring the armies of all the small north German states under her control, excluding Hanover of course, and this would certainly have political consequences after the war. Britain calmly waited for the various rulers to come to her for protection. The German states were economically devastated after the 20 years of war. They had no money and Britain's trading empire provided the means to buy their allegiance. Britain could wait for the right time to make a move. After all, the sooner the coffers of the German princelings were filled, the less compliant with British wishes they were likely to be. Britain's policy was thus to keep the German states waiting and to play them off against Prussia, even though war with France was only weeks away.

[9] Vane, *Castlereagh*, vol X, p 289 f.

The Battle for the German Contingents

It was now the turn of the rulers of Germany's smaller states to play a role in the proceedings. At the request of Austria and Prussia, they met and formed a commission. On 5 April 1815 they decided that no one power could unilaterally decide their fate, and that all decisions they made must be unanimous. They also decided that their contingents were not to be divided up individually among the armies of the great powers. Instead, their contingents were to be organised in divisions and corps consisting of troops of several states. These corps could then be placed under the command of a general of one of the Great Powers.[10] This bold move for self-determination was yet another blow to Prussian ambitions. All that Prussia had to offer these states was an end to their independence – not a particularly pleasant prospect. As Britain's offer of subsidies would fill their empty coffers, there can be little doubt who was orchestrating this act of defiance. Prussia could do little to change the situation other than attempt to apply pressure behind the scenes.[11]

Marschall also reported that the division of the German contingents agreed by Britain and Prussia on 1 April had made Prussia's aims clear and, with the exception of Weimar, had caused great concern among the minor princes, especially the Saxon Dukes in their small Thuringian states. They were still hoping for changes in these arrangements. On 11 April, Marschall reported about Prussia's continuing 'pretensions' and that there was yet to be a final agreement on the distribution of the German contingents. This was to be left to the individual princes to decide. However, on 14 April, Prussia obtained consent for control over the armies of the Saxon Duchies, Reuss, Schwarzburg, Anhalt, Lippe, Waldeck and Mecklenburg. These contingents assembled on the Lower Rhine under Prussian command, while the troops of the south German states came under Austrian command. Prussia still wanted to add the Nassau contingent to the list but now saw no hope of achieving this particular aim. These arrangements were definitively confirmed on 18 April 1815, when a decisive meeting of the Great Powers took place.

On 20 April 1815 the joint committee of the German states and the Great Powers was therefore able to draw up an outline of the composition of the Allied armies. The army on the upper Rhine was to be made up of forces from Austria, Bavaria, Württemberg, Baden, Hesse-Darmstadt, Hohenzollern, Liechtenstein, and Frankfurt. On the middle and lower Rhine troops were to deploy from Prussia, the Electorate of Hesse, Mecklenburg, Saxon Duchies, Anhalt, Schwarzburg, Reuss, Lippe-Detmold, Schaumburg-Lippe, Waldeck. The army in the Netherlands was to be made up by Britain, the Netherlands, Hanover, Brunswick, Oldenburg, and the Hanseatic towns. This army was to be joined by the Saxons and part of the Nassauers, while another Nassau contingent was to garrison Mainz.

Representatives of the German states reminded the Great Powers that it was on record that only they themselves could make decisions on the use of

---

[10] Klüber, *Acten*, vol IV, p 394.
[11] Pflugk-Harttung, *Gegensätze*, p 133.

their contingents. Sizes of the contingents were also laid down, though this was still to be subject to review. Prussia was allocated 13,400 German troops. Britain was allocated 3,000 Brunswickers, 1,600 Oldenburgers, 6,080 Nassauers and 3,000 Hanseatic troops, a total of 13,680 men. In addition to those came 17,000 Hanoverians and 9,000 Saxons plus militia.

On 22 April, a further conference determined the strength of these contingents as follows (items marked * are in the original):

For Prussia

Mecklenburg-Schwerin	3,800 men	
Mecklenburg-Strelitz	800 men	(or ⅓ as cavalry)*
Saxe-Weimar	1,600 men	
Saxe-Gotha	2,200 men	
Saxe-Meiningen	600 men	
Saxe-Hildburgshausen	400 men	
Saxe-Cobourg	600 men	(Will raise 800 men)*
Anhalt	1,600 men	
Schwarzburg	1,300 men	
Reuss	900 men	
Lippe-Detmold	1,000 men	
Schaumburg-Lippe	300 men	
Waldeck	800 men	
Total	15,600 men	

For Britain

Brunswick	3,000 men	
Oldenburg	1,600 men	
Nassau	6,080 men	(including troops already in Netherlands, but excluding 2–3,000 men for the garrison of Mainz)*
Hanseatic Cities	3,000 men	
Total	13,680 men [12]	

If he were to gain the 9,000 Royal Saxons as well, Wellington could expect about 40,000 Germans to join his forces, since he already had 17,000 Hanoverians available or promised. Even without the Saxons the British were allocated twice the number of German troops as the Prussians and also got those contingents that were of better quality. Thus, there can be no question that Wellington gained much more from these bitter negotiations than Blücher, which did little to improve the image the Prussians now had of the Duke. Much depended, of course, on the payment of subsidies by Britain, whose representatives continually used this means to apply political pressure. Finally, even after they had been authorised, payments were dragged out and made only in instalments.

---

[12] Pflugk-Harttung, *Bundestruppen*, p 108. The total 'for Prussia' is incorrectly added in the original. The sum of the figures given is in fact 15,900.

On 23 April 1815 the British representative declared that he was still unable to give a firm answer on the question of financial assistance.[13] Until British wishes were met, it was evident that no British money would be forthcoming. A further indication of British policy came about when the Commission for Matters of Supply met on 30 April. Here, the British and Hanoverian representatives, Stewart and Münster, suggested that contingents sent to the Low Countries would not be required to draw supplies from their home areas. Instead, they would receive direct assistance from Britain, leaving less money available for the other contingents. The home territories of those contingents joining Wellington would thus be freed of the obligation of supplying their own forces, relieving their economies, but those of the other German states would be worse off. This attempt to play one German state off against the other and at disrupting the agreed method of supply was met with objection.[14]

By the outbreak of hostilities, neither Wellington nor Blücher had actually received the contingents for which they had hoped. Grand Duke Peter of Oldenburg sent off his army to join the North German Federal Corps under Kleist instead of Wellington's army. As Grand Duke Peter was a relative of the czar, it would have been surprising for him to support British interests. The Hanseatic towns delayed the deployment of their contingents, and the Saxons never saw action. Wellington finally mustered a total of around 36,000 Germans, including the KGL, for his army. However, even that reduced figure was larger than the number of British troops, around 32,000, that the Duke had at his disposal. His Netherlands force consisted of 25,000 men, so the Germans were the largest contingent in Wellington's army. Had he obtained all the German troops for which he had hoped, then his army would have been predominantly German in composition.

The Nassauers

Once Napoleon had been expelled from Germany after his defeat at the Battle of Leipzig in October 1813, there was a power vacuum in the German territories between the Elbe and the Rhine. In December 1813 Willem of Nassau-Orange was made ruler of the Netherlands. He also had lands in Germany, including the principalities of Dillenburg, Dietz, Hadamar and Siegen. Here, at the beginning of 1814, he began raising the Nassau-Orange Regiment, joining the Allied coalition as the Prince of Nassau-Orange.[15] The first battalion of the regiment was completed in January, the second in April. Together, these battalions numbered over 3,000 men. They were brigaded with the existing Nassau troops, which were one line and one Landwehr regiment, six battalions and three companies of volunteers in all. This brigade formed part of the V German Corps under the Duke of Saxe-Cobourg, and was used in the blockade of Mainz. After Mainz surrendered, the two Nassau-Orange Regiment battalions entered Dutch pay. The 1st Battalion was stationed in the

[13] Klüber, *Acten*, IV p 424.
[14] Pflugk-Harttung, *Gegensätze*, p 136.
[15] Starklof, Vol I, p 168 ff.

Netherlands, from the end of August 1814. The 2nd Battalion remained at home on call. It was called up in May 1815. It arrived in the Low Countries just before the commencement of hostilities, joining the 1st Battalion in Genappe on 12 June 1815.

Other Nassau forces included the 2nd Nassau Infantry Regiment, recruited from Nassau-Usingen. This formation was three battalions strong. Many of its men had originally been recruited to fight on the French side and had a history of effective service during the Peninsular War when the regiment had fought as part of a contingent from Napoleon's Confederation of the Rhine under Oberst Freiherr von Kruse. After Napoleon's defeat at Leipzig, word was sent from Nassau to Kruse ordering him to go over to the British at the first opportunity, which he did on 10 December 1813. The regiment was transported back to Britain by sea and later went into Netherlands service.

The Nassauers objected strongly to Prussia's attempts to gain control of their forces. Particularly, they did not want to find their army amalgamated into Kleist's Prussian corps, stationed on their native Rhine. Marschall's aim was for the Nassau forces to join the Netherlands Army. After all, both states were ruled by the same royal house, and there was already one Nassau contingent with Wellington's Army.[16] Naturally, the Duke fully supported their position.

Prussian efforts to acquire the Nassauers for their own army continued in April 1815, but Marschall resisted them. He reported on 2 April that the Nassauers were to be sent to Wellington. On 4 April, he mentioned Prussian efforts to obtain the Nassauers for themselves. On 6 April, he wrote that, 'In no event will the Nassau troops become part of a Prussian Corps.'[17] On 11 April he recounted that it was up to Wellington as to exactly when the Nassauers should join his army. However, he advised that the troops should be sent to the Netherlands as soon as possible so that Nassau might qualify for British subsidies. On 14 April Marschall showed signs of giving in to the Prussians, which alarmed the British and led to more pressure from them. On 19 April, Marschall claimed to the Prussians that the Nassauers were either just about to or had indeed already marched off to the Netherlands.

However, the final decision that the Nassauers were to join Wellington only came on 20 April. The Nassau contingent was to total 6,080 men not including any troops in the Mainz garrison. The 1st Light Regiment, until then part of the V German Army Corps under the Duke of Saxe-Cobourg, was disbanded. The Prince of Nassau sent the good news off to Wellington on 24 April.[18] The British won this round, with the Prussians again going off empty-handed.

The Regiment Nassau-Orange and the 2nd Regiment were organised into one brigade. This was initially placed under the command of Oberst von Goedecke, but later, when he was injured, he was replaced by Prinz Bernhard. At the outbreak of hostilities, the Nassau Brigade totalled around 4,300 men.

[16] Pflugk-Harttung, *Gegensätze*, p 140.
[17] Pflugk-Harttung, *Gegensätze*, p 142.
[18] WSD, vol X, p152.

It was attached to the Prince of Orange's Corps, in the 2nd Netherlands Division of General Perponcher. Although it consisted of German troops, the Nassau Brigade was placed under Netherlands, and ultimately British command.

Freiherr von Kruse, now a general, was placed in charge of the newly raised 1st Nassau Infantry Regiment. He had been ordered to mobilise his forces on 25 March 1815. On 2 April, he reported that the matter was already in hand, but that his Orange Battalion was short of 200 men. More time would be required to recruit the necessary men. This force was due to become part of the V German Corps under the Duke of Saxe-Cobourg. On 22 April Kruse informed the Duke of Saxe-Cobourg that he had just received instructions that he was to march without delay to Wellington's army and link up with the 2nd Infantry Regiment. Kruse also reported to Wellington that he was going to join up with him.

Owing to delays in obtaining equipment for his men, Kruse only left his depot on 21 May. His force numbered 70 officers and 2,917 men. They reached Cologne on 27 May and Maastricht on 1 June. Once they joined up with Wellington, they were not, after all, brigaded with the other Nassauers. There were various reasons for this. Firstly, this would disrupt the existing formations, and to do so this close to the outbreak of hostilities would have been unwise. Secondly, and more importantly, while Kruse's contingent came under Wellington's direct command, the Nassau Brigade itself owed its allegiance to the King of the Netherlands, and was at its monarch's disposal. Kruse's men missed the action at Quatre Bras, but went on to take part in the Battle of Waterloo.[19]

Saxony in the Napoleonic Wars

The Saxon Army was the most tragic casualty of the Anglo-Prussian political conflict. The well-equipped Saxon Corps of 14,000 men was regarded as one of the better German formations, yet it did not participate in the campaign. Instead, it was broken up, suffered punitive executions, had one of its colours burned, and was sent home in disgrace.

For most of the Napoleonic Wars the Saxons were among Napoleon's most loyal allies. The Prussians had long had territorial ambitions in Saxony, and had occupied Saxony in the Seven Years War and press-ganged the Saxon army into Prussian service. The Saxons still regarded Prussia as their most dangerous enemy. Forced to fight alongside the Prussians again in 1806, the Prince Elector of Saxony quickly changed sides after the Battle of Jena, joining Napoleon's Confederation of the Rhine, and receiving his royal throne in reward. His forces became a significant part of the *Grande Armée* in most of the coming campaigns. King Friedrich August of Saxony did show some signs of hesitation once news of the disastrous retreat from Moscow reached him at the end of 1812. However, he was caught between the pressures of nascent German nationalism in sections of his army, and a desire for self preservation

[19] Pflugk-Harttung, *Gegensätze*, p 144.

coupled with fears of what might happen to his state should Prussia emerge as a great power again. He thus remained loyal to Napoleon during the German War of Liberation in 1813. His army shared their ally's misfortunes that summer and autumn, fighting on the losing side in battles from Grossbeeren to Dennewitz. On the morning of the third day of the Battle of Leipzig, when it became clear that defeat for Napoleon was certain, General von Zeschau, commander of the Saxon infantry, asked his king for permission to go over to the Allies. Friedrich August did not give him a clear answer. The remaining Saxon infantry did change sides, but their king was treated as a prisoner-of-war and led off to Berlin at the end of the battle.

The position of the Saxons was thus somewhat confused. Their king had remained loyal to the French, but parts of his army had joined the Allied cause. From the Allied perspective, the Saxon Army had broken its oath to its monarch, so this oath was regarded as no longer being valid. However, both the Saxon people and the men of the Saxon Army saw matters differently.

Some Saxons had divided sympathies. A good example of this was General von Thielemann.[20] A Saxon by birth, he considered his loyalty to the German nation paramount, with his oath to his king coming second to that. In Saxon service, he was made commandant of the strategic fortress of Torgau on the Elbe early in 1813. He hoped his king would join the Allies in the forthcoming campaign. However, when Friedrich August decided to stay with Napoleon and handed over this important fortress to the French, Thielemann quit. He first joined the Russians, but hoped that the Prussians would accept him into their army. This they did, appointing him commander of the Saxon corps which served with the Allies in 1814. So a Saxon who had left royal service in protest against royal policy was now back as a 'Prussian' commanding Saxon troops. His men had mixed feelings about their commander. He was now dressed in Prussian blue, and to convince his new masters of his loyalty, he would have to be more Prussian than the Prussians themselves.

At the end of the campaign of 1814, the Saxon Army was allocated to the North German Army Corps deployed in the Rhineland. This was under the command of the Prussian General Kleist von Nollendorf. In view of Prussia's territorial ambitions in Saxony, it is not difficult to imagine the friction between the Saxon and Prussian soldiers. The Saxon officer corps clearly had divided loyalties as well as insecurity over its future. Kleist attempted to handle this situation sensitively, but when Napoleon returned from Elba, the Prusso-Saxon forces were placed under the command of Blücher and Gneisenau, who had different views. Blücher always demanded total loyalty from his men. Gneisenau was not a Prussian by birth, but had pursued a successful career in the Prussian Army and, as an outsider who had been promoted over a number of jealous native Prussians, he too had to be more Prussian than the Prussians. In any difficult circumstances, both Blücher and Gneisenau were unlikely to treat the Saxons gently.

---

[20] For a life of Thielemann, see: Petersdorff, *General Johann Adolph Freiherr von Thielemann*, (Leipzig, 1894).

The Struggle for the Saxon Army

In April 1815 the Congress of Vienna decided that the Kingdom of Saxony should be divided, with the northern part being annexed by Prussia, while Friedrich August was to retain the rump of his domain. Partly because of his earlier loyalty to Napoleon, the Prussians had tried to have the king removed from his throne, and gain all of Saxony for themselves. Only Anglo-Austrian desires to check Prussian growth and the fact that part of the Saxon army joined the Allies during the Battle of Leipzig prevented this from happening. Friedrich August was reluctant to give up so much of his territory, so he held on to it for as long as possible, hoping for a change in events.

The division of Saxony obviously also opened the question of the future of its army. There were two possibilities: either the Saxon Army was to be left intact for the campaign, or it was to be divided into 'new Prussians' and 'rump Saxons'. Leaving the army intact was totally unacceptable to the Prussians, as participation by a Royal Saxon Army in an Allied victory would strengthen the case for preserving the Kingdom of Saxony. The King of Prussia thus ordered Gneisenau to divide the Saxon Army. Those Saxons hailing from territories annexed by Prussia were to join the Prussian Army, and those still from areas under Saxon rule were to be sent to the North German Federal Army. Clearly, the military cohesion of the proud Saxon Army would be destroyed by such an action, demoralising the Saxons. Kleist intervened on their behalf, strongly objecting to this.

The 'new Prussian' contingent was attached to the II Prussian Army Corps, then under the Prussian Generallieutenant von Borstell, a man of conscience. Had hostilities begun immediately, then the Saxons might have acquitted themselves well. However, the weeks dragged on, and fighting did not begin. In these weeks, the political wrangling over the future of Saxony continued, with the Saxons becoming despondent. The relationship with their Prussian commanders continued to deteriorate.

When Blücher took over the supreme command of the Prussian forces from Kleist, he attempted to gain the loyalty of the Saxons. He had two Saxon regiments, including the élite Guard Grenadiers, posted to his headquarters in Liège. Ever a leader of men, Blücher tried to gain the trust of the Saxon officers. Both Saxon and Prussian officers dined at his table. Müffling, a spokesman for Saxon interests, was sure of their loyalty. However, events in Vienna had more influence on attitudes in Liège than Blücher's hospitality. Prussia wanted to assimilate Saxony, so Blücher was pressured to assimilate the Saxon Army.

When Thielemann was transferred to take command of the Prussian III Army Corps, his replacement, the Saxon General Ryssel, also donned a Prussian uniform. Other Saxon officers were forced to decide if they wanted to enter Prussian service. Ever more, the Saxons felt that they were no longer an independent army, rather, they were being compulsorily Prussianised. The majority of the Saxon officers objected to this, and resistance began.

The Saxon party concentrated around their chief-of-staff, Oberst von Zezschwitz. It now seemed unavoidable that Prussia would dismember

Saxony, but the rump Saxons decided they did not wish to join Kleist's corps in the proposed federal army. Instead, they pressed to be allowed to join Wellington. Reports also reached the Prussian authorities that off duty Saxon troops were now drinking the health of Napoleon, not so long ago the guardian and saviour of Saxony from the Prussians. The situation was becoming tense.

On 30 April 1815 General von Grolman arrived in Liège with a dispatch from Vienna from the Prussian king. This was an order-in-cabinet dated 22 April informing Blücher that the final agreement on the details of the division of Saxony was likely to take a few more days. In the meantime, Blücher should prepare to reorganise the Saxon corps into two brigades. The first was to consist of those Saxons native to the parts of Saxony about to be annexed, whilst the second was to consist of rump Saxons. The order implied that regimental formations were to remain unaffected, which would be impossible as, even at company level, the soldiers were a mixture of new Prussians and rump Saxons. The reorganisation was to be implemented immediately, without regard to the fact that the King of Saxony had not yet released his soldiers from their oath of loyalty. The Prussian representatives in Vienna were out of touch with the situation in Liège, putting Blücher in a quandary, as such a reorganisation was likely to be difficult to implement.

The Saxon Rebellion

Blücher carried out his instructions on 1 and 2 May 1815. He expected by 5 May to have reorganised the Saxon corps into two brigades, one consisting of soldiers and officers from rump Saxony, the other of natives of Prussian Saxony with their officers in Prussian service. Blücher announced the rather confusing plans for implementing this to the Saxons on 2 May. This led to demonstrations. Soldiers of the Saxon Guard Grenadiers protested in front of Blücher's residence, crying, 'We don't want to be split up, long live our King Friedrich August'. Their officers calmed them down, but not before stones had been thrown at the blue-coated General Ryssel, who was denounced as a 'Prussian lickspittle'.[21]

Despite efforts by their officers to calm the situation down, a further demonstration took place that evening. Saxon grenadiers, still carrying their side arms after being on parade, made their way to Blücher's headquarters. Prussian staff officers and Saxon sentries tried to stop them. When their pleas were ignored, the Prussian officers drew their swords and laid into the crowd. The Saxons drew their weapons, and a fight ensued. The Saxons at the back of the crowd threw stones through the windows of the Prussian headquarters. Then they stormed the building, forcing Blücher to flee to safety. Once he was gone, the crowd broke up. On this occasion, no senior Saxon officers were in sight, and they had not attempted to calm the situation. That night, Blücher had the Saxon Guards marched off to Namur.

These events could not have occurred at a more embarrassing time for the Prussians. On the very same day, 2 May 1815, a despatch from Generalmajor

---

[21] Pflugk-Harttung, *Gegensätze*, p 149.

von Dörnberg, a Hanoverian officer who was commanding one of Wellington's outposts at Mons, arrived at the Duke's headquarters.[22] This reported stated (incorrectly at that time) that Napoleon was moving towards the frontier with his army, so it seemed as if hostilities were imminent. Wellington had already arranged to meet Blücher at Tirlemont the next day.[23] The Prussian commander, ejected from his headquarters the previous night, must have felt most uncomfortable in that meeting, giving Wellington a big advantage in their discussions, as explained in Chapter 6.

While preparing to leave for the meeting with Wellington at Tirlemont, Blücher had issued further orders for how the reorganisation of the Saxons was to continue. The two brigades were to leave Liège by 10 a.m. and march off in different directions. Thereafter, a Prussian brigade was to be posted in the town. The commander of the 'new Prussian' 1st Brigade, Generalmajor von Steinmetz, was instructed to execute this order, but it was one that could only lead to further incidents. Zezschwitz tried to reason with Steinmetz, suggesting that the regiments be allocated to the brigades on the basis of the origins of the majority of their members. However, Steinmetz insisted that he should carry his orders out to the letter. The situation exploded.

Although the 'rump Saxon' 2nd Regiment mostly marched off, the two grenadier battalions refused, demanding that they be allowed to join the Guard Grenadier Battalion in Huy. Zezschwitz conceded the point but did not want to move them out of Liège until 3 p.m. First the 2nd Grenadier Battalion, then the 3rd started to protest. Discipline and order broke down. Soldiers started running through the streets shouting insults about the King of Prussia as well as crying 'Vive l'Empereur'. A major who had joined Prussian service was chased. Only when the two battalions were permitted to march off in the direction of the Guard and the Grenadiers were promised that they could join the Guard the next day, did any movement take place. Loyal Prussian units immediately entered Liège.

There was a further development when, on his way back from Tirlemont, Blücher passed the Saxon 2nd Light Regiment. They refused to salute him and the Field Marshal took this as a great insult. Borstell, commander of the Prussian II Army Corps, was ordered to take precautions in case the Saxons marched off to France. The III Army Corps was ordered to move up to support Borstell. Blücher struck with an iron fist when perhaps gentler methods would have been more effective. The three battalions of the Guard Grenadier Regiment were separated from each other, and were disarmed. They were ordered to hand over a total of ten men, who were then executed by firing squad. The colour of the Guard, which the Queen of Saxony herself had embroidered, was burnt in public. Borstell protested and was relieved of duty for his trouble. Not only did Prussia lose a crack formation from its forces, a badly needed general of considerable experience was now not going to be available for this campaign.

[22] WSD, vol X, p 216.
[23] WD, vol XII, p 345.

Wellington and the Saxons

Wellington's involvement in the dispute over the fate of the Saxon Army was noteworthy. It had been agreed at the Congress of Vienna on 1 April that the Saxons were to be attached to Wellington's army. The Prussians kept objecting to this and it has already been explained that further meetings were held. In these discussions, Clancarty drew Hardenberg's attention to the rebellious atmosphere in the Saxon army and its objections to being in Prussian service. He argued that this was an additional reason why the Saxons should come under Wellington's command. If they were nevertheless to come under Prussian control, then Clancarty demanded that other German contingents of a similar strength should be attached to Wellington's army.[24] Hardenberg was thus placed in a difficult position. In an earlier meeting with Wellington, before a final decision on the fate of Saxony had been made, Hardenberg had been asked to estimate the size of the Saxon contingent. He had put this at 'about 12,000 to 14,000 men'.[25] After that discussion, it had been decided to divide the Saxon army in relation to the division of the Kingdom of Saxony, which would leave a royal army of 7,000 to 8,000 men. However, Clancarty now wanted Wellington to be sent the entire 12,000 men.

On 30 April 1815, Hardenberg gave Clancarty a formal answer. The Prussian representative's position was quite clear. In the meeting of 1 April, the issues had been discussed, but his side gave no firm commitments one way or the other. Although agreements on other German contingents had been defined by treaty on 25 March, the Royal Saxon army had not been part of this. By calling up further men from the relatively populous Saxony, Wellington could still get his 14,000 men. Indeed, Hardenberg had already instructed the Saxon provisional government to send three militia regiments to the Rhine. The division of the Saxon army into two brigades had already been ordered, so there was now nothing to stop the rump Saxons being added to Wellington's forces.[26] In a meeting on 1 May, Clancarty opposed this, insisting that there had been a formal agreement between Hardenberg and Wellington. Hardenberg denied that he had ever promised Wellington the entire Saxon contingent. He said he had not included Prussian subjects in this contingent and had never agreed on the number of Saxons the Duke should get.

This was the background of political conflict that had caused the Saxon army to rebel and, as we have seen, those events began on the evening before an important meeting between Blücher and Wellington. Wellington certainly made as much political capital from the Saxon mutiny as he possibly could, and continued to do so over the issue of how to remove the Saxons from the front and get them to a place where they could do no further harm. The Prussians wanted to isolate the rebellious troops, keep them out of sight from the remainder of the army and send them back to Germany with a minimum of fuss and publicity. It was in Wellington's interests, however, to maximise the embarrassment his allies were suffering.

[24] Pflugk-Harttung, *Gegensätze*, p 153.
[25] WSD, vol X, p 142.
[26] Pflugk-Harttung, *Gegensätze*, p 155.

Meanwhile, the King of Saxony requested Metternich to intervene on his behalf, so Metternich wrote to Wellington from Vienna on 23 May 1815, informing him that Friedrich August wished the Duke to take command of his army. Their exceptional behaviour had been due to mishandling by the Prussians and they were an excellent body of soldiers. If Wellington did not want command of his army then, Metternich said, the king would offer it to Schwarzenberg.[27]

The same day the Duke of Saxe-Cobourg wrote to Wellington informing him that the King of Saxony had appointed him commander of the Saxon Army and that he wished it to join Wellington.[28] Saxe-Cobourg also lobbied Lord Stewart with the British delegation in Vienna, the latter informing Wellington of this on 25 May.[29] Further pressure was put on Wellington when Zezschwitz came to Brussels to negotiate with him on 24 May. The Duke dined his guest but refused to discuss the situation. He reported the matter to Hardinge, telling him that,

> The Colonel of the Saxon dragoons [Zezschwitz] was over here the other day and dined with me… The Colonel wanted to speak to me, but I did not see him… You may mention this or not as you please. You will take care, however, not to get the Colonel into any scrape.[30]

There is no doubt that, at one stage, Wellington would have liked to take over command of the Saxons from the Prussians and had attempted to gain control of the Saxon forces for himself.[31] However, Nostitz, Blücher's ADC, noted in his diary that, when Blücher offered Wellington the entire Saxon Army at the meeting in Tirlemont on 3 May,[32] Wellington rejected this, commenting that he already had enough problems with potentially mutinous Belgians. Wellington probably realised that accepting such an offer would have led to great difficulties with the Prussians later on, which would have been counter-productive. Wellington might well have been disappointed that he had not obtained the Saxons, but at least the Prussians had not either, and the disparity in the numbers of their respective armies was not as great as it might have been.

Wellington's attitude was confirmed on 6 June when he rejected the approaches of two Saxon colonels, Leyser and Ziegler, who were acting on behalf of their king. He informed Müffling of this for the Prussian to report to Gneisenau.[33] Wellington was having nothing more to do with the Saxons.

The disaffection of early May soon spread throughout the Saxon army. Blücher sent the entire Saxon infantry off to the Rhine, hoping that the artillery and cavalry, of which his need was greater, could still be used. Oberst Raabe, commander of the Saxon artillery, expressed his unwillingness to fight for a foreign army. So the artillery was sent away, too. Only the cavalry remained, but nobody really thought they would be useful in a battle situation.

[27] WSD, vol X, p 346.
[28] WSD, vol X, p 346.
[29] WSD, vol X, p 371.
[30] WD, vol XII, p 421.

[31] WD, vol XII, p 300.
[32] Nostitz, p 11.
[33] GStA, Rep 92, Gneisenau, A 40, fol 79.

The Saxons were packed off first to the Rhine, then to Westphalia and Hesse. There was talk of the rump Saxons being sent to Hanover where they would not have to be fed by the Prussians and from where they could be sent on to Wellington.[34] The Duke, however, dropped the matter. This tragic affair was now coming to its end. Saxe-Cobourg gave up his hopes of commanding the Saxons under Wellington.[35]

The King of Saxony finally released his men from their oath of loyalty to him, allowing the division of his forces to take place. Having been left in the lurch by the British and insulted by the Prussians, he offered the services of the rump of his army to the Austrians.[36] He even went as far as to start to march them off to join Schwarzenberg. However, the war with Napoleon ended before this move was complete.

As far as Wellington was concerned, the Saxon question had served its purpose. It was a shame that he was not able to obtain their army for his own use, but at least the Prussians had not gained this advantage. Also, there was now a precedent regarding the fate of the other German contingents. If they came under Prussian command, they might rebel. Would it not be better, therefore, to put them all under British command?

Without the Saxons, Wellington had a problem raising the number of troops he required for his army. He would need to obtain other German contingents instead but it seemed as if the smaller states would not provide the answer. The British complained bitterly when the Grand Duke of Oldenburg sent his contingent off to join Kleist's North German Corps and attempts to obtain the expected 1,600 men of the contingents of Saxe-Cobourg, Saxe-Hildburghausen and Saxe-Meiningen were futile because these forces existed only on paper. Those states were bankrupt and could not raise troops without British subsidies but Britain was unwilling to commit any payments until it was certain that she would get these troops. This would mean further conflicts with Prussia over the allocation of the other contingents. The tension between the allies was not likely to ease, even as war approached.

The Hessians

Kurfürst Wilhelm I, ruler of Hesse-Kassel had been forced into exile after the French victories at Jena and Auerstedt in 1806 because of his alliance with the Prussians. His territories were then used to form part of the so-called Kingdom of Westphalia. This unpopular puppet state collapsed in 1813. Wilhelm returned home, determined to restore his domains to their former glory. It was as if his seven years of exile had never happened. His former soldiers were ordered to their depots, and told to bring all their old kit with them. Wilhelm took a dim view of any officers who had joined the Westphalian army. Those who had been promoted in Westphalian service were required to rejoin his army at their 1806 rank. His Guards were given old-fashioned tricorn hats and

[34] WSD, vol X, p 426.
[35] WSD, vol X, p 425.
[36] WSD, vol X, p 561.

long gaiters and instructed to wear their hair in queues. Wilhelm even wanted to reintroduce this uniform throughout his entire army, but was finally persuaded to adopt a more modern Prussian style, worn with the Hessian cockade, for the rest of his troops.

Wilhelm remained a bitter enemy of Napoleon, the man who had expelled him from his home. Despite his state's general impoverishment, he committed substantial resources to liberating Germany from Napoleonic imperialism. On the return of the 'Ogre' from his short exile in Elba, Wilhelm was faced with the choice of throwing in his lot with the Prussians again or joining Wellington's army in the Low Countries. His support for German nationalist ideas inclined him towards Prussia, but Hesse's economic plight made the golden guineas offered by Britain tempting. The Kurfürst was in a quandary.

The Prussians understood Wilhelm's dilemma. To advance their cause they were quick to provide his army with military advisors. On 19 March 1815, Friedrich Wilhelm III of Prussia ordered Generallieutenant von Zastrow to raise and equip as many Hessians as he could to join the Prussian army. Zastrow had not only military, but also diplomatic skills, so the scope of his mission was soon widened. On 31 March, Hardenberg instructed him not to leave Kassel until he had persuaded Wilhelm to join the Prussians and sign a treaty.[37] Zastrow was also to establish what moves the British had made in Hesse-Kassel. He was to make every effort to dissuade the Kurfürst from deciding to join Wellington and urge him instead to join his fellow Germans. What use would there be in fighting so far from home, in the Low Countries when he could join forces deployed for the defence of Germany and his principality?

The discussions about Hesse at Vienna seemed to be going well from the Prussian point of view. On 3 April 1815 Hardenberg wrote to Zastrow informing him that negotiations on the allocation of the north German contingents were as good as over.[38] It had been agreed provisionally that the German contingents would join forces with the Great Power in whose sphere of operations they lay. This meant that the Hessian forces would now come under Kleist's command. Zastrow was instructed to act on this basis.

There were some initial disagreements between the Prussians and the Kurfürst on the size of the contingent the Hessians were to provide. The Prussians wanted 12,000 men with a further 6,000 in reserve. The Hessian representatives in Vienna offered 10,000, while Wilhelm himself at first talked of 7,500. When the outbreak of war loomed closer, he showed himself more willing. As early as the end of March, he sent 4,000 men off to the Rhine, promising to send another 6,000 as soon as he could.[39]

Alarmed by this potential growth of Prussian influence, Britain now started to offer the Kurfürst financial support. At the end of March, Wilhelm received a letter from Münster, the Hanoverian minister. It was too late to stop the first batches of Hessians from joining the Prussians, so Münster offered to pay the

[37] Pflugk-Harttung, *Gegensätze*, p 171.
[38] Pflugk-Harttung, *Gegensätze*, p 172.
[39] Pflugk-Harttung, *Gegensätze*, p 173.

Kurfürst subsidies for any further troops he might like to raise for use by the Duke of Wellington. Wilhelm could not help but be tempted. By dividing the Hessian forces, Britain would at least be able to postpone the question of in whose sphere of influence this territory would end up after the war. However, due to the shortage of manpower, no more troops could be raised. In an endeavour to qualify for much needed cash, Wilhelm offered to send his contingent to the Prussian army corps that was going to be placed under Wellington's command at that stage. By doing so, he hoped to keep his powerful neighbour happy, and to obtain financial relief for his state.

Zastrow met with Wilhelm again on 6 April. The Kurfürst made it clear that he wanted to take the payments offered by Britain, and he would raise more troops with these subsidies. He had no particular preference as to whose army his contingent would join, the important point being that he was on the right side. However, Zastrow could not let these Hessians join Wellington. This contingent was, after all, the largest available from any north German state. Without the Hessians, the Prussians would lose all chance of having any say whatsoever in north German affairs, with British-ruled Hanover dominating the lesser states on the north German plain, and pushing back Prussia's sphere of influence to the Elbe river. Zastrow reminded the Kurfürst of his patriotic duties and his commitment to Prussia, insisting that any troops sent by Wilhelm to join Wellington would be over and above the number promised to Prussia. While Britain offered hard cash, Prussia could only talk about the good of the fatherland.

Further political pressure was applied. On 9 April, reports about problems with British subsidies arrived from Vienna. Zastrow used these reports to suggest to Wilhelm that payments from Britain were not certain, so the Kurfürst decided to send off his 12,000 men to join Kleist. On 11 April Zastrow was instructed by Hardenberg to speed up the Hessian mobilisation as best he could, and see that these troops indeed went off to join Kleist. Meanwhile, Zastrow was also told to thank Wilhelm for the speed and patriotism with which he had responded and say that Prussian representatives would make every effort to secure an appropriate part of the British subsidies for Hesse. It remained to be seen if the Prussians could get Wilhelm the finances he so badly needed.

This was not the last word since a final treaty had yet to be agreed and signed at Vienna, where it was now decided that the German states were to raise forces in proportion to their population. This meant that Hesse-Kassel was obliged to provide only 7,500 men, and the Hessian ambassador in Vienna insisted his country would provide no more. Hardenberg feared this would mean that Kleist would get only 7,500 Hessians with the remainder joining Wellington. However, on this occasion, Hardenberg did achieve his aims.

On 4 May 1815, a treaty was signed in Kassel in which the Kurfürst agreed to provide the King of Prussia with a contingent of 12,000 men for the front and 6,000 in reserve.[40] Fortunately for the Prussians, this treaty was signed just

---

[40] Pflugk-Harttung, *Gegensätze*, p 177.

before news of the fate of the Saxon contingent reached Kassel. In return, Prussia agreed to represent Hesse-Kassel's interests, particularly on the vital question of subsidies from Britain. The Kurfürst fulfilled his part of the agreement. On 6 May 1815 the first brigade marched off to the Rhine. The second brigade followed on 21 May. Even the third brigade reached the French border before the outbreak of hostilities, but the much needed subsidies did not arrive.

Questioning the effectiveness of Prussia's negotiations with Britain, Wilhelm sent off one of his adjutants, Major von Dalwigk, to ask Wellington for the long awaited payments. He could not expect much sympathy from that quarter, as the Hessians had, after all, joined Kleist's Prussians. The agreements the Duke was prepared to recognise as valid were those made in Vienna, and he accordingly considered the Prusso-Hessian treaty of 4 May as irrelevant. He gave permission for the payment of subsidies for only the 7,500 men agreed in Vienna, in effect, a financial penalty on the Hessians for supporting the Prussians. Kurfürst Wilhelm told the Prussians he would send no more men until this issue was resolved in his favour.[41] Events finally overtook this dispute when the war came to an end.

On this occasion, the Prussians managed to outmanoeuvre the British. Their success was owed partly to the fact that Hesse-Kassel was a neighbouring state with close ties to Prussia and partly to the Kurfürst being a conservative patriot, sympathetic to nationalistic arguments. However, Britain's trump card was money and Hesse-Kassel was one of a number of German states with a history of providing the British crown with mercenaries. Ultimately Zastrow and Hardenberg were astute enough to get Wilhelm to commit his men before the issue of subsidies had been fully resolved. For once Wellington was outsmarted, so he punished the Hessians for their loyalty to Prussian interests by not increasing their subsidy.

[41] Pflugk-Harttung, *Gegensätze*, p 179.

Chapter 3

The Prussian Army of 1815

The State of the Prussian Army

The armed forces fielded by the Kingdom of Prussia in 1815 were, in terms of quality of manpower, equipment and coherence of organisation, probably the worst Prussia employed in the entire Revolutionary and Napoleonic Wars. This is in part explained by the general deterioration of resources during this 25-year period of warfare, which affected most participants, and in part by the fact that Prussia was largely agrarian and economically underdeveloped. Yet this army held together despite early setbacks, participated in a dramatic victory, and went on to advance to the enemy capital. The main reasons for the success of Prussian arms in this campaign were its determination and superior leadership. That, in turn, was thanks to the development and training of a uniform general staff, one of the major military advances in this period.

A substantial part of the Prussian infantry in 1815 consisted of untrained, poorly equipped Landwehr (militia) troops, many of whom came from provinces which had only recently come under Prussian control. Indeed, France had ruled certain of these territories for two decades so that, for many of these young soldiers, German was almost a foreign tongue. Some of the regular formations, such as those from Berg, had recently fought as allies of France, so their new masters could not count on their loyalty. Others, such as the Saxons, were more or less press-ganged into Prussian service, as has been explained in Chapter 2. Other line regiments were new formations raised by amalgamating certain rather exotic units that had originated during the Wars of Liberation. These included the former Russo-German Legion and Lützow's Freikorps, both of limited military value owing to their irregular origins.

The Prussian cavalry was in the throes of a major reorganisation when war started in 1815. New regiments had been formed by putting together various squadrons from the legions, Freikorps and other sources. Many of these new formations lacked experience and cohesion, leaving the Prussian cavalry of 1815 in a very sorry state. The artillery fared little better, lacking much of the necessary equipment, and with new guns continuing to arrive even after the commencement of hostilities. Under-strength and under-equipped, the Prussian artillery struggled to make a mark in the campaign.

The performance of the Prussian Army was also affected by its inability to purchase or obtain sufficient supplies near its cantonments in the Netherlands, with the cash-rich British and native Netherlanders getting the lion's share of the available food. The Prussian quartermasters could only offer promissory notes when they tried to buy supplies, and few Dutch farmers or traders considered them able or even willing to honour these promises.

It was also significant that many of the élite formations and veteran units of the Prussian Army were not included in the Army of the Lower Rhine which actually did all the fighting. Instead these units were deployed nearer home, eyeing Prussia's Austrian allies with suspicion.

Poorly equipped, lacking both clothing and food, a mixture of raw levies and men of questionable loyalties in untried new formations, and without a substantial core of veterans – only strong and determined leadership would be able to pull this army through and bring it to victory. Fortunately, the Prussian Army of 1815 enjoyed commanders of the calibre of Blücher and Gneisenau, but it had few other advantages over its allies and enemies.

The General Staff

Perhaps the most significant development in the Prussian Army of the Napoleonic Wars was the birth of what was later to evolve into the German General Staff. Defeated by the single genius of Napoleon Bonaparte in the catastrophic campaign of 1806, a humbled Prussia began the long climb back to the status of Great Power. Lacking a single genius of her own with whom to counter her conqueror, Prussia founded an institution, the General Staff, thereby forming a collective genius to lead the prostrate nation out of her calamity. This collective genius set about implementing a series of reforms in the army which were not only to restore Prussia to her former glory, but which were to shape the face of modern Germany and Europe as a whole.

Gerhard von Scharnhorst and Graf Neidhardt von Gneisenau are usually described as the founding fathers of the German General Staff. Nevertheless, Oberst Freiherr von Massenbach, a Swabian nobleman, is credited with being the first to suggest that Frederick the Great's 'General Quartermaster Staff' (GQS), as it had become known, should be modernised in accordance with the current developments in warfare.

The period between the accession of Friedrich Wilhelm III to the throne of Prussia in 1797 and the outbreak of the Napoleonic Wars in 1805 was one of free-thinking open debate and liberal reform in Germany. The great changes that the French Revolution had brought to warfare and society and their meaning for the future were discussed in a plethora of military journals. Scharnhorst was the publisher of one such journal and earned himself the respect of such diverse characters as Blücher and Rüchel, a senior commander in the campaign of 1806. Though he was of Hanoverian descent, Scharnhorst's reputation as a theorist opened the door to service in the Prussian Army and he was soon appointed to the GQS. He was given the task of instructing his fellow officers and founded a 'Military Society' in Berlin. This body soon influenced the thinking of army officers such as the young Karl von Clausewitz, Boyen, later the Prussian Minister of War who introduced universal conscription to Prussia, and Grolman, later one of Blücher's staff officers at Waterloo. Under Scharnhorst's expert guidance, the 'brain' of the Prussian Army was conceived and developed.

It was on the retreat from Auerstedt in October 1806 that fate decided the form the General Staff was to take. Scharnhorst had become separated from the Royal Headquarters during the confusion and came across Blücher, who was trying to cover the withdrawal of the heavy artillery. The two men already knew each other, so Blücher did not hesitate to appoint Scharnhorst as his advisor for the rest of the campaign, in their case a fighting retreat to Lübeck on the Baltic coast.

Peace followed in the summer of 1807. Prussia, prostrate before a victorious Napoleon, was dismembered and plundered. One positive result of this defeat was that the reformers got the upper hand both in matters of state and of army organisation. The Baron vom Stein, a leading reformer and patriot, was put in charge of the Ministry of State. He saw to it that Scharnhorst would lead the recently founded 'Military Reorganisation Commission', empowered to conduct reforms of the army and its institutions. Stein also appointed fellow reformers like Gneisenau, Boyen and Grolman to posts on this commission. As leader of the commission, Scharnhorst became in effect an unofficial minister of war and chief of the general staff, particularly as the post of chief of the GQS was not filled after October 1806.

Scharnhorst's programme was clear. He aimed to introduce universal military service, though this was not implemented until 1814, and even then not without restrictions. He reorganised the army into permanent divisions of all arms, even in peacetime. However, because of the restrictions placed on the Prussian Army by Napoleon, these divisions were reduced in size, and redesignated as brigades. Scharnhorst also created a formal general staff, organised a ministry of war to which the general staff would be subordinated, opened the officer corps to men of sufficient education, and ended corporal punishment. Through all these reforms ran a thread of liberal democratic politics, a desire to reform not just one institution of the state, the army, but the state itself as a whole.

Blücher and Scharnhorst worked together again as a command team in the campaign of the spring of 1813, until Scharnhorst was mortally wounded at the Battle of Grossgörschen (known in the English-speaking world as Lützen). After this Gneisenau was brought in to replace Scharnhorst as Blücher's chief-of-staff. This type of team, with a leader to inspire the men and a brain to direct their operations, would characterise future Prussian and German General Staffs, Hindenburg and Ludendorff in the First World War being the most famous of several possible examples.

Blücher and Gneisenau were, therefore, a tried and tested team by 1815. They had ensured the Prussian Army played an important role in the decisive Allied victory at Leipzig in October 1813, and then taken their victorious Army of Silesia across the Rhine and into the enemy's heartland in the bitter winter of 1813–14. Despite suffering several checks at Napoleon's hands in 1814, they still pressed on to Paris. There were not many commanders in Europe with an equivalent record of perseverance and ultimate success.

Gneisenau was a Saxon by birth, and his father was merely a junior artillery officer, so, despite his record of accomplishment, he was not popular in certain sections of the Prussian Army. Officers of established Prussian military families tended to regard him as an upstart and an outsider, which would cause problems in 1815. General Yorck, Prussia's most capable corps commander, the victor of Wartenburg and Möckern, leader of the 'Fighting Corps' of Blücher's Army of Silesia, had proved a difficult subordinate in 1813–14. He was not willing to serve under Blücher and Gneisenau again, and in 1815 was sorely missed. Pirch, promoted to corps commander to replace Yorck, was not the best man for the job. To make room for Gneisenau, General Kleist von Nollendorf was also moved to a lesser command, as discussed in Chapter 6. General der Infanterie Graf Bülow von Dennewitz, the only full general to hold a corps command, was senior to Gneisenau in rank and length of service and came from an old military family. He had to be asked, and not told, to carry out orders from Gneisenau. This was to result, at a critical moment, in a day's delay in his corps getting to the front.

The General Staff in 1815

The General Staff was organised as follows. The Quartermaster-General, or chief-of-staff of the army was Generallieutenant Graf von Gneisenau. The staff officers included Generalmajor von Grolman, Oberst von Pfuel and Oberst von Thiele, Oberstlieutenant von Witzleben, Major von Lützow and Kapitain von Vigny. Their aides included Majors von Weyrach, von Brünneck, Graf Nostitz, and von Winterfeld, and Kapitain Sprenger. Blücher, the commander-in-chief, normally made command decisions after consultation with Gneisenau and Grolman. The staff then drafted the orders, which were taken to the relevant sub-commanders by aides from the staff. This organisation was duplicated at corps and brigade level so that each commanding general had his chief-of-staff.

The basic role of the general staff in the field was the same in principle at all levels. Its task was to receive and implement dispositions, operational orders, and routine orders (orders of the day, army, corps and brigade general orders). It also wrote the daily reports and maintained the unit war diaries. In practice these responsibilities had different effects at the various levels of command.

The Army Headquarters

Every field army had a chief of the general staff, officially known as the Quartermaster-General. For the duration of the war he was the representative of the Minister of War with the army, and was responsible for both operations and administration. The chief-of-staff and the army headquarters had three main tasks: firstly the organisation and assembly of the army, secondly its operations, that is its movements, tactics and positions, and finally its supply, including clothing, food, ammunition and accommodation. The supreme command was naturally the responsibility of the army's commanding general, with the role of his chief-of-staff being to turn the commanding general's intentions into practical plans. The chief-of-staff organised the officers available to him according to all those needs. He was himself personally responsible for dealing with political issues, drafting dispositions and issuing any necessary instructions.

The Corps Headquarters

The chief-of-staff of an army corps was responsible for all matters of organisation and leadership. He acted as an advisor to the corps commander, but the commander had the final word in any dispute. Any instructions issued by the chief-of-staff were only on behalf of and with the consent of the commander. In the event of any dispute, the chief-of-staff had the right to note his disagreement in the records. However, agreement and close co-operation were essential to the successful running of an army corps, so care was taken in choosing people who could work together.

The Staff Officer of the General Staff

This grade of officer was the representative of the chief-of-staff and was required to give his chief any support he required. Duties of this type of officer included personally leading larger formations into combat, choosing the sites for camps and bivouacs, planning reconnaissances and briefing the junior officers who would carry them out, working out the details of dispositions, and keeping the war diaries.

The Third General Staff Officer

Officers in this post, roughly the equivalent of assistant quartermaster-generals in the British forces, were responsible for dealing with all pressing matters of detail, on instruction from and in support of the commanding general and his chief-of-staff. The limited number of general staff officers made it necessary for them to be prepared to be used in every function, and thus such officers needed to have a good general training in all matters.

Brigade General Staff Officers

These officers dealt with matters such as the detailed scouting of terrain on the line of march and any resulting changes in the direction of the marching columns; the reconnaissance of the enemy positions; examination of the countryside, with a view to the supply and quartering of the troops; and the receipt and implementation of orders regarding combat, deployment and marching. And, of course, any other matter drawn to the brigade staff officer's attention by the brigade commander.

Army Organisation[1]

The Army of the Lower Rhine that was eventually assembled to fight the campaign of 1815 consisted of four army corps. They were numbered consecutively from I to IV. Three additional corps, the V, VI and VII, were not used in the campaign. The first two were deployed along the Elbe, from where they could observe the Austrians, and the Reserve (VII Corps) was stationed

[1] This section is based largely on Lettow-Vorbeck, p 469 ff.

around Berlin. Had the Army of the Lower Rhine suffered a major defeat, then it was possible that these three corps would have been sent to the front.

Each corps contained four infantry brigades, the corps reserve cavalry, and reserve artillery. The brigades each had two regiments of line infantry and one of Landwehr, together with integral cavalry and artillery support. The one exception was the Reserve Corps which included the Royal Guard and the two Grenadier Regiments. The four brigades in each corps were numbered consecutively through the corps and army. The I Army Corps thus contained brigades 1 to 4; the II Corps 5 to 8; the III Corps 9 to 12; the IV Corps 13 to 16. Each corps was a self-sufficient fighting force with a balanced component of infantry, cavalry and artillery.

No reserves, of infantry, cavalry or artillery, were held at army level. This was in part a deliberate choice from the way the army was organised, and in part owing to the fact that various Prussian corps had been attached to different allied armies in the Wars of Liberation. The Prussian Army had, in fact, not fought as one unit since 1806 and had had no need for reserves at an army level since then. In the event the IV Corps effectively operated as an army reserve because it was based to the rear of the other three army corps.

Each infantry regiment, whether of the line or Landwehr, theoretically consisted of three battalions: two of musketeers (line infantry) and one of fusiliers (light infantry). In reality the third battalions of the Landwehr regiments, though required to perform a light infantry function, had questionable expertise in this role. The two grenadier companies that had at one time been part of every regular regiment had been amalgamated to form grenadier battalions, which had been detached and formed into independent regiments. These regiments were allocated to the Reserve Corps and were not involved in the Waterloo campaign.

The Landwehr regiments came in part from the new provinces and in part from the core territories of Prussia. They consisted largely of young, raw levies with more experienced cadres. Lacking fighting experience, they tended to exhaust themselves quickly in combat. A number came from areas which until recently had been administered for some time by France. Their loyalties were questionable, but only once control had broken down after the hard fighting at the Battle of Ligny on 16 June 1815 did some actually desert, making for Liège and Aachen, where military discipline was finally restored.

The line cavalry in the campaign consisted of dragoons, hussars and uhlans (lancers). None of Prussia's cuirassier regiments participated in this campaign. Each cavalry regiment, of whatever type, theoretically included four squadrons, but certain of the new formations were under-strength. The cavalry was assembled from three sources: established regiments; new formations put together from various legions, Freikorps and cavalry of the newly acquired provinces; and finally the Landwehr. The first group was of good quality, well mounted and led by experienced officers, and acquitted themselves well. The second group lacked experience as coherent units and accordingly suffered from command problems. The Landwehr was of questionable value. They were not really suitable for use as battle cavalry.

A good example of the state of organised chaos that characterised the Prussian cavalry at this time can be found in the 8th Uhlans, part of the Reserve Cavalry of the III Army Corps. The men of the regiment were taken originally from the Russo-German Legion. The troopers continued to wear their old hussar uniforms into 1815, green for the 1st and 2nd Squadrons, black for the 3rd and 4th. Although, as its name suggests, the 8th was officially a lancer regiment, no lances were issued in 1815 and the mixture of small arms carried led to the cartridges issued having to be remade to fit the pistols that the men actually had.[2]

The artillery lacked both guns and ancillary equipment, with new supplies arriving at the front in dribs and drabs. Each battery, both foot and horse artillery, normally consisted of eight guns, six of the main battery calibre plus two howitzers. Most of the guns in both foot and horse batteries were 6-pounders, but the reserve artillery included a number of batteries of 12-pounders. The howitzers in the 6-pounder batteries were 7-pounder types; the 12-pounder batteries had 10-pounder howitzers. The Prussian artillery certainly acquitted itself well in 1815, but it was far from being at its best.

Brigade Tactics

One of the great faults in the Prussian Army of 1806 had been its lack of training at an operational level, because the army had no permanent formations larger than the regiment. The individual infantry battalions may well have out-shot their opponents and the cavalry squadrons out-ridden the enemy but, because senior officers lacked practice in matters of grand tactics, there was little co-ordination between larger formations. This problem was addressed in the subsequent reforms with brigade evolutions being included in the manual in use in 1815, the *1812 Reglement*.

The *Reglement* outlined basic principles for the operations of combined arms on the field of battle. At that time, a brigade consisted of three regiments of cavalry, two batteries of artillery, and seven battalions of infantry in all, three each from the two regiments plus the combined grenadier battalion from the two regiments. The standard tactics laid down were for the front line to consist of the two fusilier (light) battalions partly deployed into skirmish formation with the remainder forming closed supports. Particular officers were allocated to command the skirmish line, and they were designated as 'skirmish officers'. The main battle line consisted of three musketeer battalions. The reserve was made up of the grenadier battalion and the senior musketeer battalion, that is the first musketeer battalion of the senior regiment. The cavalry and artillery were deployed according to circumstances. The battle would be opened by the fusiliers, taken up by the musketeers, and supported by the reserves of infantry, cavalry and artillery.

Although the size and content of a Prussian brigade differed from the above in 1815, the basic principles remained. On 8 June 1815, Blücher had Grolman issue an 'Instruction' to the brigade commanders that summarised the system now to be employed:

[2] Förster, pp 58-59.

The brigade formation is already laid down in the regulations [the *1812 Reglement*] and its practicality has been confirmed by the experience of the last war. As the brigades now consist of nine battalions, then they will as a rule be deployed as follows:

Two light battalions

XXXXXX   XXXXXX

Four battalions

XXXXXX   XXXXXX   XXXXXX   XXXXXX

One light battalion   Two battalions

XXXXXX   XXXXXX   XXXXXX

One 6-pounder battery

† † † † † † † †

Two cavalry squadrons

XXXX   XXXX

The artillery and cavalry will be deployed according to circumstances and terrain and have no set position. As a rule, however, the cavalry should not be separated from the brigade. Only rarely may an exception be made; to pursue the enemy, or when all the cavalry is detached from the corps.

Whenever an army corps requires a vanguard, an entire brigade will be designated for this purpose and will receive the necessary cavalry from the reserve cavalry (as a rule two regiments as the cavalry regiments are weak) and one horse battery. If circumstances require, half a battery of 12-pounders can be added.

In open terrain, the reserve cavalry must immediately follow and support the vanguard. In other circumstances, the corps commanding general is responsible for its disposition.

Those Landwehr regiments that have yet to designate one battalion as the light battalion are immediately to select one, the one judged by its commander as the best suited for this purpose. This battalion as well as the third rank of all battalions must be well trained in skirmishing and individual combat.

From the moment when the troops leave their current cantonments to move against the enemy, the only horses and waggons allowed to accompany them are those permitted by regulations. The brigade commanders will be held personally responsible for this. On the other hand, the regulation waggons should not be taken away from the regiments and corps, the only possible exception being the treasury waggon. All other regulation waggons on normal marches are to remain with their battalions and regiments. On marches in the proximity of the enemy, all these waggons are to be collected together and follow the corps. Should several corps be following each other along the same route, then the waggons are to be placed behind the rear corps. Any waggons needed can be brought up when pitching camp.

Horse drawn waggons are not permitted with the troops. Should they be needed to transport supplies and forage, then they are to be attached to the brigade supply columns and every evening only the necessary number is to be sent into the bivouacs. As soon as they have been unloaded, they are to return to the column. The police directors of the various army corps, in view of the

Royal Instruction, have complete permission to enforce this regulation and have been ordered to deal with any such disorders immediately and severely to reprimand those involved.[3]

Because the peacetime brigades of 1808–12 had been enlarged with reserve and Landwehr formations during the campaign of 1813, it had become customary to divide the responsibilities of command of such a large formation among several senior officers. For instance, while Generalmajor von Pirch II was in overall command of the 2nd Brigade in 1815, Oberstlieutenant von Stach commanded its infantry.[4] The brigade commander directly controlled three sub-commanders for the infantry, cavalry and artillery, as compared with 1806, when he would have had to direct each battalion individually. This allowed the brigade commander of 1813–15 to co-ordinate all inter-arm operations more effectively and, rather than always having to lead from the front as his equivalent did in 1806, he could control his troops from brigade headquarters.

All this indicates how well the grand tactical lessons of the Napoleonic Wars had been learned in Prussia. Combined-arms operations were emphasised, with the role of the artillery and cavalry in support of the infantry being made clear. Particular attention was also paid to improving mobility, with the orders quoted above on traffic control and the supply trains only one example of this.

Mobilisation[5]

On mobilisation in March 1815, the Prussian Army underwent a number of organisational changes. The 32 line infantry regiments under arms were quickly augmented. On 25 March, in recognition of their good service, the Reserve Regiments were incorporated into the line, being numbered in turn. The Brandenburg Infantry Regiment, which had been formed from reserve battalions on 6 July 1813, was numbered 12. Reserve Regiments 1–12 were renumbered 13–24 in the line. The infantry of Lützow's Freikorps became No. 25. Part of the Elb-Regiment, which had been raised in the summer of 1813 from Prussians originating from the occupied territories west of the Elbe, became No. 26. Infantry Regiment No. 27 was formed from Reiche's Battalion, a formation raised from former Westphalian soldiers in the spring of 1813, along with the infantry of Hellwig's Freikorps and the reserve battalion of the Elb-Regiment. The two former Berg regiments were numbered 28 and 29, while the battalions of the German Legion were formed into Infantry Regiments No. 30 and No. 31. Troops originating from the recently annexed parts of Saxony were designated to form Infantry Regiment No. 32 but, because of the rebellion of the Saxon troops, this regiment was not raised.

The formation of the new infantry regiments took place largely without mishap. For example, the 25th Regiment was formed at the beginning of April on the right bank of the Meuse from the Lützow infantry and about 1,000 men

[3] Conrady, *Grolman*, p 289 ff.
[4] Conrady, *Sechsten Infanterie-Regiment*, p 238.
[5] This section is based mainly on GGS, *Heer 1814 und 1815*.

of Replacement Battalions Nos. 3 and 10, which came from Halberstadt and Westphalia, territories that had recently come under Prussian administration again. On 16 May, it was ready to march off. By 20 April, the 26th Regiment was short of only 250 men, which it received from the Rhineland. The 27th Regiment was similarly ready to join the field army by the end of April.

The Berg troops made up the 28th and 29th Regiments and had completed their formation in Aachen by 18 April, though they continued to wear their old white uniforms. The 28th Regiment consisted of the former 1st Berg Infantry Regiment, while the 29th was formed from the two battalions of the 2nd Regiment and the Grenadier Battalion. The grenadiers became the 1st Battalion of the 2nd Regiment, while the former 1st Battalion was renamed the 3rd, or Fusilier, Battalion.

The 30th and 31st Regiments were formed from the infantry of the German, formerly the Russo-German Legion. These cadres were so under-strength that men from several replacement battalions had to be allocated to these regiments, bringing them up to full strength by the end of April. It is unlikely that the former legionnaires received new uniforms; they probably continued to wear their old green Russian ones. Officers and men of the replacement battalions wore new Prussian blue uniforms. This sort of mixture was typical for the new formations.

Also mobilised for the campaign in the Low Countries was a battalion of Schützen from the province of Silesia. This was a specialist light infantry unit armed in part with rifled carbines.

New cavalry regiments were raised in various ways. Some of these new regiments included odd squadrons taken from existing regiments; others were based on units raised in the recent war or on existing squadrons in territories recently acquired by Prussia. These included:

Hussar Regt. No. 7	formed from one squadron of 1st Life Hussars and two from the Silesian National Hussar Regt.
Hussar Regt. No. 8	formed from one squadron each of 2nd Life, 2nd Silesian and Brandenburg Hussars.
Hussar Regt. No. 9	formed from one squadron each of the Pomeranian and 1st Silesian Hussars and of Lützow's Freikorps.
Hussar Regt. No. 10	formed from the three squadrons of the Elbe National Cavalry Regiment.
Hussar Regt. No. 11	formed from the three squadrons of Berg Hussars.
Hussar Regt. No. 12	formed from Saxon cavalry.
Uhlan Regt. No. 4	one squadron each from the West Prussian Uhlans, and the East Prussian and Pomeranian National Cavalry Regiments.
Uhlan Regt. No. 5	one squadron each from the Silesian and Brandenburg Uhlans, and one from the Berg Hussars.
Uhlan Regt. No. 6	three squadrons of Lützow cavalry.
Uhlan Regt. No. 7	Saxons and the cavalry of Hellwig's Freikorps.
Uhlan Regt. No. 8	the two Hussar Regiments of the German Legion.

These regiments went to war in 1815 largely in their old uniforms. Some of the uhlans had no lances – and had never been trained in their use in any case. The regiments were all under-strength, and had little time to practice as coherent formations, which restricted their usefulness.

On 28 March Boyen, the Minister for War, sent Kleist an instruction regarding uniforms,[6] pointing out, firstly, that an order-in-cabinet of 21 March called for savings in expenditure on these. Prussia simply lacked the resources to issue a large number of new uniforms in such a short space of time; everything was in short supply. Boyen told Kleist that only part of the regulation dress for the infantry and artillery could be supplied. The men should all get one greatcoat, one pair of linen breeches, one pair of shoes with one spare shoe (at that time shoes were made to be worn on either foot), a pair of soles, one pair of drill gaiters, one neck stock, two good shirts, one cartridge box, a knapsack and a bread bag. However, there were insufficient supplies to produce the cloth overalls, forage caps and shako covers which were also included in the regulation issue. Those regiments that still had grey, black or white uniforms, issued either when they were Prussian reserve formations or when they were still part of the army of another state which had subsequently come under Prussian control, would have to wait to be supplied with the regulation Prussian blue jackets. The cavalry were supposed to be supplied with one greatcoat, and one short coat, dolman or jacket. However, they would have to wait until 1816 before getting new supplies. Riding breeches were, however, supplied in 1815 along with one pair of boots, one spare pair of soles, one neck stock, two shirts, headgear, one greatcoat-bag, cartridge box, shoulder belt, sword belt and riding equipment.

Thus every soldier was apparently equipped with his basic needs, if not everything he was meant to have. However, many uniforms were old, worn out and ragged. It is most likely that many, for want of better uniforms, marched to the front wearing only a greatcoat and a pair of linen trousers. Uniforms of British and French origin were also acquired, altered and worn. The former Westphalian, Berg and other formations continued to wear their old uniforms. The reorganisation of the cavalry in particular caused further disuniformity. It was not unusual for half a dozen different uniforms to be worn by men in the same regiment. The Army of the Lower Rhine was indeed a rag-tag force that presented a sorry picture.

This army therefore went into battle on 15 June 1815 with very little in its favour, yet the greater burden of the fighting was to fall on its shoulders.

---

[6] Pflugk-Harttung, *Bundestruppen*, p 47.

Chapter 4
Wellington's German Contingents

The King's German Legion[1]

The King's German Legion, or KGL, was founded in 1803 by refugees from the Electorate of Hanover and became one of the élite formations of the British Army for the remainder of the Napoleonic Wars. Britain's King George III was also the Elector of Hanover at this time so, when Hanover fell victim to French aggression, it was natural for its émigrés to look to Britain for sanctuary, and as a base for future military action against the invader.

That summer a Hanoverian officer called Oberstlieutenant Friedrich von der Decken and the Duke of Cambridge, a younger son of George III who held general's rank in both the Hanoverian and British armies, started to organise a corps from former Hanoverian soldiers. Progress was slow at first, but later an Oberstlieutenant Bock started to organise recruitment from his estate at Elze, near Hanover. Shiploads of men started for England, including men such as Baring, Poten and Arentsschildt who, as KGL officers, would play a distinguished part in the 1815 campaign. The French tried to stop the flood of men leaving for England, but soon the depot at Lymington in Hampshire was full. Further recruits were sent to Parkhurst on the Isle of Wight. By November 1803 the King's German Regiment, as the corps was then known, numbered 450 men, under Major von Hinüber. Only a month later, the number of recruits had risen to over 1,000. They were transferred to the Hilsea Barracks, north of Portsmouth.

This level of recruitment exceeded expectations, so it was decided to form cavalry and artillery units as well. Thus, on 19 December 1803, the King's German Regiment became the King's German Legion. The Legion continued to grow throughout 1804; in February, a 2nd battalion was formed, in May a 3rd, later a 4th, and from January 1805 a 5th was raised. Members of the former Hanoverian 12th Regiment, an élite formation, were used to form the 1st and 2nd Light Battalions. A further three battalions of line infantry were formed during 1806. In all, ten battalions of Legion infantry were raised.

Initially the cavalry consisted of one heavy and one light dragoon regiment. Some of the men were former members of the Hanoverian Life Guards and Light Dragoons. By the end of 1804 each cavalry regiment had three squadrons, each of two troops. By the end of June 1805 each regiment had reached its full strength of eight troops, so a 2nd light regiment was raised.

---

[1] The best history of this formation is that by Schwertfeger. This section is based largely on his work.

Once this was complete, a 3rd light and 2nd heavy regiment were formed. At the end of 1812, the two heavy dragoon regiments were converted to light cavalry. Supporting artillery and other specialist units were also raised. The KGL infantry and cavalry became a vital component of Wellington's army in Spain, playing a major role in many of the important battles.

Throughout this time Hanover was under foreign occupation, first by the Prussians for a short time in 1806, then by the French until 1813. It therefore became ever more difficult to obtain native Hanoverians to keep the Legion up to strength. In time, prisoners-of-war and deserters from the French allied forces were recruited. Hanoverians were preferred, but soon all Germans were taken, then Swiss, then Poles, and finally almost anyone was regarded as acceptable. The less desirable recruits were the first to be let go at the end of hostilities in 1814.

The officer corps of the Legion, particularly the more senior ranks, consisted largely of former Hanoverian officers. Many a young son of the principality's leading families found adventurous ways of getting to the Iberian Peninsula. In later years, British officers joined the Legion, particularly the infantry. When Prussia again went to war against France in 1813, most of the Prussian officers in the Legion returned home.

After Napoleon's first abdication in 1814 the KGL became part of the army of occupation in the Netherlands. However, the end of the Napoleonic Empire also meant the end of the raison d'être of the Legion. Thought was given to its future. Hanover was now freed from French occupation and, as the KGL had been raised for the duration of the war, disbandment seem likely now peace had come. Officers who had spent a decade or more away from home in foreign service pondered their futures but, before any binding decisions were made, a new war loomed.

At the end of hostilities the units of the Legion made their way, in various ways, to the Netherlands, mainly from Spain and southern France. The Light (formerly Heavy) Dragoon Brigade moved from Toulouse to Mons, arriving there in July 1814, where it remained until early in 1815. The 1st Hussar Regiment moved from the south of France in March 1814 to Charleroi, arriving there on 14 July, and staying there until early 1815. The 2nd Hussar Regiment had returned to Britain in 1813 where it was remounted. In 1814, it joined the British expedition to the Netherlands, entered Antwerp and then went to Ypres, where it remained until early 1815. The 3rd Hussars were involved in the campaign in Holstein until early 1814 after which they marched to the Netherlands, fighting against the French there. After the abdication of Napoleon, they remained in Brussels.

After the campaign in south-west France, the light battalions were transported back to Britain, landing at Spithead on 23 July from where they marched to Bexhill. Early in September, they left for the Low Countries, remaining in Tournai until early 1815. The 1st, 2nd and 5th Line Battalions followed more or less the same route, but once in the Netherlands, they were quartered in Thielt and Tournai. The 3rd and 8th Battalions, having fought in Italy, were shipped via Corsica and Gibraltar to Deal, arriving there on 22

September 1814. Here, they were not disembarked, but were sent on to Ostende and wintered in Ath and Mons.

The 4th Line Battalion fought in Catalonia in the spring of 1814. From there, it marched to the south of France, embarking for Britain on 15 July. It arrived at Spithead on 26 July and then marched via Deal to Ramsgate, before going to Mons and Ath for the winter. The 6th and 7th Line Battalions together with the 3rd Foot Battery remained on service in the Mediterranean. The rest of the artillery either wintered in the Low Countries, or arrived there early in 1815. Once in the Netherlands, the Legion remained in British service, joining the Allied army under the overall command of the Prince of Orange.

On Napoleon's return to France in March 1815, the Legion was under-strength. Wellington expressed his concern about this to the Legion's founder, the Freiherr von der Decken (now a general), suggesting to him on 13 April that he make up their numbers by taking 3,000 volunteers from the Hanoverian militia. Decken rejected this suggestion as the Hanoverian forces were already short of men. Instead, he requested permission to obtain new recruits in Hanover for the artillery and cavalry, provided these recruits could, in due course, be transferred to the Hanoverian army, with the infantry being allowed to keep their depot formations but not to recruit any Hanoverians. Wellington agreed to this.

New General Orders were issued to the Legion on 25 April covering various organisational matters. Each infantry battalion was set at a strength of six companies, instead of the usual ten, giving the Legion a total of 48 companies in the Netherlands. This freed 91 officers and 104 sergeants who could now be seconded to the Hanoverian militia, for which they formed cadres. In effect, the Legion was the framework around which parts of the new Hanoverian army was being formed.

Organisation of the King's German Legion

The Legion, along with the the Hanoverian Subsidiary Corps (see p 75), came under the command of General Carl von Alten, whose headquarters was in Ghent.

The Legion was organised as follows:

1st Cavalry Brigade   (General von Dörnberg):
      1st and 2nd Light Dragoon, 2nd Hussar Regiments.
2nd Cavalry Brigade   (Oberst von Arentsschildt):
      1st and 3rd Hussar Regiments.

1st (Light) Infantry Brigade   (Oberstlieutenant von dem Busche):
      1st and 2nd Light Battalions.
2nd Infantry Brigade   (Oberst von Ompteda):
      1st, 2nd and 5th Line Battalions.
3rd Infantry Brigade   (Generalmajor du Plat):
      3rd, 4th and 8th Line Battalions.

Artillery   (Oberstlieutenant Hartmann):
      1st and 2nd Horse, 4th Foot Batteries.

As preparations for the outbreak of hostilities with the French continued, Legion formations were attached to various parts of Wellington's Anglo-Dutch-German army. Individual artillery batteries were attached to particular divisions and the cavalry regiments were each brigaded with various British light cavalry units. The infantry were formed into two brigades and attached to different British divisions.

During their years in British service, the KGL had come to adopt British drill regulations and military practices, and had even gone so far as to give its orders in English. The exception to this were the light battalions which drilled to their own regulations, and gave orders in German.[2]

The cavalry drew up in two ranks with a gap of four feet (1.2 m) between the ranks. Turns were made by threes. The senior captain of the two troops commanded the squadron, each of which was divided into four divisions. A lieutenant commanded a troop, riding on its flank; the most junior cornet rode in the centre of the squadron; the sergeants rode behind their squadrons, on the flanks of the centre divisions. The second captain and the senior cornet rode behind the front, watching the second rank. Marching was normally done by file. To attack, the order 'gallop' was given. The second rank would ride four paces behind the first. When 100 paces from the enemy, the order to charge would be given and the troopers would raise their sabres, before pressing home their attack. Cavalry skirmishers would operate 300 to 400 paces in front of their supports, at 20 to 25 paces apart with the men of the second rank ten paces behind the front rank. The front rank of skirmishers, depending on the proximity of the enemy, would have either their pistols or their carbines drawn, with their sabres hanging from their sword knots. Men of the second rank would have drawn sabres.

Each infantry company was divided for tactical purposes into two platoons, each of two sections. The company of the senior captain normally stood on the right, the others in descending order to the left, although this practice was not always adhered to. Formed infantry deployed in only two ranks, with the distance between the front and rear rank being 2 ft 6 in (76 cm). When firing, the second rank moved right and forward by 6 in (15 cm). The battalion commander and adjutant rode in front of the battalion, while the captains marched on the right flank of their respective divisions, as the companies were referred to for tactical purposes. The remaining officers stood three paces behind the second rank.

Hollow squares were formed if a cavalry attack was threatened, either three or four ranks deep with the first or the first two respectively kneeling, while the remainder gave fire. Line troops normally had their bayonets fixed throughout an engagement, while the light troops only fixed bayonets when specifically ordered. The line marched at 75 paces per minute, the lights at 108. When attacking, the first rank charged arms while the second trailed theirs. Manoeuvres were normally carried out in an open column of divisions. A column of march was normally formed by the two files making a quarter

---

[2] Poten, *Königs Deutsche Legion*, p 24.

wheel to the left or right, the second rank taking one step to the left or right. Skirmishing was in pairs with the men of the second rank deployed to the right rear of the front rank, passing them to give fire, then retiring to reload. Fifes and drums were used to convey orders.

The Hanoverians[3]

On the liberation of northern Germany in early 1813, Hanover was restored as an independent state and set about raising a new army. Three infantry battalions were raised, namely Lauenburg, the Bremen-Verden Light Battalion and the Lüneburg Light Field Battalion. They were augmented by a Feldjägerkorps recruited from foresters consisting of two companies at first, later increased to four. In May and June 1813, the infantry was reinforced by a further two battalions, Bennigsen and Roehl (later Langrehr), which had originally been intended to become part of the Russo-German Legion.

Once Napoleon was expelled from Germany at the end of 1813, further field battalions were formed. Men serving in the field battalions were usually volunteers. In January 1814, 30 Landwehr battalions were also raised from men between 18 and 30 years old who were liable for compulsory military service. Many of them were in poor health. The officers of the militia were a permanent part of the establishment and were promoted in exactly the same way as the officers of the line. Most officers were formerly from the Hanoverian, Westphalian and Prussian services.

For the purposes of raising replacement manpower, the provinces of Hanover were divided into districts from each of which a battalion was to be raised, and the districts into areas to provided the men for a company. All officers and NCOs of the former Hanoverian Army who were still capable of service, were required to join the Landwehr. Most of the NCOs were formerly from the Westphalian Army.

The strengths of the battalions varied. The field battalions were all meant to consist of eight companies, but they did not reach their full complement of 1,137 men. Thus, in May 1814, the establishment was reduced to six companies totalling around 800 men and in July 1814, after demobilisation, this was further reduced to four companies each of 150 men. The Landwehr battalions were of a similar strength. The strength of the Jäger companies was also 150 men.

In March 1813, two hussar regiments were raised, the Bremen-Verden and the Lüneburg. Towards the end of that year, they were joined by a third, the Duke of Cumberland's. The hussar regiments initially consisted of three squadrons, each of 150 men, but later this was increased to an establishment of four squadrons, but a shortage of horses meant it was unusual for more than two or three squadrons to be in the field at any one time. Each squadron consisted of two companies.

The artillery was raised around a cadre of 40 men sent from the depot of

---

[3] This section is based largely on Sichart vol 5 and articles by Schirmer in the *Zeitschrift für Heereskunde*, 1931 and 1957.

the KGL, who were sent home to form a foot battery. Its formation was completed by August 1813. In December of that year, the raising of a second and a third battery commenced. All three batteries, known as Batteries Wiering, Rettberg and Braun were thus completed in 1814.

The establishment of each battery was six officers, 15 NCOs, six artisans, 100 gunners and 66 drivers. Battery Wiering consisted of four light 6-pounders and two 5½-inch howitzers. Battery Rettberg had five 9-pounders and one 5½-inch howitzer. Battery Braun had light 6-pounders. On 5 May 1815, Battery Wiering was disbanded and its weapons and personnel divided up among the others.

Because of the exertions of the previous long years of war, the men in all types of unit were mostly very young and inexperienced. The infantry battalions were trained according to the regulations of 1802. In the line battalions, every twelfth man was trained as a skirmisher. and in the light battalions, everybody. In addition to that, the line battalions had ten Scharfschützen (sharpshooters) per company who took post on the right flank of the company when it was formed up. Orders were given via bugle horns.

Until 1 February 1814, the new Hanoverian Army was considered to be part of the British army. From then, it was no longer considered so, and Hanoverian distinctions were carried instead of British. In September 1814, the Field Battalion Osnabrück was named 'Duke of York'.

During the winter of 1814–15, a body of Hanoverian troops known as the 'Subsidiary Corps' was stationed in the Netherlands. It composition is shown below.

Field Battalions	Osnabrück, Grubenhagen, Bremen, Lüneburg, Verden (2 companies), Hoya (2 companies), Lauenburg and Calenberg.
Landwehr Battalions	Salzgitter, Bremervörde, Osnabrück, Quakenbrück, Hameln, Hildesheim, Peine, Gifhorn, Verden, Hoya, Nienburg, Bentheim, Lüneburg, Osterode, Münden.
Hussar Regiments	Lüneburg and Bremen-Verden.
Foot Battery	

On 4 February 1815, all the Field and Landwehr battalions were amalgamated into a total of ten regiments. The Field Battalion Bremen-Verden was renamed 'Bremen', the Field Battalion Bennigsen 'Verden', and the Field Battalion Langrehr 'Hoya'. Each regiment consisted of one Field and three Landwehr battalions, as shown in the table above right, though the formation of the Field Battalion Hildesheim was not completed.

In addition, 13 Landwehr battalions still based at home, and not part of the Subsidiary Corps, were sent to the Netherlands. They were commanded by General von der Decken and known as the Reserve Corps. They were employed to garrison various fortresses during the campaign of 1815. The 2nd Artillery Company was mobilised, manned by officers and men of the KGL and sent to the front as the 2nd Hanoverian Foot Battery. The Hussar Regiment Lüneburg was designated 'Prince Regent'.

Organisation of the Hanoverian Infantry

Regiment	Field Battalion	Landwehr Battalions
1. Bremen	Bremen	Otterndorf, Stade, Bremervörde
2. Verden	Verden	Verden, Bremerlehe, Harburg
3. Hoya	Hoya	Hoya, Nienburg, Diepholz
4. Osnabrück	Osnabrück 'Duke of York'	Osnabrück, Quakenbrück, Melle
5. Lüneburg	Lüneburg	Lüneburg, Celle, Gifhorn
6. Lauenburg	Lauenburg	Ratzeburg, Bentheim, Lüchow
7. Calenberg	Calenberg	Hanover, Hameln, Neustadt
8. Hildesheim	Hildesheim (incomplete)	Hildesheim, Uelzen, Peine
9. Grubenhagen	Grubenhagen	Alfeld, Salzgitter, Springe
10. Göttingen	Jäger	Osterode, Münden, Northeim

During the preparations for war these were joined by:

1 April	Feldjäger-Corps	2 companies under von Spörken
	31st Landwehr	drawn from Meppen, to replace the incomplete Field Battalion Hildesheim
	Garrison Battalion	
	Harzer Schützenkorps	2 companies under von der Decken
1 June	Volunteer Jägerkorps	30 men, attached to Feldjägerkorps

See Sichart, pp 86–7.

Hanoverian Forces in 1815

The following formations saw action in the campaign of 1815:

Field Battalions	Bremen, Verden, Lüneburg, Osnabrück, Grubenhagen, Lauenburg, Calenberg, Feldjäger-Corps.
Landwehr Battalions	Bremervörde, Osnabrück, Quakenbrück, Salzgitter, Verden, Lüneburg, Osterode, Münden, Hameln, Gifhorn, Hildesheim, Peine, Hoya, Nienburg, Bentheim.
Hussar Regiments	Lüneburg, Bremen-Verden, Cumberland.
Artillery	1st and 2nd Foot Batteries

The following units were stationed in Netherlands fortresses:

Field Battalion	Hoya.
Militia Battalions (Reserve Corps)	Bremerlehe, Melle, Northeim, Alfeld, Springe, Lüchow, Celle, Ratzeburg, Otterndorf, Hanover, Neustadt, Uelzen, Diepholz.

See Sichart, pp 89-90 ff

The uniforms worn were similar to those of the KGL. The line battalions wore red jackets, the five light battalions and the Feldjäger green. The 1st Hussars (Bremen-Verden) wore dark blue dolmans with red pelisses, the 2nd (Lüneburg) green and red respectively, and the 3rd all green. The artillery had dark blue uniforms.

The Brunswickers[4]

The Duchy of Brunswick, like Hanover, had been a victim of French aggression. Brunswick had allied with Prussia for the campaign of 1806 and the then Duke of Brunswick, a Prussian field marshal, was killed at Auerstedt. Following this defeat the Duchy of Brunswick was dissolved, with its territory being swallowed up by the Kingdom of Westphalia. The new Duke of Brunswick, in exile in Austria, formed an alliance with his Austrian hosts and went to war along with them in 1809. He raised an army in his former possessions and gave his men black uniforms so that they became known as the 'Black Corps'. The subsequent campaign ended in defeat for the Austrians at Wagram, but Duke Friedrich Wilhelm refused to surrender. Instead he led his troops across north Germany to the coast, where they boarded British ships and became another of the foreign legions that fought for the British Crown against the common enemy.

The Duke was joined by a certain Oberst Wilhelm von Dörnberg who was appointed chief-of-staff of the Brunswick corps. Dörnberg had previously been a colonel in King Jérôme Bonaparte's Westphalian Guard and later, as an officer of the KGL, would play a significant role in the Waterloo campaign.

The Brunswick infantry and cavalry fought alongside the British forces in various battles of the Peninsular War. Once Germany had been freed from French occupation, Duke Friedrich Wilhelm returned home and set about re-forming his army. Such new forces as he managed to raise in the short time available participated in the campaign of 1814 and at the end of the year the Peninsular veterans of the Brunswick infantry also returned home.

Not expecting war to break out again so soon after Napoleon's abdication, the Duke furloughed some of his men, disbanded certain formations and set about reorganising others. He had some difficulties in getting his Peninsula veterans to fit in with the new native recruits, particularly as the veterans had picked up so many habits from their British allies. To solve this difficulty, Friedrich Wilhelm issued a new set of drill regulations on 17 April 1815. These were based in part on the Prussian *Reglement* of 1812, and in part on the British Regulations of 1792. The Duke also used parts of the Prussian Light Infantry *Reglement* of 1788, particularly the two rank formation and the organisation of his battalions into 16 platoons, and he added his own rather unusual square formation, six ranks deep. The Duke was particularly fond of his light infantry, whose battle drills were based on the Prussian regulations of 1788 with certain modifications.

When Napoleon returned to France the Duke was invited to place his

---

4 This section is based mainly on: Kortzfleisch, vol 2.

Organisation of the Brunswick Corps

Commander-in-chief	**Herzog Friedrich Wilhelm**
Brigade Commander	Oberst Olfermann
Adjutants	Kapitain Morgenstern and von Zweiffel
Attached to Wellington's Headquarters	Oberst von Herzberg
Quartermaster-General	Oberstlieutenant von Heinemann
Chief-of-staff	Major von Wachholtz
Avantgarde	Major von Rauschenplat
Leichte Infanterie Brigade	Oberstlieutenant von Buttlar
Adjutant	Kapitain von Mosqua
Leibbataillon	Major von Pröstler
1. leichtes Bataillon	Major von Holstein
2. leichtes Bataillon	Major von Brandenstein
3. leichtes Bataillon	Major Ebeling
Linien-Infanterie Brigade	Oberstlieutenant von Specht
Adjutant	Kapitain von Aurich
1. Linien-Bataillon	Major Metzner
2. Linien-Bataillon	Major von Strombeck
3. Linien-Bataillon	Major von Normann

Including staff and non-combatants, the Brunswick infantry numbered 169 officers, 482 sergeants, and 5,043 men. They were supported by:

Husaren-Regiment	Major von Cramm
6 companies (3 squadrons)	
Ulanen-Eskadron	Major Pott
2 companies	
Feldartillerie	Major Mahn
Reitende Batterie	Kapitain von Heinemann (8 guns)
Fussbatterie	Major Moll (8 guns)

The total strength of the corps was 270 officers, 7,110 other ranks.

Cantonments

The cantonments of the Corps in the Netherlands were as follows:

Avantgarde	Anderlecht, Dilbeek, Itterbeek.
Leibbataillon	Molenbeek St Jean, Berchem, Ganshoren, Koekelberg.
1. leichtes Bataillon	Grand Bigard, Bodeghem, Cappelle St Ulric, Zellick.
2. leichtes Bataillon	Jette, Wemmel, Strombeek-Bever, Heembeek.
3. leichtes Bataillon	Grimberghen, Meysse.
1. Linien-Bataillon	Schaerbeek, Evere.
2. Linien-Bataillon	Wolwe-St Lambrecht, Wolwe St Stephan, Crainhem, Nosseghem.
3. Linien-Bataillon	Haeren, Dieghem, Saventhem, Steenockerzeel, Welsbroeck.

forces at the disposal of the Duke of Wellington, and eventually signed the formal agreement to do so in Vienna on 18 April. On mobilisation, furloughed troops were ordered to Brunswick and those of the 1st Light Battalion to Holzminden. The Duke reformed his Avantgarde (vanguard) at one battalion strong, and placed it under the command of Major von Rauschenplat. It consisted of four captains, 16 subalterns, 57 sergeants and corporals, 16 buglers, 586 privates, 30 hussars and 20 uhlans. The grey-clad Jäger made up two companies, the other two were from the light infantry. The remaining battalions were brought up to strength with each company including one sergeant-major, six sergeants, six corporals, six buglers and 150 Jäger. On 14 April, the battalion commanded by Major von Pröstler was honoured with the designation Life Battalion.

In addition to the troops who had joined their Duke in British service in exile, some 8,000 Brunswickers had been raised to fight alongside the French in the Westphalian army. The best part of 5,000 had perished, mostly in Spain and Russia. Brunswick's resources of manpower were accordingly running low, so it is no surprise that most of the soldiers raised for the Brunswick forces in 1815 were aged between 17 and 22. The light battalions had sergeants, even sergeant-majors, who were aged no more than 18. The officer corps in 1815 was relatively young also, the battalion commanders being on average 30 years old, company commanders 28. The entire Brunswick Corps was, therefore, rather young and inexperienced.

The Brunswick Corps began marching off for the Low Countries on 15 April 1815. Duke Friedrich Wilhelm divided it into five columns. The first four left, one after the other, over the coming days, while the last waited for missing recruits to report for duty. On 16 April Brunswick reported to Wellington that his columns would arrive in Antwerp between 10 and 18 May. When they arrived in the Netherlands, Wellington redirected them to Vilvoorde, north of Brussels. Friedrich Wilhelm set up his headquarters in Laeken.

After the strategy conference of 3 May at Tirlemont, the Brunswickers were allocated to the reserves deployed to the rear of the Allied positions for use as appropriate. The British were a little uncertain as to the loyalties of the Brunswickers; as a neighbour of Prussia with strong ties to the Hohenzollerns, but with years of close links to the British Crown, where did Friedrich Wilhelm's sympathies lie? Wellington attempted to have the corps broken up, with its constituent parts divided between his divisions, but Major von Wachholtz, the Duke's chief-of-staff, successfully resisted this, as Friedrich Wilhelm wanted his corps to act as a raiding force behind enemy lines during the planned Allied invasion of France. The Brunswickers got their way.

Some changes were made to the organisation of the Brunswick Corps on 15 May. The Avantgarde was made an independent unit; Buttlar, commander of the Light Infantry Brigade, was given the Hussars and Horse Battery in addition; and Specht, commander of the Line Infantry Brigade, received command of the Uhlans and Foot Battery. A field hospital was set up in Laeken, an ammunition depot in Vilvoorde. Supplies of musket ammunition were delivered from Britain; food and fodder came from British magazines, but was paid for by the Netherlanders. Unlike the Prussians, the Brunswickers wanted for nothing.

Daytime was spent training the troops. On 22 May Wellington inspected the Brunswickers. The fifth column arrived on 5 June, and its men were sent to their units. However, various middle-ranking officers became unhappy with the posts they had been allocated. Some left to return to Prussian service. Others who remained were also dissatisfied, but events soon overtook this affair; the youthful Brunswick Corps, dressed in its sombre black, was to see action in a matter of days.

The Nassauers

The six battalions of Nassauers raised in Nassau in 1815 consisted principally of young recruits and a few volunteers. Less than one third of the Nassauers had any experience of war. Fortunately, the officer corps was largely made up of veterans, half of the subalterns having four or five years' experience, and often the scars to prove it.[5]

The Nassau troops mobilised for the campaign of 1815 were the 1st Regiment, 2nd Regiment, Regiment Nassau-Orange and volunteers of Nassau-Orange. Some of these troops were already based in the Netherlands when preparations for war began. Others were at home in Nassau.[6]

The 1st Regiment, based at home in the Duchy, was called up on 24 March 1815, and mobilised on 1 April. Its two line battalions were augmented by a 3rd (Landwehr) battalion, and brought up from four to six companies per battalion. The regiment was raised in a mere six weeks and suffered from a number of problems. Its effective strength was 71 officers and 2,974 men but over 1,000 of the men were raw recruits.

Some of these officers were former cavalrymen since the Nassau cavalry had been disbanded. Oberstlieutenant Hagen was appointed second-in-command of the 1st Regiment at this time. The other former cavalry officers who were appointed to posts in the infantry were promoted, with the senior lieutenants becoming captains, and the senior sub-lieutenants becoming lieutenants. The captains of the Landwehr were experienced reserve officers. The remaining officer posts were filled partly from the reserves, partly by volunteers from the educated classes, mainly young civil servants. These men were keen but had no practical experience. Pressure of time meant that they and the recruits received only a minimum of training. Efforts to improve this sorry situation were made, however, on the forthcoming march to Brussels.

The regiment set off on 21 May in good spirits. Instead of going to the Prussians on the Lower Rhine as originally planned, the regiment marched on to the Netherlands where it joined its compatriots, who had already been deployed with the Allied army. It reached Brussels on 7 June and was most probably quartered there. The regiment formed the Nassau Brigade for the

5 Kolb, p v f.
6 Rössler P., *Geschichte*, p 68 ff.

Organisation of the Nassau Contingent[a]

1st Regiment

Staff

1 Oberst, 1 Oberstlieutenant, 3 Majors, 3 Adjutant-majors, 1 Auditor, 1 Regimental quartermaster, 1 Regimental surgeon, 3 Battalion surgeons, 3 Divisional surgeons
> *17 officers*

3 Colour bearers, 3 Battalion adjutants, 1 Drum major, 3 Drum sergeants, 1 Staff crescent player, 1 Music director, 22 Oboists, 1 Sapper corporal, 18 Sappers, 1 Waggon master, 2 Train corporals, 33 Train soldiers, 5 Artisans
> *94 men*

Battalions

6 Captains 1st class, 6 Captains 2nd class, 6 Captains 3rd class, 9 Lieutenants 1st class, 9 Lieutenants 2nd class, 18 Sub-Lieutenants
> *54 officers*

18 Sergeant-majors, 126 Farriers and sergeants, 216 Corporals, 45 Drummers, 9 Buglers, 2466 Privates
> *2880 men*

The total effective strength of the 1st Regiment was 71 officers and 2,974 men.

Officers

On 1 June 1815, the senior officers of the 1st Regiment were:

Regimental Commander	Oberst Ernst von Steuben
Battalion Commanders	
1st Battalion	Major Wilhelm von Weyhers
2nd Battalion	Major Adolph von Nauendorf
Landwehr Battalion	Major Friedrich von Preen

The 2nd Regiment

The 2nd Regiment's strength on 31 May was 86 officers and 2,584 men.

In June 1815 the senior officers of the 2nd Regiment were:

Regimental Commander	Oberst Friedrich Wilhelm von Goedecke
Battalion Commanders	
1st Battalion	Major Friedrich Sattler
2nd Battalion	Major Philipp von Normann
3rd Battalion	Major Gottfried Hegmann

The Regiment Nassau-Orange

The Regiment Nassau-Orange had two battalions, each of five companies, with 39 officers and 1,427 men, plus a volunteer company of 3 officers and 166 men.

In June 1815, the senior officers of the Regiment Nassau-Orange were:

Regimental Commander	Oberst Prinz Bernhard Carl von Sachsen-Weimar
Battalion Commanders	
1st Battalion	Oberstlieutenant W. Ferdinand von Dressel
2nd Battalion	Oberstlieutenant Philipp Schleyer

[a] Rössler A., *Infanterie-Regiment Nr.87*, p 114 f.; Kolb pp 89–92 f; Rössler P., *Geschichte*, p 68f.

coming campaign, commanded by General von Kruse, who arrived in Brussels on 15 May in advance of his men. Duke Wilhelm, the Hereditary Prince of Nassau, decided to participate in the campaign, and joined Wellington's staff with the rank of colonel.

The 2nd Nassau Regiment and the Nassau-Orange Regiment formed the 2nd Brigade of the 2nd Netherlands Division under Lieutenant General Perponcher, part of the I Corps of Wellington's army. Oberst von Goedecke commanded both the 2nd Regiment and the brigade with his headquarters in Houtain-le-Val. Goedecke was later injured by a horse kick and replaced by Duke Bernhard of Saxe-Weimar, until then the commander of the Regiment Nassau-Orange. The 2nd Regiment consisted of three battalions each of six companies, a total of 89 officers and 2,738 men. After Goedecke's injury Major Sattler was promoted from command of the 1st Battalion to lead the regiment as a whole and replaced by Kapitain Büsgen.

The 2nd Regiment had received its marching orders on 30 March and left Maastricht that day. It marched via Liège and Namur to Montigny-sur-Sambre. It received its orders to join the 2nd Brigade on 9 April. On 11 April, the regiment marched to Marbais. In May Perponcher's Division was deployed in the area of Nivelles, Quatre Bras and Genappe, where the Nassauers would see their first action on 16 June. In total 7025 Nassau soldiers fought in the campaign.

The Hanseatic Contingent

The Hanseatic cities of Hamburg, Bremen and Lübeck had traditionally been independent states within the German Empire. As major trading centres they had joined the commercial association of towns known as the Hanseatic League as far back as the Middle Ages. These cities were still relatively wealthy and customarily raised their own defence forces, though these civil guards were actually of little military value. In 1815 the Hanseatic contingent was allocated to Wellington's forces and on 3 April 1815 the Allies decided that the cities should raise 1,000 infantry and 200 cavalry with six guns. When insufficient volunteers were found, bounties were offered and efforts made to raise the numbers required. A corps of volunteers was founded on 26 April, supposedly to be made up of men who would provide their own uniforms and equipment.

The Hamburg force[7] comprised one infantry regiment of two battalions, each of four companies, one squadron of cavalry. one foot battery of six guns, two companies of volunteers.

The troops from Hamburg, together with the contingents from Lübeck and Bremen, formed a brigade. On 12 June, the 2nd Infantry Battalion and the cavalry marched off from Hamburg, followed on 13 June by the Lübeck Battalion of three companies. One of these companies, the volunteers under Major Winterfeldt, stayed in Hamburg a further day. On 15 June, the Hamburg regimental staff marched off, together with the 1st Infantry

---

7 Mayer, p 22.

Battalion and the Foot Battery. The two companies of volunteers followed on 30 June. The head of the column arrived in Bremen on 15 June. The Bremen Battalion of four companies under the command of Major von Weddig had left a day earlier along with a company of volunteers.

The Hanseatic contingent finally reached the Netherlands on 6 July, far too late to see any fighting. Instead they awaited orders from the Duke of Wellington. The Brigade eventually set off en route to join the Allied forces in France on 20 July. On 24 July, when they had only reached as far as Mons in Belgium, a British officer, Colonel Neale Campbell, took command and soon made himself unpopular. Campbell continued to wear his British uniform and, since he spoke no German, could only communicate with his men in French. His first order emphasised that his men were to behave in France with restraint and should not make demands on the inhabitants, or revenge themselves for the long years of French occupation of the Hanseatic towns. The brigade reached its final destination in France on 31 July, going into cantonments on the Somme. Here they remained until their return home, which started in October 1815.

The only Hanseatic troops to see action in the campaign were Bremen volunteers who had joined Lützow's Freikorps, which had been incorporated into the Prussian Army, as explained in Chapter 3.

Chapter 5

Plans to Defend The Netherlands

Initial Preparations

News of Napoleon's landing in France after his escape from Elba reached Vienna on 7 March 1815. The troops garrisoning those areas most likely to be affected by his return to France included a corps deployed south of the Moselle under the command of the Crown Prince of Württemberg and the Bavarian General Prince Wrede; one stationed between the Moselle and the Meuse under the Prussian General Kleist von Nollendorf; and another under the Prince of Orange in the Low Countries. Those troops would be the first to face any French attack.

The Kingdom of the Netherlands was one of the new states so recently created by the Congress of Vienna. It consisted of those territories that make up the modern countries of Belgium, the Netherlands and Luxembourg. The Netherlands was regarded as being in the British sphere of influence, designed to be a buffer against any future French attempts to control the Channel ports and Antwerp, all important to British commercial interests. The whole territory had been under French rule from the 1790s until 1814. The northern parts of this new kingdom were inhabited by Dutch-speaking Protestants. However, the southern part was inhabited by francophone Catholics, also known as Walloons. The Walloons favoured France and their king-to-be was a stranger to them. Frederik Willem, the Prince Sovereign, was not highly regarded by certain of his contemporaries, particularly the Prussians. He had served as a divisional commander in the Prussian Army in 1806 and been cashiered for misconduct, only narrowly escaping execution because of his family connections. His relationship with the Prussian high command was made even more difficult by the fact that General Gneisenau, soon to be chief-of-staff of the Prussian forces in this theatre, had been instrumental in the charges brought against Willem in 1806.[1] Frederik Willem's son, the Prince of Orange, had served as an aide-de-camp in the Duke of Wellington's Army in the Peninsular War. Their decisions in the forthcoming campaign wavered between their need for British protection against France and their desire to assert their authority.

At the outset of the drama, the young Prince was placed in command of the Allied forces in the Netherlands. Sir Hudson Lowe, a British general, was placed at his side to keep a close eye on him. The forces initially available to the Prince of Orange consisted of around 39,000 men, a mixture of British,

---

[1] Delbrück, *Leben*, p 138.

Germans and Netherlanders. Of these only 2,900 were Dutch and around 1,400 Belgians, hardly enough to give the Netherlands an independent voice. Furthermore, since many of the more experienced Dutch and Belgian soldiers had previously fought for Napoleon, the Prince and his father could not be certain of their loyalties. They accordingly rapidly began raising new line troops and a militia.

General Kleist summed up the difficult situation in a letter to his king on 19 March 1815,

> ....the English army in Belgium is neither strong nor in particularly good condition. Twenty-two quite incomplete English battalions including the German Legion have twenty poor cannon and amount to less than 15,000 men of the worst English troops. The Hanoverian corps has but one battery. One cannot say better of the Belgians. They are a wretched collection of riffraff. The entire army cannot consist of more than 30,000 men with 40 bad cannon. According to the report of the Dutch Ambassador General Fagel – of 14th March – Bonaparte could be in Paris any day now, so it seems to me that the English have grounds for concern over their situation.[2]

Clearly the British and Dutch forces were totally unprepared for what lay ahead – and the Prussians were hardly in a better state themselves. The line troops and militia in the provinces in western Germany had been left on a war footing after Napoleon's first abdication but in January 1815 a slow demobilisation of these forces had started.[3] The first three army corps under Kleist's command were deployed in the Rhineland. His headquarters was in Aachen. By mid March, the I Army Corps, under the command of Generalmajor von Pirch II, was down to the strength of a single brigade, stationed in and around Koblenz. The II Army Corps under Generallieutenant von Zieten had two brigades, stationed in Aachen and Verviers. The III Army Corps under Generallieutenant von Borstell consisted of three brigades placed in and around Krefeld, Kleve and Wesel. The fortress of Luxembourg was garrisoned by Prussian troops under Generalmajor von Borcke but the entire Prussian force in the theatre amounted to little more than 30,000 men. Also under Kleist's command were 14,000 Saxons, based around Cologne.

On receiving news of events in France, Kleist began some precautionary movements even before he had received any instructions from Vienna. He ordered the III Army Corps to close up around Krefeld, and to be ready, along with I Corps and the Saxons, to move on Jülich, if required. At the request of the Prince of Orange, Kleist next ordered Zieten and his corps to cross the Meuse and enter Liège, while Borstell was sent into Aachen and Thielemann's Saxons moved up behind Zieten.

At this time the Prince of Orange clearly felt himself unable to defend his father's new kingdom without foreign aid. However, it was neither in their nor in British interests to allow the Prussians to play too great a role. Neither party

---

[2] Lettow-Vorbeck, p 134.
[3] Ollech, pp 3 ff.

wanted the Prussian sphere of influence to spread too far westwards. The then Prince Sovereign had already been worried by a Prussian threat to the Netherlands before Napoleon's reappearance. In a letter dated 21 February 1815, Sir Charles Stuart, British envoy in The Hague, wrote to Castlereagh,

> M. De Nagell [the Dutch minister] has stated to me the substance of the instructions sent to the diplomatic agents of the Prince Sovereign in the principal courts of Europe... prove that a dread of the encroachments of Prussia, which Court the Prince Sovereign considers to be a mere instrument in the hands of her powerful neighbour, is most thoroughly impressed on the minds of his Royal Highness and of his Ministers.
>
> His Excellency has repeatedly mentioned to me, with some exultation, that the Russian and Prussian Envoys are alike ignorant of the measures to which the extravagant pretensions of their respective Courts have compelled the Allies to recourse [the Treaty of 3 January 1815, etc.] – which ignorance, he says, has been betrayed in discussions to which the encroachments of the Prussian troops in the Dutch territory on either bank of the Meuse have given rise.[4]

The Prussian forces involved in these moves were a mixed bag. Alongside veterans of the recent campaigns were untrained men from the depots and unsteady militia. Alongside blue-blooded Prussians and Westphalians stood Rhinelanders who had almost forgotten how to speak German in the decades of French occupation. Then there was the lack of money. Napoleon had plundered large parts of Germany to finance his wars of aggression, and little had been left behind. British blockades and Napoleon's Continental System caused further economic damage. The few uniforms available were threadbare; horses were in short supply, and food was hard to come by. Moreover, the army was also in the throes of a reorganisation. By chance, on the very day that news of the return of Napoleon to France arrived in Vienna, the King of Prussia had ordered the disbanding of the Prussian militia and a reorganisation of his infantry and cavalry formations, which caused considerable disruption. The only troops available to Kleist that were fit for war were the Saxons. However, owing to the impending dismemberment of their state and the fact they were now under the command of their traditional enemy, the Prussians, their morale was not high.

What was facing Napoleon on his north-eastern border on his return to Paris was an unstable cocktail of British, Hanoverians, Dutch, Belgians, Rhinelanders, Westphalians, Prussians and Saxons. This mixture spoke several different languages and dialects and their countries also had conflicting interests. The individual contingents were all partly demobilised or being reorganised. The Allies were thus not in a position to invade France immediately to prevent Napoleon from re-establishing his dictatorship, so there was no other option than to guard the border with France and await reinforcements.

---

4 Vane, *Castlereagh*, vol X, p 256.

Friedrich Wilhelm III of Prussia reacted to the news of Napoleon's return to France by immediately cancelling his order to disband the militia. On 11 March he ordered 13 depot battalions off to the Rhine to reinforce his troops there. Orders to prepare and improve the fortifications at Koblenz, Cologne and Wesel were issued; further depot battalions were to be raised on the Weser; garrison battalions from the provinces between the Oder and Elbe were to be sent to the Rhenish fortresses; former French soldiers in the new Prussian provinces in the west were to be mobilised; and on 12 March four militia regiments, one of cavalry and three of infantry, were sent off to the Rhine.[5] On 13 March the Prussians held a council of war. Five days later, a series of orders-in-cabinet were issued and a general mobilisation of the Prussian forces followed.

Although it was not yet certain that Napoleon would overthrow Louis XVIII, no risks were to be taken, as Germany had suffered too much from those years of French aggression. All was to be done to prevent another invasion. Furthermore, it was in Prussia's interests to secure as many advantages as possible from whatever developed, and a rapid mobilisation would place the Prussian Army in the fore. The important fortresses of Mainz and Luxembourg might be brought under Prussian command which would help make northern Germany an exclusively Prussian sphere of influence.

In Vienna, the Great Powers drew up a basic strategy for the expected war. The Russians were to assemble their forces in Poland. Austria was to place an army on the middle Rhine. They were to be joined by contingents from Bavaria, Württemberg, Baden and Hesse-Darmstadt. The Anglo-German and Netherlands forces in the Low Countries were to assemble between Namur and Mons. Prussian reinforcements were to collect around Madgeburg. Kleist was to form up between Mainz and Luxembourg. Were King Louis to require urgent assistance against the Upstart, then Kleist was to provide it. The Anglo-Netherlands forces and the Austrians on the Rhine were to move rapidly to support him.

This strategy was based on the assumption that Kleist's Prussians were the one force immediately available for action. However, a rapid intervention by the Prussians would have political effects, with the Prussians thereby expanding their sphere of influence westwards. Once the initial panic died down, these consequences were thought through. The Austrian General Schwarzenberg proposed to link Kleist's army with the Anglo-Dutch forces, with the Duke of Wellington commanding this army. An army under British supreme command would make the Austrians feel more secure and they were ready to make every effort to ensure that the Prussians did not have too much say in the affair. The political interests of the parties involved were to play the dominant role in this campaign.

Initially Louis XVIII considered his regime stable enough to deal with the threat from Napoleon. He had no desire for any allied army to intervene in French affairs, so he rejected the offers made. However, events moved so

5 GGS, *Heer 1814 und 1815*, p 115.

rapidly that Louis' government completely collapsed before the allies could move to support it.

Prince Frederik Willem of the Netherlands felt particularly threatened once this became clear. After all his Belgian subjects had been French citizens for the last 20 years, so he could not rely on their loyalty. The British and Prussians also worried about this and had agreed, on the recommendation of Brockhausen, Prussian ambassador in the Hague, that the strategic fortress of Luxembourg should remain in German hands. The British and Prussians feared that a Netherlands garrison would fail to hold it against the French.[6]

The imminent collapse of the government of Louis XVIII persuaded Frederik Willem, until then the Prince Sovereign of the Netherlands, to ascend the throne as King Willem I. In doing so the new king hoped to hold his divided realm together. However, the francophone areas received news of the founding of the new kingdom with little enthusiasm.

The picture is one of a divided country, divided by language, culture, traditions, religion, law and economic interests. A rapid advance by Napoleon was likely to bring about its collapse. The Prince of Orange was acutely aware of the potential problem, and had been for some time. He had written to Wellington as early as 13 March suggesting the available allied forces should intervene in France to prevent the collapse of Louis XVIII's government.[7] He requested Wellington's support and advice, informing him that he was sending Sir Hudson Lowe, then commander of the British forces in the Low Countries, to visit Kleist at his headquarters in Aachen to sound out the Prussians.

The Prince of Orange's strategy was to intervene in France, thus preventing any invasion of the Low Countries. He sent off messengers to Britain and to Aachen to enlist his Allies' support, mobilised his forces, armed his fortresses and assembled his army to the south of Brussels.[8] On 17 March the Prince wrote to Bathurst, Britain's Secretary of War, saying that he supported the probable appointment of the Duke of Wellington as supreme commander in the Netherlands. Reports had come in that Napoleon was intending to invade Belgium as soon as he could, but whatever might happen, the Prince said he believed the Allies should prepare to invade France, and was aware Kleist would support this. The Prince also explained that he was raising a militia in Belgium and asked for 10,000 to 20,000 muskets for them. The Prince also requested reinforcements, but altogether he seemed in a buoyant mood.[9]

The Prince's mood changed as the threat from France grew. On 21 March, on hearing of the total collapse of Louis XVIII's government, he asked Bathurst to send the weapons for his Belgian militia immediately and requested more British forces to be sent to support him.[10]

The Prussians meanwhile were busy reinforcing Luxembourg as well as concentrating their field army on Liège. Here, they could link up with the

6　Pflugk-Harttung, *Bundestruppen*, p 13.
7　WSD, vol IX, p 593.
8　De Bas & T'Serclaes de Wommersom, vol I, p 169.
9　WSD, vol IX, p 600.
10　WSD, vol IX, p 604.

Netherlands forces, which were now around 23,000 men strong. On 22 March the Prince of Orange was worried by intelligence that he received stating that Napoleon's intention was to invade Belgium immediately.[11] He pleaded with the Prussians to invade France along with his forces. He wanted Zieten's corps to move on Namur and the remainder of the Prussian army to follow him, but this was unrealistic. On 23 March Kleist wrote to him from Aachen to point out the practicalities of the situation and outlined the measures he was taking. Kleist would assemble one corps at Namur as requested, the remainder of his army between Liège and Jülich, and would ensure that Luxembourg was in a state of readiness. He considered the chances of a successful intervention in France to be almost nil and advised a withdrawal to Antwerp, Maastricht, Jülich and Mainz should Napoleon take the offensive.[12]

Both the British and Louis XVIII also objected to the Prince's proposal. King Louis, who had already fled Paris for Lille, told the Prince that he did not wish the allied forces to cross his border.[13] Stuart, the British envoy in the Hague, stated that his government wanted to employ a defensive strategy, not an offensive one.[14] On 25 March Stuart wrote further that his government was willing to do all necessary for the security of Belgium, but wished no invasion of France. The Prince's plans were put to rest.

A report from Brockhausen gave an interesting picture of the mood of the population in the Netherlands at this point.[15] By 23 March, Brockhausen said, 30 battalions and 12 batteries had been mobilised. Half of these consisted of reliable militia but, because of a shortage of money, the artillery could not be properly equipped. A total of 24,000 men, including four Belgian battalions, were considered fit for service in the fortresses where there would be little opportunity to desert. With reports of Napoleon's entry into Paris arriving, rumours were spreading that he would be in a position to invade the Low Countries within three to four weeks. Brockhausen believed that the Dutch burghers were certainly prepared to resist the expected invader, but they lacked arms. The militia battalions were reliable, but the line troops, many of whom had served Napoleon, were untrustworthy.

Also on 23 March, Prince Hardenberg informed Goltz, the Prussian representative in Paris, that the Allies would concentrate on the French border and would only cross it if expressly requested to do so by Louis.[16] That afternoon Kleist reported to Boyen, the Prussian Minister of War, that he, too, thought it unwise to invade France. He considered the forces at his disposal to be too weak and ill prepared for such a venture.[17] That evening General de

[11] Pflugk-Harttung, *Bundestruppen*, p 18. He also points out a printing error in De Bas & T'Serclaes de Wommersom, vol I, p 175 which incorrectly dates this document as 12 March 1815.

[12] Pflugk-Harttung, *Bundestruppen*, pp 19 f,. Here he reproduces the text of the entire document so that the errors in De Bas & T'Serclaes de Wommersom, vol I, p 168 are apparent.

[13] WSD, vol IX, p 620.

[14] WSD, vol IX, pp 631-2

[15] Pflugk-Harttung, *Bundestruppen*, pp 14 f.

[16] Pflugk-Harttung, *Bundestruppen*, p 21.

[17] Pflugk-Harttung, *Bundestruppen*, p 21.

Constant Rebeque, the Netherlands chief-of-staff, reported to Kleist that Louis XVIII and his government had fled to Douai or Lille, near the Belgian frontier, while all of France appeared to be shouting 'Vive l'Empereur!'[18]

Kleist's response to the situation was to issue the following Disposition on 23 March:

The Army is to concentrate as follows:

The Royal Prussian II Army Corps under Generallieutenant von Zieten: Namur and environs, that is in the Sambre and Meuse Départements, and baggage at Huy.

The Royal Prussian III Army Corps under Generallieutenant von Borstell: Liège and environs, that is in the Ourthede and Lower Meuse Départements on the right bank of the Meuse.

The III German Army Corps under Generallieutenant von Thielemann: Aachen and environs, Roer Département.

The Berg Corps under Generalmajor von Jagow: Düsseldorf and environs.

The Westphalian troops under Generalmajor von Steinmetz: Wesel and environs.

The Royal Prussian I Army Corps is to remain in its present positions [on the Rhine].

Headquarters is to remain in Aachen.[19]

Kleist reported his actions to his king on 25 March. His report, written in the hand of his chief-of-staff Müffling, read as follows:

Subsequent to my most humble report of 19 March, may I bring to Your Majesty's attention that the news of Napoleon's arrival in Paris on 20 March prompted me to issue a most humble written disposition.

Herewith, I have ordered Generals Steinmetz and Jagow and the respective districts under their command to mobilise their troops, to call up reserves, etc. The Westphalian militia has not been mobilised. I hope that Your Majesty's orders will be received before our assembly is completed.

This disposition has been issued as a result of the demands of the Prince Sovereign of Orange and because Napoleon's arrival in Paris with an army is more of a threat to the Netherlands than for the Upper Rhine. Besides, the French Army in Alsace and Lorraine is weak and the tricolour cockade has yet to be seen there.

Should Napoleon, after a few days of rest, lead the army (which according to all reports is now in the area of Paris with around 50,000 men) against Lille and the northern fortresses, and then attack the English quickly, then I believe I am carrying out Your Majesty's declared wishes if I link up with the Belgian Army in the plains around Tirlemont and, together with them, bring Napoleon to a battle, in which the numerical and other advantages will probably lie on our side.

In the meantime, I have made my intentions known to the Prince [of

---

[18] Pflugk-Harttung, *Bundestruppen*, p 22.
[19] Pflugk-Harttung, *Bundestruppen*, p 23.

Orange] and today I sent Generalmajor von Roeder to Brussels with orders to convince the Belgian Army personally and to make preparations for such an event. This plan must remain secret so that even Napoleon believes that he is only facing the Belgian Army, hoping to beat us individually in the old way.

Should we be so unfortunate as to be beaten in battle, then a well secured retreat over the Meuse would be the consequence and the Army of the Lower Rhine would, thanks to the reinforcements arriving, soon be able to go over to the offensive. Should Napoleon be defeated, then this could cost him the throne, as 12,000 good cavalry would give us the means to destroy him after the battle.

...The stockpiling of three months of provisions at Luxembourg and Jülich are being accomplished with all haste. The former will be achieved by 1 April, the latter by 10 April. Lack of time and money have not allowed us to provide these fortresses with the means to withstand a formal siege. However, they will withstand any violent assault.[20]

Also on 25 March, Kleist sent an order marked 'secret' via Müffling to Pirch I. This read as follows:

Your Honour will have seen from the Disposition of 23 March that I have taken precautions against certain events, including an attack by Napoleon on Belgium.

Should this occur, then it will be necessary for the cavalry under your command to close up on me by means of forced marches so that it can get to the battle in good time. Your Honour is, in such an event, required to march through the mountains with the infantry of the 7th Brigade with one battery, and reach Namur in six to seven days.[21]

Kleist clearly regarded the situation as serious.

On 24 March the Prince of Orange reported he had received intelligence that Napoleon had been sighted near Lille. In response, he had moved forces to Tournai, which he intended to defend as a fortified camp. The French army did not appear to be strong, so he considered his forces sufficient to hold them off until Kleist arrived.[22] Meanwhile, Kleist was concentrating his army and, as we have seen, had already sent off Zieten's corps to Liège to link up with the Prince. The fact that none of the allied armies was strong enough to withstand an assault from Napoleon on its own left them with little option but to co-operate, but this was a matter of expediency. The potential for hostility lurked beneath the surface. Their recent agreements on territorial arrangements had been made somewhat reluctantly, and all were aware that any change in circumstances could lead to alterations before the new borders became final.

On 25 March Müffling passed on his thoughts as to what to do next to Generaladjutant von der Knesebeck, Friedrich Wilhelm's senior ADC.[23]

---

[20] Pflugk-Harttung, *Bundestruppen*, p 23. Extracts from this report can also be found in Ollech, p 6 and Lettow-Vorbeck, p 136.

[21] Pflugk-Harttung, *Bundestruppen*, p 25; Ollech, p 7.

[22] WSD, vol IX, p 606 f.

[23] Pflugk-Harttung, *Bundestruppen*, p 25.

According to intelligence reports, Müffling noted, Napoleon already had 50,000 men at his disposal, which would soon increase to 70,000. Should the fortresses in northern and eastern France go over to him then he would have 100,000 men, and it was to be expected that he would, in due course, have the entire French nation behind him. Even if the Allies were to put every effort into the war, it was unlikely that they would be able to take the offensive in full strength before June. Müffling discussed whether it would be advisable to await the concentration of all the Allied forces or to start the war when only some were ready. Müffling admitted that the Allies would be sure of destroying Napoleon's regime with superior numbers if they waited, but argued that, if the Bonaparte regime were to show signs of instability, then the Allied troops already on the French borders should attack without waiting for reinforcements. Müffling accepted that, in such an event, the French border fortresses would have to be taken by assault if they did not remain loyal to King Louis but he said that the Allies could achieve this and then advance on Paris. If the British sent over their contingent quickly, then the Armies of the Netherlands and the Lower Rhine would be able to open hostilities with 80,000 to 90,000 men. In four weeks, he thought, this number could be doubled. A south German corps could also occupy Switzerland and advance from there. By June, the Allies would have a force of 200,000 men in action in France – Austrians, Russians, Prussians and Germans – which would signify the end for Napoleon. On the other hand, Müffling argued, if the Allies remained on the border with France, awaiting events and reinforcements, then Napoleon would be able to strengthen his fortresses and unite France behind him, making it that much harder for the Allies to overthrow him.

Kleist's strategy was the opposite, favouring the defensive. He advocated allowing Napoleon to invade Belgium, expecting only to face the Anglo-Netherlands army. The Prussians would then move to assist their allies and surprise the French. Once Napoleon was beaten in battle, the allied cavalry would then complete the defeat by an aggressive pursuit.

The major fault with Müffling's plan was that it was based on the British and the Netherlanders being in a better state of readiness than they actually were. This would mean that the Prussians would have to take on a French army not only superior in numbers, but also better in quality. Besides, any invasion of French territory would probably result in the population closing ranks behind Napoleon, increasing the risk that the attack would be defeated. Kleist's strategy to err on the side of caution was far better.

During the night of 25 March, Kleist's representative Roeder arrived in Brussels.[24] At 8 a.m. on 26 March, he met with Sir Hudson Lowe. Lowe had established a good relationship with the Prussians during the time he spent in their headquarters during earlier campaigns. However, as he had little to say on this occasion, Roeder next went to see the Prince of Orange. They discussed the situation over lunch, with the Prince talking about the many rumours he had heard. In particular, it seemed as if all the French border

---

[24] Roeder's reports can be found in GStA, Rep 92, Gneisenau A 48.

fortresses apart from Lille had willingly gone over to Napoleon, and Lille had apparently been stormed by Napoleon's forces. The Prince feared that Napoleon was likely to advance along the coast to cut his troops off from their supply bases at the Channel ports. Furthermore, since a French patrol had already crossed the border near Tournai, he was worried that the outbreak of hostilities was imminent. This in turn gave rise to a sense of fear and panic in Brussels, and the suspicion of treachery in high places.

Other intelligence was not quite so conclusive. Goltz, the Prussian representative in Paris, reported that Napoleon was saying in public that he had no intention of conquering Belgium. Rather, he was in favour of peace. However, Goltz had also received information that Napoleon was telling his generals he would be in Brussels shortly. Goltz, though, considered this to be unlikely as Napoleon had insufficient men and supplies for such a rapid offensive. Napoleon was moving troops to the border but Goltz thought they were going there merely to garrison the fortresses.[25]

However, it would seem that the British regarded the situation as already critical. Britain had started to land additional men and supplies in Ostend and Antwerp, and was promising to strengthen her forces in the Low Countries rapidly. Lowe also began to develop his relationship with Roeder. The two had a friendly conversation on 27 March, in which Roeder informed Lowe of Prussia's willingness to support the Anglo-Netherlands position in Belgium.

The Prince of Orange, Lowe and Roeder next met in Namur, where they drew up plans. The Prince had been unsure of Prussian support, were the French to invade, and had been considering a withdrawal to Antwerp. With Prussian assistance now certain, this was now no longer the case, so the question of a place to offer battle was considered. Roeder proposed a position between Tirlemont and St Trond, in open terrain which would suit the Prussian army better. Roeder came away from the meeting with the impression that his plan had been agreed on. His papers use phrases such as 'the plan agreed on earlier' and 'I have suggested the area of Tirlemont–St Trond and Geet without having to plead. Everybody seemed to agree with this idea.'[26] This seems a little surprising, as assembling the armies in this area would have abandoned Brussels and southern Belgium to the French. However, this area did lie roughly half way between Brussels and Aachen, so in a crisis, the Allies could have concentrated there most rapidly. As it was Kleist's responsibility to protect the German border, without clear instructions from Vienna, he could not risk leaving Cologne and Aachen open to a French thrust.

The relationship between the three allied commanders appeared to be working well. The Prince of Orange devoted much energy to his duties, visiting his outposts frequently. On 27 March, he rode from Brussels to Mons and back again. On 28 March, he inspected Antwerp, returning to Brussels in time for lunch, and a meeting with the allied representatives which rather spoiled the atmosphere of good will. The Prince announced that he had just asked Kleist

[25] Pflugk-Harttung, *Bundestruppen*, p 29.
[26] GStA, Rep 92, Gneisenau, A 48, fol 76. Cf. fols 72, 74.

to remain on the right bank of the Meuse after all, but that this should not be regarded as a sign of mistrust. He had called for assistance from the Prussians when the danger to his country seemed great, but the expected French invasion had yet to materialise so now he did not wish the Prussians to move to Namur. The Prussians regarded this change of stance as insulting, and the Prince was embarrassed by this.[27]

The new King of the Netherlands was due to visit Brussels in the coming days, and the Duke of Wellington was expected to arrive shortly. These two events indicated that a shift in the local balance of power was imminent. Reports had also arrived from Paris stating that the forces available to Napoleon were only 50,000 men strong,[28] so there were apparently no longer any grounds for panic. The Prince of Orange and Lowe now favoured a deployment on the border to cover Brussels, as opposed to Roeder's wish of a concentration in the Tirlemont–St Trond area. In any case, Wellington was now going to be making the final decision.[29]

The Anglo-Netherlanders' position had gone through a range of changes in only a few days but now seemed to be stabilising. At first, they had even considered falling back to Antwerp, abandoning Brussels to the feared invader. Then they had considered enlisting Prussian aid and even allowing the Prussians to enter Netherlands territory, accepting that, as a consequence, Brussels would be left unprotected and southern Belgium abandoned. Finally, they considered meeting the enemy on the border and keeping the Prussians out of the Netherlands for as long as possible. In all this the Prince of Orange was evidently being forced to change his military decisions as a result of political decisions made by his father. This would not be the last time in this campaign that a political decision dictated the military response.

One reason for the changes in the Dutch plans was that the situation in France also seemed to change daily. A report dated 28 March 1815 mentioned Napoleon having no more than 50,000 men at his disposal in Paris,[30] but then news from Lille on 29 March spoke of a corps of 50,000 to 60,000 men having left Paris for the Belgian frontier on 24 March. The Prince of Orange again called for Kleist's aid, via Roeder. Roeder, however, did not believe the situation was as serious as the Prince thought,[31] but that did not stop him from using this development to his advantage. The same evening he went to Lowe to protest about the way the Prussians were being treated. First, they were requested to move to Namur, then they were told not to. Now they were being asked to again. Lowe accepted that these inconsistencies existed, but pointed out that, as British representative, he did not have the final say on matters involving the territory of the Kingdom of the Netherlands. The next day, Roeder visited the Prince of Orange to repeat his complaint. The Prince agreed that, from the military point of view, it was desirable for the Prussians to move closer to him, even if it meant entering Netherlands territory. However, he pointed out that the final decision on such matters lay with his

[27] Pflugk-Harttung, *Bundestruppen*, p 31 f.   [30] GStA, Rep 92, Gneisenau, A 48, fol 72.

[28] Pflugk-Harttung, *Bundestruppen*, p 32.   [31] GStA, Rep 92, Gneisenau, A 48, fol 74.

[29] GStA, Rep 92, Gneisenau, A 48, fol 72.

father and the British. The Prince also said that, unlike the Prussians who wanted to offer battle at Tirlemont, he favoured giving battle at Nivelles since Brussels could be protected from there. In any case the Prince also confirmed that, as Wellington was due to arrive in the next day or two, no firm decisions were going to be made. Poor Roeder was running around in circles.

Next, the foreign ambassadors in Paris were expelled, an indication that war might be about to start. Rather than being allowed to cross the land border into the Netherlands, the ambassadors were sent out of France via Dieppe, to delay the receipt of any information they might be able to pass on. The Allies also suspected that this route was chosen to prevent the ambassadors seeing any war preparations that might be taking place in northern France.

King Willem arrived in Brussels on 30 March, becoming the leading allied figure there. The Prince of Orange's influence was on the wane. In a meeting with Roeder that day the Prince said that,

> According to a report from General Dörnberg, [Marshal] Ney and Napoleon have reached the border at Valenciennes with troops. Reinforcements were expected there and in Lille. Ney had already paraded 18,000 men in Valenciennes. If this is correct, then the assault on Brussels could start any day with the hope that its defenders were neither ready nor organised.[32]

The Prince asked Kleist to provide him with every assistance should the worst happen. However, he was still determined to defend Brussels and would take up positions at either Braine-le-Comte or Nivelles. Roeder repeated that the Prussians wanted to take up positions around Tirlemont and expected their Allies to join them. The Prince made it clear that he would rather suffer a defeat than give up Brussels without a fight. Roeder reported that a decision on giving the Prussians permission to cross the Meuse was going to be made by King Willem shortly. Roeder though such formalities were laughable and believed that because of the coming danger, the decision had already really been made.[33]

Sir Charles Stuart, writing from Brussels on 30 March, informed the Duke of Wellington that,

> The Prussians have manifested some ill humour upon the King's refusal to allow them to pass the Meuse: as they appear, however, now to confine their demand to the admission of one battalion into Namur, I do not think their feelings will give rise to any change of measures on the part of General Kleist.[34]

General Müffling also prepared a memorandum for Kleist on 30 March, which was to be sent on to the King of the Netherlands.[35] This discussed the measures to be taken in case of a French invasion. Müffling pointed out that, if Napoleon had already begun attacking the Anglo-Netherlands forces, they would be unable to defend Brussels. The Prussians would be unable to

---

[32] Pflugk-Harttung, *Bundestruppen*, p. 36
[33] GStA, Rep 92, Gneisenau, A 48, fol 76.
[34] WSD, vol X, p 7.
[35] GStA, Rep 92, Gneisenau, A 40, fol 37.

concentrate their forces at Liège for three or four days. The Anglo-Netherlanders would then have to fall back on the lower Rhine, and would reach a position between Tirlemont and St Trond on the second day of fighting. The best plan would be for the Prussians to be in a position to meet them there that day and they should be permitted to deploy in such a way as to allow them to achieve this. It accordingly made military sense for King Willem to allow the Prussians to enter his territory as soon as possible.

However, Müffling noted, since Napoleon's preparations were not as advanced as had been expected, the Anglo-Netherlands forces might be able to give him the impression that they intended to hold a position at Ath, between Valenciennes and Brussels. Holding Ath could only be a deception, never the real plan, as it would take the Army of the Lower Rhine seven days to reach a supporting position there. It would be better for the British and Dutch to fall back on the Prussian reinforcements while the deception helped cover the move. For their part the Prussian forces would not be able to leave their positions on the Meuse until they were certain that Napoleon was advancing on Brussels, and not on Namur or even the upper Rhine.

Kleist agreed with Müffling's arguments. He forwarded this memorandum, which he had annotated, to Roeder, who received it and handed it over to the Prince on 31 March.

Further news came in that day from Valenciennes. Apparently, Napoleon's presence there was not confirmed. However, Ney was there, and troops were arriving, and being deployed in and around Lille, Condé and Valenciennes. A nervous King Willem had Roeder present his best greetings to Kleist. It was clearly expedient to be a little more friendly to the Prussians, at least for the time being.

The situation was also difficult for the Prussians. For political reasons, they very much wanted to play a major role in the forthcoming campaign, but for military reasons they hesitated to make any deployment deep inside Belgium since this would have left them with long lines of communication vulnerable to a French attack. King Willem also dithered, constantly hoping that events would not force him to have to rely on the Prussians. Roeder expressed his frustration at having to be a diplomat, hoping that he would soon be relieved of these duties.[36]

Roeder had already held another meeting with the Prince of Orange on 31 March.[37] Here, the Prince requested the Prussians to occupy Namur, and sent orders to General Stedman to remove his Dutch garrison the next day. Roeder recommended to Kleist that he go along with this plan, even though it was different from that previously agreed. He also informed Zieten of the situation and made preparations for billeting Prussian troops in Namur. Roeder told Kleist that Napoleon was still believed to be in Valenciennes, with hostilities likely to commence within 48 hours. The Netherlands headquarters were thus to be moved to Ath, and the Prince of Orange planned to

[36] GStA, Rep 92, Gneisenau, A 48, fol 78.
[37] Pflugk-Harttung, *Bundestruppen*, p 39.

concentrate his forces at Nivelles and Braine-le-Comte. If the Prussians were to move from Namur towards Nivelles then, the Prince said, he would await the enemy with confidence. However, he feared that Napoleon would attack before these preparations were complete.

Roeder's report was sent off by a Netherlands despatch rider who had just happened to arrive with communications that were to be forwarded to Kleist. The messenger rode to Zieten's headquarters, arriving there later the same day, 31 March, and passing on Roeder's news to Zieten.

Zieten did not wish to carry out Roeder's suggestion without consulting Kleist first as he believed the move could have grave political consequences. So he wrote to Kleist, informing him that, 'General von Roeder has written to me that the Prince of Orange believes I must shortly march to Namur; this I cannot do without Your Excellency's orders, so I will await these here.'[38] Zieten considered this information so urgent that he sent this message off at 1.30 a.m.

The Prince of Orange expected a French offensive any day. On 31 March he personally wrote to Kleist, seeking urgent assistance from him. He began by apologising for his failure to answer the Prussian General's previous communication, explaining that difficulties regarding the crossing of the Meuse had delayed him. As these problems no longer existed, he stated he would be most grateful if Kleist were to cross the Meuse at Namur and Huy. The Prince's preference was for the Prussians to support his defence of Brussels; he could not abandon his country as far as Tirlemont, as his British allies would be cut off from their line of retreat to Antwerp and he doubted they would accept such a plan.[39]

Kleist answered this letter on 1 April. He replied that he could not justify fighting at Nivelles. His view was that the Allied cause was based not simply on defending Belgium, but rather the whole of Europe, against a resurgence of Napoleonic imperialism. He considered that making a stand at Nivelles would hardly cover Brussels. The Prussian position was quite simple. To advance too far into Belgium with the forces they currently had available would expose them to the possibility of a severe defeat. The destruction of Kleist's forces would leave Germany open to a French invasion. That risk could not be taken, no matter how desirable any occupation of parts of Belgium might be.

On 1 April the Prince of Orange also discussed Müffling's earlier memorandum with Lowe and Roeder. The Prince acknowledged the thoroughness of the Prussian analysis, and said that on the whole he agreed with the suggestion that the Dutch-Belgian Army should be concentrated at Nivelles, ready to march from there via Namur to join the Prussians. Even after this admission, Roeder felt he was making little progress.[40]

Later the same day Kleist's 1 April letter arrived in Brussels, but Roeder

[38] Pflugk-Harttung, *Bundestruppen*, p 40. Letter of 31 March, 1.30 a.m. [1 April] from Huy.

[39] Pflugk-Harttung, *Bundestruppen*, p 41.

[40] GStA, Rep 92, Gneisenau, A 48 fol 79.

did not expect this note to achieve much either, as he had already gone over the issue of Tirlemont with Lowe and the Prince. Roeder considered it most unwise for the Prussians to cross the Meuse until Napoleon's intentions were clear. It also seemed evident that the Prince was going to make a stand in front of Brussels come what may. As he could not abandon his new Belgian subjects to their former master without at least putting up a token fight, his political needs evidently had priority over military strategy. And if they were defeated south of Brussels, Roeder considered his Allies' line of retreat would more likely be towards Antwerp than the Prussian positions, whatever the Prince might say now. In such an event, any Prussian forces at Tirlemont would be out on a limb and have to retreat towards the Rhine.

Meanwhile, the port of Ostend was busy. Every day, more of the promised British troops were disembarked. Lord Hill, one of the officers chosen for senior command, arrived in Brussels on 1 April. He briefed the Prince of Orange with news from the Ministry of War in London. The British, too, were of the opinion that only a token resistance could be offered in front of Brussels, so the Prince was told not to place his troops too near the border.[41] The Duke of Wellington's arrival was keenly awaited.

One of Kleist's staff officers, a Major Dumoulin, prepared a memorandum for Lowe on 1 April in which he pointed out that, once news of any French offensive arrived, it would take the leading elements of the Prussian army four days to reach Nivelles. It would take a week for the entire Prussian army to concentrate there. As Napoleon could reach Brussels in those four days, there would be little point in such a Prussian manoeuvre. Lowe did not answer this memorandum, but it seems to have made its point. The Prince of Orange now realised that a junction with the Prussians at Namur was also impossible. He, too, hoped that Wellington would soon arrive so that he would not have to make the decisions in such a difficult position.[42]

In a meeting with Roeder on 3 April King Willem complained bitterly about Kleist's unwillingness to help the Dutch in the way they wanted. Roeder did his best to convince the king that, in the circumstances, the Prussians could do little else. He appears to have got his point across as the meeting ended on a friendly note with the king excusing his earlier excitement, explaining that it was hard for him to have to give up part of his realm to the enemy when there were enough soldiers available to stop this from happening. The next morning, in his regular meeting with the Prince of Orange, Roeder assured him that, in the event of hostilities, the Prussians would indeed do everything in their power to assist their Allies.

The Prussian Preparations

Kleist was making every effort to complete his army's preparations for war. The entire force needed to be reorganised. New regiments had to be formed,

---

41 De Bas, *Prins Frederik*, vol III, p 1140; De Bas & T'Serclaes de Wommersom, vol I, p 186.
42 GStA, Rep 92, Gneisenau, A 48 fol 81.

and the manpower necessary had to be raised. The new recruits had to be trained and reserve officers and militiamen called up. As early as 27 March, Kleist was in a position to tell Zieten that the army should only move when it had a minimum of ten days supplies available and that these supplies – bread for two days, flour for a further eight, one pound of rice per man, salt, brandy and meat for ten days, oats for six days – were now in fact ready. On 1 April Zieten was ordered to occupy Namur and to prepare to march on Tirlemont. On 2 April Zieten's troops secured the town while his main body under Pirch I took up positions between Huy and Havelange. On the same day, Generalmajor Graf Henckel moved his cavalry brigade from Luxembourg to Bastogne.

The forces now available to the protagonists were roughly as follows:

Allies

Army of the Upper Rhine	
Württembergers	20,000 men
Badeners	12,000 men
Hesse-Darmstadters	8,000 men
Bavarians	10,000 men
	50,000 men
Between the Rhine and Meuse	
Bavarians and garrisons of	
Mainz and Luxembourg	18,000 men
On the Meuse	
Prussians	50,000 men
Anglo-Allied Army in the Netherlands	
British and Hanoverians	23,000 men
Netherlanders	20,000 men
Total	161,000 men

French

French Army on Napoleon's return to France	230,000 men
Less fortress garrisons, troops in Paris, etc.	110,000 men
Total field army	120,000 men [43]

Kleist is Transferred

The question of who was to lead the strongest army on the lower Rhine was important not only for Prussia but for the whole of Europe. The most successful army in the forthcoming campaign would give its government a big say in any subsequent peace treaty. King Friedrich Wilhelm was thus most careful about whom he placed in the senior positions in this situation. He needed leaders who were respected both at home and abroad, experienced

[43] Pflugk-Harttung, *Bundestruppen*, p 48.

and capable of the task in hand, but he also had to take account of frictions that existed between his senior officers.

One group of senior commanders was centred around Gneisenau, and included War Minister Boyen, and the staff officers Valentini, and Clausewitz. These officers had played a major role in the recent reforms and modernisation of the army but, although they may have been the most brilliant minds in the Prussian Army, they were all also relatively young and inexperienced.

The second group included older, more senior, officers like Generaladjutant von der Knesebeck, Feldmarschall von Kalckreuth and Generals von Kleist, Yorck and Tauentzien, former corps commanders in the Wars of Liberation. These men were more conservative in their outlook, resisting changes they considered too radical.

General von Bülow was somewhere in between these two cliques, supporting Gneisenau's modernisation of the army, but disliking him personally. Müffling was another senior officer in an ambivalent position, a talented general, but one without a command. He was a supporter of Kleist, and envious of both Gneisenau and Grolman. Prince Hardenberg had contacts with both cliques but favoured the Gneisenau party. Blücher himself was largely above such politics, but his sympathies lay with the reformers.

In the final analysis the Knesebeck party was less effective because it lacked a single aim. Gneisenau and his associates pressed for reforms both in the army and the state, and had clear political objectives, both in domestic and foreign policy. Knesebeck's group lacked any of these, merely striving to maintain their positions of influence against competition from more liberal ideas.

The relationships in the high command were thus as follows. Bülow did not get on with Gneisenau. Boyen and Gneisenau could not stand the sight of Yorck. Tauentzien felt himself pushed aside by Bülow. Kalckreuth engaged in intrigues to protect his own position. The king was naturally drawn to the conservatives, but reason told him to favour the intellectuals, which explains the inconsistencies in his decision making. While Knesebeck and Kleist enjoyed the king's favour, in the end he actually trusted Gneisenau and Blücher with the most senior positions, even though he also described them as 'mad Jacobins'.

Wellington was certainly aware of the divisions at senior levels in the Prussian government and had been briefed as to how the British intended to take advantage of this. As Stewart wrote to the Duke on 28 April 1815,

> You know there is a strong party in the Prussian army, and Generals Gneisenau and Knesebeck are declared rivals, and are jealous of each other's influence. On the present occasion, however, it appears to me that General Knesebeck is ready to lend himself to counsels which emanate from you, and which he believes will have the approval of those with whom you are acting in the most immediate communication.[44]

[44] WSD, vol X, p 172.

The British were quite happy to use all these frictions within the Prussian hierarchy to further their political aims.

Thanks to the military successes of the campaigns of 1813 and 1814, the reformist party had ended the previous war with the upper hand. Throughout the diplomatic problems of the second half of 1814 and early 1815, and the possibility of war with the other Great Powers over Saxony, the reformists remained particularly critical of Kleist. Once Napoleon returned to France, they clamoured even louder for Gneisenau to replace him. Grolman used the opportunity of being in Vienna to apply pressure at the highest levels. On 13 March, he wrote to Boyen,

> With regard to the senior commands, we did not know what better to do than to suggest Blücher in his old relationship with Gneisenau. The King has agreed to this. It is very important that they both go to the Rhine together. Kleist is about as useful as the fifth wheel on a waggon there. If Blücher does not make his mind up immediately, then Gneisenau should go straight away and take over the supreme command provisionally... Kleist should then be put in command of the [other] German troops... the Chancellor agrees with this.[45]

The conservatives, however, saw matters a little differently. Kalckreuth, being in Berlin, was not at the centre of the political intrigues, but did contact Blücher, who was also in the Prussian capital city, to try to put him off accepting the command.[46] Knesebeck, the king's senior ADC, was more influential than old Kalckreuth. He planned for Kleist to be commander-in-chief of the north German contingents, which Knesebeck expected to be attached to the Prussian army, and even wanted the Austrian and Bavarian forces between the Moselle and Rhine to be placed under Kleist. Knesebeck's note on the subject read,

> The forces in northern Germany will be allocated as follows. The Prussian troops between Mainz and Luxembourg are to be transferred to General von Kleist. He is to be put in command of all troops between the Rhine, the Meuse and the French border as well as all fortresses and garrisons in this area.[47]

King Friedrich Wilhelm, however, did not agree. On 15 March he wrote to Blücher stating he hoped the Field Marshal would again put his energies into the cause. Knesebeck then started to fudge his position, stating in a memorandum of 17 March that Wellington should be given command of the Allied army in the Netherlands, while saying rather vaguely that Blücher should be put in command of Mainz.[48] Kleist was not mentioned by name in this document and exactly who was to command the German troops on the lower Rhine was not made clear.

However, on 17 March, the king finally decided on Blücher as commander-

---

[45] Conrady, *Grolman*, vol II, p 273.
[46] Pflugk-Harttung, *Stosch*, p 247.
[47] Pflugk-Harttung, *Bundestruppen*, p 52.
[48] Pflugk-Harttung, *Bundestruppen*, p 53.

in-chief, with Gneisenau as his chief-of-staff. Gneisenau was sent off to the Rhine immediately, while Blücher was instructed to remain in Berlin pending the outcome of events in France.[49] The king was in a difficult situation here. Certainly neither party could object to Blücher's appointment as he was the most senior commander available and had a right to the position, but if Blücher were to refuse the command, then it was likely that Gneisenau, Kleist and Bülow amongst others would expect to receive this posting. Gneisenau may well have been the most popular officer for second choice, but his rivals were more senior. By way of recompense to Kleist, whom Friedrich Wilhelm did not want to insult, he removed the North German Federal Corps from the Army of the Lower Rhine and placed it under Kleist's command, hoping to placate the conservatives with this decision.

The order-in-cabinet from Vienna which informed Kleist of these changes arrived in his headquarters in Aachen towards the end of the month. Kleist was insulted that Gneisenau, a foreign upstart, should be sent to remove him from office.[50] After all, he was a full general, enjoyed royal favour, was respected by his officers and men, had proved himself both as a soldier and as a diplomat, and, in addition, was a Prussian by birth. He regarded himself as the victim of a conspiracy.

Whatever Kleist thought hardly mattered now, for Gneisenau arrived in Aachen on 1 or 2 April to take up his new post and Blücher followed to take command on 11 April. The 'Jacobins' now controlled the Army of the Lower Rhine. Wellington, too, had arrived in his headquarters on 5 April. The scene was set for the forthcoming drama.

---

[49] Ollech, p 13; Unger, *Blücher*, vol II, p 252.
[50] Pflugk-Harttung, *Stosch*, p 247.

Chapter 6

Preparations for War

The Duke of Wellington Arrives

The Duke arrived at his new headquarters in Brussels during the night of 4 April 1815. On his way from Vienna, he had visited the Prussian headquarters, which were still in Aachen, and had met Gneisenau there. At 8 a.m. the next day, he wrote a report to Castlereagh, his first in his new post. In this report he told the Foreign Secretary that, 'I found the Prussians very content yesterday at Aix la Chapelle [Aachen], and I propose to write to Gneisenau this afternoon upon our plan, as soon as I shall have seen how matters are situated here, and on the frontier.'[1]

That afternoon, he wrote to Gneisenau outlining the position as he saw it,

The reports on the situation, the number, and the intentions of the enemy are excessively vague...

There is no doubt that, for him [Napoleon], it would be most important to force back the troops we have before Brussels; to force the King of France and the Royal Family to flee; and to make the King of the Netherlands and the new establishment here withdraw. This would be a terrible blow to public opinion here and in France.

My opinion is that you must take measures to assemble the entire Prussian army with the Allied Anglo-Dutch before Brussels...

With this deployment, we will be sure of saving this country which is of such interest to the Allied Powers; we would cover the assembly of their forces on the Rhine.[2]

Wellington's stratagem was to ensure that the Prussians played a secondary role, while the Austrians and their German allies formed up along the Rhine. The Duke would then lead the invasion of France, while the Austrians would protect Germany. That way, the Prussians would not have a chance of playing a significant role in military affairs, and so would have relatively little say at the peace table. Gneisenau saw through the Duke's scheme, and had Roeder reply to Wellington on 8 April,

Although the Prussian Army of the Lower Rhine would never refuse to contribute to the defence of the Netherlands in conjunction with the Anglo-Dutch Army, it is at the same time charged with guarding the security of the area between the Meuse, Moselle and Rhine...

As a consequence, orders have been given for Generallieutenant von Zieten to concentrate around Namur on 10 April, and to march on 11 April to occupy

[1] WD, vol XII, p 288.
[2] WD, vol XII, pp 288-89.

cantonments between Charleroi (including the town) and Namur (excluding the town), and in the area enclosed by the Meuse, Sambre, and the old Roman road running from Binch[e] through Ramelles [Ramillies] to Avenne[s].

The corps of Generallieutenant von Borstell will, on the same day, take over the quarters currently occupied by General Zieten, in the town of Namur. The corps of Generallieutenant Thielemann will concentrate in and around Liège. The headquarters will move to Liège on 11 April.[3]

The Prussians were certainly not willing to play a secondary role to Wellington, so they deployed as they saw fit in the circumstances.

The Secret Treaty

On 6 April, two days after the Duke arrived in Brussels, the British heard that Napoleon had found out about the treaty of 3 January 1815, the secret alliance by Britain, Austria and Royalist France against Russia and Prussia.[4] The British correctly anticipated that Napoleon would publish this treaty, as public knowledge of it would clearly be detrimental to good relations between the Allies. On 8 April, referring to a letter from Sir Charles Stuart, ambassador to the Netherlands, Castlereagh wrote to the Duke on this matter informing him that, '…you will perceive from the enclosed that Buonaparte is trying to make mischief on the subject of our Treaty of January 3rd' and instructing Wellington that, '…it is better to be silent, unless Russia or Prussia should enquire as to the fact.'[5]

The parties to the Treaty had been hoping to keep it to themselves.[6] It would be severely embarrassing if initial talks on a joint plan of campaign were clouded by the revelation of what some Prussians could term a 'British led anti-Prussian plot'. Wellington followed his instructions, writing back to Gneisenau on 10 April,[7] but only about the plan of operations.

At this time a French Foreign Department official fell into Prussian hands at Aachen with a copy of the treaty in his possession. Gneisenau soon raised the matter in a protest to Wellington. The Duke reported the position to Bathurst, Britain's Secretary of War, on 11 April, describing how the capture of this document, '…had created a good deal of jealousy and ill-temper in the minds of the Prussian officers.' Wellington also explained that he had sent a trusted officer, Lieutenant-Colonel Hardinge, to Gneisenau in an attempt to placate the Prussians. 'I have likewise desired him [Hardinge] to tell General Gneisenau that if he is not satisfied with the position in which I have placed his troops, I beg he will place them as he thinks proper.'[8] Joint operations had certainly got off to a dismal start.

The timing of this revelation could not have been more favourable to Napoleon but, at this particular time, it also suited the Prussians to have the upper hand in the negotiations with the British over the plan of operation. It is possible that this revelation was a case of the Prussians playing a card they had had up their sleeves for some while. Certainly British representatives had

---

3 WSD, vol X, p 47 f.

4 WSD, vol X, p 43 f.

5 WSD, vol X, p 43.

6 Vane, vol X, p 256.

7 WD, vol XII, p 293 ff.

8 WSD, vol X, p 62.

had indications for a time that the secret treaty was perhaps not quite so secret after all. On 27 March, Castlereagh had written to Wellington that,

> It is to be presumed, in the hurry of their departure, the Foreign Office at Paris has not been stripped by the King's Ministers of any of its contents, and consequently that our secret treaty with France and Austria... will fall into Buonaparte's hands... I flatter myself, after all he knew long since, it cannot produce any unfavourable impression on the Emperor of Russia's mind.[9]

On 19 April, Clancarty wrote to Wellington that, 'I have had little doubt for some time that the Russian government at least has long been in possession not only of the fact but of the very stipulations of the treaty of January.'[10] And, if Czar Alexander was aware of the treaty, it is very likely that his junior partner, the Prussians also knew. Whether they had known for some time or not, the Prussians now had to draw up a plan of operations with their British allies knowing the British had a hidden agenda. In such circumstances it was unlikely they were to be particularly co-operative with their ally.

Gneisenau's and Wellington's Plans

The arrival of Wellington and Gneisenau in the Low Countries in early April 1815 marked the beginning of a new phase in the Allied preparations. The vacillations of the Prince of Orange would now give way to the cool-headed military planning of two experienced generals, even if they had different objectives for the forthcoming war. While Wellington wished the campaign to be planned and executed in such a way that the Prusso-Russian axis would not dominate the affair, Gneisenau wanted the Prussian politicians at Vienna to have a stronger hand at the negotiating table.

Gneisenau began by sending off an outline of his suggested plan of campaign to his masters in Vienna. This read as follows:

1. One army in Belgium.
2. Another on the Middle Rhine.
3. A third on the Upper Rhine.
4. Behind the army on the Middle Rhine, a reserve army; this is to be the strongest.

The commanders of the first three armies are to enter France and take the direction of Paris. They are to expect to arrive there simultaneously with the neighbouring army, whether or not one of them has suffered a defeat. Each of the commanders is expected to continue his advance without stopping, leaving behind mobile detachments to observe any fortified places. The reserve army is expected to deal with any reverse suffered by one of the first line armies, be it by a flanking movement on the communications of the enemy or by direct assistance.

This plan of campaign is based on the numerical superiority of the armies of the Allied powers. France formerly had 90 fortified places whose garrisons will

---

[9] WSD, vol IX, p 626.
[10] WSD, vol X, p 107.

necessarily take up a considerable number of the enemy forces. Should Napoleon defeat one of the first line armies and pursue it, the other two will keep advancing, to gain more territory and close in on Paris. At the same time, the reserve army will attempt to make good the reverse that has been suffered by the defeated army. Should Napoleon prefer to fall on the next army after a victory instead of pursuing his success with the defeated army, he will have to fight a new battle, which, with the aid of the reserve army, will be disputed forcefully. While all this is going on the third of our first line armies will continue to advance and the beaten army will be able to reform and take the offensive again.

The three front line armies will have to avoid getting too close to each other so that the enemy will not be able to disappear from the front of one and move by surprise on another, but so that he will be forced to make a number of marches, allowing the first to learn of his departure from its front and the other to learn of his approach. The army with which he is seeking combat must only fight in very favourable terrain, and it will be well worth them retiring several marches to find such an advantage.

Any plan of campaign which takes account of the armies in Italy would be wrong because it would contain the danger of losing us time. Once the armies are assembled on the eastern border of France, then operations should be pursued vigorously.[11]

Wellington, however, produced a memorandum on 12 April 1815 which put matters differently:

The object of the operations proposed in my letter to the Earl of Clancarty, of the 10th, to be undertaken by the corps of the Allies, which will probably be assembled in Flanders and on the Rhine in the end of the month of April, is, that by their rapidity they might be beforehand with the plans and measures of Buonaparte.

His power now rests upon no foundation but the army; and if we can introduce into the country such a force as is capable either to defeat the army in the field, or to keep it in check, so that the various parties interested in the defeat of Buonaparte's views may have the power of acting, our object will be accomplished.

The Allies have no views of conquest; there is no territory which requires in particular to be covered by the course of their operations; their object is to defeat the army, and to destroy the power of one individual; and the only military points to be considered are; 1st, to throw into France, at the earliest possible period, the largest body of men that can be assembled; 2ndly, to perform this operation in such a manner that it can be supported by the forces of the Allies, which are known to be following immediately; 3rdly, that the troops which shall enter France shall be secure of a retreat upon the supporting armies, in case of misfortune.

The troops to be employed in this operation should be the Allied British, Hanoverian and Dutch troops, under the command of the Duke of

11 WSD, vol X, p 196 f.

Wellington; the Prussian troops, as reinforced, under the command of Comte Gneisenau; the allied Austrian, Bavarian, Wurtemberg [sic], and Baden troops, to be assembled on the Upper Rhine, under Prince Schwarzenberg.

The two former should enter France between the Sambre and the Meuse; the Duke of Wellington endeavouring to get possession of Maubeuge, or, at all events, of Avesnes; and General Gneisenau directing his march upon Rocroy and Chimay. The Duke of Wellington, besides the garrisons in the places in Flanders and Brabant, should leave a corps of troops in observation on the frontiers. Prince Schwarzenberg should collect his corps in the province of Luxembourg; and, while his left should observe the French fortresses of Longvy, Thionville, and Metz, he should possess himself of the forts of Sedan, Stenay, and Dun, and cross the Meuse.

The first object would then be accomplished, and we should have in France a larger body of troops than it is probable the enemy can assemble.

It is expected that the British and Dutch army would be followed in the course of a fortnight by about 40,000 men, and the Prussian army in the same period by 90,000 men; and that the allied Austrian and Bavarian army would be followed by a Russian army of 180,000. Supposing then, that the enemy should have the facility of attacking the line of communication of the English, Hanoverian, and Dutch army, by Maubeuge, and that of the allied Austrian army from their fortresses on the Upper Moselle and Upper Meuse, they could not prevent the junction of those troops. It must, besides, be observed, that the enemy could not venture to leave their fortresses entirely without garrisons of troops of the line, on account of the disgust which the usurpation of Buonaparte has occasioned universally; and the operations on our communications will therefore necessarily be carried on by a diminished body of troops.

However inconvenient, then, they may be to those troops which will have advanced, they can neither prevent the junction of the armies which will be following the first that will enter France, nor can they prevent the retreat of these upon those which are moving to their support.

According to this scheme, then, we should have in the centre of France a body of above 200,000 men, to be followed up by nearly 300,000 more, and their operations would be directed upon Paris, between the Meuse and the Oise.[12]

While the basic structures of Gneisenau's and Wellington's plans were largely similar, namely to invade France with overwhelming force, it is interesting to note their diverging war aims. Paris was the main objective for Gneisenau. Once his Prussians got there, the hated French would be made to pay for their widespread destruction of Germany. France would be weakened and, as a result, Prussia could expand westwards unhindered. For Wellington, the primary objective was to defeat Napoleon, remove him from command of the French armed forces, and restore the *status quo ante bellum*. After all, a strong France was needed to counterbalance Prussian expansionism. For Gneisenau, it was clear which one of the three armies in his first line should

---

[12] WD, vol XII, p 304 f.

reach Paris first, the Prussian-led force based on the middle Rhine. Gneisenau thought in terms of a race to Paris and feared that Wellington, with his suggested lines of advance, would have the advantage in it. The Duke did not plan such a race but British diplomats thought differently. As Stewart put it in a letter to Wellington from Vienna on 28 April,

> The possession of Paris now would, according to all ordinary calculation, finish the career of Napoleon, and give us peace: the state of the country and the government strongly leads to this belief. It is therefore of more importance to arrive there rapidly (even although the whole of the enemy's army should not be beaten) than at the former period.[13]

Whatever Wellington and Gneisenau wanted, the final decision on grand strategy was still to be made in Vienna; after all two other Great Powers also wanted their say. A quick offensive into France would give Czar Alexander little chance to obtain glory for Russia, since he clearly needed time to bring up his army. Schwarzenberg had to bear in mind the Austrian interests in Italy and also wanted the Allied supreme command for himself. To justify his claim Austria needed time to mobilise the largest army, so a quick offensive was also not in Austrian interests.

The Allied representatives had their decisive meeting in Vienna on 19 April. They resolved not to begin the offensive against France before 1 June 1815 because the armies would not be fully assembled until then.[14] Even that was too early for Schwarzenberg. He first asked for a delay to 16 June, then to 27 June and finally to 1 July. By then he expected the Anglo-Prussian forces in the Low Countries to be 250,000 strong, the Russians to have concentrated 200,000 men on the middle Rhine, with the Austrians on the upper Rhine, in Switzerland and Italy having mobilised 350,000 men. The Allies would then have put an overwhelming force of 800,000 men into the field.[15] The long-drawn-out preparations of 1814 were to be repeated and Napoleon was to be handed the initiative.

Wellington Prepares for War

Wellington had to prepare two plans for the forthcoming campaign. The first was how to deal with any French offensive that might occur before the Allies had completed their mobilisation and preparations for the joint invasion of France. The second was how to carry out this joint invasion. The Duke could not be certain which of these possibilities was more likely to become reality but his first requirement was undoubtedly to prepare his army and its defensive fortifications for a French attack.

Wellington's army was one of the most mixed bags ever to take the field. The total force available to Wellington at the outbreak of hostilities in June would number roughly 93,000 men. Roughly one-third came from the British Isles, nearly one-third were Belgians and Dutchmen, and over one-third were

13 WSD, vol X, p 172.
14 Ollech, p 34.
15 Pflugk-Harttung, *Vorgeschichte*, p 5.

Germans of various kinds, notably the Hanoverians, including the King's German Legion, the Brunswickers and the Nassauers. This army was not merely an ethnic and sartorial patchwork, there were also appreciable differences in training, discipline and general experience of war. The most reliable units were some of the British and most of the KGL who were veterans of the Peninsular War. Many of the British were new troops without any battle experience at all. The remaining German formations also contained elements of varying quality ranging from militia to experienced line units.

The Dutch troops in the Netherlands Army were largely young and inexperienced but generally determined to see the matter through. The Belgian Walloons had an appreciable conflict of loyalties, however. Many of them were experienced soldiers who had willingly served the French Emperor in the past and now found themselves in the army of a country of which they did not want to be part. Due to supply shortages, many of them even went to war dressed in their old uniforms, albeit sporting the Dutch cockade, so the technicalities of changing sides would not be difficult either.[16] The Netherlands Army was consequently plagued with desertion. Rather surprisingly, Belgian militia formations proved to be more loyal to the Allied cause than the Belgian regulars. The militia were drawn mainly from the middle classes and feared the results of another invasion from France.[17]

Desertions in the Allied forces were balanced to an extent by pro-Royalist French troops coming over to the Allies. Although relatively few in numbers, the French deserters where often of high rank, and could provide valuable information. All in all, the reliability of troops was a problem that every army in this theatre faced; the Prussians had problems with their Rhinelanders and Saxons; the British with their Hanoverian levies; the French with their Royalists; the Dutch with their Belgians. Many men of conscience had to make difficult decisions.

There was probably only one commander in Europe who could make something out of this seething bundle of contradictions and frictions, and that was the Duke of Wellington with his long and successful experience of commanding multinational forces in India and Spain. His method was to strengthen the weaker elements by grouping the more reliable units with the less reliable ones. As Wellington himself described this, 'It was necessary to organize these troops in brigades, divisions, and corps d'armée with those better disciplined and more accustomed to war, in order to derive from their numbers as much advantage as possible.'[18]

Wellington's forces were deployed from Ypres in the west, through Menin, Tournai, Mons, and Nivelles to the road junction at Quatre Bras, a front of some 100 km. The Prussians were deployed in an arc south of Charleroi, from Binche to Thuin and Gerpinnes, and then east to Liège, their front extending over 80 km. The Allied outposts met to the west of Binche, along an old Roman road. Generallieutenant von Zieten and the Prince of

[16] Müffling, *Leben*, p 223.
[17] Pflugk-Harttung, *Vorgeschichte*, p 19.
[18] WSD, vol X, p 517.

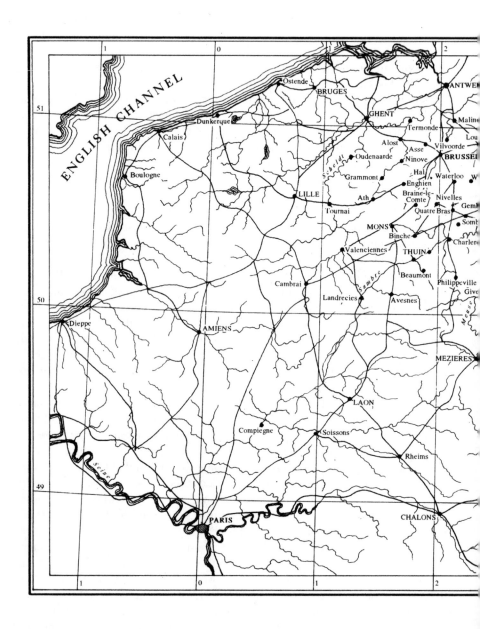

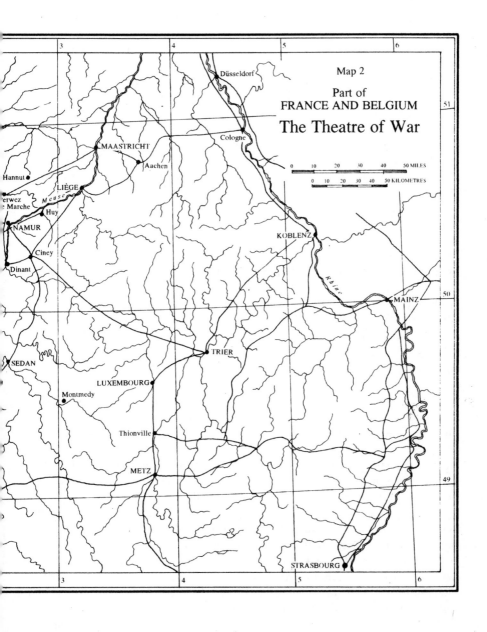

Map 2

Part of
FRANCE AND BELGIUM
The Theatre of War

Orange were the respective commanders of the forces at this pivotal point. Binche is situated to the south-west of the easternmost British positions, between Mons and Nivelles, so the Prussian front overlapped Wellington's line in this area. The Allied deployment was spread over such a wide front for two reasons. Firstly, because of supply – the Allies did not want to overburden the local population – and secondly to cover all possible avenues of approach by Napoleon. Such a deployment was necessary in the circumstances, but made the Allies very vulnerable to a surprise attack.

Despite their common cause, the intentions of this deployment were as divergent as the war aims of Britain and Prussia. Wellington's objectives were to prevent Brussels falling into Napoleon's hands, as well as to avoid the political embarrassment of the exiled King of France being forced to quit his refuge in Ghent. The Prussians' aim was to prevent an invasion of Germany. The Prussian lines of communication ran east to the Rhine while the British lines of communication ran north-west to the Channel ports of Antwerp and Ostend. The fault line of the coalition in the Low Countries lay along the axis Thuin–Charleroi–Fleurus–Gembloux–Tirlemont and this was where Napoleon would eventually decide to attack.

There were only four major paved roads along which Napoleon could advance against Wellington. One ran from Lille via Menin, to Courtrai, Ghent and Brussels; the second went from Lille to Tournai and then Ghent; the third road which went from Condé through Tournai via Ath and Enghien to Brussels; the fourth road began from Condé or Valenciennes and ran via Mons to Brussels.[19] The Duke attempted to cover all these approach routes. A fifth possible line of attack lay along the road running via Beaumont and Charleroi to Brussels. The Prussians under Zieten covered this front. Their rear, and a variation on this possible line of advance from Binche to Nivelles and Brussels, was guarded by the Netherlanders.

Wellington's deployment was weakest on its north-west, becoming more concentrated from Leuze to Ath, and strongest between Mons and Binche. This, too, was where the strongest concentration of Blücher's army could be found. His lines weakened as they went to the east. Though the Allies placed considerable strength at this point because the main French forces seemed to be gathering opposite, around Maubeuge, Valenciennes and Philippeville the join between the Allied forces was still potentially a weak link.

Wellington's intention was to deploy his troops in such a way that his men could be concentrated at the required point in the shortest time. The Duke's plan was to cover his entire front until it was absolutely clear where the enemy was making his main attack. Put another way, Wellington would prefer to make no move at all rather than a false move. This strategy was indisputably the best one for these circumstances, but was to have almost fatal consequences when problems arose in its execution on 15 June 1815.

Ypres, Ghent and Antwerp were the strongest fortified places. The citadel of Ypres alone boasted some 117 cannon, and a major survey of Antwerp's

---

[19] WSD, vol X, p 523.

fortifications had been carried out in March.[20] In the event of a defeat by the French and the fall of Brussels, this city would be the point to which the bulk of Wellington's forces would retire. Some 20,000 labourers in British pay were involved in improving the various defenses up to June 1815, and this work was largely completed by the outbreak of hostilities. Wellington also fortified the major routes, 'Each of these was a great paved road, upon which there was no obstacle of a defensive nature, excepting the field works of which it appears the Duke of Wellington ordered the construction.'[21] Specific orders for the defence of the fortified places were issued, the Prince of Orange being sent his copy on 7 June 1815.[22]

The Allied forces each deployed small detachments of mounted troops near the border, watching the enemy outposts and supported by companies and battalions of infantry placed in the nearby villages. These, in turn, were backed by larger bodies of infantry together with artillery to their rear, and so on to Brussels where Wellington's reserve and headquarters were positioned. Brigade and divisional headquarters were located in the second and third lines. The Prince of Orange, commander of I (Allied) Corps, had his headquarters in Braine-le-Comte, roughly halfway between Mons and Brussels, from where there was a good road to Binche and the Prussian lines.

Since Wellington's army was smaller than Blücher's and guarded the important prize of Brussels, it was reasonable to assume it would be the focus of Napoleon's attention and the most likely first target for attack. Both Allied headquarters therefore initially expected the French offensive would be against Wellington. Gneisenau had made it quite clear that in the event of a French offensive, he intended to operate in conjunction with the British. As Roeder wrote on 9 April, 'General Gneisenau has certainly indicated that he sincerely wishes to operate in concert with the Duke of Wellington and to move the troops under his orders to the places required without awaiting a general plan...'[23] Gneisenau confirmed this in a letter to Wellington on 13 April, '...but you may, my Lord Duke, in the event of an attack, count on the assistance of all our available forces here, and we have decided to share the lot of the army under the orders of Your Excellency.'[24]

Wellington's army was organised into two corps, one on each flank, plus the reserve and the cavalry. On the basis of that organisation and these assurances from Gneisenau, Wellington drew up a plan of campaign that he communicated to various of his subordinates in a secret memorandum at the end of April 1815,

> 1. Having received reports that the Imperial guard had been moved from Paris upon Beauvais, and a report having been for some days prevalent in the country that Buonaparte was about to visit the northern frontier, I deem it expedient to concentrate the cantonments of the troops with a view to their early junction in case this country should be attacked, for which concentration

[20] WSD, vol X, pp 723 f.   [23] WSD, vol X, p 52.
[21] WSD, vol X, p 523.   [24] WSD, vol X, p 70.
[22] WD, vol XII, pp 450-52.

the Quarter Master General now sends orders.

2. In this case, the enemy's line of attack will be either between the Lys and the Scheldt, or between the Sambre and the Scheldt, or by both lines.

3. In the first case, I should wish the troops of the 4th division to take up [demolish] the bridge on the Scheldt, near Avelghem [Avelgem], and with the regiment of cavalry at Courtrai, and fall back on Audenarde [Oudenaarde], which post they are to occupy, and to inundate the country in the neighbourhood.

4. The garrison of Ghent are to inundate the country in the neighbourhood likewise, and that point is to be held at all events.

5. The cavalry in observation between Menin and Furnes are to fall back upon Ostend, those between Menin and Tournay upon Tournay, and thence to join their regiments.

6. The 1st, 2nd, and 3rd divisions of infantry are to be collected at the head quarters of the divisions, and the cavalry at the head quarters of their several brigades, and the whole to be in readiness to march at a moment's notice.

7. The troops of the Netherlands to be collected at Soignies and Nivelle[s].

8. In case the attack should be made between the Sambre and the Scheldt, I propose to collect the British and Hanoverians at and in the neighbourhood of Enghien, and the army of the Low Countries at and in the neighbourhood of Soignies and Braine le Comte.

9. In this case, the 2nd and 3rd divisions will collect at their respective head quarters, and gradually fall back towards Enghien with the cavalry of Colonel Arentschildt's and the Hanoverian Brigade.

10. The garrisons of Mons and Tournay will stand fast; but that of Ath will be withdrawn, with the 2nd division, if the works should not have been sufficiently advanced to render the place tenable against a *coup de main*.

11. General Sir W. Ponsonby's, Sir J. Vandeleur's, and Sir H. Vivian's brigades of cavalry will march upon Hal.

12. The troops of the Low Countries will collect upon Soignies and Braine le Comte.

13. The troops of the 4th division and the 2nd hussars, after taking up the bridge at Avelghem, will fall back upon Audenarde, and there wait for further orders.

14. In the case of the attack being directed by both lines supposed, the troops of the 4th division and 2nd hussars, and the garrison of Ghent, will act as directed in Nos. 3 and 4 of this Memorandum; and the 2nd and 3rd divisions, and the cavalry, and the troops of the Low Countries, as directed in Nos. 8, 9, 10, 11 and 12.[25]

Wellington also explained an essential aspect of the whole scheme in a letter to Lord Uxbridge, his cavalry commander, on 30 April,

All the dispositions are so made that the whole army can be collected in one short movement, with the Prussians on our left.[26]

[25] WD, vol XII, pp 337-38.
[26] WD, vol XII, p 338.

Prussian Positions

The Prussians were also developing detailed plans to be implemented should the French attack. Zieten gave new orders to his I Corps on 2 May, outlining the role they were to play in such a situation:

In the event of the enemy pushing forward along the road from Binche or Maubeuge with superior numbers, thus forcing back our outposts and making it necessary to place the entire corps on alarm, the brigades are to assemble as follows: 1st Brigade behind Fontaine l'Evêque

2nd Brigade behind Charleroi

3rd Brigade behind Fleurus

4th Brigade behind Onoz

Reserve Cavalry behind Gembloux where it is to await further orders.

Reserve Artillery behind Eghezée.

2nd Brigade is to leave one battalion each in Châtelet, Charleroi and Marchienne, and 1st Brigade is to leave two companies in Fontaine l'Evêque with which the outposts are to link up. The latter are to be ordered to do so.

With regard to the outposts, two Schützen companies of 1st Brigade are to deploy behind the Haine defile. The main body of the 1st Silesian Hussar Regiment is to draw up behind Lerunes. The outposts of this regiment are to deploy diagonally to here. The outpost at Lobbes is to go right back to the left bank of the Sambre. The main body of Uhlan Regiment No 6 is to retire to Charleroi and link up with 2nd Brigade. The outposts from this regiment at Thuin are to wait to be joined by the outpost from Lobbes and are then to withdraw together with them to the left bank of the Sambre to Marchienne. All other pickets stationed between Thuin and Ham-sur-Heure are to retire to Marchienne via Montigny-le-Tilleul. Those between Ham-sur-Heure and Gerpinnes are to retire directly on Charleroi.

The 1st and 2nd squadrons of the Westphalian Landwehr Cavalry Regiment, stationed in Presles and Sart-Eustache, are to cross the Sambre at Châtelet to join 2nd Brigade. The 3rd and 4th squadrons are to cross the Sambre at Fallisole, their outposts are to take the same route and rejoin their squadrons. They are then to rejoin the 1st and 2nd squadrons when on the left bank of the Sambre. The crossing points over the Sambre which are in the jurisdiction of the respective brigades, are to be occupied until ordered by their brigades to march to their assembly points. The baggage and the trains are to be sent back to Temploux.

Should the enemy push us back even further, then:

1st Brigade, after having sent its artillery to Gosselies, is to retire via Roux to Jumet and Gosselies and then take up positions behind Gosselies as vanguard and in support of the outposts along the Piéton.

2nd Brigade is to deploy before Fleurus with this town to its rear.

3rd Brigade is to deploy behind Fleurus, to the right of the road.

4th Brigade is to deploy to their left in column.

If the brigades are ordered to continue the withdrawal to Fleurus, then the 1st and 2nd Brigades are to hold the crossings of the Piéton; the 2nd Brigade from Roux to the junction with the Sambre; the 1st Brigade from Roux to the Roman Road. The 1st Silesian Hussars and 6th Uhlans are to remain in support of the infantry deployed along the Pieton. The Reserve Cavalry is to move to Sombreffe, the Reserve Artillery to the Roman Road in the direction of the defiles this side of Gembloux. Here, should battle be given at Fleurus, they would then be in a position to be used. Also, should a further withdrawal be ordered, they would be able to reach the main road to Namur via Gembloux and Temploux.

The baggage of both brigades is to go to Namur directly if a further withdrawal becomes necessary. One officer per brigade with the necessary support should accompany it.

Should the enemy advance from Beaumont or Philippeville, then the same deployment will be used.

The 2nd Brigade is to hold the crossings over the Sambre at Marchienne, Charleroi and Châtelet until 1st Brigade coming from Fontaine l'Evêque is level with their position. The remainder of 2nd Brigade is to remain in support of the three named outposts, and as vanguard of the army corps assembled at Fleurus, take up position behind Gilly on the road from Charleroi to Fleurus, and there await further orders.

Should the enemy come from Philippeville, forcing back the outposts of 4th Brigade, then this brigade is to defend the crossings over the Sambre until the Army Corps has assembled.

Should individual armed French troops approach the outposts, then they are to be directed to go away so long as they are not deserters. However, should they not do so, then they should where possible be taken prisoner and brought to headquarters. In no event should any picket retire in a peaceful manner.

In the event of I Army Corps falling back on Fleurus, then headquarters is to be moved there.[27]

Zieten's orders indicate that his intention was to fight as long a delaying action as possible with his corps to gain the remainder of the Prussian army enough time to concentrate and move up in support. This valuable time would also be used by Wellington to concentrate his army. Every village, every river crossing was to be contested but Napoleon still had the initiative because of the widespread Allied deployment.

The Invasion Threat

On 2 May intelligence came in that Napoleon was on his way to the frontier, adding to the rumours of an impending French invasion.[28] Wellington passed this information on to Britain and to the Prince of Orange, whom he placed on alert.[29] The Duke then went to Tirlemont for a meeting with Blücher on the 3rd to develop the Allied plans. Unfortunately there is no official protocol of

[27] Plotho, pp 21 ff.
[28] WSD, vol X, p 216.
[29] WD, vol XII, p 344.

this meeting, nor any comprehensive account of what was deliberated there. The only way to achieve an outline of what was agreed is to examine the accounts of various participants where these exist, the orders given to various units around this time, and the subsequent actions of the Allied commanders.

The Allies had not actually agreed on a plan of campaign before this meeting. Gneisenau had made proposals, but Wellington wanted to establish himself as the dominant partner in the Allied hierarchy and was helped in the negotiations by the problems the Prussians were having with the Saxon army at this time. Wellington's own records of this meeting are sparse, but it seems that he came away with a promise from Blücher that, in the event of a French invasion, Blücher would come to the Duke's assistance as soon as possible. This is confirmed in the letters that Wellington wrote that evening to the Prince of Orange, to Hardenberg and to Clancarty. He told the Prince that, 'My meeting with Blücher was very satisfactory'[30] and expressed similar sentiments to Hardenberg, saying, '...as it appears that Prince Blücher and the Prussian officers are not disposed to let me be beaten by superior numbers, I am satisfied.'[31] To Clancarty, he wrote,

We hear of Buonaparte's quitting Paris, and of the march of troops to this frontier, in order to attack us. I met Blücher at Tirlemont this day, and received from him the most satisfactory assurances of support.[32]

In his account, Nostitz, Blücher's ADC, merely mentioned that the topics discussed at the meeting, included the Saxon rebellion, the future of the Saxon contingent, and the plan of campaign. He gave no details of the conversation.[33] All that is on record of Gneisenau's participation in this meeting is his comment, 'The Prussian army is determined to share the fate of the English army',[34] while the Bavarian representative Prince August of Thurn und Taxis, who was not personally present at the meeting but arrived at the Prussian headquarters on 5 May, was told that, '...two days earlier, in Tirlemont, a meeting had taken place with the Duke of Wellington in which it had been agreed, in the event of an enemy offensive, the armies would be united and a battle offered.'[35]

As well as the various assurances of assistance Wellington seems to have had from his Prussian allies, there were also matching changes in the Prussian deployment. Blücher moved his headquarters forward from Liège to Namur to be closer to Wellington, and, as we have seen, Zieten's corps had already been given orders to deploy its outposts around Charleroi. Unbeknown to Zieten he had now positioned himself at the very point the French assault was to strike.

The Duke was convinced that, in the event of a French offensive, Napoleon would attack him first and that Blücher's role should be to support him. But why was there only one offensive possibility, namely an assault on the Anglo-Dutch-German Army? When the events of 15 June 1815 started to unfold, the Duke took some time to realise the error he had made, which led

---

[30] WD, vol XII, p 345.
[31] WD, vol XII, p 345.
[32] WD, vol XII, p 346.
[33] Nostitz, p 11.
[34] Ollech, p 44.
[35] Thurn und Taxis, p 313.

to a dangerous delay. Making up for that delay was going to have far reaching consequences.

Blücher issued new orders for the concentration of his forces on 5 May which throw further light on what was probably was on the 3rd. Zieten was told to concentrate his I Army Corps at Fleurus so that he could move off at short notice. Blücher specifically ordered him,

> I request Your Excellency, as you have suggested, after reading this message, to concentrate at Fleurus in such a way that you can march off in a few hours after receiving orders, which will be sent to you once your reports to me are confirmed by the Duke of Wellington. You are to follow the enemy's moves with counter moves. It is entirely up to you if you bivouac your troops or place them in billets.
>
> General von Borstell has received a similar order to concentrate his army corps at Namur.
>
> I also request you to keep in close contact with the Anglo-Dutch army and with II [Prussian] Corps. If you are attacked, you should in any event await the enemy deployment at Fleurus, and immediately inform the Duke of Wellington, as well as myself. I will then move towards Your Excellency's corps and take command there.[36]

The II Army Corps (to be commanded by Pirch I, but for the moment still under Borstell) was ordered to concentrate in Namur, '…so that Your Excellency can march off with six hours of the receipt of orders.' The III Army Corps was ordered nearer to the front, from Trier and Diekirch to Arlon and Bastogne, while IV Army Corps was ordered to march from Koblenz to Malmédy.

Zieten reported to headquarters on 6 May that his deployment was progressing as ordered,

> The close cantonments of the I Army Corps have been arranged in such a way that it can deploy at Fleurus. 1 and 2 Brigade have been assembled as vanguard between Charleroi and Fontaine l'Evêque and are ready, depending on enemy movements or further orders from Your Highness, to move on Fleurus. To be nearer to any news of the enemy, I shall stay here in Charleroi.

Thus, Blücher's plan in the event of a French attack via Charleroi was for I Army Corps to stage a rearguard action, falling back to Fleurus, where Blücher would arrive with the remainder of the army and take command. In the meantime Wellington would move in support of the Prussians.

The Supply Situation

It was not only the possible enemy moves that influenced the Allied deployment but also their supply situation. Supply problems were prominent in the minds of the Prussian high command in the Netherlands from the start. They knew they were unwelcome guests, known to have territorial ambitions in this

---

[36] Ollech, pp 45 f.

part of the world, and unable, unlike the wealthy British, to pay cash for the supplies they wanted. It is thus no surprise that the Prussians had considerable problems actually obtaining the supplies they required.

The General Staff was concerned with this issue from the outset but the problem became particularly acute after 5 May when the III and IV Corps were ordered to march from the Rhineland to join their comrades in the Netherlands. A letter of 8 May from Gneisenau to Boyen, the Prussian Minister of War, illustrated how the questions of deployment and supply were closely linked,

> My worries about supplies grow daily. The lands between the Meuse, Moselle and Rhine are exhausted. We are soon going to have to leave this area and find another where we can live. At the moment, only Brabant offers us this possibility. Merchants in this province only supply us when we can pay. But we have no money at all. If we cross over to the left bank of the Meuse [to Brabant], we can live from the supplies available there and pay with promissory notes. This measure will lead to another. Our first two corps are at Fleurus and Namur respectively. If the enemy pushes forward quickly from his fortresses, he will attack with superior numbers. If we were to move the IV Army Corps to the left bank of the Meuse, and place it one march from Gembloux it would be available for such a battle. The III Army Corps, still weak in numbers, can, in such an event, be deployed at the Ciney cross-roads to cover any movement by the enemy from Givet to Liège. The terrain here is difficult... [37]

The dispersed deployment of the Prussian Army necessary because of the supply problems was a hindrance to the rapid concentration that would be needed to deal with Napoleon's invasion. This deployment would be partly responsible for the failure of Bülow to be able to arrive with his corps at Ligny on 16 June.

The hoped-for easing of the supply situation through the policy of dispersal was slow in coming. The Netherlands government had agreed to establish magazines for the Prussians and at times supplied both bread and meat. However, the Prussian Commissary was expected to supply salt, vegetables and all other requirements, but had no cash available for this. On the one hand, King Willem of the Netherlands needed the Prussians to protect his fragile realm. On the other, he did not do enough to feed them. Not only did the magazines not contain the agreed three days' supply, there was often no bread at all. This resulted in supplies being sought from the local inhabitants, which did little to improve Prussia's popularity. The locals indeed received promissory notes, but the Netherlands authorities either refused to honour these, or were slow in doing so.

Gneisenau wrote to Dörnberg on 25 May, describing the complaints he had received from the locals regarding the indiscipline and demands of his troops,

---

[37] Lettow-Vorbeck, p 179 ff.

... the troops... are referred to the communes. The latter are not able to meet what is required of them. The soldiers then demand loudly what they believe they are entitled to. Many locals have already left the area and more will do so unless the situation changes. The King of the Netherlands is continuing to amass wealth and has little concern for his subjects. His hostility to the Prussians causes bad will towards us, not to speak of his minister with his background in administering for the French and his sympathy towards them. Day by day, relationships are getting more bitter. The delays in opening hostilities are causing more harm than a defeat on a field of battle... [38]

Gneisenau was particularly annoyed by a complaint from King Willem about the burden that the Prussians were on his land. Hardinge reported the situation to Wellington in his letter of 22 May,

General Gneisenau informs me a letter has just been received from the King of the Netherlands, the substance of which announces the Prussian troops are felt to be a very heavy charge on this part of the country, and that it is desirable to consider of means to alleviate the pressure. It is intended to answer that the Prussians did not come uninvited, or purely for Prussian objects; and that if the King is decidedly of the opinion that their services are no longer required, they will move on the Moselle, where, he added, the right bank afforded abundant subsistence, and where the entrance into France presented none of the impediments of fortified places with which the Belgian frontier was crowded. [39]

Gneisenau's message to Willem was clear. Without proper assistance from the Netherlands authorities, the Prussians would not be able to assist in their defence. Prusso-Netherlands relationships were certainly at a low.

Wellington's answer to Hardinge stated,

In regard to the King of the Netherlands, his case is a very hard one...

The King does not complain of subsisting them; and I believe they have been, and will be, as well taken care of in his country as on the Moselle or elsewhere; but he complains of the expense, which ought not to fall upon him, but partly on the King of Prussia, and partly on the countries forming the *rayon* [area of supply] of the Prussian army. [40]

The Duke's point was partly valid, but only partly. The financial arrangements agreed in Vienna had yet to be communicated to all parties, let alone implemented. As Hardinge replied on 25 May,

I spoke with General Gneisenau this forenoon on the subject of the subsistence of the Prussian troops by the King of the Netherlands. I introduced the conversation by asking if the General had received the Vienna arrangements for the subsisting of the Allied armies by *rayons* of countries. He said he had not... I then explained the points, according to your Lordship's instructions,

[38] Lettow-Vorbeck, p 180 f.
[39] WSD, vol X, p 337.
[40] WD, vol XII, p 422.

which render the case of the King of the Netherlands a hard one. The General admitted the expense to be very heavy: his reasoning on the question was, that when circumstances rendered it expedient that the Prussian troops should enter Belgium, it was stipulated that their subsidence should be provided at the expense of the King of the Netherlands, and that your Lordship was a party, or a guarantee, to this stipulation, and the principal cause of the readiness with which the movement was made without magazines or means to supply their troops...[41]

Gneisenau believed he was being let down by the Duke. When the Prussians had entered the Low Countries, Wellington had promised Willem would pay for their supplies, and that he would personally guarantee this. Now that the Prussians were there, Gneisenau evidently felt that the Duke had not applied sufficient pressure on Willem.

General Müffling, who had recently arrived in Brussels to take up a post as the Prussian liaison officer in Wellington's headquarters, also raised the issue with the Duke, reporting on 27 May that,

> ...the Duke informed me of the whole discussion at Vienna on the question of the *rayons* and said he had requested the King of the Netherlands to obtain the required supplies and to request payment through diplomatic channels.
> There is certainly no shortage of food in this country.[42]

Brockhausen, the Prussian ambassador to the Netherlands, also reported on 29 May that King Willem had again promised to deal with this issue. Gneisenau did not hesitate to point out that he had heard that promise before.[43] However, Wellington apparently believed the issue had now been dealt with, telling his Commissary General that, 'The conferences with the Prussian Commissaries have already produced an arrangement satisfactory to them for the formation of their magazines... '[44] That was not the case as, the very same day, Blücher had issued a printed decree for his field officers informing them that due to the inconsistency of supply from the magazines, he was allowing his troops to live at the cost of the local inhabitants. This decree was sent to Bülow on 9 June together with a note from Blücher instructing him to point out to the local population who was really at fault for this situation.[45]

The difficulties experienced by the Prussians with supplies contrasted sharply with the situation of their British allies. The British troops, the King's German Legion and the Hanoverian Subsidiary Corps obtained many of their supplies direct from Britain, and those items obtained locally and all billets were paid for in cash. Such guests are always welcome. The Hanoverian Landwehr, posted in the fortresses, was likewise not a burden on the land. Only the Brunswickers, arriving in mid May, had any problems, although on a much lesser scale. The Nassauers, from territories already ruled by the House of Orange, had no such problems.

---

[41] WSD, vol X, p 368 f.
[42] Lettow-Vorbeck, p 510 f.
[43] Lettow-Vorbeck, p 182.

[44] WD, vol XII, p 444 f.
[45] Lettow-Vorbeck, p 182 f.

Blücher's Visit to Brussels

In part because of their supply difficulties the Prussians were not keen to sit back and wait for Napoleon to attack. Blücher was under pressure from all sides to commence operations, but without Wellington's support, he could not move. His soldiers wanted the war to end as soon as possible and his government was virtually bankrupt, unable to finance a long wait. Blücher naturally did his best to win Wellington over to his point of view and accordingly welcomed a second meeting between the two leaders when Wellington took steps to arrange one. On 23 May Wellington invited the Prussian senior commanders to visit him[46] and mentioned this to Hardinge in a letter the next day,

> General Roeder promised me he would ask the Marshal to come over and dine with me on Sunday; to take this little tour on Monday; and he might return on Tuesday; and I can only repeat that I should be most happy to see him.[47]

On the 27th, in preparation for the visit, Müffling gave the Duke a list of topics which Blücher wished to discuss. The crucial point, as far as the Prussians were concerned, was when hostilities were to be commenced. As Müffling put it:

> The first four army corps of the Prussian Army will be up to full strength in a few days. Indeed, they will be stronger than required by treaty. As the Belgians are causing us so many problems with supplies, it would be desirable to commence the war as soon as possible. Would Your Grace kindly give me his opinion as to when this would be likely?

According to Müffling, Wellington replied that he saw only two possibilities,

> Firstly, if Napoleon's forces in front of us at Maubeuge were to be significantly reduced by detachments to the Upper Rhine or to the Vendée. Secondly, as soon as the Austrian Army had reached Langres.

Müffling continued,

> He [the Duke] then showed me a report of 17 May from the captain of an English ship anchored off the west coast of France. According to this report, the royal party in the Vendée had formally opened military action. Were matters here to become serious, forcing Napoleon to make significant detachments, then one should put him under pressure so long as this was not too far in advance of the arrival of the remaining armies.[48]

The meeting went on with a discussion of how to implement any invasion of France. Müffling outlined two possible strategies to end the war. The first was to head straight for Paris, fighting the necessary battles en route. The second was to advance methodically, besieging fortresses on the way, living off the local resources and awaiting Napoleon's attack. Wellington supported the

---

[46] GStA, Rep 92, Gneisenau, A 48, fol 133.
[47] WD, vol XII, p 422.
[48] Lettow-Vorbeck, p 510 f. Here, the memorandum is printed in full.

first option.[49] He wanted a rapid offensive to avoid any unnecessary suffering for the French population.

After these preliminary talks, the main discussion between the two commanders commenced. Blücher actually arrived in Brussels and dined with Wellington on 28 May. inspected the Allied troops on the 29th, and returned to Namur on the 30th after having paid the King of the Netherlands a visit. The two commanders discussed their plans for both defensive and offensive operations. They agreed that Napoleon's main objective in this theatre would be the capture of Brussels. If he chose a more westerly line of advance the Anglo-Dutch-German Army would be his first target. In that event, it would concentrate on Ath, Braine-le-Comte or Nivelles, while the Prussians would assemble at Sombreffe, on the flank of the enemy line of operation, and support Wellington according to circumstances. If Napoleon's main thrust on Brussels were to be via Charleroi, then the Prussians would be struck first. They were to accept battle at a place where they could be sure of Wellington's support. The likely point was again Sombreffe. In such an event Wellington was to concentrate at Quatre Bras.[50]

Blücher itched to take the offensive. His army was more or less ready. His ambition was to get to Paris as rapidly as possible so that this time he, and not the diplomats and politicians, could make good what he saw as the wrongs perpetrated in Vienna. Furthermore, while his army was unwelcome in the Netherlands and was having problems obtaining supplies from the local population, in France he could use whatever force he wanted to obtain supplies.

The Duke was in no such hurry and wanted to co-ordinate operations with the other Allied forces. On 2 June he wrote to Schwarzenberg that,

> Marshal Blücher is ready and very impatient to begin; but I told him today it appears to me that we will not be able to do anything until we are certain of the day you will commence and have a general idea of your plans.[51]

Wellington finally agreed with Blücher to commence offensive operations on 1 July, the date by which all the Allied forces would be prepared.[52] He was not going to commence hostilities with just the Prussians ready. The Duke preferred to wait for the Austrians to complete their preparations, before he would go to war.

---

[49] GStA, Rep 92, Gneisenau, A 40, fols 57–60.
[50] Damitz, vol I, p 38; Hofmann, p 23; Siborne, *History*, p 24.
[51] WD, vol XII, p 437.
[52] Damitz, I, p 40.

Chapter 7

The Outposts

The Frontier

As we have seen, the Allied forces along the border with France were spread thinly to guard against the many possible lines of attack and because of their supply problems. However, these were not the only reasons why the Allied outposts were in a rather difficult situation.

Officially, the Allies were not at war with France. Napoleon had been declared an outlaw, and the Allied armies were assembling in part to support the claim to the throne of Louis XVIII, the legal head of state of France, but the Allied troops could not cross the border to gain information on French movements. Their only role was to act as a trip wire, giving the alarm in the event of an attack. Intelligence gathering was left to spies, and what could be gleaned by interrogation of people crossing the border from France. The Franco-Netherlands border was open for most of the time leading up to the outbreak of hostilities – after all, France and the Netherlands were not officially at war.

Each side's outposts usually respected the other's borders, in a fairly friendly style at first. Officers of the Prussian 25th Regiment were involved in one such incident,

> On 1 May, we rode, after a merry dinner with fellow officers, through our outposts and over the French border to the village of Falmignoul where we stopped at the tavern and ordered good wine. Soon, a crowd of curious locals gathered around us. Only a little later French soldiers and customs officials came up, indicating, some politely, some gruffly, that we had crossed the border, and would have to come to Givet as prisoners. The officers protested forcefully, and were supported by the local farmers, who, fearing a fight would break out, called out: "Let them be, they are only refreshing themselves!", and stated that the gentlemen had paid for what they had drunk. The incident ended with the French soldiers escorting the Prussian officers back to the border with all politeness and courtesy, pointing out, as if they did not already know, where it was.[1]

As the armies began to assemble, and tension increased, attitudes changed. On 12 May a French column coming from Longwy was intercepted crossing the German border. Rittmeister von der Horst of 2./8th Uhlan Regiment had them chased off, but not before a French chasseur was taken prisoner. This was the first action of the war, and the first prisoner taken.[2]

---

[1] Stawitzky, pp 34–5.
[2] Förster, p 60.

The Netherlands Outposts

Lieutenant-General Baron de Collaert, commander of the Netherlands Cavalry Division, was responsible for the outposts on the Anglo-Dutch sector of the front. His headquarters was in Boussoit-sur-Haine, to the north of the road that ran west from the Prussian positions at Binche to Mons and about half-way between the two. Collaert's division consisted of three brigades, one of heavy and two of light cavalry, with two half batteries of horse guns. The heavy cavalry, commanded by Major-General Baron Trip was placed in cantonments in Houdeng-Gœgnies, Le Rœulx and Mignault, to the rear of the divisional headquarters, and the light cavalry were deployed in positions closer to the front from where they could perform patrol duties.

The 1st Light Cavalry Brigade, commanded by Major-General Baron de Ghigny, had its headquarters in Havré. Its cantonments nearby were:

4th Light Dragoons	Havré and Obourg
8th Hussars	Gottignies and Saint-Denis.[3]

The 2nd Brigade, under Major-General Baron van Merlen, had a more southerly location, nearer the French, with its headquarters in St Symphorien, to the east of Mons. Its cantonments also nearby were:

5th Light Dragoons	Harmignies, Harveng, Spiennes, Bougnies, and Asquilles.
6th Hussars	Estinne-au-Val, Estinne-au-Mont, Maurage, Bray, St Symphorien, Villers, and St Ghislain.[4]

The two half batteries of horse guns were billeted in Ville-sur-Haine, St Symphorien, Thieu, Boussoit-sur-Haine and Villers-sur-Haine.[5]

The 2nd Brigade was on a particularly vital sector of the front, giving first warning of an advance along the road from Mons to Brussels, the most direct of Napoleon's potential invasion routes, and linking up with the Prussian outposts at Binche. This gave Merlen a dual responsibility for detecting a French assault and keeping communications open with the Prussians. Merlen was a soldier with 26 years of military experience, much of it fighting for Napoleon's forces, including some years in the prestigious 2nd Regiment of Lancers of the Imperial Guard.[6]

Until 6 June only a few vague reports of French intentions came in to the Netherlands outposts. However, from that day, the number of reports increased so dramatically that Collaert sought instructions from corps headquarters in Braine-le-Comte. The Netherlands' chief-of-staff, Constant Rebeque, ordered him to keep his light cavalry in its quarters, apart from those on patrol, and, above all, not to occupy any villages west of the paved road from Maubeuge to Mons, except for Asquilles and Bougnies. Clearly, he feared that small detachments might be overwhelmed and cut off by a sudden French advance. In the event of an enemy attack in overwhelming numbers, the two light cavalry brigades and associated artillery were to fall back to join

---

[3] De Bas & T'Serclaes de Wommersom, vol III, p 100.
[4] De Bas & T'Serclaes de Wommersom, vol III, p 101.
[5] De Bas & T'Serclaes de Wommersom, vol III, p 101.
[6] De Bas & T'Serclaes de Wommersom, vol III, p 33.

the Netherlands 3rd Infantry Division at Fayt where they would be able to keep in contact with the Prussians. The heavy cavalry would assemble at Casteau. Collaert was reminded to be very alert.[7]

Changes in the troop positions were made on 9 and 10 June in response to more information becoming available about the French threat. As it seemed that the French were going to invade from the direction of Maubeuge, the heavy cavalry brigade and the 3rd Netherlands Infantry Division were moved farther east, closer to the Prussians, and to a position from where they could better cover any French move on Nivelles. Constant Rebeque issued orders to both the 2nd and 3rd Netherlands Divisions on 9 June to be prepared to march off at short notice.

The daily routine of the battalions from now on was to gather at their assembly points every morning so that they could move off quickly should the need arise, and only to return to their billets for the night. Cooking facilities were made available at the assembly points so that the troops did not disperse during the day. Nothing at all was to be left in the cantonments during the day; all waggons were to be loaded and everything made ready for the troops to march off immediately. The cavalry received similar orders and the horse artillery from the cavalry division was instructed to assemble at Frasnes at 5 a.m. every day, remaining there until 7 p.m. The sections were to take turns to cook and eat, and the horses were to be changed at noon. This way, part of the battery was ready for action all the time.

Thus, the entire Netherlands army held itself ready for an immediate reaction to any French offensive. This must have been strenuous and tedious for the troops. However, when the French offensive did indeed start, the Netherlanders were able to react immediately.

The Prussian Outposts

Earlier chapters have explained how the Prussian forces were assembled from late March and gradually deployed into the Netherlands. The foremost Prussian formations at the outbreak of hostilities were the 1st and 2nd Brigades of Lieutenant-General von Zieten's Prussian I Army Corps. The 1st Brigade was posted to the most vital area of the front, the hinge between Wellington's and Blücher's forces, and had its headquarters in Fontaine l'Evêque. Major-General von Steinmetz commanded the brigade when fighting began but he did not in fact take up this post until the second week of May, by which time his brigade was already in position.

Unfortunately for Steinmetz, his troops were thin on the ground and had to cover an extensive section of the front. This meant that a strong French attack anywhere along the line was likely to gain local superiority quickly, and there was great danger of a breakthrough with outposts being cut off.

The 2nd Brigade was commanded by Major-General von Pirch II. Pirch's brigade had its headquarters in Marchienne-au-Pont and covered 1st Brigade's

---

[7] De Bas, *Prins Frederik*, vol IV, p 1160.

line of communication with corps headquarters in Charleroi as well as Charleroi itself.

An early priority was to set up a warning system. An instruction of 30 April from Pirch to one of his artillery outposts, at Mont-sur-Marchienne, shows how this was done,

> This artillery outposts of two cannon is to fire off three warning shots should the enemy, against expectations, break through our outpost chain threatening the brigade's cantonments.
>
> Two guns of the 1st Brigade are posted at Fontaine l'Evêque for the same purpose. As they are nearer to the French border than those at Mont-sur-Marchienne, it is more likely that the alarm will come from there; in such an event, the alarm shots must be repeated without delay at Mont-sur-Marchienne, and be repeated by the alarms at Charleroi and Châtelet... [8]

The artillery outposts were made responsible for ensuring that the whole corps was not alarmed without good cause. A cavalry detachment was stationed in front of the artillery post at Nalinnes as a further precaution. Its men were to ride to the artillery post to warn it to fire off the three shots when this was necessary. As the wide dispersal of the cantonments made a prompt assembly even more essential, the importance of these warning shots cannot be underestimated.

The Deployment

We have seen in Chapter 6 how the whole Allied strategy was clarified at the meeting between Blücher and Wellington at Tirlemont in early May. For the leading formations this took effect with a disposition issued from I Corps headquarters by General Zieten on 6 May,

> Our commander, His Highness Prince Blücher, has ordered the concentration of I Army Corps. Thus, I request the brigade commanders to move their troops into close cantonments near to the rendezvous points of their respective brigades... so that, when required, the brigades can be immediately assembled to march to Fleurus. All baggage is to be sent to Temploux immediately, moving along both sides of the road, and, wherever possible, not over crops, supervised by one lieutenant from each brigade, and commanded by a senior captain from the 3rd Brigade.
>
> The troops will be supplied as before from their appointed magazines, the quarters left by the troops must continue to be used to supply the necessary vegetables. The brigade commanders, as soon as their assembly is complete, are to send a mounted officer here to receive further orders.
>
> The outposts are to remain where they are, and measures will have to be taken so that they can fall back to their brigades soon. [9]

Colonel von Hofmann, chief-of-staff of the 1st Brigade, told Zieten in his

---

[8] MWBl., vol XXX, p 20.
[9] MWBl., vol XXXI, p 162 f.

128

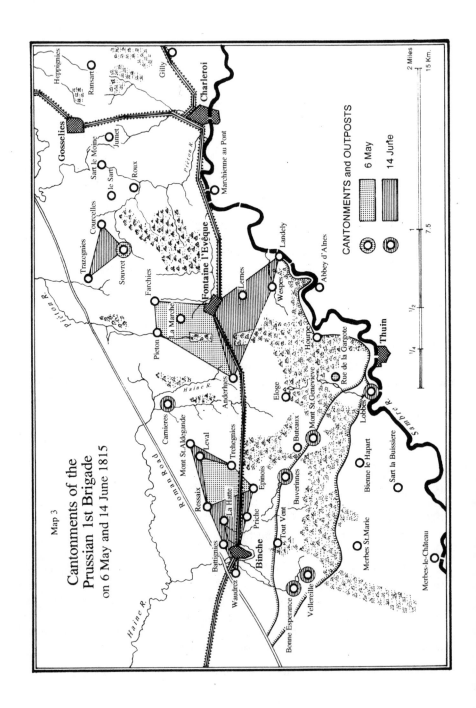

Map 3

Cantonments of the
Prussian 1st Brigade
on 6 May and 14 June 1815

CANTONMENTS and OUTPOSTS

6 May

14 June

reply from his headquarters in Fontaine l'Evêque later the same day that no changes were actually necessary,

> As the troops of the brigade in my trust are already billeted partly close to the rendezvous, partly on their allocated marching route via Gosselies – then I am already in a position to execute Your Excellency's orders in an instant. The outposts, which remain where they are, are deployed in such a way that they can quickly rejoin the main body.[10]

The deployment of the 1st Brigade that was actually in force was based on an instruction of 2 May, as follows:

Outpost chain from Binche to Lobbes
Under the command of Major von Engelhardt of the 1st Silesian Hussar Regiment.

Right flank
From Binche to Buvrinnes under Major von Hertel of the 1st Silesian Hussars.
At the abbey of Bonne Espérance – an observation post of one sergeant and twelve hussars. This post to keep in contact with the left flank of the Dutch forces at Haulchin.
At Binche – an observation post of one corporal and three hussars on the road from Binche to St Marie.
At Tout Vent – an observation post of one sergeant and nine hussars on the road from Binche to Bienne-lez-Happart.
At Buvrinnes – a picket of one officer, one sergeant, one trumpeter and six hussars.

Left flank
From Buvrinnes to Lobbes under Major von Neumann of the Silesian Schützen.
At Buvrinnes, in the bushes – a picket of one officer, five Schützen and nine fusiliers.
At Mont St Geneviève – a picket of one officer, one sergeant, one bugler, 24 fusiliers and 14 Schützen, and a warning post of one corporal and three hussars.
At Lobbes – a picket of one officer, one sergeant, one bugler, eight Schützen and 24 fusiliers and an observation post of one corporal and three hussars.
At Tru de Lobbes and the outskirts of Thuin – one officer, two sergeants and 40 men.

At night, the 1st Squadron of the 1st Silesian Hussars, stationed in Ressaix, shall deploy a picket of one officer and 20 troopers at the château at La Hutte near Ressaix. The 4th Squadron shall deploy a picket of one officer and 20 troopers at the château of Epinois.

---

[10] MWBl., vol XXXI, p 163.

In support of the outposts

In Ressaix	1st Squadron	1st Silesian Hussar Regiment.
In Leval	2nd Squadron	1st Silesian Hussar Regiment.
In Epinois } In Trahegnies }	4th Squadron	1st Silesian Hussar Regiment.
In Fontaine l'Evêque	1st Battalion	1st Westphalian Landwehr Regiment.
In Anderlues	2nd Battalion	1st Westphalian Landwehr Regiment,
	2 companies	Silesian Schützen Battalion.
In Piéton	3rd Battalion	1st Westphalian Landwehr Regiment.
In Forchies-la-Marche	4th Battalion	1st Westphalian Landwehr Regiment.
In Souvret	Horse Battery	No. 7,
	Foot Battery	No. 7.

Outpost chain from Lobbes to Gerpinnes

Under the command of Lieutenant-Colonel von Lützow.

In La Maladrie – an observation post with one sergeant and six troopers, keeping in touch with Lobbes.

In L'Houzée – one officer, one sergeant, one carabineer [each cavalry squadron had a number of such men armed with rifled carbines], 12 troopers, keeping in touch with La Maladrie. The officer in L'Houzée shall command the posts in La Maladrie, L'Houzée, and Fleur en Champ.

In Fleur en Champ – one sergeant, six troopers, keeping in touch with L'Houzée.

In Nalinnes – one officer, one sergeant, one carabineer, 12 troopers, in communication with Fleur en Champ. The officer in Nalinnes shall command the posts at Nalinnes, Böchon, and Les Flaches.

In Böchon – one sergeant, one carabineer, nine troopers, keeping in communication with Nalinnes and Les Flaches.

In Les Flaches – one sergeant and six troopers, in communication with Gerpinnes where there was a warning post manned by Westphalian Landwehr cavalry.

In support of the outposts

In Gozée and Marbaix	4./6th Uhlan Regiment.
In Jamioulx	Staff and 2./6th Uhlan Regiment.
In Loveral and Acoz	3./6th Uhlan Regiment.[11]

An important element in the defensive plan was taking account of the various rivers in the area. On 11 May Captain Decker, Pirch's chief-of-staff, issued important instructions to the 2nd Brigade for the defence of the Sambre crossings,

As the bridges are of stone, and cannot be destroyed and cannon should not be placed on them, their defence has to be limited to an effective skirmish fire.

The organisation of the defence of the town of Marchienne is left to the discretion of the commander of the Fusilier Battalion of the West Prussian

[11] MWBl., vol XXXI, p 163 f.

Infantry Regiment. [This battalion was replaced there by the 2nd Battalion of the same regiment before the outbreak of hostilities.]

As the battalion will not be able to retire across the Sambre without the support of the 1st Brigade, it is to send a mounted officer to Colonel von Hofmann in Fontaine l'Evêque. This officer is to keep riding back and forth, bringing the commander news of what the 1st Brigade is doing, particularly if 1st Brigade withdraws behind the Piéton stream.

If 1st Brigade abandons Fontaine l'Evêque to withdraw to Gosselies, and reaches somewhere around Judonsart, then the battalion in Marchienne should pull back its posts at Monceau and Zoone, and retire to Dampremy [north of Charleroi]. Should, however, the enemy attack Marchienne with superior numbers, then the 1st Brigade must be warned that these posts can no longer be held, and will have to be given up. Only then can the withdrawal to Dampremy be started, otherwise the 1st Brigade would be abandoned... [12]

The vital task of communication with the high command was also emphasised. On 13 May Blücher ordered his corps' commanders to establish courier relay posts for communications purposes to his new headquarters in Namur. His order to Zieten was clear and specific, 'As there is no military post chain from Charleroi to Namur, Your Excellency is to establish one immediately and to inform me where the stations are.'[13]

One use for these lines of communication was to pass on intelligence. The commanders of the leading brigades were very active in this respect, sending scouts secretly behind enemy lines. An example of information received by one of Steinmetz's spies can be found in a report of 28 May,

The headquarters formerly in Avesnes have gone, nobody knows where, but one suspects into the interior of France. All cavalry in this area have marched off with it, and neither new troops, nor a new commander have arrived. In Avesnes, there are 2,000 young conscripts with neither weapons nor uniforms, but there are many infantry veterans in the area. Work on the fortifications is continuing uninterruptedly, with paths being cleared and batteries built, but no cannon have arrived for them. In the fortress of Maubeuge, there are mainly conscripts and national guardsmen, armed with shotguns. There are not many troops around this fortress. There are only national guardsmen in Beaumont. In its immediate area are one infantry and one light cavalry regiment. The 1st Regiment of Lancers "Duc de Berry" has gone back into the interior of France. The majority of the national guardsmen are simply waiting for the first chance to desert without getting their families into trouble. The entire Département du Nord is in chaos due to the requisitioning and delivering of supplies. The mayor of one village told us, that if he were to sell the whole village, he could still not pay as much as was demanded. Furthermore, all live-stock and grain is to be moved into the interior of France, and it seems as if Bonaparte intends to leave the Département du Nord in one march.[14]

---

12 MWBl., vol XXX, p 19 f.
13 MWBl., vol XXX, p 21.
14 MWBl., vol XXX, p 22.

A little imagination had sometimes to be used to obtain information of the French positions and intentions. One example of this took place on 10 June when Schütze (Rifleman) Wilhelm Friedrich II of the Silesian Schützen, attached to the outpost at Fontaine l'Evêque, crossed into France disguised as a French customs official. He spoke no French, but still managed to get to the encampment at Beaumont, and returned to his post with detailed information on the French strength and dispositions.[15]

Steinmetz actually inspected his outposts for the first time after he took up his new command on 12 May and after the inspection he reviewed his positions, making various minor changes on 17 May.[16] Other alterations followed the reorganisation that took place in the Landwehr in early May when they had their complement of battalions per regiment reduced from four to three. This fed through to changes in the disposition of the front line brigades that can be seen in a listing of 21 May.[17] However, it was not until 9 June, when a new disposition was issued, that there was significant movement. One reason for this new disposition was the arrival of more troops, namely the 12th Infantry Regiment on 4 June. The 12th Regiment joined 1st Brigade. These extra mouths to feed exacerbated the existing supply problems, making a new disposition highly desirable. Even more important, however, was responding to the increasing flow of reports which indicated that the French offensive would start soon. The troops on the right wing were seen as especially vulnerable, as the list of 9 June makes clear:

1st Silesian Hussar Regiment
Staff	in Epinois.
1st Squadron	in Battignies, castle of La Hutte, and Priches.
2nd Squadron	in Waudrez.
3rd Squadron	in Leval.
4th Squadron	in Ressaix, Trahegnies.
2 cannon & Jäger detachment	in Mont Ste Aldegonde.

12th (2nd Brandenburg) Infantry Regiment
Fusilier Battalion	in Binche.
1st Battalion & Jäger Detachment	in Trazegnies.
2nd Battalion	in Courcelles.

24th Infantry Regiment
1st Battalion	in Anderlues.
2nd Battalion	in Carnières.
2 companies of Fusilier Battalion	in Binche.
1 company of Fusilier Battalion	in Bonne Espérance, and Vellereille-les-Brayeux.
1 company of Fusilier Battalion	in Buvrinnes.

[15] Otto, p 77.
[16] MWBl., vol XXXI, p 173 f.
[17] MWBl., vol XXXI, p 174.

Silesian Schützen Battalion
   2 companies — in Buvrinnes.

1st Westphalian Landwehr Regiment
   1st Battalion & Jäger Detachment — in Fontaine l'Evêque.
   1 company of 2nd Battalion — in Mont St Geneviève.
   3 companies of 2nd Battalion — in Lobbes.
   3rd Battalion (Fusiliers) — in Leernes, Wespes, and Landelies.

  Foot Battery No. 7 — in Courcelles.
  Horse Battery No. 7 — in Souvret.
  ½ company engineers — in Piéton.[18]

Steinmetz reported his actions to Zieten that day. The message read,

> Should the enemy advance from Bienne-lez-Happart on the road to Fontaine l'Evêque, the posts in the direction of Binche would have difficulties in getting to their assembly points. Thus, I have ordered that the first position for these troops to take up is on the plateau between Piéton and Carnières, with their left flank on Fontaine l'Evêque and the paved road leading to Marchienne. From these positions, I believe I will be able to maintain an overview of the progress of the enemy movements, and should the circumstances arise, either continue my retreat to Gosselies, the position allocated to me in the disposition, or, should the enemy's movements be a bluff, then to move forward again.[19]

When, from 12 June, it was clear that a French offensive was imminent, further changes in the dispositions at the front were considered. However, all that was done was to recommend the outposts to be more alert. The various detachments were moved into so-called 'alarm houses' at night, and the troops were ordered, in the event of an attack by superior numbers, to assemble rapidly at their rendezvous. Despite such provisions, the wide dispersal of Steinmetz's brigade meant that any outposts not attacked would arrive at their rendezvous relatively late. This, in turn, would mean that the main bodies of these units would have to wait some time for their outposts to come in before they could fall back on supporting troops from other brigades. Steinmetz was in a dangerous position which could lead to some of his outposts being overwhelmed, others being cut off, and his entire brigade being isolated from the corps.

Zieten and his brigade commanders sent various reports to Blücher and Wellington throughout the 12th, 13th and 14th. They also exchanged information regularly with the Dutch cavalry outposts to the west. These reports dealt extensively and in detail with the increasingly threatening French deployment and are fully discussed in Chapter 8. Steinmetz actually gave orders to concentrate his battalions on the night of 13 June as the positions to his front were so packed with enemy troops that an offensive on 14 June was considered almost inevitable.

---

[18] MWBl., vol XXX, p 12.
[19] MWBl., vol XXX, p 19.

Other I Corps' Outposts

According to a listing of 14 June 1815 the 2nd Brigade was deployed in the following cantonments:

6th (1st West Prussian) Infantry Regiment

1st Battalion	Charleroi, Marchienne-au-Pont, and Monceau-sur-Sambre.
2nd Battalion	Montigny-le-Tilleul, and Mont-sur-Marchienne.
Fusilier Battalion	Montignies-sur-Sambre and Couillet.

28th Infantry Regiment

1st Battalion	Châtelet, Bouffioulx.
2nd Battalion	Châtelet, Châtelineau, Pont-de-Loup, Grand Champ, and Aiseau.
Fusilier Battalion	On outpost duties on the left flank, in Acoz, Joncret, Villers-Poterie, and Gerpinnes.

2nd Westphalian Landwehr Infantry Regiment

1st Battalion	Charleroi and Gilly.
2nd Battalion	Charleroi, Dampremy, and Marcinelle.
Fusilier Battalion	On outpost duty on the right flank, in Thuin and Ham-sur-Heure.
Foot Battery No. 3	Lodelinsart.
2 alarm guns at	Mont-sur-Marchienne.[20]

The 1st West Prussian Dragoon Regiment from the Reserve Cavalry of the I Army Corps probably had the following cantonments:

Jäger Detachment	Reûmont.
1 squadron	Gozée.
1 squadron	Jamioulx and Haies.
1 squadron	Loverval and Gerpinnes.[21]

This regiment performed observation duties at the outposts of Thuin, Ham-sur-Heure and Gerpinnes.

The Westphalian Landwehr Cavalry Regiment performed outpost duties for the 4th Brigade, and on 7 June had the following cantonments:

Staff	St Gérard.
1st Squadron	Presles and Les Binches.
2nd Squadron	St Gérard and district.
3rd Squadron	Bossière and Maison.
4th Squadron	Graux and Denée.
½ company engineers	Dampremy.[22]

---

[20] MWBl., vol XXX, p 12.
[21] MWBl., vol XXX, p 12.
[22] MWBl., vol XXX, p 12.

The increasingly frequent and convincing information about an imminent French attack persuaded Pirch to issue warning orders on the 14th to his 2nd Brigade to,

> move into close cantonments immediately. As all battalions quartered in communes will remain there, all distant outposts in remote farms must evacuate these. The troops in the village with the parish church must be quartered in such a way as to be able to assemble at the first alarm, and ready to move on their allocated places as in the disposition previously issued... [23]

Battalion Gillhausen (II./1st Westphalian Landwehr) in Lobbes was also placed on full alert during the 14th.

The French Attack Begins

When the offensive began the next morning, I. and F./1st Westphalian Landwehr assembled on the cobbled road leading to Marchienne-au-Pont, after hearing the alarm cannon firing from the windmill at Fontaine l'Evêque. The campaign had started. Battalion Gillhausen was the first to suffer. The first fighting of the campaign fell to German soldiers, as did the bulk of the fighting for the Allied cause.

Thus both sets of Allied outposts were ready for the French offensive and had passed detailed information to the Allied headquarters from the front. The use the Allied leaders made of this dangerous work and the degree to which they were or were not surprised by Napoleon's advance will be the subject of the next chapter.

[23] MWBl., vol XXX, p 34.

Chapter 8
Intelligence and Communications

Wellington's Intelligence Network

The Duke of Wellington had two major advantages over his Prussian allies in gathering information. He had an extensive network of agents throughout France and ample funds with which to finance their operations. In addition the Duke had made and kept good contacts in royalist and government circles during the time he spent as British ambassador in France. As the protector of Louis XVIII and his court in exile in Ghent he was likely to be kept informed by them also. He was well placed to be the best informed senior commander in Europe.

It is known that Wellington received news from Paris almost daily from informants using the express post, which ran to Belgium from Paris almost until the outbreak of hostilities.[1] However, the whereabouts of most of these documents are uncertain. Some were published in Wellington's *Supplementary Despatches*, but this is not a full collection and more can be found in the 'Wellington 'Papers' held in the University of Southampton.[2] Even so, it is difficult to be certain which information in fact came to the Duke's attention, especially since the nature of espionage in any case is that records are often incomplete or deliberately misleading. One can only speculate, based on the documents that are available, about what Wellington did and did not learn through his network of informants.

The first judgement that can be made is that the quality of the information supplied to Wellington must have been high as he had spies in both the Ministry of Police and in Général Bertrand's Cabinet. Bertrand was Grand Master of the Palace and a close adviser of the Emperor while Wellington's agent in the Ministry of Police was no less a person than Fouché, the Minister himself, whose game of double-dealing was designed to insure him against all eventualities.[3] Général Bertrand's wife was the niece of one Colonel Henry Dillon, a serving British officer, who used this family connection to obtain sensitive information.[4] Dillon even obtained an outline of Napoleon's plans from Bertrand in person.[5] This intelligence, received in Wellington's headquarters by 15 June, stated with some accuracy that, '...probably the first attack would be towards Avesnes'.

The Duke's own opinion of his intelligence system is confirmed by a

---

[1] Müffling, *Leben*, p 221 f.
[2] For instance, WP 1/459 includes an anonymous document dated 1 May 1815 containing a report from Paris.

[3] Pflugk-Harttung, *Vorgeschichte*, p 27.
[4] WSD, vol X, pp 471, 479.
[5] WSD, vol X, p 480.

discussion Müffling mentioned he had with the Duke on this question. Here, he stated, 'The Duke of Wellington, informed by me that Prince Blücher's espionage was badly organised, was himself very certain of his, and that he would hear immediately of everything in Paris that was on the march to the Netherlands.'[6]

Clearly, the Duke believed he had a significant advantage over the Prussians when it came to knowledge of the enemy's movements. However, Napoleon used double agents to feed the Duke with misinformation. He also caused false rumours to be spread, and teased Wellington's whole front with troop manoeuvres all the way from Lille to Maubeuge. This made the Duke hesitate to commit too many of his troops to support the Prussians, and always aware of the need to secure his lines of communication via the Channel ports.

The hub of Wellington's intelligence-gathering operation was at Mons, an ideal location close to the border on the main road from Paris to Brussels. A Hanoverian officer, Major-General Freiherr von Dörnberg, a Peninsular veteran of standing and experience, was placed in charge of intelligence operations there. Being based so close to the French border, Dörnberg had every reason to take news of any French advance seriously to avoid capture. In Mons, he amassed a wealth of useful information, which he passed on to Brussels daily, or sometimes even more frequently. These reports can be found throughout Volume 10 of the *Supplementary Despatches*. Dörnberg used spies, scouts, farmers, travellers and the large number of French citizens crossing the border as his sources.

The headquarters of the Prince of Orange was at Braine-le-Comte, farther back along the road towards Brussels. Here, the Prince took note of the contents of the intelligence before sending it on to Wellington's headquarters. Although Dörnberg had certain special responsibilities to collect and disseminate information, all the generals posted along the frontier were equally active. Major-General Behr, commandant of the fortress of Mons, and Major-General Merlen, with the Netherlands cavalry in St Symphorien, played their part. They were also in constant contact with their Prussian neighbours, notably Zieten in Charleroi, and Steinmetz, commander of Zieten's 1st Brigade in Fontaine l'Evêque. As Zieten also reported directly to Wellington, it was considered that all eventualities were covered.[7]

Wellington's Headquarters[8]

Wellington's management style was autocratic; he was, in effect, his own staff, at least in the sense that he had no military advisors with whom he would discuss strategic matters. He had no chief-of-staff with whom he worked in tandem, as Blücher did with Gneisenau. The officers on the Duke's staff were simply there to execute his orders. Wellington himself was his own head of each department of the staff, including intelligence and did not welcome unsolicited advice from others.

---

6   Müffling, *Leben*, p 221.
7   Pflugk-Harttung, *Vorgeschichte*, p 28.
8   This section is based largely on Pflugk-Harttung, *Vorgeschichte*, p 185 ff.

The posts of Military Secretary and Quartermaster-General were the two most important on Wellington's staff. By June 1815 Wellington had filled these with experienced and trusted officers. Lieutenant-Colonel Lord Fitzroy Somerset (later known as Lord Raglan) was the Military Secretary. He usually read all incoming letters and reports and kept a register of all incoming and outgoing documents. Indeed much of the correspondence intended for the Duke's information was addressed to Fitzroy Somerset. Fitzroy Somerset also drafted certain of the replies as well. The non-British contingents were brought into Wellington's staff system under Fitzroy Somerset's guidance, and their communications to the commander-in-chief ran through his office. The Duke's staff is said to have, 'executed its duties with the regularity of a machine'.[9]

The role of Acting Quartermaster-General was filled by Colonel Sir William Howe de Lancey. His office actually wrote Wellington's orders and organised their despatch but, unlike the Prussian chief-of-staff Gneisenau, de Lancey did not have the authority to issue his own orders, he merely saw to it that his master's orders were put on paper and sent out. De Lancey's office was also responsible for matters such as quarters for the troops, ammunition, food, equipment, horses, and so on. It is interesting to note that both these officers, the most senior members of Wellington's operational staff, were of relatively junior rank. Gneisenau, was a lieutenant-general and their closest Netherlands equivalent, Baron de Constant Rebeque, a major-general.

Two experienced staff officers whom Wellington specifically requested were Lieutenant-Colonel Colquhoun Grant of the 11th Foot, who was to be employed as head of intelligence, and Lieutenant-Colonel George Scovell, an experienced staff officer and Peninsula veteran, who was to be head of military communications.[10]

The Duke himself had complained about the quality of his staff when he first took up the command in the Netherlands, writing to Lieutenant-General Lord Charles Stewart on 8 May that he had, '...a very inexperienced staff'.[11] That may have been the case at the beginning of May, but Wellington set about changing this situation rapidly. Of the 33 senior officers on his staff at Waterloo, 31 were Peninsula veterans with appreciable staff experience, one had served five years as an ADC, and only one appeared to have no staff experience at all.[12]

The Liaison Officers

Lieutenant-Colonel Sir Henry Hardinge, another Peninsula veteran, was Wellington's chief liaison officer with Blücher's headquarters. Hardinge arrived in Blücher's headquarters to take up his post on 12 April 1815.[13] Wellington had admired Hardinge's talents for some time, and learned to trust

---

[9] anon, *Life of Lord Raglan*, p 21 f.
[10] WD, vol XII, p 336.
[11] WD, vol XII, p 358.

[12] See Edmonds, 'Wellington's Staff at Waterloo', *JSAHR*, vol XII, p 239 ff, for an examination of this issue.
[13] WSD, vol X, p 79.

him with sensitive matters.[14] The post in Blücher's headquarters was clearly a delicate one, one where Wellington required a man on whom he could rely. Hardinge was to be the Duke's ears and eyes in Blücher's headquarters, sending frequent reports to his master.

The equivalent Prussian officer in Wellington's headquarters was Major-General Baron von Müffling. Müffling arrived to take up his role as liaison officer for the Prussians in Brussels on 19 April.[15] In his *Life* Müffling published a detailed account of his activities which is a vital source of information about the Waterloo campaign. He described the arrangements he made for his staff work as follows, 'I had four aides, an office and orderlies, couriers, the military postal service and as many mounted officers as I required at my disposal. General von Grolmann [sic] replaced me in the post of Quartermaster-General of the Prussian Army in Blücher's headquarters.'[16]

The arrangements for communications between the two allied headquarters were thus clear. Hardinge was to act as Wellington's representative in Blücher's headquarters, providing Blücher with information from the Duke and passing on messages from the Prince to Wellington. Müffling was to carry out the same role in Wellington's headquarters on behalf of Blücher. There was a direct line of communication between the two headquarters, one in Brussels, one in Namur. The distance between them was around 60 km; that is around five to seven hours' distance by mounted messenger.

Courier Relay Stations[17]

The Prussian army routinely set up lines of relay stations for military communications in any potential theatre of war. An officer was placed in charge of each relay station, and they in turn were under the orders of the commanders of larger main relay stations. The ordinary stations were normally sited in smaller towns or villages and the larger ones in major towns or at any other important points. A depot was established at each relay station and equipped with horses and other suitable means of transport.

The towns in which relay stations were based were regarded as fortified places for the purposes of martial law. All military personnel and civilians were subject to the orders of the post commander. Neither soldiers nor civilians could obtain private quarters or stay in a hostelry without his permission. Those given permission were required to hand over their passes to the landlord until their departure. All officers and detachments using these routes were required, regardless of rank, to produce written orders in support of their activities, or suffer arrest. They would then be given a pass to use that route. At each relay station, the pass would be inspected by the local commander who would write on it 'passed according to orders', and then add his seal to the pass. If the detachment was at the wrong place, this would also be noted on the pass.

14 WD, vol IV, pp 744, 749, 773.
15 Müffling, *Leben*, p 212 ff; Priesdorff, vol 4, p 309.
16 Müffling, *Leben*, p 215.
17 This section is based largely on MWBl. Vol XXVII, p 378 f.

The station commanders were instructed to ensure that sufficient horses and despatch riders were always at hand to send on messages swiftly. The commander had to know how many horses he had available and ensure that nobody used any of these without his express permission, unless they were military despatch riders with the correct passes. Forage also had to be readily available and the main relay stations were required to hold larger quantities of supplies of various sorts, administered by the commissariat.

The relay stations also served as bases for military security. All soldiers found off the approved roads were treated as marauders, arrested on the spot and brought to the nearest relay station. Small garrisons were kept at hand to escort prisoners, deserters and captured enemy soldiers.

Dörnberg's Listening Post

Major-General von Dörnberg himself was pleased with the amount of intelligence he was able to gather at his outpost in Mons. His later description of his sources reads,

> Through my travellers as well as a large number of French arriving here almost daily, I was very well informed of the movements of the French army, their concentration at Beaumont and Bonaparte's arrival there.[18]

The full extent and value of the information and intelligence sent in to Wellington's headquarters by Dörnberg can only be fully appreciated by examining all those messages contained in Volume Ten of the *Supplementary Despatches*. Below are extracts from the most important items sent to Brussels by Dörnberg.

April 9 By one of the confidential persons employed by me, just returned from the frontiers, I find the French have not yet assembled anywhere in our neighbourhood a considerable corps.[19]

April 16 By the report of a man I sent to Paris, and whose original report I send herewith, it appears that no camp, neither at Beauvais, Amiens, nor Abbeville, has been formed, and that no more troops are put in motion towards this frontier.[20]

April 22 There is a report that troops are assembling between Bavay and Landrecy. I have sent a confidential person to ascertain it.[21]

April 25 The man I send to Bavay, Cambrai, &c, just now returns, and reports that the greatest part of the troops in that neighbourhood have just marched towards Lille.[22]

April 30 A man I send along the frontier, and who left Valenciennes yesterday, gives the following intelligence:- From Dunkerque to Givet there are about 60,000 men, all garrisons included.[23]

---

[18] Pflugk-Harttung, *Vorgeschichte*, p 291 ff.   [21] WSD, vol X, p 140.
[19] WSD, vol X, p 52 f.   [22] WSD, vol X, p 157.
[20] WSD, vol X, p 81 ff.   [23] WSD, vol X, p 188 f.

May 1 I have the honour to inform you that a Dutch gentleman, who left Paris the day before yesterday, assures to have seen himself on that day a very strong column of French troops, which he estimates at about 40,000 men, taking the road towards Rheims... [24]

May 2 Travellers from Paris say that Buonaparte was to leave that place today... [25]

May 4 On Tuesday morning about 6000 men, also of the Guards, left Paris and were destined to go with forced marches to Charleville... between 60,000 and 80,000 men might be assembled in that neighbourhood. [26]

May 8 I have the honour to inform you that the mail from Paris, did not arrive this morning; and it is probable that the French have stopped all communication. [27]

May 9 The day before yesterday General Bertrand arrived at Condé; and as they were firing yesterday at that place, it is supposed that Buonaparte himself arrived. The French don't allow anybody to pass the frontier. [28]

May 11 It appears certain to me that the French have collected the greatest part of their forces between Valenciennes and Charleville, and that they are forming a reserve at Laon. [29]

May 16 already about 20,000 men are at Laon... [30]

May 21 At Laon he found about 8000 infantry and 1200 cavalry... [31]

May 23 French patrols have shown themselves yesterday afternoon before our piquets at Boussu and Pâturages... [32]

May 25 Two officers of the 8th Line came this morning from Valenciennes; they say that Buonaparte has postponed the Champ de Mai [The *Champs de Mai* was a major military parade, the holding of which could be a signal that war was about to start] for two days, so that it is to be on 28th. [33]

May 26 I believe I have been led into an error by the officers from Valenciennes, in reporting that the Champ de Mai was only to be on the 28th. A gentleman (the brother of the commandant of Mons, Duvivier) who arrived here yesterday directly from Paris, say it is going to be on this day, the 26th... [34]

May 27 A captain of the 6th Chasseurs arrived here last night. He was with the depôt at Compiègne, where, when he left it, three squadrons and two battalions of Buonaparte's Guards, with part of his equipages, were, and a division of the Guards were immediately expected. [35]

[24] WSD, vol X, p 214.
[25] WSD, vol X, p 216.
[26] WSD, vol X, p 222.
[27] WSD, vol X, p 262.
[28] WSD, vol X, p 263.
[29] WSD, vol X, p 274.
[30] WSD, vol X, p 311.
[31] WSD, vol X, p 336.
[32] WSD, vol X, p 344.
[33] WSD, vol X, p 367.
[34] WSD, vol X, p 379.
[35] WSD, vol X, p 386.

May 31 It appears always more certain that troops from the French frontier are marching to the interior... The French papers, which I enclose to the 26th, confess that serious troubles are in the Vendée and Bretagne... The Champ de Mai is postponed indefinitely.[36]

Dörnberg also sent intelligence both to Müffling in Brussels,[37] as well as to Blücher.[38] The originals of many such reports were formerly held in the Prussian War Archives but these have been missing since the Second World War. However, certain papers have been found, and others are known to be held in Moscow and may again become accessible to scholars. Although they cannot be consulted at the moment old research before they were lost showed that Dörnberg and the Prussian I Army Corps exchanged information on a daily basis,[39] in line with instructions from Wellington to the Netherlanders to keep Zieten informed of any developments.[40]

News from Hardinge and Blücher

Although most of the information Hardinge supplied to the Brussels head-quarters was on the question of the state of preparedness of the Prussian Army, he was, of course, also involved in forwarding Blücher's intelligence to Wellington. Some extracts are given below.

May 5 With regard to intelligence of the movements of the enemy on this front, I cannot ascertain that there is any information to be relied on excepting some reports, not of a very clear nature, that the enemy is collecting a large force in the neighbourhood of Maubeuge.[41]

May 6 We have no distinct intelligence of the enemy in our front.[42]

May 16 The reports from Charleroi of last night have just been received, in which General Zieten says that a person employed by him, who was at Givet on the 5th, and left Philippeville the 6th, reports that the regular troops of both those places (the numbers not stated) had marched on the 5th for Maubeuge and Valenciennes... [43]

May 16 No news of the enemy has been received in the course of the day.[44]

Clearly, the information on French movements received directly from Blücher's headquarters was sparse.

Zieten and Wellington

Wellington also received information from Zieten. Zieten wrote all the messages personally in French as none of his staff had a good enough English and he was the only one reasonably fluent in the only common language with Wellington and his staff.[45] Zieten's messages to Brussels included the following:

36 WSD, vol X, p 393.
37 Pflugk-Harttung, *Vorgeschichte*, p 327.
38 De Bas & T'Serclaes de Wommersom,
   vol I, p 353.
39 MWBl., vol XXX, p 12.
40 WD, vol XII, p 367.

41 WSD, vol X, p 239.
42 WSD, vol X, p 246.
43 WSD, vol X, p 261.
44 WSD, vol X, p 311.
45 Pflugk-Harttung, *Berichterstattung*, p 44.

May 10 I have found the means to procure the number of the enemy to be found in Maubeuge, around this fortress and up to Beaumont... I send herewith the report of the people coming from Condé.[46]

This report was a most valuable document containing dates, places and numbers of French troops. Wellington wrote back at 9 a.m. on 11 May to thank Zieten for this information.[47]

May 12 The news I have just received from the border confirms that the enemy is on the defensive.[48]

May 15 I have the honour of placing before the eyes of Your Highness the report of a person who, coming from Chaumont, arrived today at Charleroi.

Wellington noted on the despatch, 'Write him that I am very much obliged to him.'[49]

May 23 the enemy from Givet to the North Sea amounts to around 60,000 men...

Wellington noted on this despatch, 'Acknowledge the receipt; and I am very much obliged to you for the news you have given me, which agrees with that I have received.'[50]

Zieten continued to send intelligence to the Duke in early June. These messages are included in the discussion below but surprisingly, this message of 9 June is the last one from Zieten contained in the published *Supplementary Despatches* and there are no further unpublished messages from Zieten in the 'Wellington Papers'. If this is taken at face value, it would appear that Zieten suddenly and inexplicably broke off communications with Brussels at the vital time. However, as Zieten's records and those of others contain mentions of despatches sent to and received from Wellington in the remaining days prior to the outbreak of hostilities, the explanation for this gap in the Duke's records must be sought elsewhere.

Information Available in Brussels and Namur

An examination of the messages passing between the two Allied headquarters and the various outposts in the first half of June 1815 gives a good impression of the information that was to hand, as well as how the various commanders were reacting to it. The Allies were uncertain of Napoleon's real intentions. Some believed he would launch an offensive into the Netherlands and towards Brussels at the first opportunity. Others believed that, as in the previous year's campaign, Napoleon would adopt a defensive strategy, dealing with each Allied army in turn as it advanced into France. Reports of royalist risings were continually being received, and some accordingly thought an offensive by Napoleon unlikely until he had established his government more firmly. Reports on Napoleon's personal whereabouts were important; any mention of his presence at the front would be a strong indication that an invasion was

---

46 WSD, vol X, p 269.   49 WSD, vol X, p 303.
47 WD, vol XII, p 373.   50 WSD, vol X, p 318.
48 WSD, vol X, p 280 f.

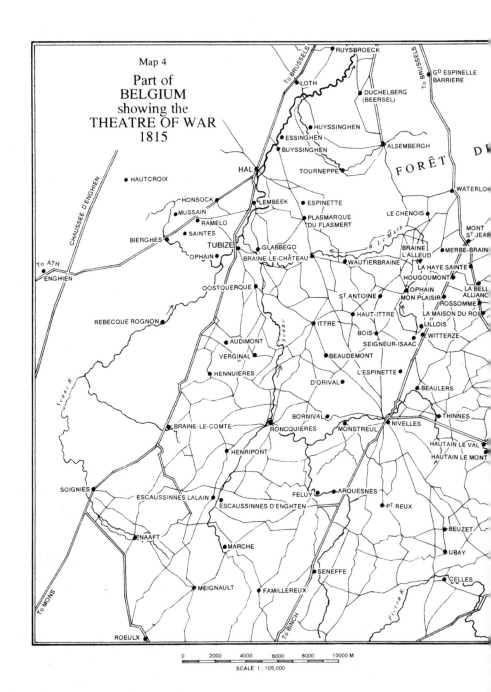

Map 4

Part of
BELGIUM
showing the
THEATRE OF WAR
1815

SCALE 1 : 105,000

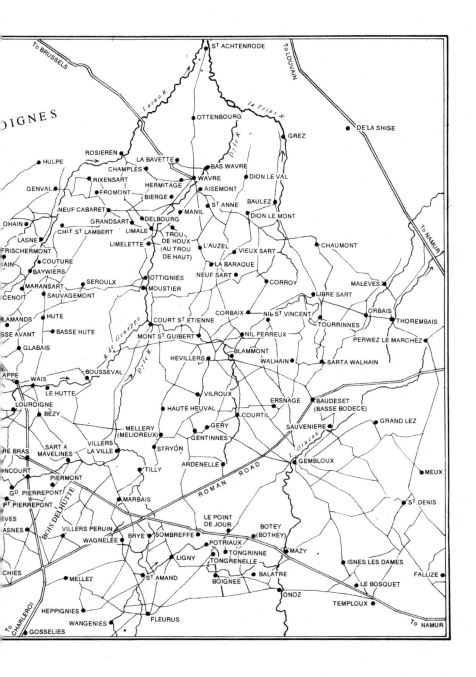

imminent. Equally, news of troubles in France and any retrograde troop movements could be taken as an indication that an invasion was unlikely.

In the early days of June, a mixed bag of information came in. It seemed as if Napoleon himself was not quite sure whether he could risk going to the front just yet, or if he should spend more time in Paris establishing his rule. In the second week of June, the threat of a French attack developed appreciably, yet there was some information to the contrary coming in to the Allied posts. Napoleon wanted to surprise the Allies, and some of this information came from a deception campaign he conducted before stealing away from Paris in the early hours of 12 June.

The messages sent and received by the various Allied posts in the first half of June included the following:

1 June

Some French troop movements were again reported at the border, but more information suggested that the French were taking defensive measures and withdrawing troops into the interior to deal with the royalists. Thus Dörnberg wrote to Brussels from Mons that, 'The French have strengthened their line in front of Valenciennes... 16,000 men... arrived at Chimay, and Buonaparte at Laon.'[51] While, from Charleroi, Zieten reported to headquarters in Namur that General Vandamme (who was correctly believed to be one of the French corps commanders) was rumoured to have withdrawn his men from the frontier into the interior of France, that several major roads had been cut with trenches and that the French border towns had been prepared for defence. The French headquarters had arrived in Laon, but without Napoleon.[52] Müffling confirmed this picture of withdrawals, reporting from Brussels to Namur that,

> Apparently a telegraphic despatch has arrived in Valenciennes ordering 4 regiments of infantry to be sent by waggon to the Vendée. News from Paris is that the uprising in the Vendée is significant.[53]

2 June

Reports of a French withdrawal continued to come in. Dörnberg, for example, reported to Brussels that, 'By smugglers that have been in the neighbourhood of Chimay, I have got the following intelligence... [they have been told that] 17,000 men from the line between Lille and Maubeuge had been sent to the interior, but these men do not believe it.'[54] Hardinge told Wellington that all the information to this effect was making Blücher very restless, 'The reports of insurrections in France, together with the marching of troops from our front into the interior, have made this head-quarters very impatient to begin operations.'[55]

---

[51] WSD, vol X, p 408.

[52] Lettow-Vorbeck, p 513.

[53] Pflugk-Harttung, *Vorgeschichte*, p 313.

[54] WSD, vol X, p 413.

[55] WSD, vol X, p 413.

3 and 4 June

Basically, there was no change in the situation since the previous day but Wellington clearly did not intend to support Blücher's wish for an immediate offensive.

Müffling reported to Namur on the 3rd that,

I do not know if the Duke of Wellington has informed Your Excellency that according to his information everything has been done to,

1. Bring Napoleon's Guard by special means from Paris to Maubeuge in two days.

2. that, weather permitting, the news of the outbreak of hostilities can be in Paris in four hours using telegraphic despatches.

3. that the enemy IV Corps (also known as the Army of the Moselle) has joined up with the III.[56]

Other reports received in Namur indicated that the Young Guard had been sent on waggons to the Vendée on 25 May, and that most troops of the line in Condé, Valenciennes, le Quesnoy, Maubeuge, Landrecies and Avesnes had been sent to Paris.[57] In fact, the importance of the royalist uprising in the Vendée was exaggerated, especially by the French court-in-exile in Ghent. In the end, Napoleon sent only two regiments of Young Guard there, and it was suppressed by a force of less than 15,000 men, largely scratch formations of gendarmerie, and the like. Even so, on 4 June Dörnberg reported to Brussels that, 'The 49th and 45th infantry of the line are certainly gone to the interior from Valenciennes and Condé. A deserter of the Grenadiers à Cheval, of Buonaparte's Guard, arrived here yesterday from Paris. He also assures that the Young Guard is sent from Paris to the Vendée.'[58]

5 June

Again, there was a mixed bag of information, with reports of troop movements, and continuing unrest in France, but more evidence that the *Champs de Mai* had indeed taken place.

Lieutenant-Colonel August von Wissel of the 1st Hussars of the KGL wrote to Lord Hill that, '...the enemy has evacuated the town and citadel of Lille... All the mentioned troops have taken the road to Maubeuge and Valenciennes.'[59] This story was given further credence by the Duc de Feltre, Louis XVIII's Minister of War in Ghent, who wrote to Wellington with the following information, 'I enclose herewith for Your Excellency details concerning Lille... It appears that the garrison of Valenciennes consists only of national guards... The affair in the Vendée is serious, despite the set back the Royalists experienced at Aizenai.'[60]

However, other reports had the opposite sense. The Prince of Orange informed Brussels that, 'It seems by the French papers, and by the reports I have received, that the *Champ de Mai* was to take place on 1st... [and it is likely

[56] Pflugk-Harttung, *Vorgeschichte*, p 319.
[57] Lettow-Vorbeck, p 513.
[58] WSD, vol X, p 416.
[59] WSD, vol X, p 416.
[60] WSD, vol X, p 417.

that] the French army expects to attack us within a few days.'[61] In the same vein Zieten informed Namur that an officer of the French 11th Chasseurs had told his staff that Vandamme's Corps was now 18,000 men strong, and that the *Champ de Mai* had taken place on 1 June.[62]

6 June

Information on French strengths and intentions appeared to be more precise, even though there were further reports on the movement of the Young Guard to put down the royalist uprising. Dörnberg's information about the French build-up was especially exact,

> I have the honour of transmitting to you herewith French papers of the 2nd and 3rd inst., as it appears by them that Buonaparte is expected to leave Paris this day, the 6th... My man from Laon returned yesterday, not thinking it safe to stay any longer there. He assures that the head-quarters are removed to a château in the vicinity... In coming here he found a great number of National Guards coming from the interior... There are also more troops of the line on the frontier near Valenciennes, which he estimates at 30,000; but I think that is exaggerated.[63]

The Prince of Orange partly confirmed this view in his report to the Duke,

> I send March [a staff officer] with the two enclosures from General Dörnberg and General Behr, which I thought you might wish to have without loss of time. I received, besides, this morning a report from General Collaert, in which he says that he knew of General Albert, who commands the French cavalry, having said that if we did not attack on the 7th, they would attack us on the 8th or 9th.[64]

Reports from the Prussians had similar information about growing French strength. Thus Zieten wrote to Brussels that,

> A French officer, lieutenant of the 11ème Chasseurs à Cheval, has arrived here... The officer claims that Vandamme's Corps is only 18,000 men strong, being 10 regiments of infantry and 4 of cavalry. He claims that d'Erlon's Corps consists of 60,000 men, Reille's 25,000... [65]

The report from Behr forwarded by the Prince of Orange had a different effect, 'the Young Guard has left Paris for the Vendée... ',[66] but Wellington disagreed, writing to Hardinge in Namur that, 'All accounts which I receive from the frontier appear again to concur in the notion of a collection of troops about Maubeuge.'[67]

There was also another interesting, but inaccurate, report. The Comte de la Porterie informed Namur that a man sent by him to Paris had heard from Général Bertrand that Napoleon planned to leave on 6 June and arrive in

[61] WSD, vol X, p 417.
[62] Lettow-Vorbeck, p 514.
[63] WSD, vol X, p 421 f.
[64] WSD, vol X, p 422 f.

[65] WSD, vol X, p 425.
[66] WSD, vol X, p 423 f.
[67] WD, vol XII, p 449.

Douai on the 7th. The report also alleged that Napoleon planned to make a fake attack on Charleroi and then move against Mons and Tournai.[68] This seems to have been deliberate misinformation from the French.

7 June

The signals coming in to the Allied posts were again confused. On the one hand the French appeared to be making preparations for an offensive, while at the same time there were signs of an impending withdrawal from the frontier. Possibly, they were intending to make a show of force on the border, even a large raid, to cover a withdrawal into the interior of France. This thought may have been one of the causes for Wellington's hesitation when the French offensive indeed began only a few days later.

8 June

Several messages concerned Napoleon's whereabouts. Dörnberg wrote, 'I have no intelligence till yet of Buonaparte's arrival on the frontier. By the *Gazette de France* of the 5th, which I have the honour to enclose, it appears that he is going from Paris directly to Laon.'[69]

Zieten's message to Brussels anticipated a more cautious French strategy:

Yesterday the French withdrew their outposts at the border around Maubeuge, placing them not far from the fortress. I do not believe that Buonaparte has left Paris, but I must add that the delay in the commencement of hostilities has led to a considerable increase in his forces.[70]

A report from a French officer also suggested a defensive plan. General Bournonville informed Namur that he had deduced from Napoleon's current actions that the Emperor was intending to hold a line between the frontier fortresses, fearing the superiority of the Allied cavalry.[71]

However, later that day Dörnberg sent a second report which mentioned,

A man who left Valenciennes last night reports, "At Valenciennes are 6000 to 7000 National Guards and 1500 troops of the line; from 4000 to 5000 troops of the line arrived in the villages near Valenciennes, mostly infantry. The Young Guard was expected last night at Valenciennes, and a report spread that the Old Guard was marching to Maubeuge."[72]

In fact the news of Napoleon's departure from Paris for the front was premature and, as it was published in a censored French newspaper, one can only assume that it was deliberate misinformation. Otherwise French intentions were still unclear. The stories about the French falling back to their fortresses could indicate a defensive posture but that conflicted with the news that Napoleon's personal troops, the Old Guard, were on their way, usually an indication that the Emperor himself was not far behind.

---

[68] Lettow-Vorbeck, p 514.
[69] WSD, vol X, p 428 f.
[70] WSD, vol X, p 429 f.

[71] Lettow-Vorbeck, p 515.
[72] WSD, vol X, p 432.

9 June

In the morning Müffling reported various items of news to his headquarters, writing,

> General von Dörnberg believes that Napoleon will attack us. He is said to have left Paris on the 6th, arriving in Valenciennes on the 7th, saying that he would attack and destroy us here before the Russians arrive. The reserves at Paris and 4 battalions of Young Guard have gone off to the Vendée, the rest are on their way towards us.[73]

Müffling also gave Wellington a report with information from Prussian sources in France that,

> An emissary who left here on the 31st of last month, passing Mons, Valenciennes and Péronne, has sent us the following news. The garrison of Valenciennes is 4000 men... on the northern frontier there are 40,000 men; but one should add that 60,000 men are marching to reinforce them.[74]

Dörnberg sent two despatches to Brussels that day. These included the information that,

> A peasant arriving from Maubeuge assures that Buonaparte came there yesterday at two o'clock, and that he left it this morning at seven o'clock for Valenciennes, from whence, it was said, he was to go to Lille... The Dutch outposts on the Maubeuge road, near Havay, have been reconnoitred this morning by a French party... This instant (half-past nine) a gun firing is heard in the direction from Maubeuge, which is supposed to signify Buonaparte's arrival at the army.[75]

In reaction to the various pieces of information the Netherlands forces made some changes to their deployment. At 7 a.m., Constant Rebeque sent an officer to Baron Chassé, commander of the 3rd Netherlands Division, with orders to have his division march off as soon as it could be prepared, leaving its cantonments in Le Rœulx, Gœgnies and Houdeng, villages a good 10 km north of the nearest Prussian positions at Binche, and move to Fayt, Beaume and Saint-Paul. The new positions would be nearer to the Prussians and would cover the crossing of the Haine River. At 3 p.m. Collaert was ordered to move his heavy cavalry brigade under Major-General Trip, from around Bauffe into Chassé's now abandoned cantonments, which were 20 km nearer the border, and keep his men in a state of alert. At 7 p.m. Constant Rebeque sent Perponcher orders to keep his men at full readiness and to Trip to occupy Chassé's cantonments for the night..[76]

That night, the Prince of Orange reported (inaccurate) news of Napoleon's appearance, adding, 'Napoleon having arrived, I think he is likely to attack in a very few days, if he means to attack at all.'[77] The Prince

---

[73] Pflugk-Harttung, *Vorgeschichte*, p 327.
[74] WSD, vol X, p 432 f.
[75] WSD, vol X, p 436.

[76] De Bas & T'Serclaes de Wommersom, vol I, p 360 f.
[77] WSD, vol X, p 437.

supported his views by enclosing a report from Behr, which stated, 'This morning he [Napoleon] arrived in Maubeuge... A man coming from Maubeuge said that the French may attack today.'[78]

New information was also reaching the Prussian commanders. Zieten informed Wellington that,

> The enemy has sent several regiments, I believe about 4,000 men, from the area around Marienbourg to Maubeuge where there are about 60 cannon in the fortified camp, and where Général Vandamme is to be found today... A young man who left Paris on 4th assures that Buonaparte has not dared to leave the capital... [79]

Oberst von Clausewitz, chief-of-staff of the Prussian III Army Corps, told Namur of news from his agents that Vandamme had gathered his corps at Convin from where he could march to Philippeville, if necessary.[80]

Hardinge also reported to Wellington that French forces were moving nearer the Prussian lines, 'I am informed by General Gneisenau that he has received intelligence, on which he relies, of the march of [the French] 4th corps from the neighbourhood of Thionville, and of the arrival of part of it at Mézières.'[81] Gneisenau confirmed that this was indeed his assessment in a letter to Knesebeck, saying that, 'Through two travellers coming from different directions, we have just received information that the 4th Corps is linking up with the 3rd Corps at Mézières. The travellers have seen the troops on the march.'[82] Surprisingly, however, Gneisenau also wrote to General von Dobschütz that, 'The enemy will not attack us, but will fall back on the Aisne, Somme and Marne and concentrate his forces there.'[83]

There were now stronger grounds to expect a French offensive shortly as Napoleon himself and increasing numbers of men were seemingly reliably reported near the border. It seems incongruous that Gneisenau was apparently of the opinion that the French were intending to fall back and, despite Gneisenau's scepticism, the Prussian headquarters played it safe by ordering Kleist to move his North German Army Corps closer to the front.[84]

10 June

The Netherlands ambassador at the French court-in-exile in Ghent sent a report to Constant Rebeque apparently based on information originating from Napoleon's Ministry of War. This indicated that the main French forces were positioned between Rocroi and Lille, that is along most of the border with the Netherlands. This intelligence included a full order-of-battle of this army, a total of 120,000 men excluding the Imperial Guard of 14,000 men that had yet to join them. The report said that Napoleon wanted to attack that day from Rocroi, but had insufficient cavalry.[85]

Dörnberg sent two despatches that day, including the information that,

[78] WSD, vol X, p 437.
[79] WSD, vol X, p 437 f.
[80] Lettow-Vorbeck, p 515.
[81] WSD, vol X, p 437.
[82] Lettow-Vorbeck, p 515.
[83] Lettow-Vorbeck, p 515.
[84] Pflugk-Harttung, *Bundestruppen*, p 100.
[85] De Bas, *Prins Frederik*, vol III, p 1153.

A deserter of the 3rd Lancers coming here just now from Roisin, near Valenciennes, says that they had it in general orders Buonaparte was arrived at Laon… A man from Valenciennes says that the news there was that Buonaparte left Paris on the 6th with 80,000 men… Count Rouvroix… says that French officers assured him yesterday positively that Buonaparte was at Maubeuge… and General Zieten writes that 60 guns are arrived in it.[86]

There were further reports about Napoleon's location, too. Lionel Hervey, the British representative with the exile court in Ghent, sent Wellington the following message, 'I have just heard that General Mattisowitch, the Belgic Governor of this place, received an estafette [a courier] in the course of the night informing him of the arrival of Buonaparte at Lisle [Lille] on the night of the 8th.'[87] The Duc de Feltre, also in Ghent, added, 'The officer who has arrived here believes that Buonaparte has left Paris and thinks he will be able to attack around the 19th, pushing towards Namur.'[88] Wellington took more note of Hervey's information and subsequently wrote to Hardinge that, 'I have received intelligence that Buonaparte arrived at Maubeuge yesterday, and I believe he has gone along the frontier towards Lille.'[89] The Duke was always a little nervous about reports of any movements on his right flank and their potential threat to his communications with Britain.

Though we now know that they were incorrect, there was seemingly solid evidence from the various reports that the 'Corsican ogre' had arrived at the front in person. This could only mean that the outbreak of hostilities was imminent, but there were as yet no clear indications of his plans.

11 June

There was more uncertainty about where Napoleon was. Wellington wrote to the Prince of Orange that, 'It appears certain, by reports from Paris, that Buonaparte had not left that city on 7th.'[90] Müffling also passed this opinion on to Gneisenau,

> After the Duke of Wellington saw the news I gave him from General von Ziethen, the Duke told me he has firm indications that Napoleon was still in Paris on 7 June. This is also reported in [the French newspaper] *Le Moniteur* of 7 June.[91]

However, a contrary view came in Dörnberg's report that, 'The Hon. H. Dillon… arrived here last night. He left Paris the 2nd, and was detained five days at Valenciennes. He says he is quite certain that Buonaparte was yesterday at Avesnes… '[92] There was also activity on the border where, the Prince of Orange reported, 'A small French party attacked yesterday morning the post at Bois Bourdon, occupied by the Belgian chevaux légers, which is at the point where the Roman road crosses the high road from Mons to Maubeuge, and we took three prisoners.'[93]

86 WSD, vol X, p 439.
87 WSD, vol X, p 440.
88 WSD, vol X, p 449 ff.
89 WD, vol XII, p 457.

90 WD, vol XII, p 458.
91 Pflugk-Harttung, *Vorgeschichte*, p 327 f.
92 WSD, vol X, p 454 f.
93 WSD, vol X, p 455.

12 June

Dörnberg sent two reports to Brussels in the course of the day which both emphasised the extent of French preparations. His message of 9.30 a.m. reported that,

> The French outposts along the frontier, between the Valenciennes and Bavay roads, have been strengthened with infantry. A French patrol of cavalry coming on Belgian ground last night, near Warquignies, was too inconsiderately pursued by some of the Bremen and Verden hussars, two of which have been taken.[94]

While at 7 p.m. he added,

> A French gentleman, coming from Maubeuge to join the King, gives the following intelligence. The corps of General Reille is come yesterday to Maubeuge and vicinity. The head-quarters of the army are transferred from Laon to Avesnes, where a division of the Guards is to arrive to-day... He estimates the forces between Philippeville, Givet, Mézières, Guise, and Maubeuge at more than 100,000 troops of the line... The general opinion in the army is, that they will attack, and that the arrival of Buonaparte at Avesnes will be the signal for the beginning of hostilities.[95]

At 7p.m. the Baron de Roisin wrote to Wellington, stating that,

> I have the honour to send some interesting details to Your Excellency... General Soult arrived today in Valenciennes, he arrived incognito. It would appear that preparations are being made to attack after tomorrow... The villages of Beuvry, Crillon, Lunda, Sameon, Aunon and the small towns of Orchie and St Amand are empty of troops, they all left for Valenciennes this morning... [96]

In response to the continuing flow of information Wellington instructed de Lancey to draft new orders for the concentration of his army, though these were not to be sent out until the Duke's gave a specific instruction to do so.[97] News of an impending French offensive also spread throughout Wellington's headquarters. Lieutenant the Hon. George Cathcart, a junior officer on the Duke's staff, wrote to his mother that day,

> I am going to a place 7 miles off to dine with an Officer of Horse Artillery at which I shall meet Charles [his older brother] – I shall come back tomorrow to breakfast, for as Bonaparte is come to Maubeuge not above 60 miles [96km] from Bruxelles, it will not do to be long about.[98]

Blücher's headquarters was also receiving word of French troop movements. News had arrived via the II Army Corps, for example, from General Thielemann of III Army Corps that Vandamme had assembled his corps in Philippeville, that is to say farther north and west and closer to the front than

[94] WSD, vol X, p 455 ff.
[95] WSD, vol X, p 463.
[96] WSD, vol X, p 457.
[97] PRO, WO 37/12.
[98] Cathcart Papers, Folio C.

before.[99] General Zieten also informed Namur that his outposts had reported numerous enemy troop movements at Givet and between Roty, Marienbourg and Couvin, but did not give their strengths.[100]

13 June

The first message of the day was one from Steinmetz at Fontaine l'Evêque to Zieten in Charleroi, timed at midnight 12/13 June, and reporting that Napoleon would arrive in Maubeuge with his Guard on the evening of 13 June, and that the French II Corps was already there. Four French battalions had crossed the Sambre at noon on the 12th towards Merbes-le-Château and Sabinissière had been occupied in force. A French deserter claimed the French would attack either on 14 June or the day after.[101]

General Collaert wrote to Constant Rebeque forwarding reports he had received from General van Merlen's outposts along the frontier. These reports contained information such as a claimed sighting of Napoleon in Maubeuge by a deserter of the French 5th Lancers, and a detailed outline of a French deployment between Beaumont, Maubeuge and Avesnes.[102]

Dörnberg sent a message to Brussels at 8 a.m. with similar information,

> General Zieten writes to me that troops coming from Mézières are marching to Maubeuge by Beaumont. A woman from Quivrain assures that all the troops of the line at and near Valenciennes have also taken the road towards Maubeuge, only leaving the customary piquets; so that it appears without doubt that the whole army is concentrating near Maubeuge... A man coming this instant from Quivrain confirms the report of the troops marching from Valenciennes to Maubeuge.[103]

The Prince of Orange also supported this assessment, writing that, 'A person coming from Maubeuge says that the head-quarters had been transferred from Laon to Avesnes, where a division of the Guards was to arrive yesterday and Napoleon daily expected.'[104]

Dörnberg included the following accurate summary of the situation in a letter to Uxbridge,

> The whole french [sic] Army it appears is concentrating at & near Maubeuge – the troops near Valenciennes marched yesterday afternoon at 3 o'clock, leaving only their Picquets. The troops near Mézières have passed Beaumont for Maubeuge, and those from Avesnes & Laon march in the same direction, so I think the whole Army may [?] there to-day – Soult was at [?] yesterday – Jérôme Bonaparte has [his Head?] Quarters at [?] le Château.
> But Bonaparte himself though hourly expected was not yet arrived.
> There is a considerable body of Cavalry with this Army, a great part of it was reviewed by Genl. Grouchy near Hirson two days ago.[105]

[99] Lettow-Vorbeck, p 516.
[100] Lettow-Vorbeck, p 516.
[101] Lettow-Vorbeck, p 517.
[102] De Bas, *Prins Frederik*, vol III, p 1157.

[103] WSD, vol X, p 470.
[104] WSD, vol X, p 471.
[105] Paget Papers, 644/A/21.

Despite all this information Wellington was not convinced. He wrote to General Lord Lynedoch on the 13th telling him that,

> There is nothing new here. We have reports of Buonaparte's joining the army and attacking us; but I have accounts from Paris of 10th, on which day he was still there; and I judge from his speech to the Legislature [on the 7th] that his departure was not likely to be immediate. I think we are now too strong for him here.[106]

Blücher seems to have thought differently, for Kleist, commanding the North German Federal Army Corps, received orders to move westwards from Trier to Arlon, closing the distance between him and the four corps of the Army of the Lower Rhine.[107] The Prussians were beginning to react.

Slightly different information came from Behr who sent a report, timed at 8 p.m., to the Prince of Orange which was then forwarded to Brussels, with the information that, '...last night 20,000 men, troops of all arms, arrived at Valenciennes. General van Merlen, coming from the outposts at Bois Bourdon on the paved road to Maubeuge, informs me that many troops have arrived at Maubeuge... '[108]

There was some uncertainty in two Prussian reports of the 13th which both arrived in Namur on the morning of the 14th. One, from the Prussian II Army Corps to Namur, gave the news from Oberst von Borcke, commander of the Neumark Dragoon Regiment, that Vandamme had not concentrated at Philippeville,[109] as had previously been thought, and the second from Clausewitz in Ciney corroborated this by suggesting that Vandamme was still in Rocroi.[110]

However, a third mainly accurate report to Blücher from Zieten in Charleroi, which likewise arrived on the morning of the 14th, contained information from the outposts that 60,000 French were drawn up at Givet, Marienbourg, Chimay and Maubeuge, with Jérôme in Beaumont and Murat in Avesnes.[111] This was also the gist of another night-time despatch from Merlen at Fontaine l'Evêque. This message reached Steinmetz at about 1 a.m. on 14 June and was later passed on to Zieten. This reported that,

> ...a large army is assembling around Maubeuge. Yesterday[12 June], Napoleon arrived around 4 o'clock... Général Vandamme with his corps, and Général Reille with his, have arrived there. A column of all arms, 20,000 men strong, passed Valenciennes yesterday on its way to Maubeuge.[112]

Zieten forwarded Steinmetz's intelligence on to Blücher on the morning of the 14th, reporting that on receiving it, he had warned his brigades to be ready to concentrate at short notice.[113]

106 WD, vol XII, p 462.
107 De Bas, *Prins Frederik*, vol III, p 518.
108 WSD, vol X, p 471 f.
109 Lettow-Vorbeck, p 517.
110 Lettow-Vorbeck, p 517.
111 Lettow-Vorbeck, p 517.
112 De Bas & T'Serclaes de Wommersom, vol I, p 353 f.
113 Lettow-Vorbeck, p 517.

In summary, most reports at this point appeared to indicate that the French forces were moving to the east, massing around Maubeuge, from where they could advance either on Mons or on Charleroi, that Napoleon was there in person, and that an attack was likely in the very near future. Gneisenau would seem to have ceased to doubt this; Wellington's was the only voice denying the weight of evidence. He still doubted that Napoleon had left Paris. One wonders if this was a case of Napoleon managing to fool Wellington with false information, or of the Duke not wishing to believe the information he had to hand.

14 June

There was some continuing uncertainty in Dörnberg's first report, timed at 9.30 a.m., which stated that, 'It appears that the troops have only been concentrated near Maubeuge to be reviewed. They began yesterday again to march in different directions, some to Beaumont [nearer the Prussians], and some to Pont-sur-Sambre [farther away], where it is said a camp will be formed.'[114] However, Dörnberg withdrew these reservations in a message timed at 3 p.m.,

> I have just now got the following intelligence, which I copy literally:– "The headquarters of I Corps left yesterday for the Sambre. Général d'Erlon is expected there. Buonaparte's kitchen arrived at 4.30 p.m. in Avesnes yesterday, but he himself was not seen. All the troops are concentrating at Maubeuge and Beaumont. The army is estimated at 80,000 men up to Beaumont and 100,000 up to Philippeville..." A man coming from Lille saw the garrison of that place march out, and also that of Dunkerque passing Lille, they shall both have passed Valenciennes, crying "Vive l'Empereur!" Nothing of his arrival was known till yet... *Moniteur* has not yet arrived, but your Lordship will have seen in the *Journal de Paris* that Buonaparte left it in the night from 11th to 12th instant.[115]

A message from the Prince of Orange, sent at 5 p.m., reported no activity on his front but gave good reason to think an attack somewhere was imminent: 'I return from my outposts where everything is calm and in order. According to the *Gazette de France*, Napoleon left on 11th for the Belgian frontier.'[116]

However, other Dutch and British reports suggested where this attack might fall. Merlen in St Symphorien told Constant Rebeque in Braine-le-Comte that,

> I have the honour to forward you a letter from a French captain [Baron Niel] which is self explanatory. It appears that a blow is being prepared against just one point. The French posts at Bettignies and Gœgnies [Gœgnies-Chaussée] have left. There is only one vedette left at Villers-sur-Nicole this evening. I believe it would be good to inform the Prince of this affair so he can take

---

[114] WSD, vol X, p 476.
[115] WSD, vol X, p 477 f.

[116] De Bas & T'Serclaes de Wommersom, vol I, p 353.

measures. It would seem that they are going to go for the Prussians. All the troops have food and forage for a week... [117]

Lord Hill, commanding Wellington's II Corps, had similar news in a message timed at 9 p.m., and sent from his headquarters at Grammont to the Prince of Orange. This stated that he had received several reports from the border which confirmed that the enemy had concentrated a sizeable force at Maubeuge. These troops had marched from Laon, Valenciennes and Mézières. It appeared that Napoleon had not been to the border, but Marshal Soult was certainly with the army.[118]

The British were also continuing to pass information on to the Prussians. At 9.30 p.m. Dörnberg sent a message to Blücher from Mons, which arrived at 1 a.m. on 15 June, stating that, '...according to the French, the attack will be early tomorrow morning',[119] while Müffling in Brussels wrote to Gneisenau, telling him that according to the reports that had come in that night (13/14 June), the entire enemy army would be concentrated at Maubeuge on 14 June.[120]

Zieten was again involved in passing on messages from the Netherlanders to Namur, this time from Merlen. This indicated that Jérôme was in Maubeuge, but that all troops from around this town had marched off to the east towards Beaumont and Philippeville, leaving only a weak screen covering Merlen's front. Zieten added the comment that, judging by the camp fires his men could see, a large body of the enemy appeared to be concentrated at Thirimont, north of Beaumont, and another behind the wood at Marpent, about 8km east of Maubeuge near Solre-sur-Sambre.[121] A final report arrived from Zieten informing his headquarters that Napoleon had arrived in Maubeuge the previous evening and that, according to the latest information from Merlen, the French offensive would begin on the 16th with the Prussians receiving the main blow.[122] Zieten also reported the sightings of numerous campfires to Wellington in Brussels, where the news arrived at 7 a.m. the following morning.[123]

Hardinge summed up this intelligence in a letter written to Wellington at 10 p.m. which would have arrived in Brussels on the morning of 15 June. This informed the Duke that,

A report from General Zieten of this day's date, just received, encloses a letter from General Merlen of the Belgian Army of this morning, in which he states that the troops collected at Maubeuge are in movement from thence on the road to Beaumont, being provided with eight day's provisions and forage... The fires of a body of troops, he reports, were seen last night in the direction of Thirimont, near Beaumont, and also in the vicinity of Mirbes...

[117] De Bas & T'Serclaes de Wommersom, vol I, p 351.
[118] De Bas, *Prins Frederik*, vol II, p 517.
[119] De Bas & T'Serclaes de Wommersom, vol I, p 353.
[120] Lettow-Vorbeck, p 518.
[121] Lettow-Vorbeck, p 517 f.
[122] Pflugk-Harttung, *Vorgeschichte*, pp 39 f. Merlen's report is also referred to in De Bas, *Prins Frederik*, vol II, p 517.
[123] Gleig, G.R., *Life of Wellington*, pp258–9.

158

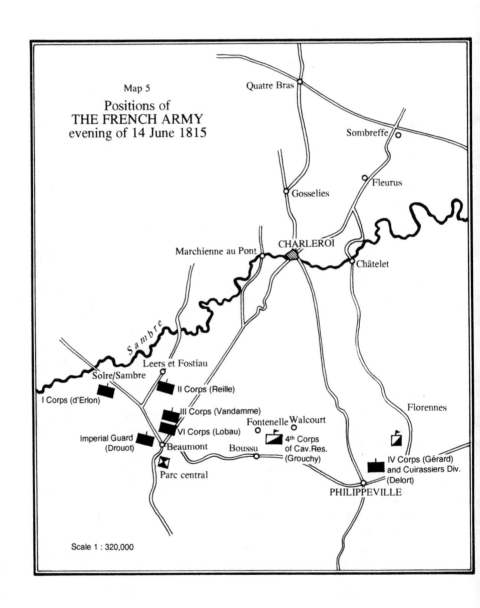

Map 5

Positions of
THE FRENCH ARMY
evening of 14 June 1815

Quatre Bras

Sombreffe

Fleurus

Gosselies

CHARLEROI

Marchienne au Pont

Châtelet

Sambre

Leers et Fostiau

Solre/Sambre

II Corps (Reille)

I Corps (d'Erlon)

III Corps (Vandamme)

Florennes

Fontenelle Walcourt

VI Corps (Lobau)

Imperial Guard
(Drouot)

4th Corps
of Cav.Res.
(Grouchy)

Beaumont

Boussu

IV Corps (Gérard)
and Cuirassiers Div.
(Delort)

Parc central

PHILIPPEVILLE

Scale 1 : 320,000

General Gneisenau credits the intelligence he has received from different quarters of the arrival of the two divisions of the 4th corps from the neighbourhood of Thionville at Sédan and Mézières on the 12th... The prevalent opinion here seems to be that Buonaparte intends to commence offensive operations.[124]

As the outbreak of hostilities seemed imminent, Blücher sent Oberst von Pfuel, an officer on his staff, to Brussels to ask Wellington what his intentions were. The Duke told Pfuel that he had taken all measures to ensure that his army would be able to concentrate either at Nivelles or at Quatre Bras 22 hours after the first cannon shot.[125]

The weight of all the available intelligence therefore supported the view that the French forces were poised for a major attack on the Prussian positions; that Napoleon had left Paris to direct this offensive in person; and that the French forces had mostly moved east from Maubeuge and no longer threatened an advance against the Anglo-Dutch-German positions before Mons. Wellington's guarantee to support the Prussians in strength within 22 hours shows that the Duke accepted this as the reality of the situation.

The war was about to begin.

Napoleon's Movements and Intentions

At the beginning of June, Napoleon was in Paris, continuing to work on assembling his army and dealing with affairs of state but at 4 a.m. on the 12th he left the capital, arriving in Laon that evening. There, he inspected the fortifications and by the 13th he had moved on to Avesnes. The next day he arrived in Beaumont.[126] It is interesting to compare these movements with the records of allied intelligence. Although there had been rumours of Napoleon's departure from Paris for some time, Wellington's information on 11 June was that Napoleon was still there on the 7th, which was correct. Rumours of Napoleon's movements continued to come in but on the 13th Wellington wrote he had information that Napoleon was still in Paris on 10 June, which was also correct.

By midnight on 12/13 June Steinmetz had heard that Napoleon was expected at the front the next evening. As Wellington had orders for a concentration of his army drafted at around the same time, he may well have had similar information. On the evening of 13 June Merlen was aware of Napoleon's arrival near the front earlier that afternoon. He informed Steinmetz who passed this intelligence on to his corps headquarters early on the morning of the 14th. On the basis of this information Zieten then ordered his brigades to be prepared for an immediate concentration. Dörnberg was also aware on the 14th that Napoleon had probably been in Avesnes the previous day and told Wellington. It would seem that, overall, the Allies had a fairly accurate picture of Napoleon's movements.

---

124 WSD, vol X, p 476.
125 Damitz, vol I, p 70. The original documentation was at one time in the Prussian War Archives, and is missing, presumed destroyed in World War Two.
126 Charras, vol I, p 85 f.

However, Napoleon was convinced that the Allies were unaware of his movements and that he had stolen a march on them. He believed that they did not have a clear picture of his troop movements and thought they were unaware of his departure from Paris. While he was completing the preparations for his offensive, he believed that, 'The Allied armies were resting in their cantonments with a feeling of security.'[127]

Napoleon was clearly unaware of how good the Allied network of spies actually was, and how much the Allies knew of his movements. He based his view of the situation on reports from his spies in Brussels and Namur who reported that all there was quiet.[128] This information was misleading. Although no significant troop movements had taken place, the various Allied headquarters were buzzing with reports coming in from all directions. Napoleon commenced his offensive in the firm belief that he had taken his enemies completely by surprise. That was his first error, and it would not be his only one in this campaign.

Poised to Advance

By the evening of 14 June the French army had formed into three great columns, stretched out along the roads leading to Charleroi. The left column consisted of the Reille's II and d'Erlon's I Corps; the centre column was made up of Vandamme's III Corps, Lobau's VI Corps, the Imperial Guard, the Reserve Cavalry and Artillery; Gérard's IV Corps formed the right column. Reille's bivouacs were on the right bank of the Sambre, around Leers; d'Erlon's camps were to Reille's rear, around Solre-sur-Sambre; Vandamme, Lobau, the Guard and the Reserves were placed along the road leading from Beaumont to Charleroi; the right column was in and behind Philippeville.[129]

Chesney summed up the position eloquently in his Waterloo Lectures,

> So passed the short night which preceded Napoleon's last campaign, the French, impatient for the light in which to fall upon their foes, and redeem, by some new Austerlitz or Jena, the disasters of the last three years; the Prussians, no less vigilant, preparing in all haste to meet the shock; the English, save only their reticent chief and a few trusted officers, resting unconscious of the storm gathering before them.[130]

At dawn the next day, the French offensive began.

---

[127] Gourgaud, pp 35-7.
[128] Charras, vol I, p 126.

[129] Charras, vol I, p 124 f.
[130] Chesney, p 67.

Right: Arthur Wellesley, the first Duke of Wellington. One of the great captains of history and a most successful soldier, statesman and politician, Wellington was one of the leading figures in the anti-Prussian party in British politics. There was very little he would not do to restrict Prussian expansionism.

Right: Napoleon Bonaparte (*after a painting by David*). In pursuit of personal ambition and glory, Napoleon plunged Europe into more than a decade of war. This period, together with the years of the French Revolutionary Wars, saw vast areas of Europe suffering devastation and great economic hardship.

Overleaf: 'Napoleon on the Road from Grenoble' (*after a painting by Charles Steuben*). It was the return of the 'Corsican Ogre' from exile on the island of Elba that led to the 'Hundred Days'. Napoleon was not recognised by the Allies as the legal ruler of France. Instead, he was officially referred to as 'Bonaparte' and outlawed.

Gebhard Lebrecht von Blücher (*after a painting by Gebauer*).
One of the prime movers in the overthrow of the Napoleonic Empire,
Blücher was admired throughout Europe for his great leadership skills and
blunt honesty. A good soldier but a poor politician, he was little match for
the Duke of Wellington when it came to astute political manoeuvring.

Above: Neidhardt von Gneisenau, Blücher's chief-of-staff. Along with Scharnhorst, he was one of the great military thinkers of this era, and one of the founders of the general staff in the modern sense. His attempts to out-manoeuvre Wellington on the political front were largely unsuccessful.

Above right: Hans Joachim von Zieten, commander of the Prussian I Army Corps. Zieten's men were the first to come to blows with the French in this campaign. The skilful manner in which he conducted his retreat in the face of the initial French attack bought the Allies enough time to complete the concentration of their forces. However, the Duke of Wellington wasted these hours through inaction.

Right: Friedrich Graf Kleist von Nollendorf. One of the accomplished generals of this era, Kleist was originally the commander of the Prussian Army of the Lower Rhine until, for political reasons, he was replaced by Blücher.

Above: 'The News Reaches the Ball' (*after a painting by C. J. Stadler*). A dramatic but rather inaccurate portrayal of the events of midnight 15/16 June. Müffling is shown delivering the news of the breakthrough to Quatre Bras by the French, when in fact the messenger was Webster, and somehow Blücher, who was actually in Sombreffe at the time, has appeared at the Duchess of Richmond's Ball as well.

ight: Johann Adolph Freiherr von Thielemann, commander of the Prussian III Army
. After years in the Saxon service, Thielemann left in protest over his king's alliance
the French in 1813. For some, he was a turn-coat. For others, he was a great patriot.

ove right: Karl Leopold Heinrich Ludwig von Borstell, one of Prussia's more able
nders. He protested so fiercely about the handling of the Saxon problem that he was
ed from command of a corps in the Army of the Lower Rhine. He was sorely missed.

The British attacking the French right wing at Quatre Bras.

Above: The Battle of Ligny (*after a drawing by Martinet*).
This would appear to show the final French attack on the evening of 16 June
and the subsequent destruction of the Prussian centre.

Above: Jean Victor Baron de Constant Rebeque, chief-of-staff to the Prince of Orange. It was Constant Rebeque who violated Wellington's orders to hold the vital road junction at Quatre Bras on the evening of 15 June 1815.

Right: Lieutenant-General Henry Paget, the Earl of Uxbridge. As commander of Wellington's Reserve Cavalry, Uxbridge managed to get his men to the field of Quatre Bras for the end of the fighting on 16 June, after a long and exhausting march in blistering heat.

Blücher's fall at Ligny, after he had led a cavalry charge. For several hours the Prussians were unsure of their commander's fate, and in this state of uncertainty Gneisenau, the chief-of-staff, ordered a general retreat to Wavre.

Right: Friedrich Wilhelm III, the King of Prussia. A rather melancholic person whom history has deemed a weak ruler, he nevertheless guided Prussia through one of the greatest crises in its history, and restored it to its place as a great European power.

Below: Carl von Clausewitz. Later to become famous for his military theories, Clausewitz, a pupil of Scharnhorst and Gneisenau, was Thielemann's chief-of-staff in this campaign.

Above: Major-General Jean Baptiste van Merlen, commander of the 2nd Netherlands Cavalry Brigade. Merlen's men were crucial to securing the vital position of Quatre Bras on 16 June.

Below: Freiherr Carl von Müffling. Appointed Prussian commissioner in Wellington's headquarters, Müffling did not understand English. Wellington was thus able to keep him at a safe distance from the more sensitive events in his headquarters.

Above: Prinz August von Thurn und Taxis. As the Bavarian representative at the Prussian headquarters, Thurn und Taxis witnessed many of the dramatic moments in the campaign at first hand.

Below: Lieutenant-General Sir Thomas Picton served as the commander of the British 5th Division. The arrival of his forces at Quatre Bras in the afternoon of 16 June was essential to the Allied resistance.

Above: Friedrich August, King of Saxony. A rather unfortunate figure in this period, he had a habit of supporting the losing side. Just before the outbreak of hostilities in 1815 his kingdom was dismembered and part of his army required to swear an oath to the Prussian crown. This led to demonstrations and, later, a mutiny.

Below: Graf Henckel von Donnersmark, commander of the 4th Brigade of Zieten's I Army Corps.

Above: Friedrich Graf Bülow von Dennewitz, commander of the Prussian IV Army Corps. Due to poor staff work and a misunderstanding, Bülow failed to reach Ligny in time for the battle on 16 June.

Below: Prinz Wilhelm, a cavalry commander in Bülow's IV Army Corps. He succeeded to the throne as King of Prussia in 1861 and became Emperor of Germany in 1871.

Chapter 9

The Advance on Charleroi

A Significant Day

The events of 15 June 1815 were to prove significant for the outcome of the campaign. While Napoleon engaged the Prussian advance guard under Zieten at Charleroi, Wellington continued to ponder the meaning of the information he was receiving. The war had indeed started, but the Duke hesitated. While Blücher set about concentrating his forces in accordance with the agreement reached at Tirlemont on 3 May, Wellington waited for confirmation that the attack on Charleroi was not merely a clash of outposts, a spoiling attack, or a diversion, with the main thrust being against his positions at Mons. One factor in the Duke's calculations was that Brussels, with its large population of French royalist émigrés and aristocratic British tourists, was a nervous city. Wellington did not want to cause an unnecessary panic by making a premature movement. His delay in taking decisive action on 15 June, however, caused his Prussian allies a number of problems, contributing to their defeat at Ligny the next day.

Napoleon's Orders

Through his new chief-of-staff, Marshal Soult, the Emperor Napoleon issued the following order to his army from his headquarters at Beaumont on 14 June,

Tomorrow, the 15th, at 2.30 a.m., General Vandamme's division of light cavalry [Domon's 3rd] is to mount up and move onto the road to Charleroi; it is to send detachments in all directions to scout the countryside and to clear away the enemy outposts; but each of these detachments must be less than 50 men. Before having his division march off, General Vandamme is to check that it has sufficient cartridges. At the same hour, Lieutenant-General Pajol is to gather together 1st Cavalry Corps and follow the movement of General Domon who is to be under the orders of General Pajol at this stage.

The divisions of 1st Cavalry Corps are not to deploy any detachments; these are to be provided by [Domon's] 3rd Division. General Domon is to have his battery of artillery march behind the first battalion of the III Infantry Corps; Lieutenant-General Vandamme is to give him any subsequent orders.

Lieutenant-General Vandamme is to sound reveille at 2.30 a.m.; at 3 a.m. he is to have his army corps march off towards Charleroi; all his baggage wagons are to be parked to the rear and are not to move off until VI Corps and the Imperial Guard have passed by; they are under the orders of the Waggon Master General who is to unite them with those of VI Corps and the Imperial Guard and give them orders to move. Each division of III Army Corps is to

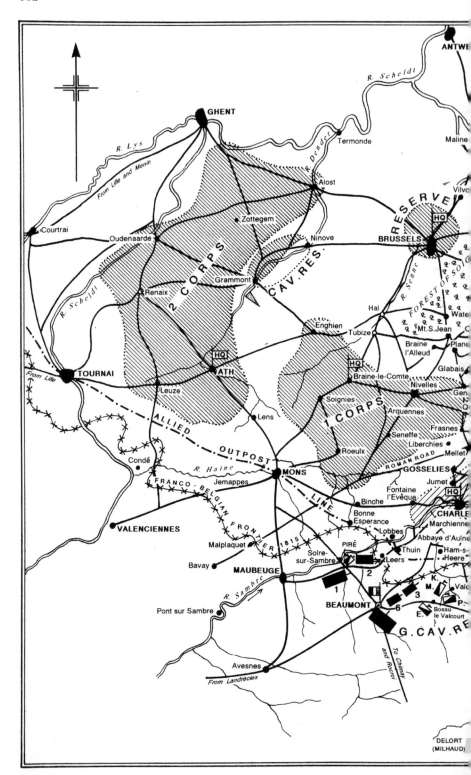

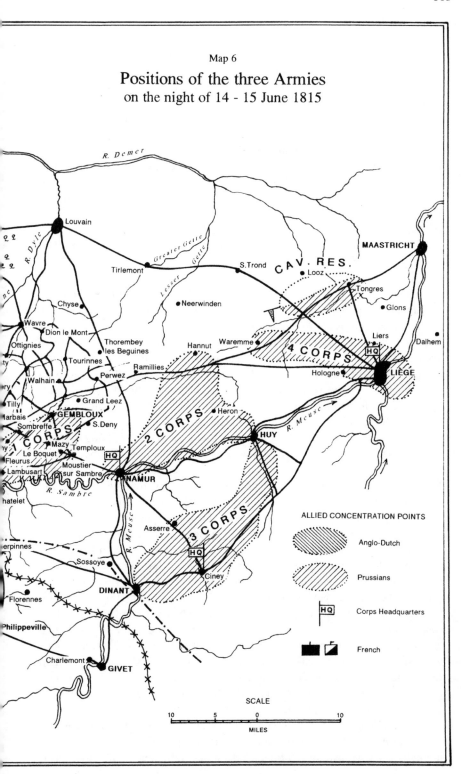

Map 6

Positions of the three Armies
on the night of 14 - 15 June 1815

R. Demer

Louvain

MAASTRICHT

R. Dyle

Greater Gette

Tirlemont

S.Trond

CAV. RES.

Looz

Chyse

Neerwinden

Tongres

Glons

Wavre

Dion le Mont

Thorembey
les Beguines

Waremme

Liers

Dalhem

Ottignies

Hannut

4 CORPS

HQ

Tourinnes

Ramillies

Hologne

LIÈGE

Walhain

Perwez

Grand Leez

Heron

Tilly

GEMBLOUX

S.Deny

2 CORPS

HUY

R. Meuse

arbais

Sombreffe

1 CORPS

Mazy Temploux

HQ

Le Boquet

Fleurus

Moustier
sur Sambre

NAMUR

Lambusart

R. Sambre

hatelet

3 CORPS

Asserre

ALLIED CONCENTRATION POINTS

erpinnes

Sossoye

R. Meuse

HQ

Ciney

Anglo-Dutch

DINANT

Prussians

Florennes

Philippeville

HQ

Corps Headquarters

Charlemont

GIVET

French

SCALE

10   5   0   10

MILES

take along its batteries and ambulances; any other vehicle found with the troops is to be burned.

Count Lobau is to sound reveille at 3.30 a.m., and he is to have VI Army Corps march off at 4 a.m., following General Vandamme's movements and supporting him; he is to observe the same order of march for his troops, artillery, ambulances and baggage trains as prescribed for III Army Corps. The baggage of VI Corps is to be united with that of III Corps, and placed under the command of the Waggon Master General.

The Young Guard is to sound reveille at 4.30 a.m., and march off at 5 a.m.; it is to follow the movement of VI Corps on the road to Charleroi. The Chasseurs à Pied of the Guard are to sound reveille at 5 a.m., and march off at 5.30 a.m., following the movement of the Young Guard. The Grenadiers à Pied of the Guard are to sound reveille at 5.30 a.m., marching off at 6 a.m., following the movement of the Chasseurs à Pied. The same order of march prescribed for III Army Corps is to be observed by the Imperial Guard. The baggage trains of the Guard are to be joined with those of III and VI Army Corps, under the orders of the Waggon Master General who will move them.

Marshal Grouchy, along with the other cavalry corps, is to mount up at 5.30 a.m., with his corps to the fore, and follow the movement to Charleroi; the two remaining corps are to depart one after the other at hourly intervals; but Marshal Grouchy will take care to have the cavalry march on the side roads to avoid any encumbrance of the principal route being used by the infantry column, and also because the cavalry keeps better order; all baggage is to remain parked at the rear, and is only to move when the Waggon Master General gives it the order to do so.

Count Reille is to have reveille sounded at 2.30 a.m., and have II Corps march off at 3 a.m.; he is to direct it to Marchienne-au-Pont, reaching there by 9 a.m. All the bridges across the Sambre are to be guarded, with nobody being allowed to cross them. The outposts are to be relieved successively by I Corps. Every attempt is to be made to prevent the enemy from destroying the bridges, especially that at Marchienne, over which it is probable the river will be crossed, as it would be necessary to repair it if it were damaged.

At Thuin and Marchienne, as in all the villages on the route, Count Reille is to interrogate the inhabitants to gain news on the positions and strength of the enemy; letters at the post offices are to be opened and scrutinised, and any information is to be sent to the Emperor immediately.

Count d'Erlon is to have I Corps march off at 3 a.m., and he is to direct it on Charleroi, following the movement of II Corps, which is to move to the left as soon as possible so as to support and assist it when needed; he is to hold one cavalry brigade to the rear to cover himself and to maintain communications with Maubeuge with small detachments; advance parties are to be sent to there, and in the direction of Mons and Binche as far as the border to obtain news of the enemy and report it as well. These advance parties are neither to place themselves in danger, nor to cross the frontier.

Count d'Erlon is to occupy Thuin with one division; and if the bridge in this town is destroyed, he is to repair it as soon as possible, while at the same time immediately establishing a bridgehead on the left bank. The division at

Thuin is also to guard the bridge at the Abbey of Alnes, where Count d'Erlon is likewise to build a bridgehead on the left bank.

The same order of march as prescribed for III Corps, the artillery, the ambulances and the baggage, is to be observed by the I and II Corps which are to have their baggage sent on, moving to the left of I Corps, under the command of the most senior waggon master.

The IV Corps (Army of the Moselle) has received orders to take up positions before Philippeville today. If its movements are implemented, and if the divisions of this army corps are concentrated, then the Lieutenant-General [Count Gérard] is to set out at 3 a.m. tomorrow, and direct them on Charleroi; care is to be taken to keep level with III Corps with which he is to communicate so as to arrive at more or less the same time at Charleroi; but General Gérard is to scout to his right, along all the passes that lead to Namur; he is to march in order of battle, leaving all his baggage and encumbrances at Philippeville so that his army corps is free to manoeuvre easily. General Gérard is to give orders to the 14th Cavalry Division arriving at Philippeville today to follow the movement of his army corps to Charleroi where this division is to join 4th Cavalry Corps.

Lieutenant-Generals Reille, Vandamme, Gérard and Pajol are to keep in regular communication by means of small parties, and are to organise their march in such a way that they can arrive and assemble before Charleroi; as far as possible, they are to place Flemish-speaking officers with the vanguard to interrogate the inhabitants and to obtain intelligence; but these officers are to present themselves as commanders of advance parties without saying that the army is behind them.

Lieutenant-Generals Reille, Vandamme and Gérard are to place all the sappers of their army corps (having ensured they have their bridging equipment with them), immediately behind the leading regiment of light infantry, and are to give orders to the engineer officers to have any poor roads repaired, to open lateral communications, and to bridge any rivers where the infantry would get wet crossing them.

Sailors and Engineers of the Guard and engineers of the reserve are to march behind the leading regiment of III Corps with Generals Rogniat and Haxo at their head; they are to take only two or three vehicles with them; the remainder of the engineer park is to march on the left of III Corps. If the enemy is encountered, these troops are not to be used for combat, rather Generals Rogniat and Haxo are to use them to work on the passage of rivers, bridgeheads, repairing roads, opening communications, etc.

The Cavalry of the Guard is to follow the movement on Charleroi, leaving at 8 a.m.

The Emperor will be with the vanguard on the road to Charleroi. The lieutenant-generals [the corps' commanders] are to send His Majesty frequent reports on their movements and the intelligence they are receiving; they are advised that it is His Majesty's intention to cross the Sambre before noon and to have his army on the left bank of this river.

The pontoon trains are to be divided into two sections; the first section is to be divided into three parts, each of five pontoons and five boats with the

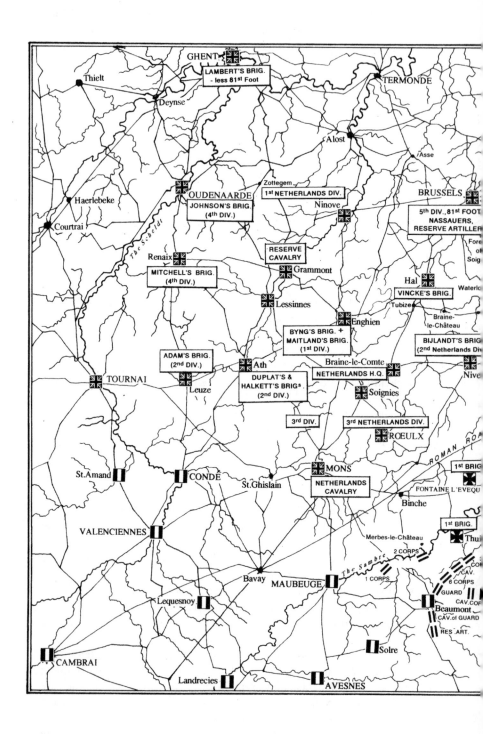

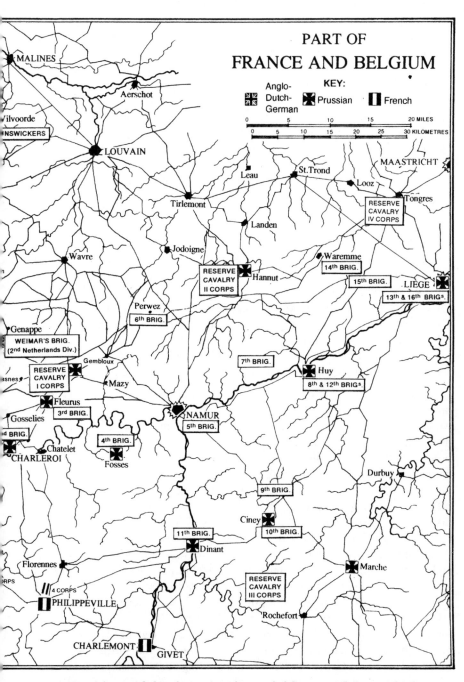

Map 7. Positions of the three Armies at 2.30 a.m. 15 June 1815

vanguard so as to place three bridges across the Sambre; each of these parts is to have one company of pontoniers. The first section is to march with the engineers, behind III Corps. The second section is to remain with the park of the artillery reserve, by the baggage column; it will be accompanied by the fourth company of pontoniers.

The Emperor's train and the baggage of the Grand Headquarters are to join together and march off at 10 a.m. As soon as they have passed, the Waggon Master General is to send off the baggage trains of the Imperial Guard, III and VI Corps; at the same time, orders are to be sent to the equipment column of the Reserve Cavalry to march in the direction already taken by the cavalry.

The army's ambulances are to follow the Headquarters, marching at the head of the baggage trains; but, the baggage trains, and with them the trains of the Reserve Artillery, and the second section of the pontoon trains are not to cross the Sambre without explicit orders. The Waggon Master General is to form sections of baggage and place officers in charge of them so as to be able to detach them if so ordered by Headquarters or for serving officers. Those vehicles which are held back are to move to the left and are not to change their position without orders from the Waggon Master General.

The Emperor orders that all equipment vehicles found in the infantry, cavalry or artillery columns are to be burned, as are any vehicles of the equipment column that leave their position and interfere with the march without the express permission of the Waggon Master General. For this purpose, the Waggon Master General has a detachment of 50 gendarmes at his disposal. They are responsible for the execution of his orders, as are all gendarmes and their officers, for the success of the campaign depends on this.[1]

The French advance on Charleroi was thus to be made by a central column protected on its left and right by smaller bodies of troops. These columns would commence their marches before dawn, advance towards Charleroi en masse, take this town, and cross the Sambre. So that their movement could proceed without delay, the baggage was to be kept to the minimum necessary, with strict penalties being imposed for anybody violating that rule.

The centre column was led by III Corps (Vandamme), of about 16,000 infantry and 38 guns, preceded by 3,800 cavalry with 12 guns (Domon's division and Pajol's corps). The left column was headed by Reille's II Corps, 25,000 men, including 1,800 cavalry and 46 guns. The right column was to be formed by the IV Corps (Gérard), with 15,800 men, including 1,600 cavalry and 38 guns. Thus, a total of more than 60,000 men with 134 guns were to draw up before the narrow defile at Charleroi by midday.

These three columns were followed by the remainder of the army. The I Corps (d'Erlon), with 20,400 men, including 1,700 cavalry and 46 guns, formed the reserve of the left column. Delort's 14th Cavalry Division, 1,700 men with 6 guns, marched behind the right column. The centre was supported by the Imperial Guard, 19,000 men, including 3,600 cavalry and 128 guns; VI Corps (Lobau) consisting of 10,300 men and 32 guns; and the Reserve

---

[1] Taken from Delhaize & Aerts, p 241 ff.

Cavalry under Grouchy, some 8,500 men and 30 guns. The reserves thus amounted to a further 60,000 men with 242 guns.

The Terrain

The area between the Sambre and Meuse rivers where the fighting began is cut by deep, narrow watercourses with steep sides. The villages were few and far between in 1815, and linked only by poor paths. In the quadrilateral formed by Beaumont, Solre-sur-Sambre, Charleroi and Philippeville, there was not a single stretch of cobbled road that could be used to facilitate the French advance across the border. Woods covered much of the area in 1815, with one large forest stretching from Lobbes to Sart-Eustache, across the whole line of the French advance, and with smaller woods elsewhere. Because of these woods the French artillery had some difficulties in moving in places, particularly to the south of Jamioulx on the route of the central column.

These already poor conditions were made worse by the Prussians who had cut trenches across certain roads, as well as blocking them with trees and abatis. The French engineers needed to spend much of the night of 14/15 June clearing the way for their army to march.

Dawn to Daybreak

The campfires of the night of 14 June 1815 gave way to dawn. The 3rd Cavalry Division and Pajol's corps moved off at 2.30 a.m. as ordered. At 3 a.m. Reille's Corps set off in the direction of Thuin from its bivouacs at Leers-et-Fosteau, followed by d'Erlon's Corps.[2] At 3.30 a.m., the French crossed the border at Leers-et-Fosteau, Cour-sur-Heure and Thy-le-Château. The left column advanced towards Marchienne-au-Pont via Thuin; the centre moved through Ham-sur-Heure, Jamioulx and Marcinelle; the right via Florennes and Gerpinnes.[3] However, Vandamme at the head of the centre column started late, causing delays to the formations following behind.

Fighting at Thuin began shortly after sunrise, at about 4 a.m., when a battery of Reille's corps opened fire on the 2nd Battalion of the 1st Westphalian Landwehr Regiment.[4] The Westphalians were expecting the French attack and were already under arms.[5] The warning cannon placed on the windmill hill near Fontaine l'Evêque, had been fired at 3.30 a.m. This was the signal for the 1st and 3rd battalions of the 1st Westphalian Landwehr to assemble on the cobbled road to Marchienne-au-Pont.[6]

The noise of the fighting could be heard as far away as Zieten's headquarters in Charleroi. Expecting the French offensive at any time, Zieten had tried to snatch a few hour's sleep, and anticipating having to react quickly to events, he had gone to bed fully clothed. The cannon fire at 4 a.m. woke him. He wrote,

---

2 Charras, vol I, p 124 ff.
3 Houssaye, p 60.
4 Ollech, p 96. Ollech is however in error as he wrote that it was the 2nd Regiment. It was, in fact, the 1st.

5 Charras, vol I, p 124 ff.
6 MWBl., vol XXXI, p 180.

I sprang out of bed, fully clothed, woke all officers, ordered Kolonnenjäger [supply train provost] Merinsky, Kapitain von Felden, and Major Graf Westphal to ride to me immediately, dictated one letter in German, one in French, that hostilities had begun and sent Westphal with the first to Namur to Field Marshal Blücher, Merinsky with the second to Brussels to the Duke of Wellington.[7]

Using the inevitable confusion of the early morning movement as cover, one of Gérard's divisional generals, Bourmont, took the opportunity to cross to the Allied lines with his staff and their escort of five lancers, surrendering themselves to the outposts of the Prussian 4th Brigade. He was brought to Fosses-la-Ville where Colonel von Schutter, second-in-command of 4th Brigade, was in cantonments with part of the 19th Regiment. Here, Bourmont revealed the French plans and intentions to the Prussians, but added little to what they already knew or could work out. His intelligence was passed to Blücher by Zieten in a message from Gilly timed at 1.30 p.m.[8] but the events of the day and the probable French intentions were already clear before Bourmont's information arrived, so his defection was of little importance.

The three French columns bore down on the Prussian positions and the Prussian pickets fell back on their supports. Zieten's 1st Brigade held a line between the Roman Road and the Sambre from Binche to Lobbes with outposts at Bonne Espérance and other villages. The link between 1st and 2nd Brigades was at Thuin, held by part of F./2nd Westphalian Landwehr from 2nd Brigade. The front line of 2nd Brigade stretched east from Thuin through Ham-sur-Heure to Gerpinnes and was held by F./28th Regiment. Other 1st and 2nd Brigade positions are listed in Chapter 7, pages 129 to 134. The 3rd Brigade covered the Sambre east of Charleroi from Châtelet to Tamines, with the 4th covering the Meuse farther east still. The outposts of both these brigades were deployed towards Phillippeville, between Gerpinnes and Sosoye. The Reserve Cavalry was quartered between the Piéton and the Dyle. Its assembly point was Gosselies.

First Blood at Thuin

Two battalions, four to five squadrons and three cannon from Jérôme Bonaparte's 6th Division of II Corps attacked the area around Thuin. Captain von Gillhausen commanded the defence of Lobbes and noted the following in his report,

At 3.30 a.m. the large body of French that had assembled before my outposts at Lobbes the previous night, clearly intending to attack and force us back, began firing at these outposts one by one. I was present myself, and had already deployed my entire battalion to take account of the broken and hilly terrain. The enemy moved more and more to the right, joining up with some others who had taken the direct way to Thuin on my left. They threw back the cavalry's advanced observation post and, at about 4.30 a.m., began

---

[7] Hafner, *Militärisches*, p 252.
[8] Ollech, p 100 f.

bombarding the outpost at Maladrie to our east with four cannon. After a hard fight lasting 1½ hours, they forced back our troops, taking Thuin...

Although I knew that Thuin had definitely been lost, and that I myself must withdraw, I nevertheless stayed for another half hour securing the far heights and withdrawing my various outposts which the enemy did not fire on much. I did, however, in the meantime, hold the bridge over the Sambre with one company. When I withdrew the battalion I occupied the wood at Sars-de-Lobbes. After the posts at Hourpeses had been taken by the enemy, I continued my withdrawal, on orders from my brigade commander, on the left to Anderlues, on the right to Fontaine l'Evêque.[9]

After this early encounter two stragglers from the outpost at Thuin reported to Steinmetz that there was not a single man left from II./1st Westphalian Landwehr. Steinmetz grinned, and said, 'There, there, one man is bound to be left over.' He sent them back to their unit with the words: 'See how many there are left, and tell Captain von Gillhausen, that if the battalion is pushed too hard, he should fall back to the woods at Anderlues.' Here the two discovered that they had panicked unnecessarily when they found their battalion reformed and waiting at the edge of the wood.[10]

At 8 a.m., Zieten sent Steinmetz the following orders, which arrived at Fontaine l'Evêque at 9 a.m.,

I thank Your Excellency most deeply for the news [of the attack on Lobbes]. Should the enemy push farther forward, then the terrain is, according to the strength of the enemy advance, to be evacuated slowly in the direction of Fontaine l'Evêque without getting involved in heavy, isolated actions. The right flank is to be withdrawn only as far the enemy advance requires. Your Excellency is then to withdraw his brigade to Courcelles, in line with that of General von Pirch [II]. If General von Pirch is forced to evacuate Marchienne[-au-Pont], then you are to fall back in collaboration with the 2nd Brigade, that is with the 1st Brigade in the position behind Gosselies, the 2nd Brigade around Charleroi. Your Excellency is to report further movements of the enemy from time to time, along with his strengths and types of forces.[11]

At the same time, Zieten also sent Pirch II the following orders,

As the enemy has taken possession of Thuin, and as it cannot yet be judged if he intends to cross the Sambre, or advance along the right bank, I request Your Honour to note precisely on which side of the Sambre or on which road the enemy advances.

General von Steinmetz has orders, if pushed back and his flank threatened, either by the enemy crossing the Sambre at Thuin or by their moving forward along its right bank, to draw up the 1st Brigade at Courcelles, level with Marchienne-au-Pont. Should the enemy push farther forward, then the 2nd Brigade is to hold the crossings down river from Marchienne [i.e. at Charleroi

---

9 MWBl., vol XXX, p 36 fn; vol XXXI, p 180.
10 MWBl., vol XXXI, p 180.
11 MWBl., vol XXX, p 39 f.

and to the east] long enough for the positions at Gosselies and Gilly to be taken up by the 1st and 2nd Brigades respectively. In this event, Charleroi and Châtelet are to be held as long as possible until a further withdrawal to Fleurus becomes necessary. Until such time, I will remain on the heights at Gilly.[12]

At 8.15 a.m. Zieten reported the latest news to Namur,

The enemy has already taken Thuin and forced back our outposts this side of Montigny-Lestigneis. On the left bank of the Sambre, he is pushing forward with equal force. He is too strong to be engaged in individual actions. Thus, the 1st and 2nd Brigades will fall back to a line from Gosselies to Gilly.

Napoleon is present with his entire Guard. It is thus probable that he has serious intentions. The enemy also has a considerable amount of cavalry. The troops that defended Thuin have many wounded...

P.S. A report just come in says that the enemy is not pressing on beyond the road via Nalinnes.[13]

By 9 a.m. the main body of F./28th had managed to assemble at Châtelet, having moved through the wooded valley of the Boussioux brook unnoticed by the advancing French. Here, the 3rd company was positioned to guard the Sambre crossing. The I./28th was on the north side of the river, and II./28th farther to the rear in reserve. At 9 a.m. the regiment received the order to retire to Gilly, where the 2nd Brigade was to assemble.[14]

At 9.30 a.m. Pirch II reported the events to Steinmetz,

The fusilier battalion in Thuin has been thrown back with the cavalry to Montigny-le-Tilleul with heavy casualties. I am withdrawing it to Marchienne as the enemy appears to have much cavalry, and from there to Marchienne is open ground. I hope this information is of use. Your Honour should now, according to the opinion of General von Zieten, start your march to Courcelles.[15]

Captain Monsterberg was leading a company of the 28th that had been deployed in support of the outpost at Thuin. He held his positions for about one hour before falling back on Montigny-le-Tilleul. There, he joined up with Lieutenant-Colonel Woiski, commander of the West Prussian Dragoons, and F./2nd Westphalian Landwehr. Heavy fighting developed around 9 a.m. and the Prussian infantry were driven out of Montigny. At first they retreated in good order, covered by the cavalry. However, a charge by French cavalry threw back the Prussian dragoons and the Westphalian Landwehr were then ridden down and scattered, losing a couple of hundred prisoners and a hundred or so dead and wounded. The remnants fell back to Marchienne-au-Pont from where Pirch II withdrew the broken battalion from the front. Woiski was wounded in this action, but remained with his troops.

Around this time, Steinmetz received a report from Pirch II promising that,

The 2nd Battalion of the 1st West Prussian Regiment will hold Marchienne

12 MWBl., vol XXXI, p 184. 14 Neff, pp 22–3.
13 GStA, Rep 92, Gneisenau A 48, fol 32. 15 MWBl., vol XXX, p 40.

until the 1st Brigade reaches Gosselies and is in line with it. To co-ordinate these moves I am sending Your Honour an officer, whom you will be so kind as to send back to me to give the signal when it is time to withdraw. I have just received a report that the observation post at Nalinnes has been attacked. I hear nothing else to my front.[16]

At St Martin, near Marchienne-au-Pont, the retreating troops were joined by II./6th (1st West Prussian) Regiment. Colonel von Stach, commander of the 1st West Prussian Regiment, described the situation in his report. According to Stach the French drew up at the windmill of St Martin and deployed about two battalions of infantry. At first these made little progress at the entrances to the village. The Prussians hastily erected barricades over the bridge in Marchienne and several French assaults were beaten off. However, the lack of artillery support and the superior numbers of the French forced a withdrawal across the Sambre. When describing the defence of Marchienne-au-Pont, Stach wrote, 'Only after having received a report from the 1st Brigade that they had reached the same level as Marchienne-au-Pont on their retreat from Fontaine l'Evêque did the 2nd Battalion fall back... '[17] In fact the II./6th Regiment held its position in Marchienne-au-Pont until the French had almost taken Charleroi itself. They only started to fall back, first to Dampremy then to Gilly, at 10 a.m.

The regimental history of the 1st West Prussians gives the following account of the battle,

Under Lieutenant von Hülfen, the skirmishers of the 2nd Battalion successfully defended the approaches to Marchienne-au-Pont against the advancing enemy. The French then moved their columns against the windmill hill in front of the village, and brought up artillery with which they bombarded it. Once the detachments ejected from Thuin had rejoined the battalion, Kapitain von Krentzki, on orders from the brigade commander, abandoned the right bank of the Sambre and fell back over the bridge. The bridge was then barricaded, with Lieutenant von Hülfen and Feldwebel Theidel placing their skirmishers behind it in very good positions. One determined attack by the enemy was beaten off, as was a second, and a third. The enemy had great superiority in numbers, which he gradually brought into play, and finally caused Kapitain von Krentzki to fall back to Dampremy where he received the order to retire on Gilly.[18]

About 10 a.m., it became clear to Steinmetz from Pirch II's movements that he should start withdrawing. He sent Rittmeister von Goschitzky, who had arrived earlier from Zieten's headquarters, back with a report on his intentions. Steinmetz also sent an officer to Colonel von Hofmann, his chief-of-staff who was commanding part of the brigade, warning him he was in danger of being cut off, and that he should withdraw his units from between Château-la-Marche and Piéton to the Piéton bridge as fast as possible. Were

16 MWBl., vol XXX, p 43.
17 MWBl., vol XXX, p 43 fn. This report is dated 18 June 1815.
18 Conrady, *Sechsten Infanterie-Regiment*, p 241 f.

this part of the brigade to reach the defile before Steinmetz and his men, then Hofmann was ordered to deploy to cover the bridge against any attempt by the enemy to take it. Hofmann had his men move off at the double through the wood at Courcelles and le Sart, to Miaucourt, and reached the Piéton at Sart-les-Moines about ten minutes before Steinmetz. By then the French had taken Marchienne-au-Pont so the brigade drew up along the Piéton. It waited there for a little while to be joined by the outpost chain of the 1st Westphalian Landwehr retiring via Roux and to reconnoitre the Gosselies defile to ensure that had not been taken by the enemy, too.

The Advance on Charleroi[19]

The French advance on Charleroi began in earnest at 8 a.m. when Pajol's 1st Cavalry Corps and Domon's 3rd Cavalry Division encountered the Prussian outpost at Ham-sur-Heure. Two companies of fusiliers of the 28th Regiment were thrown back with heavy losses when attacked by the 4th and 9th Chasseurs à Cheval. The regimental history gives the following account of what happened to one of them,

> While the battalion on outpost duty in Thuin deployed to the right of our fusiliers was being pushed back, Regiment No. 28 received the order to assemble at Châtelet. Here, the musketeers had already occupied the Sambre crossing. Kapitain Schwemmler's 11th Company had hardly left their outposts in Ham-sur-Heure when they were suddenly attacked by Domon's cavalry division, followed by Pajol's cavalry corps.
>
> By skilful use of terrain, the company was able to reach Couillet, 1½ leagues [11km] away, with only minor losses. Here, however, the small number of men had to cross open ground, and were soon surrounded by a crushing mass of the enemy and overwhelmed by superior numbers, after an heroic defence. Those men not cut down, fell, exhausted by the struggle, into the hands of the cavalry regiments. Only Lieutenant Schröder with his 36-man picket, which had already marched off for Charleroi, escaped this fate. Here, they later participated in the heroic battle for the Sambre bridge.
>
> The sacrifice of the 11th Company was not in vain. The French advance was stopped and our troops had the opportunity to form up without interference.[20]

The Fall of Charleroi

Charleroi is situated on both sides of the Sambre river. In 1815 the lower town, on the right bank, was linked to the village of Marcinelle by a dike some 400m long, and bordered by hedges. This dike crossed undulating terrain and ended as a road running into a tree-planted square beside the Sambre bridge. The river was 30m wide and the northern bank sloped up steeply. The whole town was dominated by the old citadel, situated in the upper part. The road sloped up steeply into the centre of the upper town and then on to a cross-roads with

---

[19] This section is based largely on Wagner, *Plane*, p 13 ff; Charras, vol I, p 124 ff; Plotho, 1815, p 26 ff; Ollech, p 93 ff; Damitz, p 69 ff; Delhaize and Aerts, p 261 ff.
[20] Neff, p 21 ff.

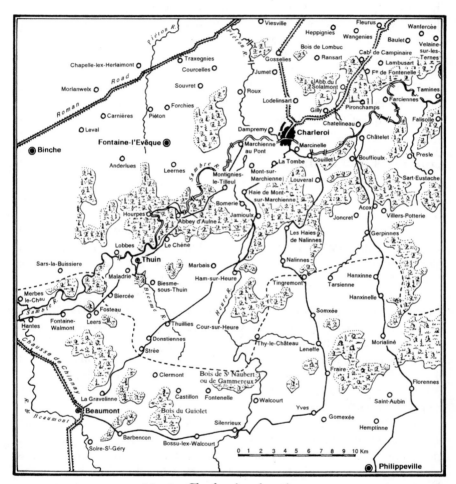

Map 8.   Charleroi and environs

routes leading to Brussels and Fleurus. However, despite the natural strength of the position, the town fortifications were in a state of disrepair, and Charleroi was no longer considered a fortified place. Places like Marcinelle, Dampremy, Lodelinsart, Gilly and Montignies-sur-Sambre are suburbs of Charleroi now, but in 1815 were outlying villages in the outskirts of the town.[21]

Once the 11th Company had been ridden down, Domon's light cavalry rode up to the dike leading into Charleroi from Marcinelle, where it was driven off by fire from Prussian skirmishers hidden behind hedges and in ditches. Part of Marcinelle, which had in the meantime been occupied by French infantry, was also recaptured. French reinforcements then arrived, driving back the Prussians. Once again Marcinelle fell to the French, this time along with the dike and the Sambre bridge, even though it had been barricaded. Charleroi was now open to a French assault. Major von Rohr, in command at Charleroi, decided that it was time to fall back towards Fleurus to the main position. He accomplished this in an orderly fashion despite pursuit by Pajol's cavalry. By 11 a.m., the French were in possession of Charleroi.

Gosselies and Jumet

Once the French had taken control of Charleroi, they began to fan out to the north and east towards Jumet and Gosselies, towards Ransart and towards Gilly. Gilly was defended by 2nd Brigade but 1st Brigade was still in the process of retiring east over the Piéton towards Jumet. Colonel Clary led the advance of Pajol's 1st Cavalry Corps against Jumet with his 1st Hussars and got there before the 1st Brigade had managed to cross the Piéton. Clary then advanced on Gosselies, only to find it stoutly defended.

The Reserve Cavalry of the I Army Corps had assembled at Gosselies, according to its original orders, by 9 a.m. About noon General von Roeder, commander of the Reserve Cavalry, was ordered to move off towards the main position at Fleurus. Roeder left Lieutenant-Colonel von Lützow, the former Freikorps leader, with his 6th Uhlans there to maintain the link with 1st Brigade. However, Zieten had already ordered Major-General von Jagow's 3rd Brigade to send Colonel von Rüchel with his 29th Regiment to Gosselies to help 1st Brigade's retreat.

The 29th Regiment started to arrive at Gosselies from 11 a.m. Rüchel met up with Lützow and placed Lützow in command of the defence of the village, giving him the 29th's 2nd Battalion. Rüchel kept the remaining two battalions of the regiment under his own command. The four skirmish platoons of the 2nd Battalion, under Kapitain von Rohr, were thrown out towards Jumet with the 7th Company being placed at the south-west exit from Gosselies in support. The three remaining companies were drawn up in line south of the road to Fleurus, several hundred paces east of Gosselies. Lützow's Uhlans were with them. The F./29th posted flank guards to the left in the wood running from Gosselies to Ransart, while the I./29th was held in reserve,

[21] Delhaize & Aerts, p 261 ff.
[22] Wellmann, p 69.

between Heppignies and Ransart. About midday, the skirmish platoons of the I./29th also occupied Wagnée.[22]

When Clary and his hussars moved towards Gosselies, a few of Lützow's lancers formed the first line of defence. They were at a distinct disadvantage, outnumbered two to one and with only one pistol each against French cavalry with carbines. However, the French were very cautious, as one eyewitness described,

> On the whole, contrary to their normal habits, the French went into action tepidly and with almost amazing caution. Their infantry was in place, they had superiority of numbers, and, at this time, the possession of Gosselies was most important to them.[23]

The French were soon driven back behind Jumet. To strengthen the Prussian position the 7th Company of the 29th Regiment was moved up closer to the 2nd Battalion's skirmishers, while the 5th Company covered the exit from Gosselies. This action provided the 1st Brigade with the opportunity of crossing the Piéton. Its battalions started to relieve those of the 2nd Brigade. Major von Chevallerie of II./29th described this as follows,

> After a battalion of Brandenburgers arrived to relieve our skirmishers, I received the order to withdraw mine, so rode to our left and right with the battalion ADC, Lieutenant von Fuchsius. As this relief action was not yet finished, I went forward to the windmill at Jumet, taking the 7th Company under the command of Kapitain von Buttler. Here, I linked up with the skirmishers, but only after the enemy was thrown back again. Major von Hymmen and his ADC, Lieutenant Feege, joined us here. The skirmishers of the 8th Company led by Lieutenant Hartwig, still fighting with élan and in good order, pulled back by themselves after having beaten off the enemy...
>
> Kapitain von Rohr with the four skirmish officers, Lieutenants Hartwig, Preuss, Kühlen, who was wounded, Meese and ADC von Fuchsius, all distinguished themselves here.[24]

This rebuff of the French advance was achieved despite the growing strength of their forces in this sector. General Lefebvre-Desnoëttes moved up to assist Clary with the Guard Light Cavalry and two artillery batteries. Duhesme's Young Guard Division moved up the road behind them in support. One regiment advanced towards Gosselies to provide Lefebvre-Desnoëttes with a reserve.

Around 12.30 p.m. the 1st Brigade was ready to start crossing the Piéton, thanks to the time bought by the repulse of Clary's first attack. Gillhausen's battalion was deployed on their right towards Jumet as a covering force. The other battalions of the brigade crossed the river and deployed with Gosselies on their left flank. Gillhausen's official report continued,

> Near Gosselies, I had to draw up my battalion with its right on a bridge to

[23] MWBl., vol XXX, p 44.
[24] Wellmann, p 71.

cover the troops who were crossing the river. When they had finished doing so, I was ordered by General von Steinmetz to move around Gosselies, cutting off the French advance on it. Hardly had I moved right, on to the heights, when I clearly saw that some of our troops were already there. Thus, I moved the battalion farther to the right, over a hill and down a valley, to around Chimay [Jumet], my skirmishers to the fore of the battalion.

At the farthest end of this place I split my battalion into two, to the left and to the right because of the narrow road. As soon as the road started widening, I had my men deploy into sections, with the rear platoons spreading out to the left and right. The enemy skirmishers there were thrown back, and I pursued them, while my skirmishers deployed on the right behind houses, and on the left in the gardens, and some at the head of the battalion.

On the far side of Jumet, I found two battalions of French, one of them deployed in such a way that it would be very easy for it to cut off my battalion. After exchanging several volleys with the enemy, I fell back at a slow pace towards the main road of Jumet on the left from where I expected an attack by our troops at any moment. The enemy pursued the battalion without pause, firing at it continuously, which would have had more effect if they had not aimed so high, at the adjutant and myself.

Knowing from previous experience that one must not withdraw too quickly in front of the French, I maintained a steady pace and retired along the whole long road through Jumet, where there was no place to turn to the left, nor to the right. During this withdrawal, part of the skirmishers on the right under Kapitain von Rappart were cut off from the battalion, only rejoining us the next morning, just as we were breaking camp at St Amand...

At the north end of Jumet, we met a Prussian battalion with red collars [29th Regiment], which fell back before we got up to it, evidently to cover our retreat into an open field. This battalion moved east of Jumet on a path running by a mill, meeting several black hussars [6th Uhlans, who still wore the uniforms of Lützow's Freikorps]. Shortly after that, enemy cavalry deployed from Jumet, forcing their way down our chosen route. Several of my men, who had been under arms the previous night, and had been on the move the whole day, fell exhausted and were taken prisoner by the enemy. However, the French cavalry still did not dare attack the battalion, which thus managed to join up with another Prussian battalion.[25]

Gillhausen's manoeuvre stopped the French advance for the time being. Covered by the 6th Uhlans and 1st Silesian Hussars, Steinmetz then started his withdrawal to Heppignies at about 4 p.m. Two skirmish platoons of II./12th Regiment under Lieutenant Rössel were ordered to cover the exit from Gosselies leading to Heppignies, and to leave only when the Landwehr skirmishers had withdrawn. The history of the 1st Westphalian Landwehr described the resulting action as follows,

When the skirmishers of the 12th Regiment were just about to march off, the

---

skirmishers of Landwehr Battalion Gillhausen under Lieutenant Harkort I fell back from Jumet under close pursuit from hussars and voltigeurs, and joined up with the 12th. An inspiring example to everybody was one officer of the Brandenburg skirmishers, who fought like a lion, and, after having his horse shot from under him, carried off the saddle and bridle on the sheath of his sabre.[26]

The French voltigeurs were forced back at bayonet point, and the Prussians restarted their withdrawal, though this was hindered by the tall crops. The French skirmishers followed up but kept their distance, as did a regiment of cavalry. The II. and F./12th Regiment then occupied Heppignies. The French advance continued and Girard, commanding the 7th Division of the 2nd Corps, took the village of Ransart. Next he tried to eject the Prussians from Heppignies but was thrown back, being pursued along the road to Gosselies.

Nonetheless, by 5.30 p.m. it was clear to Steinmetz that his men, now in action for 12 hours, were too fatigued to be able to offer much more resistance. He thus ordered a definitive withdrawal to Heppignies, covering this with two regiments of cavalry and one horse battery, along with a rearguard consisting of the two companies of Silesian Schützen under Major von Neumann and Gillhausen's Landwehr battalion. Neumann's Schützen were posted behind the hedges running along the road.

Steinmetz's men completed their withdrawal to Heppignies and Fleurus largely without interruption. However, a detachment of 1st Silesian Hussars was cut off near Gosselies and fell back to Quatre Bras, where, under the command of the Netherlands General Perponcher, it took part in the next day's battle there.

The 1st Brigade reached the heights behind Heppignies about 7 p.m. and Steinmetz decided to hold this position until nightfall. However, about 8 p.m. the French attacked, throwing back the Prussian skirmish line. Lieutenant-Colonel von Othegraven, commander of the 2nd Brandenburg Infantry Regiment, counter-attacked immediately, holding them off for about an hour. The 1st Brigade then continued its withdrawal unmolested in the dark, the first troops arriving at St Amand between 8 p.m. and 9 p.m., the last by about midnight.

Steinmetz summed up the events of the day for 1st Brigade in his official report,

> Informed of the assembly of the French army at Avesnes and Beaumont, I expected the French offensive any day... the offensive started on 15 [June] on the section of the front covered by the 2nd Brigade. This was the centre of the army corps, so the fall of Marchienne-au-Pont and Charleroi would have a disadvantageous effect on the garrisons of Binche and Fontaine l'Evêque. Everything depended on the brigade uniting at Gosselies to which the enemy was closer than my brigade. Thus they reached Jumet before I had crossed the Piéton.

---

[26] Mueller, p160.

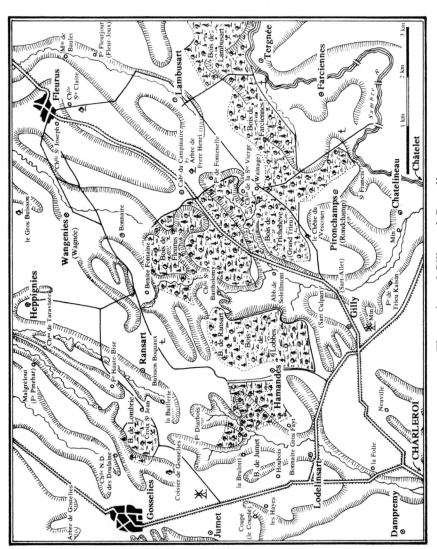

Map 9. The region of Gilly and Gosselies

For a time, it seemed doubtful if the brigade would be able to unite with the army corps at Fleurus. The 6th Uhlan Regiment, responsible for maintaining communications between the 1st and 2nd Brigades, performed a most valuable service when, with the help of an infantry battalion of the 2nd Brigade, it held off the enemy at Jumet.

Having gone around the defile, the 1st Brigade accepted battle. This turned to our advantage when, under orders, the 3rd Battalion of the 1st West Prussian Landwehr Regiment under the command of Kapitain von Gillhausen took the enemy in the left flank, after they had pushed too far forward. This was not quite as successful as expected because the enemy had too much time to deploy his troops, which far outnumbered ours. Nevertheless, the enemy was made to stop, giving us the opportunity to reach our allocated position at St Amand via the defile of Heppignies.

The 6th Uhlans, the 1st Silesian Hussar Regiment and Horse Battery No. 7 under Kapitain Richter, joining up behind Gosselies, covered our withdrawal. Here, the battery caused the enemy significant losses. The 6th Uhlan Regiment also suffered significant casualties, but held fast, performing worthily under Lieutenant-Colonel von Lützow. The enemy did attempt to storm the defile of Heppignies, and was not just repelled, but driven back as far as Gosselies, which gave us the opportunity of continuing our withdrawal to behind St Amand according to orders. The 1st Silesian Hussar Regiment covered the plain between Mellet, Heppignies and St Amand. The 6th Uhlans linked up with the 2nd Brigade.[27]

The Combat at Gilly

The village of Gilly consisted of a long unbroken row of houses. As such, it would be a problem for cavalry.[28] Pirch II had brought his brigade together around Gilly, occupying this village with four battalions of infantry supported by one battery of artillery. Their right flank reached as far as the cobbled road. The II./28th Regiment deployed on the far side of the cobbled road in the abbey of Soleilmont. The Fusilier Battalion of 6th Regiment held a small wood at the front. The 1st West Prussian Dragoons took up positions towards Châtelet. The II./2nd Westphalian Landwehr was held in reserve behind Gilly. The 1st Battalion of this regiment was on the march from Dampremy to Fleurus. The Westphalian Landwehr Cavalry, originally stationed in Moustier, was also on its way there. A barricade in the wood behind Gilly blocked the main road to Fleurus.

The history of the 6th Regiment described its positions as from 10 a.m. as follows,

> The fusilier battalion was deployed in a small copse at the forward slope of the heights of Gilly. Four cannon were placed on a mound to the right, with two cannon between this point and the cobbled road to Fleurus and the remaining two cannon on the road facing towards the exit of Gilly. The battalion's skirmishers were placed behind hedges between the cannon to protect them. The

---

[27] MWBl., vol XXX, p 49 f.

28th Regiment stood straddling the road to Lodelinsart, the regiment's two musketeer battalions 200 paces behind the front in the second line. Communications with the 1st Brigade (von Steinmetz), deployed at Gosselies, could not be maintained as the village of Ransart was too far away from the positions of both brigades for either of them to occupy it. The right flank of the brigade was all the more exposed when the French occupied the village with light infantry. The road towards Gilly was blocked by abatis.[28]

The brigade stood in these positions until 6p.m.

Vandamme's corps actually reached Charleroi by 3 p.m. after its delayed start and was ordered to support the cavalry's pursuit of the Prussians along the cobbled road through Gilly to Fleurus. However it took Vandamme's men some time to pass through Charleroi because there was only the one bridge over the Sambre available. Marshal Grouchy was up with the leading French cavalry, however, and personally reconnoitred Pirch II's positions before returning to Charleroi for further orders. Napoleon himself then rode to Gilly and drew up his troops for the assault. Vandamme's infantry was ordered to storm the village while Exelmans' 2nd Cavalry Corps was to hit the Prussians in their right flank, cutting them off at the defile through the Bois de Fleurus.

Because of the time the French preparations took the 2nd Brigade positions were untroubled at first but at 5.15 p.m., Pirch II sent Zieten the following message from Gilly, showing that he was aware of this threat,

> I have sent to General von Steinmetz to request him to occupy Ransart because my right flank will otherwise be exposed. He had me told that he could not do so, because it was too far forward and to his left. I have already placed one battalion in the Abbey of Soleilmont, and am having the wood and valley between this abbey and Ransart patrolled, as is the enemy. The cannon fire [of the 1st Brigade action] is at Jumet and is getting louder every minute. I request orders as to whether I should leave this position if the enemy moves on Ransart. I have established contact with the 3rd Brigade.[29]

As Pirch feared, the French soon established that Ransart was the weak point in the Prussian dispositions, being the hinge between the 1st and 2nd Brigades.

The French generals organised their attack from the windmill near the farm of Grand Drieu. At 6 p.m. two batteries opened fire, beginning the battle for Gilly. Pirch saw three columns of infantry advancing in echelon by the right. The first column moved on the wood occupied by the Fusiliers of 6th Regiment, the second on the Prussian centre to the north of Gilly, with the third skirting around the village to the south. The dragoon brigades of Burthe and Bonnemains of Exelmans' corps moved up in support of this attack. One moved on Châtelet, threatening the Prussian left. The other advanced up the cobbled road until it was halted by the barricade.

The fighting had already begun when Pirch II received an order from

[28] Conrady, *Sechsten Infanterie-Regiment*, pp 241–2.
[29] MWBl., vol XXX, p 49.

Zieten to withdraw, which he then tried to carry out. The 6th Regiment's Fusiliers had only just begun to pull back when they were charged by French cavalry. The history of the 6th Regiment described the situation as follows,

> Major von Haine, with our Fusilier Battalion, covered the withdrawal initially with his skirmishers under Kapitain von Wohlgemuth. On the plain behind Gilly, the enemy deployed significant formations of cavalry so the skirmishers were reunited with the main body and the battalion then retired in square.
>
> To the right of our battalion, the Fusilier Battalion of the 28th Regiment also fell back. The enemy cavalry immediately advanced at a trot, so both battalions halted and formed square, about 500 paces from the wood at Lambusart [probably the Bois de Trichehéve]. What now needed to be done was to hold off the cavalry with calmness and determination until the woods were reached. Fortunately, the cavalry was not accompanied by artillery. Major von Haine showed himself an excellent commander in this dangerous situation. He spoke to his fusiliers, called on them to remain calm and finished with the words: "No man is to fire unless I give the order."[30]

The destruction of F./28th was witnessed by the 6th Regiment. Their regimental history also gave a graphic description of that attack and of what followed,

> The cavalry attacked the Fusilier Battalion of the 28th Regiment. It was destroyed by this attack, and cut to pieces in full view of this battalion. This frightening experience however did not shake the Battalion von Haine [F./6th]. A number of men from the broken square sought refuge with this battalion which was now calmly awaiting the cavalry. It was not long before the first attack followed. Major von Haine let them advance to within 30 paces, gave the order to fire, and the Dragoons of the Imperial Guard were repelled in disorder. The subsequent attacks were no more successful as each repulse added to the confidence of our Fusiliers. The enemy cavalry, however, were out of control and carried out one violent attack after the other, all without success and with great loss.
>
> Although they were surrounded by enemy cavalry Major von Haine and his men held them off with the bayonet, and succeeded in reaching the wood of Lambusart just as the enemy infantry were advancing. The wood was occupied by the skirmishers of Lieutenants von Gerdtel and von Diecelski, while the rest of the battalion fell back to the brigade. The skirmishers now came under heavy attack from the enemy infantry. They were extraordinarily brave, holding out for a long time, despite heavy losses. During the action however, they became spread out throughout the wood and many of them failed to hear the signal to withdraw so that when they were eventually pushed back by the enemy infantry, they were taken prisoner by some enemy cavalry, who had moved around the wood in the meantime...

[30] Conrady, *Sechsten Infanterie-Regiment*, p 242.
[31] Conrady, *Sechsten Infanterie-Regiment*, pp 242 f.

Kapitain von Owitzki was killed, Lieutenant Krögelmann fell into the enemy's hands wounded, and the battalion also lost 9 NCOs and 205 fusiliers dead, wounded and missing.[31]

Woiski counter-charged with the 1st West Prussian Dragoons. This allowed the bulk of the infantry to complete its withdrawal through the Bois de Fleurus. Only the Fusiliers of the 28th Regiment failed to escape, losing two-thirds of their men to the Dragoons of the Imperial Guard and a squadron of the 15th Dragoons. The regimental history of the 28th Regiment (a former Berg regiment) described the action,

These were the brigade's positions at 6 p.m. Right in front of their eyes the enemy cavalry corps of Pajol and Exelmans along with large numbers of infantry and artillery crossed the Sambre for the attack. The artillery duel had already begun, as had a skirmish fight in which Major von Quadt had a horse shot from under him, when the order arrived to break off the battle and fall back on Fleurus. This order was made all the more difficult to carry out because the artillery limbered up and then withdrew immediately, leaving the first line of the infantry to withdraw across an open field in front of the French Cavalry Corps. Formed in a closed square, the remaining 600 men of the Fusiliers began the march to the wood to their rear. The French cavalry used this opportunity to make one daring charge after another. The fusiliers halted and faced front each time, courageously throwing back three charges. Although several cavalrymen managed to break into the square, they were all bayoneted.

Even after such a show of resistance, the enemy tried to persuade the troops to change sides. General Letort, commander of the French Guard Dragoons, recognised the Fusiliers by their Berg uniform. He thought that, since the hopelessness of their position would be obvious to them, their loyalty might waver. He rode up and demanded they desert the Prussian Army. A shot rang out and Letort fell dead from his saddle. Fusilier Kaufmann of the 12th Company had leapt out of the square and given the enemy general his answer, in powder and lead.

The battalion continued to withdraw but just before it reached the wood, the enemy cavalry approached again. The 10th Company faced front while the others continued their movement. At this critical moment, the full force of the enemy cavalry charge hit home. In a matter of moments, 120 men lay on the field of battle, including Lieutenants von Mach and Neumann. The 10th Company rallied in groups, kneeling around its officers and opened a lively fire by section. Lieutenant Scherbening, with 20 men around him, let the attacker approach to within a few paces before ordering volley fire, which was most effective. They held on for a long time, but inevitably their resistance grew weaker, until even the very last of them, Sergeant Selbach, succumbed.[32]

The F./28th Regiment lost 13 officers and 614 men that day. The loss of

---

[32] Neff, p 23 ff.

officers was particularly high because their Prussian blue uniforms contrasted with the white of their men, making them stand out as targets for French fire. The next day, the survivors were ordered to don their darker greatcoats so this would not happen again. They were then reorganised into a new 'Combined Battalion' with the survivors of the 3rd Battalion of 2nd Westphalian Landwehr which had suffered heavily on the retreat from Thuin earlier on.

At 6.30 p.m. Pirch II reported again to Steinmetz, 'I am withdrawing, as I am being attacked by superior numbers, and will deploy to the rear of Lambusart where I will link up with my rearguard.'[33]

Zieten then sent the Brandenburg Dragoons in again to support the 2nd Brigade. They charged the French several times, throwing them back and forcing them to break off their attacks. The 2nd Brigade was able to form up in front of the village of Lambusart which was now held by a few battalions from 3rd Brigade. General von Roeder moved up to support them with his three remaining regiments and Horse Battery No. 2. Seeing his advance, the French cavalry fell back, while they in turn brought three horse artillery batteries into play.

The regimental history of the 6th Regiment described this last phase of the day's action,

> The brigade had moved through the wood of Lambusart and deployed in front of this village. Shortly beyond the edge of the wood is a path to the Sambre valley. Here, General von Pirch [II] had placed Major von Rohr with the 1st Battalion to cover the flank of the withdrawal.
>
> The 2nd Battalion relieved the Fusiliers, taking over the rearguard of the brigade. The entire regiment was deployed directly behind the wood. The enemy, meeting such determined resistance, did not stop attempting to pursue, but had to wait for substantial reinforcements of infantry which gave the regiment time to fall back slowly to positions at Lambusart, threatened only by cavalry. From here, the regiment marched via Bault to Fleurus where it was ordered to bivouac at Ligny.
>
> Since 6 a.m. the regiment had fought superior numbers of enemy with great courage and endurance. Totally exhausted, it reached Ligny at 11 p.m.[34]

The 3rd Brigade

The 3rd Brigade was less heavily involved in the fighting than the 1st and 2nd. We have already seen, however, how the 29th Regiment was deployed to assist the 1st Brigade withdrawal. Other units of the brigade had been deployed to cover the crossings of the Sambre east of Charleroi. Among these were the two companies of Silesian Schützen and the F./7th (2nd West Prussian) Regiment in Farciennes and Tamines, covering the left flank of the position at Gilly.

The West Prussians had received their orders from Jagow to fall back about 6 p.m. The F./7th moved through the woods on the left of the Sambre

---

[33] MWBl., vol XXX, p 49.
[34] Conrady, *Sechsten Infanterie-Regiment*, p 243 f.

towards Lambusart, while the rearguard of four skirmish platoons held Farcienne for a time. Once the battalion had all but cleared the wood, French skirmishers suddenly appeared to its rear. Kapitain von Finance immediately took Lieutenant von Casimir's platoon against them, driving them back. The battalion was able to continue its movement unmolested until more French skirmishers came into action. So that Kapitain von Missbach with the rearguard, and the 1st Platoon could finish moving through the wood, Finance and the skirmishers of the 6th Company were sent in support. In the end the battalion was able to withdraw with minimal losses, although the skirmish platoons of Lieutenants Graf Rödern and Merker became separated from the main body. However, by taking to the side roads, were able to rejoin later.[35]

The I. and II./7th Regiment had assembled at Fleurus in the morning. The skirmishers of the 2nd Battalion, commanded by Kapitain von Berg, were sent off to Lambusart where they later linked up with the Fusilier Battalion. The skirmishers of the 1st Battalion, under Kapitain von Witten, occupied the last houses in Fleurus on the Charleroi road, while the 2nd Company covered the exits. The remaining companies were placed in the market place in reserve. Later in the day when the Fusiliers pulled out of Lambusart to Fleurus Berg withdrew his men alongside them.[36]

Night Positions

With this last flurry the day's fighting came to an end. I Army Corps had lost around 1,200 men, half of them from the Fusilier Battalion of the 28th Regiment. The French had lost less than half that number. Though his losses had been greater, Zieten had managed to concentrate his corps in the face of a numerically superior enemy advancing with great determination.

His troops bivouacked as follows:

1st Brigade	South of St Amand, cavalry vedettes towards Heppignies and Mellet.
2nd Brigade	South of Ligny, having been taken out of the front line and placed in reserve.
3rd Brigade	Replaced 2nd Brigade at the front. Occupied Fleurus with two battalions. Outposts were deployed towards Wangenies, Martinrou and Lambusart as well as north of Fleurus with the right flank as far as the cobbled road leading from Fleurus to le Point-du-Jour and Gembloux.
4th Brigade	North of Wanfercée at the farm of Le Fay.
Reserve Cavalry	In the gap between 3rd and 4th Brigades.
Reserve Artillery	Behind 2nd Brigade in Ligny.

Zieten's own station for the night was on the Tombe de Ligny, a mound that provided a vantage point, with his headquarters protected by two 12-pounders, since his pickets could see very little because of the tall crops in

---

[35] Lewinski & Brauchitsch, vol I, p 147–8.
[36] Lewinski & Brauchitsch, vol I, p 148.

which they stood. Lieutenant-Colonel von Reiche, Zieten's chief-of-staff, was concerned about his corps' positions. He considered the position around Fleurus fine for an assembly point, but not suited for a battle. As Reiche wrote,

> The night dragged on and there were still no signs of the arrival of II Corps. I started to become concerned about the possibility that I Corps could find itself caught up in a battle quite alone. I myself had indeed chosen our current position, but under quite other considerations. I started to think it a priority to find a better one.[37]

With Zieten's permission, Reiche rode to Blücher's headquarters, which was now in Sombreffe. Here, he told Gneisenau his worries, asking for permission to fall back over the Ligne stream immediately. Gneisenau refused. He said there was little to gain from disturbing I Corps' rest, since the French would themselves be exhausted by the day's fighting. They would not make a further move until the morning and when they did I Corps would have to cover the assembly of the remainder of the army in the Sombreffe position. To do so, it would have to remain in its current positions. Besides, Gneisenau said, he was also anxious not to give his Allies the wrong impression. As Reiche reported their conversation,

> General Gneisenau stated with conviction that, even though it was isolated, I Army Corps had to accept battle to allow the army to concentrate. A withdrawal over the Ligne brook could not in any event be allowed, since this would risk the English taking such a movement to be an intention to fall back to the Rhine, and themselves retire to Antwerp and embark in their ships.[38]

Blücher's Decisions

Even before he had definite news from the front that the French had actually begun to advance Blücher had responded to the threat with a promptness and decision that contrasts greatly with the Duke of Wellington's reaction over the hours to come. He sent out orders at 11.30 p.m. on the 14th to II Army Corps to concentrate at Onoz and Mazy during the 15th and to III Army Corps to assemble similarly at Namur. The matching order to IV Army Corps was sent by Gneisenau to Bülow from Namur at midnight of 14/15 June 1815 and is worth quoting in some detail

> I have the honour of humbly beseeching Your Excellency to attempt to concentrate the IV Army Corps in Hannut tomorrow, 15th of the month, in close cantonments. Incoming reports make it ever more probable that the French army has assembled before us, and that an offensive can be expected at any moment.
>
> I also beseech Your Excellency to instruct the commandant of Liège that as from tomorrow, troops or personnel marching to join the army are not to be directed via Huy and Namur, but instead on the left bank of the Meuse, along the old Roman road.

[37] Weltzien, *Reiche*, vol 2, p 171.   [39] Ollech, p 91.
[38] Weltzien, *Reiche*, vol 2, p 172.

Also, it would be advisable to send any sick in the quarters of IV Corps back to Aachen. I would also beseech Your Excellency to instruct the commandant of Liège at the same time to empty the hospitals of Liège as far as is possible, and have the sick sent back to Aachen and Jülich.

For the time being, the Field Marshal's headquarters will remain in Namur. Your Excellency may find it advisable to move your headquarters to Hannut. I would then beseech Your Excellency to set up communication posts between here and Hannut so that we may communicate by letter.[39]

Gneisenau's extremely polite and careful way of addressing Bülow is quite different to the tone he used with other corps commanders. The reason for this is that Bülow was senior to Gneisenau in the Prussian Army. Gneisenau had to request Bülow to carry out an instruction, he could not insist. There is also little emphasis in the wording of the message on the urgency of the situation. This was to have serious repercussions, which will be explained in Chapter 11.

We have already seen how Zieten's first action on being awakened by the noise of the French attack was to send off warning messages to Blücher and Wellington. Zieten's news reached Blücher in Namur at 8.30 a.m. The message read,

Since 4.30 a.m. several cannon shots and now musketry have been heard on our right flank. I have received no reports. As soon as these arrive, I will not neglect humbly to forward them to Your Highness. I have ordered my entire force to the position at Charleroi. If need be, I will concentrate at Fleurus.[40]

At 9 a.m. Blücher had Grolman write the following reply,

I have just received Your Excellency's report of 4.30 this morning that cannon and musket fire have been heard. Last night, I already ordered the II, III and IV Corps to concentrate. II Corps is to concentrate at Onoz and Mazy, III Corps at Namur and IV Corps at Hannut. The corps will have taken up those positions by this evening. Today, it is of prime importance that Your Excellency observe every movement of the enemy so as to recognise the direction and strength of his columns. Take special notice of the area of Binche and the Roman road. Your Excellency is to note the exact time of despatch on his reports.[41]

Blücher's headquarters continued to be active for all of that day. At 11 a.m. the Field Marshal had Grolman send the following message to Zieten, confirming how his plans were developing,

I request Your Excellency to execute your movements in such a way that you do not, if possible, fall back farther than Fleurus today, as I am planning to concentrate my army around Sombreffe tomorrow. I will be transferring my headquarters to Sombreffe.[42]

[40] Ollech, p 96.
[41] Ollech, p 96 f.
[42] Ollech, p 99.

At 11.30 a.m. Blücher then sent new orders to carry out this concentration to Bülow, commander of the IV Army Corps,

> This morning, the enemy commenced hostilities. He is pushing back the outposts of I Corps with force on Charleroi. Buonaparte himself is present with his Guard. I therefore request Your Excellency, as soon as your corps has enjoyed the necessary rest in Hannut, to break camp tomorrow morning, at dawn at the latest, and to march in the direction of Gembloux, informing me of the exact time of your arrival. I will move my headquarters today to Sombreffe where I expect further reports.[43]

Around the same time, the II Army Corps was also commencing its concentration. The Silesian Uhlan Regiment, for example, received news of the outbreak of hostilities and orders to commence moving just after having finished its morning exercises. It had completed its preparations by 2 p.m. and began its march to Onoz at once.[44]

By moving on Sombreffe in these ways, Blücher was carrying out his part of the agreement reached with Wellington at Tirlemont on 3 May. The Duke, by contrast, did not issue orders to do so until that evening. In view of the wide dispersal of his troops, such inaction by Wellington would have very serious consequences. How and when news of the attack reached Wellington and what communications there were between the British and the Prussians during that day will be discussed in the next chapter but messages sent elsewhere by Blücher late in the day provide further evidence of his intentions at that time.

At 10 p.m. that night Blücher sent a report on the day's events to Schwarzenberg, in the Austrian headquarters in Heidelberg. This read,

> I wish most humbly to draw to Your Highness' attention that hostilities against me by the French have begun. I am told that five army corps and the Guard are moving against me. The enemy has pushed forward to Fleurus, advancing via Charleroi. By daybreak tomorrow my army will be concentrated in this area. There is now longer any doubt that the main enemy forces are moving against the Netherlands. Thus, it is all the more safe for the armies on the Rhine to continue their operations. I hope that current circumstances will accelerate these operations.
>
> At the time of writing I have yet to receive any news from the Duke of Wellington. However, his left flank was engaged in combat today, so it seems as if the enemy intends to push between the Duke's army and mine.[45]

The same day that this news arrived in Heidelberg, Lord Stewart, the British representative at the Austrian headquarters, wrote to another British diplomat. This letter contained even more detailed information than the report above, so it is evident that Blücher sent a further message to Heidelberg. Part of this letter reads,

---

[43] Ollech, p 99.
[44] Dziengel, p 385.
[45] Ollech, p 105 f.

The News just arrived is, that Blücher's advance [guard] of a Battalion of Landwehr at Thuin and Lob[bes] was attacked on 15th by 5 Corps d'Armée, the Prussian Troops were still in Cantonments, the French shewed an immense Force of Cavalry and Artillery. The Landwehr made a good resistance and allowed time for the Prussian Troops in the Cantonments to collect. Blücher fell back on Sombref, where he had on the 15th 2 Corps d'armée before the night of that day, 2 other Corps in the rear could not have joined him, he would then have above 100,000 collected. The enemy moved at the same time in Force from Phillippeville into Charleroi which they possessed themselves and established themselves on the Sambre. No direct intelligence had reached Blücher of the Duke of Wellington, but his left was attacked on the same day. It is believed he was collecting at Soignées. The movement of the Enemy seems evidently to force the Centre, separating the 2 Armies. If nothing disastrous occurs on 16th the position of the French between both Wellington & Blücher on the 17th may make them bitterly repent their boldness. Blücher writes [he is] determined to attack the 17th when he is sure that Wellington will do the same.[46]

This document contains several important and significant items of information. It is evident that Blücher intended initially to fight a defensive battle in the Sombreffe position with all that he could assemble of his army. He intended to hold this position on 16 June, and then, once Wellington had assembled all his forces, and Bülow had arrived, to go over to the offensive on 17 June.

At 11.30 p.m. Blücher sent a report to his king finally setting the scene for the next day,

Your most humble servant wishes to report to Your Majesty that the enemy commenced hostilities today. He advanced on the Sambre at 4.30 this morning and has taken possession of Charleroi. I Corps under General von Zieten fell back fighting to the area around Fleurus. At the moment, it is holding the terrain around Heppignies and Lambusart. II and III Corps will join me here around Sombreffe tomorrow morning. IV Corps will be here by tomorrow afternoon. I still do not have any news of events affecting the army of the Duke of Wellington. However, the enemy appears to have pushed forward as far as Frasnes on the Charleroi to Brussels road. Tomorrow will decide if the enemy will turn against me or the Duke of Wellington. Tomorrow will in any case be the decisive day.[47]

So ended the day for the Prussian headquarters in which Napoleon had begun his offensive. Blücher had ordered an immediate concentration of his army around Sombreffe as agreed with Wellington at Tirlemont on 3 May. By the end of the day one corps was covering this position and two more corps were close to reaching it and would do so the next day. The IV Corps had been sent its orders, though unknown to Blücher these had not arrived. Müffling, and through him Wellington, had been informed of the movements and the

---

[46] BL, Add MS 20,114, fol 112.
[47] Ollech, p 106.

transfer of headquarters to the front at Sombreffe. Reports had been sent to the Prussian king and to the most important of the other allies. The Prussians had every reason to believe that they were ready to implement their part of the Allied plan on schedule.

Chapter 10

The Breakthrough to Frasnes

The Delay at Brussels

Chapter 8 showed how, by the evening of 14 June, the information available in Wellington's headquarters suggested that the French offensive would begin the next morning and that the main thrust would be against the Prussians. As a consequence, Wellington had gone so far as to assure the Prussians he would be able to concentrate his army either at Nivelles or Quatre Bras within 22 hours of the first cannon shot and had already had the orders drawn up for such a concentration.

Further information that made this picture even more definite soon arrived on the morning of the 15th. Around midnight of the 14th/15th, Zieten sent a report to Wellington, received in Brussels about 7 a.m. on the 15th, that numerous campfires before his positions confirmed a large concentration of French forces.[1]

Müffling reported the mood in Brussels that morning in a letter to Blücher,

> General Dörnberg's reports have confirmed those sent by Lieutenant-General von Zieten yesterday. I attach a copy of one of these [Dörnberg's second report of the 14th[2]] herewith. The French newspaper reports indicate that Napoleon left Paris on the night of 11 to 12 June. It is not known where he went. As we were not attacked yesterday, it seems that the enemy wants only to mislead us by masking his front to hide the movements he really intends.
>
> The King of France said to [an officer], who came here yesterday, that he had reports of significant successes of the Royalists in the Vendée, and that they had taken Angers but Napoleon himself has sent the Young Guard there, so it is feared that the Vendée will be crushed before we begin. If this is really true, it could be that Napoleon wants to attract our attention, perhaps to make us take up a central position around St Menehould with the main army, so as to be able to attack us, the Austrians and the Russians.
>
> The Anglo-Netherlands army is, according to the attached order-of-battle, drawn up in such a way that the two flank corps under Lord Hill and the Prince of Orange are positioned from Enghien via Braine-le-Comte to Nivelle[s] and can be concentrated in a short time. The corps of the centre, better called the reserve, is in and around Brussels, has 15,000 infantry, and can move in any direction.

[1] Gleig, *Life of Wellington*, pp 258–9.
[2] Quoted earlier on p 156.

Should the enemy invade between the sea and the Schelde [Scheldt], the army will be able to move to the offensive over the Schelde [Scheldt] at two points (where there are bridgeheads). Should the enemy advance on the right bank of the Meuse, the Duke is prepared either to move with us against him, or (as I have suggested to him in certain circumstances) to move on the rear of the enemy through the French fortresses.[3]

However, even before this letter was sent, Wellington's headquarters had already had more accurate information. Zieten's account, quoted on page 170, tells how he had been awakened by the noise of the French attack early that morning and immediately sent off news of the outbreak of hostilities to Blücher and Wellington.

Zieten's memory seems to have been at fault on one or two details of this. We know from his own account elsewhere that he was the only person in his headquarters proficient in French (the only common language with Wellington's staff), and that he wrote every communication to the Duke personally. Those communications to Wellington from Zieten preserved in the Wellington Papers are indeed in French and apparently in Zieten's hand[4] so it is unlikely that he dictated this message as his later account says.

This lapse of memory also helps explain why the exact time when this message was sent is a little uncertain. The printed version of Zieten's Journal states 2 a.m. As the French were still in bed at that time, this is clearly an error of some kind, perhaps a hand-written '2' being mistaken for a '5'. Zieten wrote a letter on this subject in 1819 in which he gives the time he heard the cannon shots to be 3.45 a.m. This also seems to be incorrect, as Zieten's message to Blücher gives the time when the firing started as 4.30. It seems most likely, therefore, that Zieten's messages to Blücher and the Duke were written and dispatched after 4.30, probably by about 5 a.m.

The despatch sent to Wellington has not been preserved in the Wellington Papers, but there seems little doubt that it was sent since, as well as the reference in Zieten's Journal, it is mentioned in a report Zieten sent to Blücher at 8.15 a.m. In this report Zieten says,

> I have informed the Duke of Wellington of the situation, and requested him to concentrate at Nivelles. According to a report received from General von Müffling yesterday, he would be willing to do this.[5]

Zieten's 5 a.m. message to Blücher had a little over 30 km to travel to Namur and arrived at around 8.30 a.m.[6] That timing is consistent with the rule of thumb in those days that a mounted courier could travel 10 km to 15 km an hour, depending on distance, weather conditions and changes of horses. The message to Wellington, travelling roughly 50 km, seems to have taken about four hours and arrived by 9 a.m.

There are a a number of inconsistencies in the Duke of Wellington's own accounts of exactly when he received the news. Writing to the Duke of Feltre

3 Pflugk-Harttung, *Vorgeschichte*, p 47 f.
4 See WP 1/466 for examples of this.
5 GStA, Rep 92, Gneisenau A 48, fol 32.

6 De Bas & T'Serclaes de Wommersom, vol I, p 375.

at 10 p.m. that evening he indicated that he had heard this news about 9 a.m. that day.[7] However, when writing his report to Bathurst on 19 June, he claimed that he '...did not hear of these events till in the evening of the 15th'[8] In his *Life of Wellington*, Gleig, an admirer and associate of the Duke, explained, presumably from information received from Wellington himself, that,

> Intelligence came in from Charleroi, at seven that morning... that in the morning the outposts at Lobbès [sic] and Thuin had been attacked. But no further tidings followed, and the Duke naturally assumed that this was a feint to cover some serious operations elsewhere.[9]

There is further evidence the early arrival of this news in other accounts. Basil Jackson, then a lieutenant on Wellington's staff, recalled that, 'Early on the 15th June 1815, we learned that the French were crossing the frontier at Charleroi.'[10] The recollection of Lieutenant-Colonel Scovell, Wellington's head of military communications, also supports this view. In his 'Memorandum of Service at the Battle of Waterloo' Scovell states 'On the 15th, about 3 o'clock p.m. there no longer remained any doubt on the subject... ',[11] which must mean that Wellington did receive the news earlier, but had doubts as to its importance until 3 p.m.

In his 'Memorandum on the Battle of Waterloo', written in 1842, Wellington gave a rather different version of what happened. Wellington was replying in this document to criticisms of his handling of the campaign made in recent posthumously-published writings by Carl von Clausewitz. He was insistent about the time at which he first heard of the attack on Zieten,

> It appears by the statement of the historian [Clausewitz] that the posts of the Prussian corps of General Zieten were attacked at Thuin at four o'clock on the morning of the 15th; and that General Zieten himself, with a part of the corps, retreated and was at Charleroi at about ten o'clock on that day; yet the report thereof was not received at Bruxelles till three o'clock in the afternoon.[12]

Yet even this statement conflicts with others made by the Duke which suggests that his testimony on this issue cannot be regarded as reliable. One of the most thorough investigations of the matter was conducted by the historian William Siborne, who had the advantage of working when most of the leading participants were still alive and could be contacted. In the third edition of his *History* his conclusion is unequivocal, 'His [Zieten's] report to the Duke of Wellington arrived in Brussels at 9 o'clock in the morning.'[13] Thus, there seems little doubt as to when Wellington did receive this news and that he simply did not take it as seriously as he should have done.

The Duke's response was certainly very different from Blücher's. Blücher

[7] WD, vol XII, p 473.
[8] WD, vol XII, p 478.
[9] Gleig, *Life of Wellington*, pp 258–9
[10] Jackson, p 12.
[11] PRO, WO 37/12, fol 2.

[12] Wellington, vol X, p 524.
[13] Siborne, *History*, p 36. The correspondence that led Siborne to this conclusion can be found in BL Add MS 34,708, fols 263–74, 280 and 284–7.

had already ordered the assembly of his remaining three corps and now developed this plan into a concentration of his whole force towards Sombreffe. Wellington did nothing, even though, as we have seen, appropriate orders had already been prepared.

The atmosphere of tension that existed in the Duke's headquarters the day before seems to have given way to a sense of absolute calm and normality. Wellington wrote Clinton a letter discussing the renumbering of the army's divisions.[14] This was followed by a long letter to the Czar of Russia discussing the general military situation.[15] Even Müffling, who was evidently not informed of the news by Wellington, was overcome by this atmosphere. He wrote the rather complacent letter quoted on p 192 above and then, acting on behalf of Blücher, took up matters such as the uniform a Captain von Scharnhorst should be wearing, the issue of British supplies of arms to the Prussian army and other similarly vital topics.[16]

It seems incredible that while Zieten's men were hard pressed trying to hold back a substantial assault from the French army, Müffling's account shows Wellington relying more on information from the French court and his informants than the overwhelming evidence of the French offensive gathered by his outposts. It is difficult to be sure what the real reason for the Duke's hesitation was. What is certain is that he dallied, either believing that Napoleon was actually going to retire from the frontier, or because he was waiting for news from Paris.

At 3 p.m. the Duke started to question his earlier decision to ignore the reports of French movements when further news of the French offensive arrived in Brussels. These reports were addressed to the Prince of Orange and Müffling, the message to the former announcing the outbreak of hostilities, that to the latter reporting the capture of Charleroi and the crossing of the Sambre. It was now clear to Wellington that the news was known to others, and that a reaction on his part was required.

The information received by the Prince of Orange was originally sent by Steinmetz to Major-General van Merlen's headquarters in St Symphorien, arriving there at 8 a.m.[17] Thence, it was forwarded to Dörnberg at Mons, who received it at 9.30 a.m.[18] It may seem surprising that the Anglo-Netherlands headquarters nearest the point where the French offensive began should be so slow to hear of it. However, the atmospheric conditions prevented the sound of the French cannonade from reaching even the right wing of Steinmetz's own brigade. Thus Major von Arnauld, the officer Steinmetz sent to communicate the news to his Allies, had to spend time spreading the alarm among the Prussian outposts he passed along his route. That was why Arnauld only arrived in St Symphorien at 8 a.m.

As soon as this information had been passed to Mons Dörnberg sent it on immediately to Braine-le-Comte, where it arrived around midday.

---

14 WD, vol XII, p 469 f.

15 WD, vol XII, p 470 ff.

16 GStA, Rep 92, Gneisenau, A 40, fols 94–6.

17 BL Add MS 34,708, fol 265.

18 WSD, vol X, p 481.

Wellington's representative there, Lieutenant-Colonel Sir George Berkeley then did nothing for two hours. At 2 p.m. Berkeley at last passed the message on to Brussels. He explained the delay as follows,

> H.R.H. the Prince of Orange having set out at 5 o'clock this morning for the advanced posts, and not being returned, I forward the enclosed letter from General Dörnberg. General Constans desires I would inform you that the reports just arrived from different quarters state that the Prussians have been attacked upon their line in front of Charleroi; that they have evacuated Binch[e], and mean to collect first at Gosselies. Everything is quiet upon our front... [19]

Fortunately, Major-General Baron Behr, commandant of the outpost at Mons, had already communicated the situation to the Prince of Orange in Brussels with his despatch of 10.30 a.m. which arrived around 3 p.m.[20] This letter included the following information,

> ...2nd Prussian Brigade was attacked this morning. Alarm cannons have been fired along the entire line. It appears the attack is directed on Charleroi where the musketry is very heavy.
> All is quiet at General van Merlen's outposts.
> P.S. The outposts before Mons are also very quiet.[21]

Even regiments at some distance from the front came to hear of the events that morning. The (British) 1st Guards at Enghien were brought, '... the information of the passage of the river [Sambre] by Napoleon, and of his attack upon the Prussians... by a dragoon about two o'clock on the same afternoon [15 June].'[22] It is unclear from this account if the message arrived from Brussels, or from elsewhere, perhaps Braine-le-Comte. It is possible that it may have come from Brussels since Fitzroy Somerset, Wellington's military secretary, was an officer in this prestigious regiment and could have passed on the news.

Müffling seems to have received two important reports that afternoon. The reports were one sent by Zieten from Charleroi which arrived at about 3 p.m., and one from Blücher from Namur which arrived later, but some time before 6 p.m. There is some uncertainty about the timings since Müffling's own version of events is rather vague,

> On 15 June, when General von Zieten was attacked before Charleroi, thus opening the war, he sent an officer to me who arrived in Brussels at 3 p.m.
> Later, the same report of the opening of hostilities, coming from Charleroi via Namur, arrived a second time here. The Field Marshal informed me of his concentration at Sombreffe and ordered me to give him news of the concentration of Wellington's army as quickly as possible.

---

[19] WSD, vol X, p 480.
[20] De Bas & T'Serclaes de Wommersom, vol I, p 388; WSD, vol X, p 524.
[21] WSD, vol X, p 481 gives the text. De Bas & T'Serclaes de Wommersom, vol I, p 388 gives the time of its dispatch.
[22] Hamilton, vol. III, pp 14–5.

I informed the Duke of this immediately. He was in full agreement with Field Marshal Blücher's arrangements.[23]

It is important to emphasise that the earlier of these messages was the first that Müffling had heard of the day's events, as the earlier reports sent to Wellington had not been forwarded to him.

There is some doubt which message from Zieten was the one that was actually the first Müffling received. We know that shortly after 10 a.m. Zieten reported the news of the assault on Charleroi at least to Namur and this report may also have been sent to Brussels. Logically, Zieten would have made his next report after this only once there had been a significant change in circumstances, such as the fall of Charleroi. Zieten later wrote that, after sending this message, he had time to have some breakfast,[24] before Charleroi fell at around 11 a.m. His report of this event may be the one Müffling refers to. Certainly an arrival at 3 p.m. is consistent with a ride of four hours or so from Charleroi.

Both the timing and the content of the message are confirmed by Captain John Gurwood of the 10th Hussars, later the editor of Wellington's published *Dispatches*, who mentioned,

> I recollect the account of the passage of the Sambre at Charleroi having arrived at Bruxelles about dinner time on the 15th [To the British officers of this period 'dinner' was a meal taken in the afternoon, as the next quotation also notes. We know that Wellington himself dined at 3 p.m. that day.], for I was then at HQ... [25]

However, as Wellington himself appeared to have been unaware of the fact that the French had crossed the Sambre until later – certainly in his letters to the Dukes of Berri and Feltre that evening, timed at 9.30 p.m. and 10 p.m. respectively, he gave no indication of knowing this – it is possible that Müffling did not communicate all his information to the Duke.

There is further confirmation of the timing at least in the account of an officer of General Sir Thomas Picton's 5th Division who was also in Brussels,

> About three o'clock of the afternoon of that day, our officers were sitting at Dinner at the Hotel de Tirlemont, where we had our mess, when we heard of a commotion, or greater stir than usual, having arisen in the city; presently some Belgian gentleman came in and told us, that there had been "an affair of posts" on the frontier, and that the French suffered a repulse. This was the picquet affair of the Prussian General Ziethen, who had gallantly resisted the enemy's advanced guard, coming in the direction of the grande chaussée to Brussels, but was driven back, or fell back, as all outposts do, as a matter of course.[26]

The second report that Müffling received was one sent from Blücher's headquarters at noon which arrived before 6 p.m. This read,

[23] Müffling, *Leben*, p. 228.
[24] Hafner, p. 253.
[25] BL Add Ms 34,706, fols 460–1.
[26] *USJ*, 1841, Part II, p. 172.

This morning at 4.30, the enemy opened hostilities and is advancing in force down the Sambre. Buonaparte and his Guards are said to be there. The latter certainly are. General Zieten has been ordered to observe the enemy and, if possible, not to fall back farther than Fleurus. Tomorrow, the army will be concentrated at Sombreffe, where the Prince [Blücher] desires to accept battle. Last night, the three army corps received orders to concentrate as follows: II Corps at Onoz and Mazy, III Corps at Namur, IV at Hannut. It is necessary that II Corps advances as far as Sombreffe today, III Corps to Onoz. Headquarters is moving to Sombreffe in two hours. Here, I expect from you as quickly as possible a report on where and when the Duke of Wellington is concentrating, and what he has decided. A line of communication via Genappe is now to be opened.[27]

Namur is about 60 km from Brussels so a journey time of five hours or so is entirely reasonable but again there is other evidence as to when this report arrived. The same officer of Picton's division quoted above continued his account,

After dinner we strolled, as was our custom in the afternoon, into the park, where the great world promenaded every evening. Towards six o'clock, sauntering about the walks, I encountered two Prussian aides-de-camp, who had come from Blücher with intelligence of the advance of the French army, pointing towards Brussels, or in that direction; we were instantly ordered to hold ourselves in readiness to march to the front in the morning.

About seven o'clock, the orderlies were seen flying about with their books, that there might be "no mistake," each in search of his own officer, to show him the orders.[28]

There are several interesting observations to make on the build up of tension in Brussels that afternoon. Rumours of the commencement of hostilities had certainly spread throughout Brussels by about 3 p.m. That, too, would confirm that the news had indeed arrived there earlier in the day. These matters will be discussed in more detail later in this book.

Blücher's message showed that he was clearly intending to gather his entire army in the Sombreffe position and offer battle there. He urgently needed to know what Wellington's plans were because he knew that he would be able to do little more than fight a defensive action himself. The Allies could only defeat Napoleon if they acted in concert. With all four of his corps in a defensive position, it was likely that the Prussians could hang on for long enough for the Duke to bring his forces into play. However, up to the time when this message arrived, the Duke had done nothing, and his troops would not begin their march to the front until the next day.

Müffling's account of his conversations with Wellington on the afternoon of 15 June contain several mentions of the Duke's fixation with Mons. Wellington waited, expecting to hear from other sources that the main French

---

[27] Ollech, p 99 f.
[28] *USJ*, 1841, Part II, p 172.

thrust was going to be via Mons after all. As Müffling noted the Duke telling him,

> If part of the enemy does come via Mons, then I must concentrate more to my centre. This is the reason why I must await the report from Mons before I determine my rendezvous.[29]

The Duke seemed simply unable to believe that the main French thrust was coming via Charleroi and only began to change his mind when he had received information to that effect from every one of his own sources, particularly Berkeley. He did not take the reports from the Prussians and Netherlanders too seriously. Only when the Duke had confirmation from an Englishman, did he start to react. Berkeley's delayed despatch arrived in Brussels some time before 6 p.m. and Wellington finally began issuing orders between 6 p.m. and 7 p.m. What effect these orders had and how accurately they were communicated to Blücher will be discussed in the next chapter.

The Netherlands Headquarters

The Netherlands' headquarters at Braine-le-Comte had certainly not been idle. While Wellington was renumbering his divisions, catching up on his paperwork, ignoring intelligence from the Prussians and enjoying a good lunch, his Netherlands allies were gathering their forces together to counter the French threat. Its is fortunate that they showed so much initiative, otherwise matters would have been much worse for the Allies.

At around midday, shortly after having received news of the opening of hostilities, Constant Rebeque began issuing orders for the concentration of the Netherlands forces, a task that became more urgent when further news reached him.

Baron Chassé, commander of the Netherlands 3rd Division, sent the following message from Haine La Pierre at 11 a.m.,

> We have received certain news that the enemy has crossed our border. The Prussians have evacuated Binche. The division has assembled at Fayt and is awaiting further orders from His Royal Highness.[30]

There was also a despatch from Major de Paravicini, on Merlen's staff at St Symphorien, repeating the news from Steinmetz. This message read,

> ...General Steinmetz has just sent me an officer to inform me that the 2nd Prussian Brigade was attacked this morning... alarm cannons have been firing along the entire front. Heavy musket fire has been directed on Charleroi. The Prussians intend shortly to evacuate Binche and the neighbouring villages to take positions with their brigade behind the Piéton river at Gosselies. Should they be forced back from there, their army corps will take up positions at Fleurus.[31]

---

29 Müffling, *Leben*, p 229.
30 De Bas & T'Serclaes de Wommersom, vol I, p 393.
31 De Bas & T'Serclaes de Wommersom, vol I, p 394.

By 3 p.m. Constant Rebeque had issued his orders. General Perponcher, commander of the 2nd Netherlands Division in Nivelles was instructed,

> His Royal Highness has charged me to write to you that on receipt of the present message, you are to assemble your division as rapidly as possible. You will keep one brigade ready for action on the paved road at Nivelles. The other is to be placed at Quatre Bras. These dispositions are to be maintained until you receive further orders from His Royal Highness.[32]

Collaert, the cavalry commander at Boussoit-sur-Haine, was also mobilised,

> H.R.H. the Prince of Orange has charged me to request you to assemble immediately General de Ghigny's 1st Brigade of light cavalry at Havré, and General Trip's brigade of carabineers behind Strépy where they are to await further orders. This morning, His Royal Highness gave General van Merlen orders concerning his brigade.[33]

Thus, while his Netherlands troops started to concentrate, the Duke of Wellington had yet to react.

Following the general orders of 7 May and 9 June Perponcher had routinely assembled his men in their cantonments of the morning of 15 June. According to this plan the 1st Brigade's positions covered the road from Binche to Nivelles, while the 2nd watched that from Charleroi to Brussels. The 1st Brigade, on receipt of its new orders, was able to take up the positions it had been assigned virtually immediately. The 5th Militia Battalion south of Obaix provided the outposts covering the main body. The remaining battalions and Battery Stevenart were around Nivelles. The 27th Jager Battalion was held in reserve in Nivelles, on the Place Saint-Paul. Small detachments covered the approaches.

The 2nd Brigade was made up of Nassauers. Colonel von Goedecke, the appointed brigade commander, had been injured several days previously by a horse kick, and been replaced temporarily by his aide-de-camp. The aide did not think he was up to his new responsibilities and around midday on the 15th he wrote to Perponcher asking to be relieved by Duke Bernhard of Saxe-Weimar, commander of the Nassau-Orange Regiment. This change was confirmed later in the day. The two battalions of the Nassau-Orange Regiment were then in Genappe, Bergmann's volunteers at Thines, the I./2nd Nassau Light Infantry under Captain Büsgen at Houtain-le-Val, III./2nd under Major Hegmann at Sart-Dame-Avelines, and II./2nd under Major de Normann and Bijleveld's horse artillery battery at Frasnes. Normann's battalion provided the outposts.

The Combat at Frasnes

During the morning of 15 June, the pickets before Frasnes and Houtain-le-Val heard numerous cannon shots coming from the direction of Charleroi. They

---

[32] De Bas & T'Serclaes de Wommersom, vol I, p 395 f.
[33] ibid.

took little notice of this, as the Prussians had indulged in firing practice several days previously. No news came to Frasnes, Genappe or Nivelles of a French offensive at this point.[34] However, around midday, the outposts at Frasnes saw local farmers moving their families and possessions on their waggons and driving their livestock before them, as fast as they could towards Genappe and Nivelles. At little later, they saw clouds of dust from the south. At about 3 p.m. cannon and musket fire were heard coming from the direction of Jumet. These were clear indications that something serious was happening.

Bijleveld first ordered his guns harnessed up and then a little later, he had his waggons harnessed, too. Normann reinforced his pickets on the Charleroi–Brussels road, as well as those thrown out towards Rèves and Liberchies. He placed one company in the village of Frasnes. and deployed the remainder of his battalion and the battery on the heights to the north, near the road. Bijleveld set up two of his guns on the road itself, three to the right, and three to the left on the crest of a knoll, covering the ground to the south. It was now around 3.15 p.m.

Around the same time, Normann sent a horse artilleryman to Genappe to warn Major Sattler, his regimental commander, and a Captain de Mahlmann, to Perponcher in Nivelles. Mahlmann arrived at divisional headquarters around 4 p.m., just before Constant Rebeque's 3 p.m. orders also got there.

Duke Bernhard of Saxe-Weimar, at Houtain-le-Val, then heard from a gendarmerie officer coming from Genappe that it was certainly true that the French were marching north from Charleroi. The Duke, realising the urgency of the situation, immediately issued his own orders for his battalions, already assembled in their cantonments, to concentrate at Quatre Bras. He spoke to his battalion commanders, saying: 'Gentlemen, I have been given no orders whatsoever, but I have never heard of a campaign beginning with a retreat, so let us make a stand at Quatre Bras.'[35] Duke Bernhard then informed Perponcher of his movements and the position of his brigade. The brigade was concentrated at Quatre Bras by between 6.30 p.m. and 7 p.m.

When he reached Quatre Bras, Duke Bernhard found I. and III./2nd Nassau Regiment had also just arrived there. He placed some of these troops in the farm buildings south of the road junction that gave Quatre Bras its name and some in the Bossu Wood to the south-west where they linked up with the 2nd Battalion. The rest of the two newly-arrived battalions were placed east of Quatre Bras. Shortly thereafter, firing was heard coming from Frasnes.

About 6.30 p.m., the pickets of II./2nd Nassau Regiment on the Charleroi road south of Frasnes observed French cavalry advancing directly towards them and to their left. These were some of General Colbert's 'Red Lancers', part of Napoleon's Imperial Guard. Only a few of them approached the Allied positions at first, but when more arrived they attacked. Some dismounted and gave fire support with their carbines, others moved forward on horseback. The Nassauers' picket was driven back. Normann sent the flank company under

---

34 De Bas & T'Serclaes de Wommersom, vol I, p 399.
35 Starklof, vol I, p 182.

Forces around Frasnes on the Afternoon of 15 June 1815

2nd Netherlands Division   Lieutenant-General Perponcher
Headquarters in Nivelles

1st Brigade
Headquarters in Nivelles

27th Jager Battalion			
in Nivelles		23 officers	786 men
7th Line Battalion			
in Feluy, Arquennes and Petit Rœulx		23 officers	678 men
5th Militia Battalion			
in Obaix and Buzet		22 officers	460 men
7th Militia Battalion			
in Nivelles and Baulers		24 officers	651 men
8th Militia Battalion			
in Monstreux and Bornival		23 officers	543 men
Horse Battery			
in Frasnes	8 guns	7 officers	104 men
Train			
in Frasnes		2 officers	110 men

2nd Brigade
Headquarters in Houtain-le-Val

1st Battalion Nassau Regiment			
in Houtain-le-Val, Vieux-Genappes and Loupoigne		30 officers	895 men
2nd Battalion Regiment			
in Frasnes and Villers-Perwin		28 officers	857 men
3rd Battalion Regiment			
in Baisy and Sart-Dame-Avelines		28 officers	871 men
1st Battalion Nassau-Orange Regiment			
in Bousval, Thy and Glabais		22 officers	666 men
2nd Battalion Nassau-Orange Regiment			
in Genappe and Ways		28 officers	865 men
Volunteer Jäger			
in Thines		5 officers	172 men
Foot Battery			
in Nivelles	8 guns	3 officers	116 men
Train			
in Nivelles		2 officers	137 men
Total	16 guns	270 officers	7,907 men

Based on: Pflugk-Harttung, *Vorgeschichte*, p 294;
De Bas & T'Serclaes de Wommersom, vol III, p 96 f.

Captain Müller with the volunteer detachment under Lieutenant Höelschen to support the threatened picket. The main body of the battalion and the artillery stayed to the north of the village and a few rounds from Bijleveld's guns deterred the Lancers from making any further forward movement for the time being.

Lefebvre-Desnoëttes, the French commander, saw that it would not be possible for his cavalry to force the Netherlanders from their positions without help and therefore called for infantry support. The first available infantry were from 5th Division, commanded by General Bachelu. They did not reach the outskirts of Frasnes until at least 9 p.m. Bachelu's troops, the 11th, 61st, 72nd and 108th Line Regiments, numbered over 4,000 men but had marched some 40 km since leaving Leers that morning. And as well as covering that 40 km to Frasnes on poor roads on a hot day, they had been almost continuously engaged in combat. They were exhausted.

While the vanguard clashed with the Nassau outposts, Colbert bypassed Frasnes to the east with a squadron of the Lancers of the Guard. They advanced almost as far as Quatre Bras before being stopped by the Nassau infantry. The remainder of the French cavalry approached Frasnes parallel to the main road from Charleroi but a little way to the east. Only the fire from Bijleveld's artillery battery prevented them from moving any farther in that direction though the French line soon extended east in the direction of Villiers-Perwin.

Normann was concerned that this sort of flanking movement might cut his men off from the main position at Quatre Bras and therefore ordered a withdrawal towards the farm of Gemioncourt and the wood of Bossu, just south of Quatre Bras itself and where the rest of the brigade was deployed. Normann accomplished the move in good order with the pursuing French chasseurs and Red Lancers being deterred by his fire and that of Bijleveld's battery.

The Nassau infantry and the Netherlands horse battery lost 1 officer, 39 men and 30 horses that day.[36] The Guard Lancers lost some 29 troopers and 30 horses in this combat.[37]

Night fell. The French did not push farther because they were uncertain how strong the forces facing them were. The undulations in the ground and the woods hindered reconnaissance and the French cavalry lacked infantry and artillery support. When Lefebvre-Desnoëttes reported the results of his reconnaissance he seemed to believe he was up against a much stronger force than was really the case. Napoleon had put the French forces approaching Quatre Bras under the command of Marshal Ney earlier that day and for the moment Ney was also content to be cautious.

Meanwhile Normann and Bijleveld completed their withdrawal. The 2nd Brigade deployed and bivouacked on its positions. The I./2nd Nassau Infantry held the road to Houtain-le-Val, sending two companies to the west of the Bossu Wood in support of Bergmann's volunteer Jäger. Three companies of

---

[36] De Bas & T'Serclaes de Wommersom, vol I, p 403.
[37] Delhaize & Aerts, p 315.

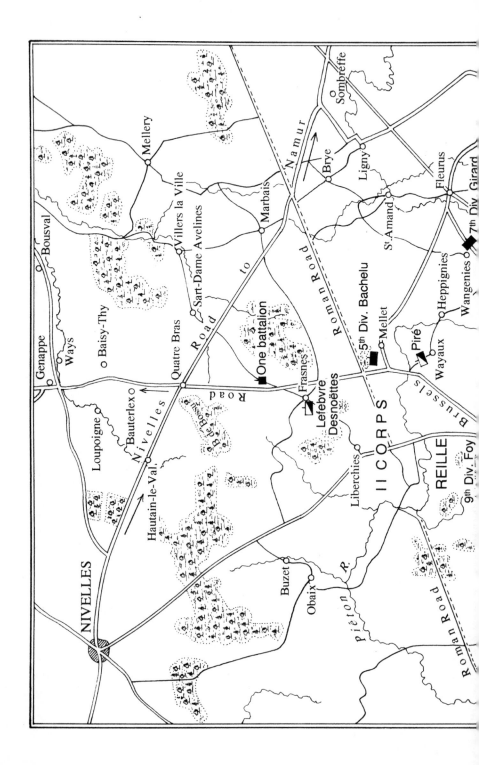

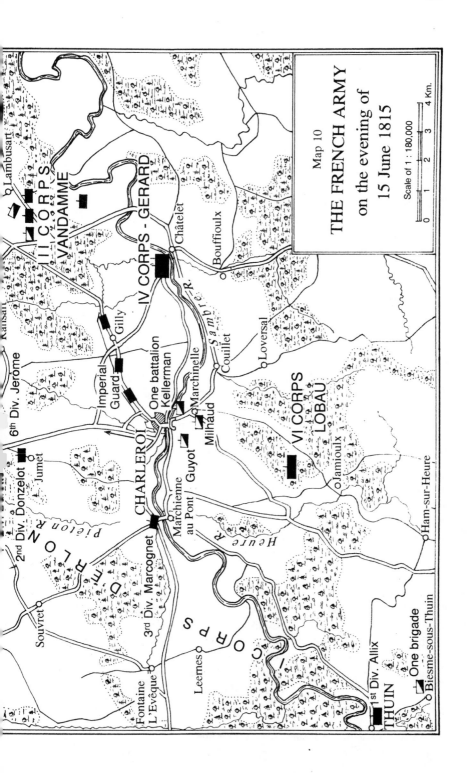

Map 10

THE FRENCH ARMY
on the evening of
15 June 1815

Scale of 1 : 180,000

0   1   2   3   4 Km.

the 2nd Nassau Regiment and two companies of II./Nassau-Orange Regiment moved to reinforce Normann's battalion near Gemioncourt, spreading their outposts along the line Grand-Pierrepont–Piraumont. The remaining companies of the Nassau-Orange Regiment occupied the hamlet and plateau of Quatre Bras, extending along the cobbled road to Namur. Bijleveld positioned three of his guns at Quatre Bras, the other five in front of Gemioncourt, one of which was with the picket on the main road to the south of this farm. The train bivouacked behind the farms of Quatre Bras.

A battalion of the 2nd (French) Light Infantry of Bachelu's Division camped opposite Saxe-Weimar. Behind them were the Lancers and Chasseurs à Cheval of the Guard who had their vedettes on the heights immediately to the north of Frasnes, with patrols going as far as Thyle and Sart-Dame-Avelines. But the French made no further attempts to sweep aside the tiny force blocking their advance.

The headquarters of the 2nd Division in Nivelles had been on alert since that afternoon when Constant Rebeque's orders arrived. They had also had a warning note from Major Normann about 4 p.m. However, news had yet to arrive of Zieten's retreat to Fleurus and the French capture of Gosselies in the afternoon. It was this development that had left open the road to Brussels, seriously exposing the left flank of the Dutch troops, as Normann and his men had since found out.

Perponcher's 2nd Brigade had waited under arms. About 7 p.m. he learned from Prussian stragglers coming from Thuin and Lobbes that there had been fighting at Gosselies. However, the strength, direction of advance and the intentions of the French Army were still unknown. A French deserter next brought news of the fall of Charleroi, and told the Dutch that Napoleon was on his way to Brussels with 150,000 men. One of Perponcher's aides, Captain Gagern, who had earlier taken orders to Duke Bernhard, arrived back in headquarters while this deserter was being questioned. Captain Gagern reported that Normann had evacuated Frasnes and corroborated the deserter's tale that the French were marching on Quatre Bras. It was now between 8 and 8.30 p.m.[38] Perponcher instructed Gagern to take the news of the French offensive to Netherlands headquarters in Braine-le-Comte.

At 9 p.m. Duke Bernhard sent his report on the day's events to Perponcher at Nivelles,

> All measures have been taken for our security this night. I must confess to Your Excellency that I am too weak to remain here for long. The 2nd Battalion of Nassau-Orange has French muskets and is down to ten rounds per man. The volunteers have carbines of four different calibres and ten rounds per carbine. I will defend the post entrusted to me as well as possible and for as long as possible. I expect an attack at daybreak. The troops are in good spirits but there are no reserves of infantry ammunition in the waggons.[39]

[38] De Bas & T'Serclaes de Wommersom, vol I, p 406.
[39] De Bas & T'Serclaes de Wommersom, vol I, p 405.

Since Gagern had not long left, Perponcher was still waiting for new orders from Braine-le-Comte when he heard this. He sent Colonel van Zuylen van Nyevelt, his chief-of-staff, to Quatre Bras to implore Duke Bernhard to hold his positions for as long as possible, to retire only when attacked by greatly superior forces, and then to go in the direction of Mont St Jean where he would be joined by 1st Brigade. Zuylen also told Duke Bernhard that two battalions were being sent to him that night and that he was to take command of them personally.

The French Reach Quatre Bras

Captain Gagern arrived at Braine-le-Comte at about 10 p.m. He reported the events at the front and the information received from the French deserter, and requested that reinforcements be sent to the 2nd Brigade in Quatre Bras. Constant Rebeque had difficulty believing the news of the French attack on Frasnes. He knew that the road from Charleroi to Brussels should not be abandoned but he was still of the opinion that the French were going to invade via Binche and Mons and knew this was the Duke of Wellington's fear also, so he did not order a complete evacuation of Nivelles.

As Gagern's mount was too exhausted to make the return journey to Nivelles, Constant Rebeque sent Major Count O. de Limbourg-Stirum with the following message to Perponcher timed at 10.15 p.m.,

> At present, His Royal Highness is in Brussels. I am expecting his return at any moment. I believe it will be important to support the 2nd Brigade with 1st Brigade and, if necessary, with the 3rd Division, which is at Fayt, and also the cavalry of General Collaert, which is in the neighbourhood of Rœulx. The hospital and the military court are to withdraw to Brussels.
>
> In any case, General Perponcher should send an officer to General Chassé in Fayt to give him information on the situation and to have him communicate with General Collaert.[40]

Constant Rebeque also ordered the Count to tell Perponcher that,

> If the report you have given me – that is to say through the intermediary Captain Gagern – is precise, the Duke of Wellington must already have been informed of the events by Marshal Blücher. He would not delay in taking the necessary measures. It is imperative to hold Quatre Bras and Nivelles for as long as possible. I cannot order General Perponcher to abandon Nivelles to march to Quatre Bras with all of the 1st Brigade. However, if he considers it appropriate, he should reinforce it with several battalions.[41]

At 10.30 p.m. the Netherlands chief-of-staff also wrote to the Prince of Orange,

[40] De Bas & T'Serclaes de Wommersom, vol I, p 408 f.
[41] ibid.

At this instant, Captain Baron Gagern has arrived from Nivelles with a report that the enemy has already pushed as far as Quatre Bras.

I believe it necessary to take upon myself to inform General Perponcher to support his 2nd Brigade with the 1st, and to have the hospital and military court evacuated to Brussels.

I have sent an officer to Nivelles and to Fayt to make sure of the state of affairs in the former place and then to advise Generals Chassé and Collaert to join and support the 2nd Division if needed.[42]

Lieutenant Webster of the 9th Light Dragoons then took this message to Brussels. Wellington was soon to be disturbed with shocking news.

---

[42] De Bas & T'Serclaes de Wommersom, vol I, p 409 f.

Chapter 11

The Night of 15 June

The Little Paris

In the first half of June 1815 Brussels was a flourishing social centre. Along with wealthy officers from Wellington's army, the metropolis was teeming with aristocratic British tourists and French royalist émigrés. Parties were thrown most evenings and social events dominated the agenda, but beneath this façade of jollity were some deep anxieties. Rumours were constantly sweeping the city. Napoleon's approach was not only feared by the émigrés, but also by some of the local population who had supported the new regime in the Netherlands or who were known to be friendly to the British. Merriment could, at any time, give way to panic. Wellington was well aware that he needed to be seen to be calm and in control of the situation, even when, as was going to happen, events moved on rapidly and unexpectedly.

A new crop of rumours was making the rounds in Brussels from the evening of 14 June but as so many unsubstantiated stories had passed around over recent weeks, not everybody took the current ones seriously. Even officers like Major-General Sir Hussey Vivian, commander of a cavalry brigade, who had just inspected his troops at the front, paid little attention to what he was told there. As he wrote to his wife,

> On June 13th I went to Tournay to inspect the 1st Hussars. I there heard that the whole French Army had concentrated at Maubeuge, and the persuasion in France was that Buonaparte would arrive from Paris and advance on the 15th. We treated this with contempt, supposing that he would hardly dare such a thing, &c.[1]

The morning of 15 June was quiet in Brussels. Tension started to mount during the course of the day. Despatch riders were seen coming and going. Rumours spread of a major incident on the border and by the evening, Bonapartists in Brussels were claiming to be able to hear cannon fire.[2]

Wellington's Orders

In the morning and early afternoon Wellington had received reports from Zieten of the French concentration opposite the Prussian positions, heard the news of the outbreak of hostilities direct from Zieten, and then received confirmation of this via the Prince of Orange, but still did not react.

[1] Siborne, *Waterloo Letters*, p 147.
[2] Müffling, *Leben*, p 230.

210

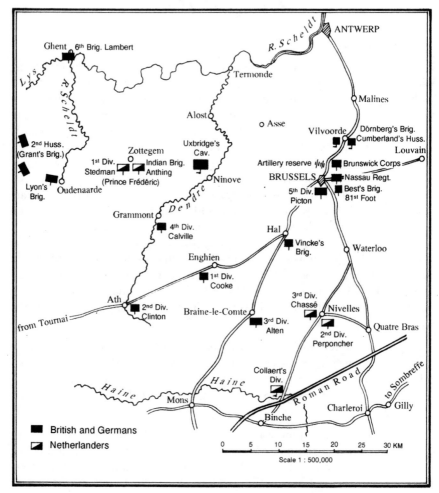

Map 11. Positions of the Anglo-Dutch-German Army
according to orders issued at 6 - 7 p.m. on 15 June 1815

Even as late as 6 p.m. this lack of urgency still prevailed. The Prince of Orange, for example, sent a message to Constant Rebeque saying,

> Unless you have received news since this morning which makes it necessary to leave the troops out all night, I request you to send them an order in my name to go to their billets, but to assemble at 4 a.m. tomorrow morning at the points fixed. Please say to Abercromby [a British staff officer attached to the Prince's headquarters], in my name, to do the same for the English troops. The Duke of Wellington wants me to stay here this evening. I will thus not leave until midnight or 1 a.m.[3]

When this message arrived at the Netherlands' headquarters at 9 p.m. the Nassauers were already in action around Frasnes.

Soon after this message was sent Wellington finally received the delayed despatch from Berkeley. By then had also heard from Blücher that he was concentrating his forces and moving to the front. Only then, between 6 p.m. and 7 p.m. on 15 June, did the Duke issue his first set of orders. These read as follows:

> General Dornberg's [sic] brigade of cavalry, and the Cumberland Hussars, to march this night upon Vilvorde, and to bivouac on the high road near to that town.
>
> The Earl of Uxbridge will be pleased to collect the cavalry this night at Ninhove, leaving the 2nd hussars looking out between the Scheldt and the Lys.
>
> The 1st division of infantry to remain as they are at Enghien, and in all readiness to march at a moment's notice.
>
> The 2nd division to collect this night at Ath and adjacent, and to be in readiness to move at a moment's notice.
>
> The 3rd division to collect this night at Braine le Comte, and to be in readiness to move at the shortest notice.
>
> The 4th division to be collected this night at Grammont, with the exception of the troops beyond the Scheldt, which are to be moved to Audenarde.
>
> The 5th division, the 81st regiment, and the Hanoverian brigade of the 6th division, to be in readiness to march from Bruxelles at a moment's notice.
>
> The Duke of Brunswick's corps to collect this night on the high road between Bruxelles and Vilvorde.
>
> The Nassau troops to collect at daylight to-morrow morning on the Louvain road, and to be in readiness to move at a moment's notice.
>
> The Hanoverian brigade of the 5th division to collect this night at Hal, and to be in readiness at daylight to-morrow morning to move towards Bruxelles, and to halt on the high road between Alost and Assche for further orders.
>
> The Prince of Orange is requested to collect at Nivelles the 2nd and 3rd divisions of the army of the Low Countries; and, should that point have been attacked this day, to move the 3rd division of British infantry upon Nivelles as soon as collected. This movement is not to take place until it is quite certain

---

[3] De Bas & T'Serclaes de Wommersom, vol I, p 396 f.

that the enemy's attack is upon the right of the Prussian army, and the left of the British army.

Lord Hill will be so good as to order Prince Frederick of Orange to occupy Audenarde with 500 men, and to collect the 1st division of the army of the Low Countries, and the Indian brigade [a formation of Netherlands colonial troops] at Sotteghem, so as to be ready to march in the morning at daylight.

The reserve artillery to be in readiness to move at daylight.[4]

It is evident from these orders that Wellington had still not grasped the reality of the situation. He was not convinced that the French intended to drive a wedge between him and Blücher even though, by then, they had already done so. The orders only instructed his units to concentrate and make ready to move. They were not movement orders. The Duke was going to wait until he was certain of the direction of the French attack.

The orders were also badly flawed. The Duke was leaving Quatre Bras undefended and thus playing into Napoleon's hands for, if they captured Quatre Bras, the French would be poised on the main road to Brussels and would also have cut the only good west-east route by which Wellington could move to support Blücher. Fortunately for the Duke, his Netherlands subordinates were making the right decisions and would plug the vital gap.

Finally, it was clear from these orders that the Anglo-Dutch-German army would have to march long distances from its concentration points to get to the right positions to support Blücher. At daybreak on 16 June Dörnberg's men would be over 40 km from the front, Uxbridge and most of the cavalry a good 60 km, 1st Division over 50 km, 2nd Division a good 50 km, 3rd Division 25 km, parts of 4th Division up to 60 km, 5th Division 30 km, Brunswick around 40 km, the Nassauers nearly 40 km, the Hanoverians 30 km, the rest of Hill's troops up to 70 km, and the reserve artillery a good 30 km. Taking 30 km to be a good day's march, Wellington was not going to complete his concentration at Quatre Bras until 17 June. If there was going to be a battle on 16 June, most of his army would not be there.

At 7 p.m. after these orders were drawn up Müffling was at last able to send a report about Wellington's plans to Blücher,

> News has just arrived [this must be Berkeley's message] that Lieutenant-General von Zieten has been attacked.
>
> The Duke of Wellington has ordered his entire forces to assemble at their rendezvous. The Prince of Orange will inform him if the [enemy] columns are directed to Nivelles. The enemy is either moving along the Sambre to join the columns coming from the direction of Givet, or he is going to attack at Fleurus, in which case it is likely that he will also attack at Nivelles.
>
> As soon as the moon rises, the Reserve will march off, and if the enemy does not attack Nivelles immediately, then the Duke will be in the area of Nivelles with his entire army tomorrow from where he can support Your Highness, or should the enemy have already attacked Your Highness, then, after appropriate discussion, to move onto his flank or rear.

---

4 WD, vol XII, p 472 f.

I believe Your Highness will be pleased with this explanation and the actions of the Duke. I hope that we can celebrate victory on 17th.[5]

This letter was sent on British Army notepaper and its envelope was marked with the word 'immediate' along with three crosses indicating that it was sent by Müffling directly from Wellington's headquarters by a top-priority British courier. There can be little doubt that the information it contained came direct from Wellington and that the Duke asked Müffling to send it. Its assurances of support from Wellington's 'entire army' conflicted with the orders the Duke had just finished issuing and in hindsight this can be seen as the first phase of the Duke's deception of Blücher that was to continue the next day.

Around 10 p.m. Müffling received a further despatch from Blücher confirming that the entire Prussian army was moving to concentrate on Sombreffe.[6] This message probably mentioned the fall of Charleroi, and may have been the first that Wellington heard of that particular event. This news caused Wellington to issue a new set of instructions, known as the 'After Orders'. Yet even those orders, timed at 10 p.m., did little to improve the situation. They read as follows,

The troops in Bruxelles (5th and 6th Divisions, Duke of Brunswick's and Nassau troops) to march when assembled from Bruxelles by the road of Namur to the point where the road to Nivelles separates; to be followed by Gen. Dornberg's [sic] brigade and the Cumberland hussars.

3rd division of infantry to continue its movement from Braine le Comte upon Nivelles.

The 1st division to move from Enghien to Braine le Comte.

The 2nd and 4th divisions of infantry to move from Ath and Grammont, also from Audenarde, and to continue their movements upon Enghien.

The cavalry to continue its movement from Ninhove upon Enghien.

The above movements to take place with as little delay as possible.[7]

These attempts to accelerate the concentration were too little too late. Even when they were carried out most of the troops would still be a long way from Quatre Bras.

Had Wellington issued his first set of warning orders at 10 a.m., by which time he knew of the commencement of the French offensive, then he would have been able to issue movement orders shortly after 3 p.m., when confirmation of the French offensive arrived. Part of his army, particularly the Reserve in Brussels, would have been able to march closer to the front that day, possibly as far forward as Nivelles. Such movements could have catered for both the strategic possibilities. By moving on Nivelles Wellington's army would have been in a position either to give Blücher the support he needed at Ligny on 16 June, or to counter the feared French thrust supposedly coming via Mons against Wellington's centre and right.

5 GStA, Rep 92, Gneisenau, A 40, fol 93.
6 MWBl, vol XXIX, p 11; Damitz, vol I, p 103; Müffling, *Leben*, p 229.
7 WD, vol XII, p 474; WD (1847 ed.), vol VIII, p142

214

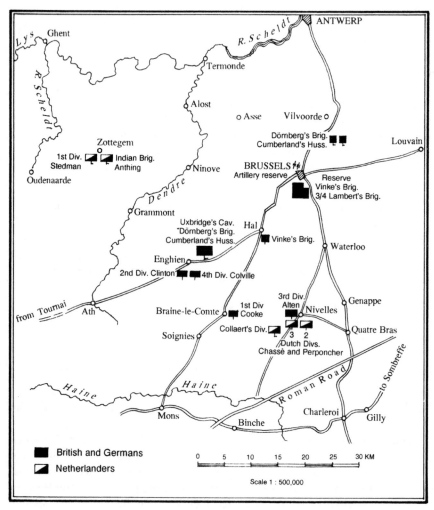

Map 12. Positions of the Anglo-Dutch-German Army
according to After Orders' of 10 p.m. on 15 June 1815

After delivering the message he received at 10 p.m. Müffling returned to his lodgings, and prepared a reply to Blücher. He wrote it in such a way that all he needed to do was enter the names of the places to which Wellington's forces were going to march. He had a courier wait at his door. Towards midnight, Wellington entered the Prussian's room, telling him that, on the basis of information just received from Dörnberg in Mons, he had now ordered his forces on Nivelles and Quatre Bras.[8] Müffling completed his report, and sent it off. It contained assurances that Wellington's army would be concentrated within 12 hours, and the Duke would have 20,000 men at Quatre Bras by 10 a.m.[9] Those promises were again inconsistent with the orders that Wellington had just issued.

The Duchess of Richmond's Ball

Wellington had kept calm throughout the day. He insisted that all his senior officers should attend that evening's ball to keep up that impression and so that he would have all his senior officers to hand that evening, should he need them. The Duke went to the ball at about midnight.[10] He had not been there long when news of the French advance to Quatre Bras arrived. This was the message, timed at 10.30, which was given to Lieutenant Henry Webster of the 9th Light Dragoons at Braine-le Comte, and which is quoted at the end of the last chapter. There is some doubt as to when this message actually left, despite the timing given on it, since according to the letter-book kept at Braine, Webster left at 10 p.m.[11] Webster had raced to Brussels with this urgent news, changing horses on the way. His recollection of the ride, given some years later, and a little inaccurate in places, was as follows,

> At ten o'clock [name bowdlerised], the minister, came to me, telling me that the advanced guard of the Prussians had been driven in at Ligny [actually Charleroi]; and ordering me, without a moment's delay, to convey the despatch he put in my hand to the Prince of Orange. "A horse ready-saddled awaits you at the door," he said, "and another has been sent on, half an hour ago, to a half-way house, to help you on the faster. Gallop every yard! You will find your chief at the Duchess of Richmond's ball." [It is more likely he was told to go to Wellington's headquarters.] "Stand on no ceremony; but insist on seeing the Prince at once." I was in my saddle without a second's delay; and thanks to a fine moon and two capital horses, had covered the ten miles [actually nearer 20 miles/30 km] I had to go within the hour! [He took two hours.] The Place at Brussels was all ablaze with light; and such was the crowd of carriages, that I could not well make way through them on horseback; so I abandoned my steed to the first man I could get hold of, and made my way on foot to the porter's lodge.[12]

When Webster arrived around midnight, he found the Prince had departed for the Duchess of Richmond's ball. A servant led him there where he handed

[8] Müffling, *Leben*, p 229.
[9] Nostitz, p 22 fn.
[10] Müffling, *Leben*, p 229 f.
[11] De Bas & T'Serclaes de Wommersom, vol I, p 410 fn.
[12] Young, p 307.

the despatch to the Prince. His arrival was witnessed by an officer of Picton's 5th Division who described it as follows,

> About half-past nine or ten [this time has to be quite wrong, it was nearer midnight] an orderly dragoon, covered with dust and foam, arrived at the hotel of the Commanding General, bearing despatches from the front, and earnestly inquired of the Duke of Wellington. He was taken to the house of the Duke of Richmond... [13]

Webster's recollection continued,

> On my telling the Suisse I had despatches of moment for the Prince, he civilly asked me if I would wait for five minutes; "for," said he, "the Duchess has just given orders for the band to go upstairs, and the party are now about to rise. If you were to burst in suddenly, it might alarm the ladies." On that consideration I consented to wait. I peeped in between the folding doors and saw the Duchess of Richmond taking the Prince of Orange's arm, and Lady Charlotte Greville the Duke's, on their way to the ballroom. The moment they had reached the foot of the stairs, I hastened to the Prince's side and gave him the despatch. Without looking at it, he handed it behind him to the Duke, who quietly deposited it in his coat-pocket. The Prince made me a sign to remain in the hall. I did so. All the company passed by me, while I hid myself in a recess from observation for fear of being asked awkward questions. As soon as the last couple had mounted the première étage, the Duke of Wellington descended, and espying me, beckoned me to him, and said, in a low voice, "Webster! Four horses instantly to the Prince of Orange's carriage for Waterloo!"' [Actually, he went back to Braine-le-Comte.] [14]

This version conflicts slightly with the Prince of Orange's own account that he opened the note himself and then discreetly whispered the news to the Duke, who apparently did not want to believe his ears.[15] The crucial sentence of the message read, 'At this instant, Captain Baron Gagern has just arrived from Nivelles with a report that the enemy has already pushed as far as Quatre Bras.'

This news must have stuck like a bolt of lightning. Wellington's orders had left the vital cross-roads at Quatre Bras unguarded and the road from Charleroi to Brussels open. Not only that, but direct communication with the Prussians in the Sombreffe position might now be cut off. This was devastating. It underlined the series of errors the Duke had made that day. Then, and only then, did the full seriousness of the situation finally dawn on Wellington. Napoleon had driven a wedge between the two Allied armies in the Netherlands and his plan to separate them and defeat them individually was well under way.

There was now no more time to lose but little that could actually be done

---

13 *USJ*, 1841, Part II, p 173.
14 Young, p 307 f.
15 Pflugk-Harttung, *Vorgeschichte*, p 82 fn.

that night. The Prince was sent back to Braine-le-Comte with such haste that
he even left his sabre behind. Between midnight and 1 a.m. on 16 June, the
remaining officers at the ball or in Brussels were sent back to their units one
by one.[16] Picton's division was ordered to march off at 2 a.m., instead of at
4 a.m. as had previously been the case. Even then, it was not sent to Quatre
Bras, but only as far as Waterloo. One of his officers related,

> Whatever these despatches [as carried by Webster] contained, the arrival of
> which would soon be whispered around the room, and create a sensation, no
> further change was made in the chief's arrangements as concerned us, than
> altering the hour of departure in the morning from four to two o'clock.[17]

That done, Wellington retired to bed at some time between 2 a.m. and
3 a.m., determined to get what sleep he could. He might have slept a little
more easily if he had known that some of his Netherlands subordinates had
already taken steps to mitigate the damage that had been done.

At about 10.30 p.m., shortly after Lieutenant Webster had left Braine-le-
Comte with his fateful message, a Captain Russel arrived at Braine with
Wellington's orders. Russel had left Brussels at 8 p.m. These orders, as we
have seen, were for the 2nd and 3rd Netherlands Divisions to concentrate at
Nivelles, which would have meant withdrawing the forces already positioned
at Quatre Bras or on their way there through Constant's and Perponcher's
recent decisions. Constant was convinced that Wellington would never have
issued such orders were the true situation at the front known in Brussels and
bravely and correctly decided to disobey them. Instead, at 11.30 p.m., he
amplified his earlier instructions to the 2nd Division with the following orders
for his other divisional commanders,

> To General Collaert
>
> On receipt of this order, Your Excellency is to put your division of cavalry
> with movement orders and occupy the heights behind Haine-Saint-Pierre,
> detaching one brigade with the artillery necessary to cover the passage of the
> Haine near Saint-Paul.

> To General Chassé
>
> Your division is to march immediately to Nivelles to support the 2nd
> Division if required. You are advised that General Collaert is taking up
> positions behind the Haine.[18]

French Positions Overnight

The French Army camped, as the previous night, in three columns. The
vanguard of the left wing, the Guard light cavalry, stood in Frasnes. II Corps
with Piré's light cavalry was between Mellet and Gosselies, Girard's Division
at Wangenies. I Corps stood in echelon between Marchienne and Jumet. III

---

[16] Siborne, *Waterloo Letters*, p 148.
[17] *USJ*, 1841, Part II, p 173.
[18] De Bas & T'Serclaes de Wommersom, vol I, pp 436 ff.

Corps and Grouchy's cavalry were in the Fleurus wood as follows: 1st Cavalry Corps in Lambusart, one division around the farm of Martinroux, General Domon's light cavalry at the exit from the Fleurus wood, and 2nd Cavalry Corps between the light cavalry and III Corps. The Guard was by the paved road between Charleroi and Gilly. VI Corps and the cuirassiers of 3rd and 4th Cavalry Corps were south of Charleroi. IV Corps and the other formations of the right wing were just north of the bridge over the Sambre at Châtelet. Napoleon's headquarters was in Charleroi and Ney's in Gosselies.

Prussian Movements

Chapter 9 showed how the Prussian II and III Army Corps were sent orders late on the 14th to concentrate, at Onoz and Mazy, and at Namur respectively. To achieve this their troops were on the move throughout the 15th. Only Bülow's IV Army Corps would fail to execute its concentration orders on time.

We also left I Army Corps bivouacked for the night of 15/16 June between Fleurus and Ligny. Reiche, Zieten's chief-of-staff, had already gone to army headquarters once that night to express concerns about the exposed position in which the corps was placed. Even after returning to corps headquarters with an assurance from Gneisenau that the rest of the army would shortly arrive at Sombreffe, Zieten and Reiche continued to be anxious.

Blücher and Gneisenau did not yet know that both II and III Army Corps had been late concentrating that day. Although their orders had gone out from Namur at 11.30 p.m. on the 14th, they took their time filtering down to the brigades, regiments, battalions and squadrons. For instance, the units of the 8th Brigade in Jodogne, Château d'Huy, etc., received theirs at 9 a.m., the 5th Hussars in Hannut by noon. Parts of the 25th Infantry Regiment, who got their orders by 9 a.m., only managed to arrive in Namur in dribs and drabs starting from 5 p.m. and continuing throughout the night. The regiment then marched on to Wagnelée early on the 16th and had to take part in the battle without the men having had the chance even to cook a meal.[19]

The experience of the 22nd Regiment, billeted in seven villages halfway between Liège and Namur, was even worse. It received its marching orders at 2 p.m. on 15 June, but only managed to concentrate at Héron by 9 p.m., and arrived at Ligny shortly before the battle commenced on 16 June. Premier-Lieutenant von Becker of the 2nd Company, related the events in his diary,

> At 3 p.m. I marched off with the company from Borlez. While marching, we heard occasional cannon fire coming from Fleurus. By 9 p.m. the regiment was assembled at its rendezvous in Héron. After a pause of one hour, it moved off again and marched the whole night. At 4 a.m. on 16 June we reached Namur. Tired out by the night march, we rested for two hours under the beautiful lime and chestnut trees. The entire military road was covered with troops that were marching to the army's assembly point at Sombreffe. The residents of Namur were standing in crowds on the main road, watching the troops march

---

[19] MWBl, vol XXX, p 20.

by. We set off again about 7 a.m. and continued our march in the direction of Nivelles. We soon met a waggon full of wounded of the I Army Corps, that had suffered significant losses the previous day at Fleurus; its baggage trains were also going back to Namur. These encounters obstructed and delayed our march. There was not a cloud in the sky, the June sun was burning hot, the dust suffocating, and we were all suffering from thirst; the wells in the villages we passed through were already dry. Our men were already falling down with exhaustion, and with every hour the numbers of stragglers increased. It was past noon when the regiment stopped in a village, partly to wait for the stragglers to catch up, partly to quench its thirst from a pond; the water tasted wonderful, despite the fact that artillery and cavalry horses had drunk there, mixing it up with mud. A despatch rider arrived with the order to hurry to reach the battlefield, as the honour of the regiment depended on it. We marched off immediately, even though more than half of the stragglers, exhausted by their 24-hour march, had yet to catch up. We marched past the III Army Corps which was already deployed at Sombreffe and reached the far right flank of the II Army Corps near Brye at 3 p.m.[20]

Blücher and Gneisenau did not yet know of these problems so the orders Gneisenau sent II Army Corps at 11.30 p.m. only set out how Pirch I and his men should come into action. As far as Gneisenau was aware at that time II Army Corps was spending the night in Mazy and Onoz, about 6 km from Sombreffe. Pirch's orders read,

Your Honour is to move II Army Corps in such a way that, at 4 a.m., it arrives in Sombreffe. Colonel von Aster [II Corps' chief-of-staff] should come here before then, to receive further details of the deployment of the corps. Two regiments of the Reserve Cavalry are to move to assist Lieutenant-General von Zieten via Onoz to Le Fay.

Lieutenant-General von Thielemann has been ordered to organise III Corps in such a way that it arrives at Mazy on the Orneau at daybreak. Your Honour is to withdraw Colonel von Borcke to the left bank of the Sambre at Namur and to instruct him to reconnoitre the right bank with outposts and patrols. The detachments of III Corps on outpost duty are to move off with their corps.

Fleurus is still in our hands.

General Count Bülow will move to Gembloux tomorrow [16 June]. You are to send the baggage of II Corps back to Liège.[21]

By later in the night Gneisenau had heard about II Corps' problems and wrote to Zieten describing the slightly revised situation,

I report herewith to Your Excellency that orders have been given for II Corps to arrive tomorrow morning in Sombreffe and for III Corps to arrive in Mazy. IV Corps is marching to Gembloux. II Corps was late concentrating today. It is thus not yet certain if it will really arrive by daybreak. So that the

[20] *Infanterie-Regiment Nr. 22*, p 112 f.
[21] Ollech, p 121.

concentration behind the Ligne stream can be made with complete safety, it is important that Your Excellency hold the positions you have occupied this evening. I have again ordered Generalmajor von Pirch I to move two cavalry regiments via Onoz to La Fay, on Your Excellency's left flank. I also beseech Your Excellency to order Generalmajor von Steinmetz that he uses every means to reconnoitre his right flank, observes the Roman road, and seeks to establish communications with the Dutch army.[22]

Despite this instruction Zieten sent Reiche back to Sombreffe towards the end of the night to request once again that I Army Corps be withdrawn behind the Ligne brook. Once drawn up behind the stronger defensive positions offered by this brook and the nearby villages, Zieten felt he would be better able to hold off the French advance. Gneisenau finally granted this request in new orders issued at 5 a.m.,

> 1st Brigade is to occupy the village of St Amand, 3rd Brigade the village of Brye, 4th Brigade Ligny, and 2nd Brigade is to form up in reserve in the centre behind the windmill hill [south-east of Brye, the Mill of Bussy].
>
> The I Corps' Reserve Cavalry is to draw up behind the village of Ligny, leaving the left of it free for the Reserve Artillery to move into position. To cover this movement, the 12-pounders on the Tombe de Ligny are to remain there until it is completed, and are then to leave.
>
> Those parts of the brigades, which are not required to occupy the villages are to form up in support behind them. The villages are to be placed in a state of defence forthwith and the necessary barricades built. As they lack sufficient local knowledge, the brigades are permitted to assist one another in occupying the villages and terrain.[23]

These positions were taken up by around 8 a.m. The outposts and the brigade cavalry were positioned south of the Ligne rivulet. By then it was clear that the rest of the army was far from assembled, making it particularly important to keep control of the section of the Roman Road from Mazy through Sombreffe as II and III Corps would be moving along it.

Bülow's Failure to Join Blücher

The first major error made by the Prussian General Staff in this campaign was to fail to ensure that Bülow moved his IV Army Corps to be in a position to support the three remaining corps on 16 June. Both the original order to begin the concentration, sent at midnight of 14/15 June, and the subsequent message, sent at 11.30 a.m. on the 15th, are quoted in Chapter 9. In both of them Gneisenau had to be excessively polite to Bülow, his senior in rank, and failed to convey the urgency of the situation. This was not the only reason for the failure, however, for Bülow was also being deliberately awkward and obtuse.

Blücher and Gneisenau first realised that their orders were not being carried out on the night of 15/16 June when Captain von Below, of Bülow's

---

[22] Ollech, p 105.
[23] Ollech, p 120.

staff, eventually found their new headquarters in Sombreffe after having gone to the old location in Namur. He carried a letter from Bülow, about the initial concentration order, written in Liège earlier on 15 June. This letter explained that his corps would only reach Hannut on 16 June, still nearly 40 km from Sombreffe and a day's march from where it was required. Bülow excused this sorry situation as follows,

> I am sending Captain von Below to Your Excellency so that you can give him the necessary instructions as, in the orders sent to me, nothing was said about the other Army Corps on my borders...
>
> As far as both myself and my chief-of-staff Major-General von Valentini understand, all four corps will be concentrating at Hannut in which case I do not consider it appropriate to take the troops out of their cantonments today to march to the cantonments in Hannut... Had the points of concentration of the other three army corps been stated in the orders, then I would have been able to understand what Field Marshal Blücher intended. In the event of the actual outbreak of hostilities, I would have expected to have been given this information in advance.[24]

This is a rather flimsy explanation for this series of events. The truth is that Bülow was a member of an established Prussian military family and was probably simply reluctant to carry out orders from a junior non-Prussian. Had Gneisenau been a little more informative and more forceful in expressing himself to a man to whom he did not want to cause offence, then it is most likely that Bülow would have reacted immediately which would have helped the situation significantly.

The misfortune did not end with Bülow's wilful misunderstanding of the concentration order. The orders sent by Blücher to Bülow at 11.30 a.m. on 15 June also failed to arrive in time. The despatch rider entrusted with their delivery took his instructions too literally. He was told to deliver them to Bülow at Hannut and tried to do just that. He rode to Hannut and when he found that Bülow was not there, he awaited his arrival, which he was told was imminent. Only when Feldjäger [courier] Rothe arrived later, with oral information for Bülow that the army was concentrating at Sombreffe, was this situation rectified. Rothe reported to Grolman that he found the written orders in Hannut and personally took them to Liège. His report, written at 11.30 p.m. in Hannut, read,

> The situation now makes it impossible for IV Army Corps to reach the heights of Gembloux by tomorrow [16 June].[25]

This error was to cost the Prussians dearly.

At this juncture Blücher might have done better to consider a fighting withdrawal instead of a major battle on 16 June. With only three corps at his disposal, and as yet no news of Wellington's intentions, he could not expect to

---

[24] Ollech, pp 106–7.
[25] Ollech, p 107.

be able to hold off the entire French army. It would make sense for Zieten to fall back into a defensive position and act as rearguard while the entire army concentrated for battle on 17 June around Gembloux, to the north-east of Sombreffe. Here, the Prussians could hold a defensive position while Wellington moved from Quatre Bras into the flank and rear of the advancing French.

Nostitz described the dilemma facing the Prussian headquarters on the night of 15 June, and explained the reasons for Blücher's decision,

> As there was no longer any doubt that we would be facing the main enemy force the next day, and could be certain neither of support from the English, nor expect the arrival of IV Corps, justifiable concerns for the result of the battle arose. One asked the question if it were not more advisable to join up with the English by means of a flank march, or to fall back towards IV Corps. Some commanders, in such circumstances, would have chosen one or the other way out of a battle, particularly as only part of the forces were concentrated; I can affirm that the Field Marshal made his decision without a moment's hesitation, and that nobody in headquarters uttered a word against this.
>
> It is indisputable that it would have made a bad impression on the army if such a courageous commander, trusted by all, and at the head of 80,000 men, largely experienced soldiers, had avoided a battle in a position chosen by himself and where the Duke of Wellington had agreed in detail to give him substantial support.[26]

Now, more than ever, Wellington's support on 16 June was necessary.

[26] Nostitz, p 22 f.

Chapter 12

The Morning of 16 June

Wellington Leaves Brussels

Wellington got to bed about 3 a.m. on 16 June and was awakened after only a couple of hours sleep. The Duke first had a conference with Fitzroy Somerset and the Duke of Richmond, then gave Picton his orders to march off,[1] and finally set off south from Brussels himself.

Müffling was with the Duke's party and described the journey '...at 5 a.m., we rode off. We overtook the marching troops and were in Quatre Bras by 11 a.m., where the enemy had placed his outposts opposite the troops of Perponcher's Division.'[2] Müffling's recollection is inaccurate as to the time at least. Wellington probably left Brussels rather later than 5 a.m. and certainly seems to have first reached Quatre Bras at about 10 a.m., having ridden via Waterloo and Genappe, stopping briefly on the way. He passed the troops of his Reserve on their march to the front at Waterloo and left them there, preparing their breakfasts. Some accounts say that he passed by at about 9 a.m. Again this time may be incorrect, with 8 a.m. possibly being more accurate. What is certain, however, is that Wellington, having ridden past the 5th Division, was aware that it was halted just beyond the Soignes Forest enjoying its breakfast, and that he had yet to order it to move on beyond Waterloo. He did not send it an order to move on to Quatre Bras until later, probably about 11 a.m.

Reference to a number of accounts of members of this corps will help illuminate this point. Captain Leach, then an officer in the 95th Rifles, wrote, 'Our division and the Brunswick troops, after a halt of an hour or two near Waterloo, were directed to advance; and we arrived at Quatre Bras about two hours after mid-day.'[3] Private Costello, also in the 95th Rifles, is a little more specific in his account,

> We halted at the verge of the wood, on the left of the road, behind the village of Waterloo, where we remained for some hours... About nine o'clock the Duke of Wellington with his staff came riding from Brussels and passed us to the front... [4]

Kincaid, then a subaltern of the 95th, added,

> The whole of the division having... advanced to the village of Waterloo, where, forming in a field adjoining the road, our men were allowed to prepare

[1] Gronow, vol I, p 66.
[2] Müffling, *Leben*, p 230.
[3] Leach, p 374 f.
[4] Brett-James, p 150 f.

their breakfasts... Lord Wellington joined us about nine o'clock... About twelve o'clock an order arrived for the troops to advance... [5]

Dörnberg joined Wellington's party at Waterloo, from where they continued south to the road junction at Mont St Jean.[6] Here, the road forked, one arm going in the direction of Nivelles, the other to Quatre Bras. Dörnberg wrote that Wellington, 'remained at Mont St Jean for a while, enquiring where the various roads led.'[7] It would seem that Wellington had yet to make a final decision as to where to send his troops that day.

The Dutch and the Prussians

While Wellington was catching a few hours sleep, the Prince of Orange had made his way back to his headquarters. The Duke's 'after orders' had arrived in Braine-le-Comte at 2.30 a.m. Constant Rebeque had already begun to implement them when the Prince arrived at 3.30 a.m. When briefed on the situation and the measures taken in his absence by his chief-of-staff, the Prince approved them. He told Constant that Wellington only finally began to accept the reality of the situation when the despatch carried by Webster arrived, and that the Duke had told the Prince in response that he intended to move all of his forces to Quatre Bras.[8]

The Prince instructed Constant Rebeque to leave for Quatre Bras immediately, taking with him all the troops still at Nivelles. Shortly before 4 a.m., the Netherlands chief-of-staff rode off. At Nivelles Constant ordered those units of Bijlandt's 1st Brigade who were still there, two battalions of infantry and a foot battery, to prepare to leave for Quatre Bras.

Constant Rebeque reached Quatre Bras at 5.30 a.m. and met Perponcher. Perponcher had left Nivelles for Quatre Bras at 2 a.m. but only with part of his 2nd Division as he did not want to leave that important town totally unguarded. On moving off from Nivelles, Perponcher had met a troop of Prussian cavalry, men of the 1st Silesian Hussars under Lieutenant Zehelin, who had been cut off from their army in the fighting on the 15th. Colonel van Zuylen, Perponcher's chief-of-staff, sent them to Houtain-le-Val. Perponcher had arrived at Quatre Bras about 3 a.m., and immediately inspected Duke Bernhard's positions, which he approved.

The Prince himself rapidly changed his dress and quickly set off with the rest of his headquarters staff for Quatre Bras,[9] where they arrived towards 6 a.m. At Quatre Bras Constant Rebeque and Colonel Abercromby presented Major von Brünneck, an officer on Blücher's staff, to the Prince. Brünneck briefed the Netherlanders on the measures the Prussians were taking.

Brünneck then wrote Blücher the following report at 6.30 a.m. from Quatre Bras,

> I wish to report most humbly to Your Highness that the Prince of Orange is here with seven battalions. The combat which could be heard on our far right

---

5 Kincaid, p 154 f.

6 Pflugk-Harttung, *Vorgeschichte*, p 292.

7 Pflugk-Harttung, *Vorgeschichte*, p 292 f.

8 Journal of Constant Rebeque.

9 De Bas & T'Serclaes de Wommersom, vol I, p 446.

last evening took place at Frasnes, which had been at first in the hands of Belgian troops. The enemy has taken Frasnes and, during the night, sent his patrols as far as Sart-à-Mayelines [Sart-Dames-Avelines on modern maps], across the Namur–Nivelles road, thereby breaking communications between our two armies during the night. They are now being maintained by only one officer and 30 troopers at Marbais. The position of Quatre Bras and the woods near it were held in yesterday's action and are still in the possession of Belgian troops.

The occasional cannon and small arms fire heard by Your Highness from time to time, are coming from French and Belgian troops at Frasnes. There have been no significant changes with regard to the enemy since last evening. He is still resting and showing no signs of movement.

The Prince of Orange believes that within the next three hours the entire Belgian army and the bulk of the English army can be concentrated at Nivelles. Seventeen English battalions have marched off from Brussels to support Quatre Bras.

I will remain here with the Prince of Orange's outposts to observe the enemy here, and to be able to report events to Your Highness.[10]

It would seem from this letter that the Prince of Orange expected the bulk of Wellington's army to be in a position to intervene at Quatre Bras that day. He indicated that most of Wellington's forces would be concentrated at Nivelles by 9.30 a.m. As the distance between Nivelles and Quatre Bras is only 10 km, that meant that the bulk of the Duke's forces could be expected at Quatre Bras by early that afternoon. As the Prince had spent the previous afternoon and evening in Brussels in Wellington's headquarters, it is likely that this was the source of his information.

Wellington Arrives at Quatre Bras

Wellington's party arrived at Quatre Bras at 10 a.m. The Duke's account noted,

I reached the field of Quatre Bras twice on the day in question, the first time at about ten o'clock in the morning, having quitted Bruxelles before daylight. I found there the Prince of Orange with a small body of Belgian troops, two or three battalions of infantry, a squadron of Belgian dragoons, and two or three pieces of cannon which had been at the Quatre Bras – the four roads – since the preceding evening.[11]

Dörnberg's account continued,

Arriving at Quatre Bras, we found the Dutch troops under the Prince of Orange skirmishing with the French around Frasnes, with the odd cannon shot being fired. Here, the Duke wrote an order to Lord Uxbridge to move his cavalry assembled at Enghien immediately to Quatre Bras.[12]

[10] Lettow-Vorbeck, p 298.
[11] Jennings, vol III, p 175.
[12] Pflugk-Harttung, *Vorgeschichte*, p 292 f.

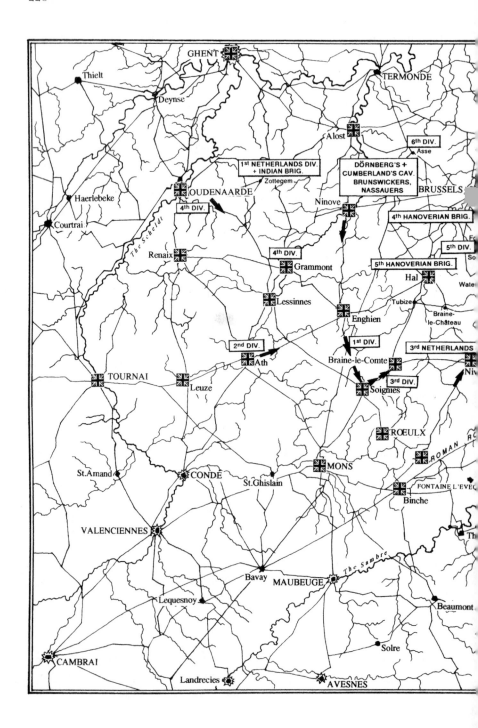

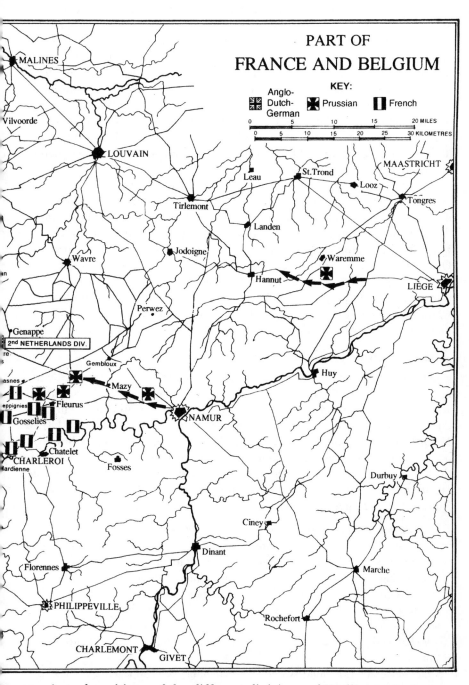

Map 13. Actual positions of the different divisions of Wellington's Army
at 7 a.m. 16 June 1815, and of the French and Prussian Armies

However, it is doubtful that Wellington actually ordered Uxbridge as far as Quatre Bras this early in the day since the way the cavalry actually moved followed a different pattern. Captain Thomas Wildman of the 7th Hussars, an 'extra aide-de-camp' to Uxbridge, in a letter to his mother written in Brussels on 19 June 1815, mentioned meeting Uxbridge near Enghien on the 16th. Uxbridge sent him on to Braine-le-Comte and, as he did not find the Duke there, he went on to Nivelles. Arriving there about 4 p.m., Wildman made towards the sound of the guns. Reaching Quatre Bras, he was then ordered to Braine to bring up all the cavalry and another, unnamed, British division.[13] This was probably the 3rd Division, as the 1st Division evidently marched to the sounds of the guns on its own initiative.[14]

Even when he reached Quatre Bras Wellington appeared not yet to be convinced that the main French force was moving against Blücher. The orders issued by the Duke that morning merely brought his troops closer to the front, rather than committing them to a certain line of action. Other than 5th Division, Wellington appears not to have instructed a single unit to march to Quatre Bras that day until later that afternoon, after the fighting had begun. The Duke had ordered certain infantry divisions to march to various places on the route to the front, including Braine-le-Comte, Nivelles and Waterloo, and when the orders to move to Quatre Bras were issued that afternoon some units, particularly the 1st Division, seem to have been omitted.

The de Lancey Disposition

Colonel de Lancey, Wellington's acting Quartermaster-General, who evidently remained behind in Brussels for a while, apparently wrote out a 'Disposition' summarising the army's positions for Wellington's information at 7 a.m. The document was supposedly copied down by Major de Lacy Evans, ADC to Major-General Ponsonby, a cavalry brigade commander. Its validity has been questioned but is accepted by some historians. According to their interpretation, de Lancey handed this document to Wellington at some time before 10.30 a.m. and, using the information provided by it, the Duke then wrote to Blücher from Frasnes at 10.30 a.m.

Disposition of the British Army at 7 o'clock A.M., 16th June.

1st division	Braine le Comte	marching to Nivelles and Quatre Bras
2nd division	Braine le Comte	marching to Nivelles
3rd division	Nivelles	marching to Quatre Bras
4th division	Audenarde	marching to Braine le Comte
5th division	beyond Waterloo	marching to Genappe
6th division	Assche	marching to Genappe and Quatre Bras
5th Hanoverian Brigade	Hal	marching to Genappe and Quatre Bras
4th Hanoverian Brigade	beyond Waterloo	marching to Genappe and Quatre Bras

[13] Paget Papers, 644 A/21.
[14] Hamilton, p 15.

2nd division ⎱	army of the Low Countries	
3rd division ⎰	at Nivelles and Quatre Bras	
1st division ⎱	army of the Low Countries	
Indian brigade ⎰	Sotteghem	marching to Enghien

Major-General Dörnberg's brigade and Cumberland Hussars

	beyond Waterloo	marching to Genappe and Quatre Bras

Remainder of the cavalry

	Braine le Comte	marching to Nivelles and Quatre Bras

Duke of Brunswick's corps

	beyond Waterloo	marching to Genappe
Nassau	beyond Waterloo	marching to Genappe

The above disposition written out for the information of the Commander of the Forces by Colonel Sir W. de Lancey. The centre column of names indicates the places at which the troops had arrived or were moving on. The column on the right of the paper indicates the places the troops were ordered to proceed to at 7 o'clock A.M., 16th June, previous to any attack on the British.

De Lacy Evans [15]

For a graphic comparison of the positions given in this document and the reality, refer to the appendix on page 357 and the maps accompanying this chapter.

Wellington's Orders [16]

Whether the de Lancey Disposition is accepted as genuine or not there is further evidence that de Lancey and the Duke were well aware of where their troops really were on the 16th. Between 5 a.m. and 10 a.m. that morning, Wellington had de Lancey issue orders to Lieutenant-General Lord Hill, commander of II Corps which consisted principally of the British 2nd and 4th Divisions, and Sir John Lambert, commander of a brigade in 6th Division, part of the Reserve.

These orders read as follows:

To General Lord Hill, G.C.B.

The Duke of Wellington requests that you will move the 2nd division of infantry on Braine le Comte immediately. The cavalry has been ordered likewise on Braine le Comte. His Grace is going to Waterloo.

Presumably, this order was issued before the Duke left Brussels.

To General Lord Hill, G.C.B.

Your Lordship is requested to order Prince Frederick of Orange to move, immediately upon receipt of this order, the 1st division of the army of the Low Countries, and the Indian brigade, from Sotteghem to Enghien, leaving 500 men, as directed, in Audenarde.

[15] WSD, vol X, p 496.
[16] See WD, vol XII, p 474 f for each of the orders quoted in this section.

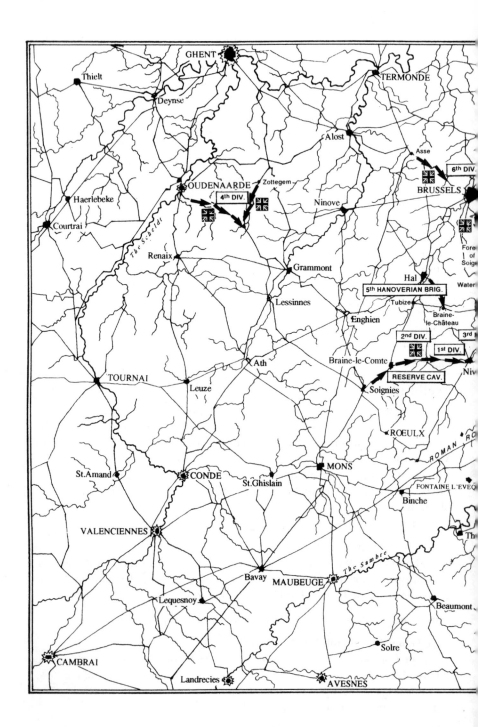

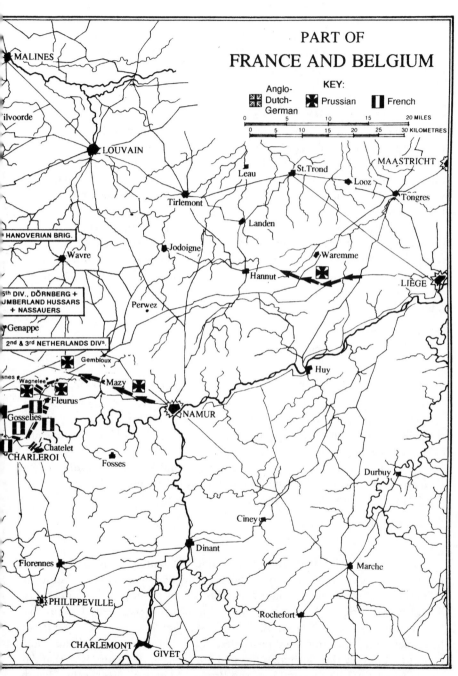

Map 14. Positions of the different divisions of Wellington's Army
7 a.m. 16 June 1815, as given in the 'Disposition of Sir W. De Lancey',
and of the French and Prussian Armies

These orders, evidently issued early on 16 June, indicate that de Lancey, who signed them, and Wellington, who had them drawn up, knew where their troops were. They must have been aware that those troops could not arrive at the front until the next day. These orders are certainly inconsistent with troop positions and movements apparently noted by de Lancey in his 'Disposition' of 7 a.m.

The Frasnes Letter

The next important document is a letter from Wellington to Blücher written from Frasnes that morning. None of Wellington's papers, printed or manuscript, contains a copy of it. Neither Dörnberg nor Müffling, who had accompanied Wellington to the front that day, indicate they were aware it had been written. Throughout the rest of his life, the Duke never made a reference to having written it.

It was first located in the mid-nineteenth century by the German historian Ollech, after detailed research in the Prussian War Archives. Ollech then reproduced it in facsimile form in his history of the campaign published in 1876. It is now lost or at least missing but comparisons of Ollech's version and other documents that are still available confirm it is in the Duke's own hand. The text reads,

> On the heights behind Frasne[s],
> 16th June 1815, at 10.30 [a.m.].
>
> My dear Prince,
>   My army is situated as follows. The Army Corps of the Prince of Orange has one division here and Quatre Bras, the remainder at Nivelles. The Reserve is on the march from Waterloo on Genappe where it will arrive at midday. The English cavalry will be at Nivelles at the same time. Lord Hill's Corps is at Braine le Comte.
>   I do not see much of the enemy before you, and I await news from Your Highness and the arrival of troops to decide my operations for the day.
>   Nothing has appeared near Binche, nor on your right.'
>
> Your very obedient servant.
> *Wellington*[17]

Wellington's claim that Hill was at Braine-le-Comte is particularly strange when de Lancey had spent part of the previous five hours issuing a series of orders to Hill, which would only result his arrival at the front the next day. There can be little doubt that Wellington knew just as well as de Lancey that Hill was a day's march from Braine. This belief is confirmed by Fitzroy Somerset's account which indicates that the Duke knew that all he could expect to reinforce the Netherlanders and 5th Division at Quatre Bras that day were the cavalry, the remainder of the Prince of Orange's Corps, the Guards and Alten's 3rd Division. The Duke's military secretary was surely in a

---

17 Ollech, p 125.

position to know and he makes no mention of Hill's troops being available there that day.[18]

Wellington and Blücher

Wellington had a good personal relationship with Blücher, the Field Marshal trusting the Duke implicitly. When Major Count Nostitz, Blücher's ADC, once questioned the honesty of Wellington's intention to come to the aid of the Prussians, Blücher dismissed the accusation. Nostitz's account read, 'I received the answer that it was a crime to doubt, even in the slightest, the word of a man like the Duke, who had such a glorious record.'[19]

Nostitz had first expressed such misgivings before the campaign began, when Wellington had shown no signs of moving his army into a position where it could better support the Prussians. He related,

> ...the Duke can certainly be accused in all conferences, in which either the Prince himself [Blücher] or officers representing him, discussed the common measures to be taken at the opening of hostilities, of having expressed every time the certainty that he was fully prepared in the event of the Prussians being the first to be attacked by the main French force, to be in a position to give rapid and substantial support. We can be accused of having unquestioningly believed these assurances.

> ...Thus no further attempt was made to get the Duke of Wellington to move his army into other quarters that would have given us a more certain assurance of the promised support.[20]

Wellington now rode to the Prussian headquarters for a personal meeting with Blücher, where he was again to repeat his promises of support. As the Field Marshal had such a high regard for the Duke, there can be little doubt that Blücher would believe whatever he would be told.

The Meeting at Brye

Having sent off his letter from Frasnes, Wellington continued his reconnaissance of the French positions, accompanied by Fitzroy Somerset, until about 11 a.m.[21] Seeing that there was apparently no major threat from the French there he then ordered part of his Reserve to Quatre Bras. Müffling's memoirs then take up the story,

> As the enemy was being quiet [at Frasnes], and as meanwhile a report had come to me that the Prussian army was assembling at Ligny, the Duke was of the opinion that it would be best to ride to the Field Marshal [Blücher] and to agree with him orally what measures were to be taken for a decisive battle with united forces.[22]

Dörnberg's account confirmed this, adding,

[18] Raglan Papers, A 24–31.
[19] Nostitz, p 18.
[20] Nostitz, p 17.

[21] *Life of Lord Raglan*, p 22.
[22] Müffling, *Leben*, p 230.

A patrol of Prussian hussars arrived, informing the Duke that Marshal Blücher was at Sombreffe. He said to me he wanted to ride there and I should accompany him. Along with several of the Duke's adjutants, General von Müffling rode with us.[23]

About 12.30 p.m., Wellington and Müffling inspected the troops at Quatre Bras before they rode to meet Blücher at his headquarters at the Windmill of Bussy at Brye.[24] The Duke was accompanied by Müffling, Dörnberg, Fitzroy Somerset and others, and escorted by a detachment of hussars. Müffling again takes up the story,

…while on our way, the Duke said to me, "If, as it seems, what the enemy has standing at Frasnes opposite Quatre Bras, is so insignificant, and should only mask the English army, then I can use my entire strength to support the Field Marshal, and everything he wishes as a joint operation, I will gladly carry out."

I was firmly convinced that what the Duke had said was his honest, firm will. I knew, however, of General von Gneisenau's mistrust of the Duke and was concerned in advance this would influence the discussions we were about to have.[25]

However, the situation existing while this conversation took place was that, other than one division of Netherlanders already engaged and 5th Division which he had just ordered to move on Quatre Bras, Wellington had yet to commit any further troops in support of the Prussians. Before his visit to Blücher's headquarters, his perception of the situation seems to have been that part of the French forces were before Blücher's positions, but no forces of note appeared to be threatening the Anglo-Dutch at Quatre Bras. Thus part of Napoleon's army was accounted for, but part was not. The Duke probably still worried that French troops could be manoeuvring around his right flank at Mons, making the feared move that would cut him off from the Channel ports and threaten Brussels and his line of retreat to Antwerp. In such circumstances, he would have been unwise to have committed a substantial part of his army to support the Prussians. However, as he had been tardy with the concentration and movement of his army, he would need the Prussians to tie down the bulk of the French forces to gain him the time to complete this.

The Duke also knew from information received by Müffling from Blücher, that the Prussians should have three army corps available to them at Sombreffe and that the fourth had been ordered to join them. As Blücher only discovered early on the morning of 16 June that the IV Army Corps would be unable to arrive that day, then it is unlikely that Wellington knew of this before his meeting with the Prussians at Brye. Thus, the Duke probably believed that the Prussians would be strong enough to hold out for a day against the French troops immediately before them, and that their need for his aid was not crucial. At that time, he may well have believed that the small body of men available at Quatre Bras, albeit not the 20,000 men he would

---

[23] Pflugk-Harttung, *Vorgeschichte*, p 293.   [25] Müffling, *Leben*, p 230 f.
[24] Scriba, pp 293–4.

consistently promise, would be sufficient for the task in hand, and could move to support the Prussians at Ligny, while he did not need to commit the rest of his troops until he was sure of the whereabouts of the remainder of the French army.

The party arrived at Blücher's headquarters at about 1 p.m. Here, the Duke met Blücher and various other Prussian officers including Gneisenau, Blücher's chief-of-staff; Reiche, Zieten's chief-of-staff; Clausewitz, chief-of-staff of the III Army Corps; Nostitz, Blücher's ADC; and Grolman, a senior officer on Blücher's staff. One more or less impartial participant was the Prince August of Thurn und Taxis, a Bavarian who was attached as an observer to Blücher's headquarters. Hardinge, the Duke of Wellington's representative in the Prussian headquarters, was also present. A number of these eye-witnesses have left accounts of this meeting, conducted, ironically, in French, as neither Wellington nor Hardinge could speak German, and only Dörnberg of the Germans could speak English. The possibility that misunderstandings may have arisen should not be discounted. The various accounts were as follows:

Müffling

The Duke of Wellington met the Field Marshal at the windmill of Brye. His army corps had just been allocated their positions whilst several officers observed Napoleon moving onto the Tombe de Ligny [the same vantage point Zieten had used the previous night]. The Duke examined the measures taken and appeared to be satisfied with them. As the heads of Napoleon's attack columns started to move towards St Amand, the Duke asked the Field Marshal and General Gneisenau: "What do you want me to do?". I had already informed General Gneisenau briefly that the Duke had every good intention and would do everything he could to support the Field Marshal bar dividing his army, this being against his principles. Only a few troops had got to Quatre Bras, and the English Reserves (which had been directed there) would not be able to arrive before 4 p.m. It thus seemed important to me that Wellington's troops concentrate to the fore, on the other side of Frasnes, and from there advance towards the Prussian right flank (Wagnelée), taking up a position at right angles to that of the Prussians, thereby flanking Napoleon on his left. General Gneisenau shook his head, but I did not know what he had against my proposal.

In answer to the Duke of Wellington's question, General Gneisenau replied that it would be most desirable for the Prussian Army if, "The Duke, once his army had assembled at Quatre Bras, was to march left down the Namur road and place itself in reserve behind the Prussian Army at Brye... "

The Duke of Wellington looked at his map and did not answer. I saw that this proposal did not please him and thus made the following remarks, "According to this proposal, the English Army would, until it had completed its assembly, be standing at Quatre Bras, 12,000 paces from the Prussians, doing absolutely nothing and without being of the slightest use. If, however, the English Army were to advance to the point where the Roman road meets the road from Quatre Bras to Charleroi (1½ hours), then it would be no more than 6,000 paces from the right flank of the Prussians and would thus, if it marched to the left, join up with Marshal Blücher as well as having favourable terrain in which to fight and manoeuvre. The Prince of Orange's Corps would have less distance to cover from Nivelles than to Quatre Bras and the right flank at Ath would be even nearer."

In this way, I avoided commenting about the Duke's erroneous calculations of the time it would take to assemble his army as well as General Gneisenau's incorrect assumptions of when the English Army would arrive at Brye. The Duke immediately accepted my proposal, saying: "I will brush those forces before me at Frasnes aside and head for Gosselies."

General Gneisenau rejected everything that was in favour of this course of action with the few words: "This would take too long and is uncertain. However, the march from Quatre Bras to Brye would be safe and decisive". The Duke exclaimed: "Very well! I will come so long as I am not attacked myself."[26]

Dörnberg

We found Marshal Blücher at the mill near Brye. After having spoken a few words, the Duke said to General Gneisenau, "Do tell me your opinion as to what you wish me to do." Gneisenau took the map in his hand and said, "If you push the forces before you at Quatre Bras out of your way and advance quickly, this would put you in the position of being able to move on the rear of the French Army. However, as there are only narrow roads running in that direction, it would be safest if you were to tie down those forces immediately facing you and then to move to your left with the remainder of your army, so coming onto our right flank and taking the French in their left." The Duke answered, "Your reasoning is correct, I will see what is standing against me and act on that basis", without saying one way or another what his decision was and without promising anything.[27]

Reiche, Clausewitz and Thurn und Taxis

Reiche's account of the meeting is relatively short, as he was clearly more concerned with getting his troops into position for the forthcoming battle.

At 1 p.m. Blücher appeared on the heights at the mill of Bussy where he was joined shortly after by the Duke of Wellington... He [Wellington] stated that he was convinced that the bulk of the enemy's forces were drawn up against us and not against Quatre Bras and there could thus not be any further doubts as to the enemy's intentions... Promising us substantial support and assistance, Wellington returned to his army at 1.30 p.m.[28]

Clausewitz's account was equally brief.

At 1 p.m. the Duke of Wellington met Field Marshal Blücher at the Windmill of Brye. The Duke told the Field Marshal that at this very moment his army

[26] Müffling, *Leben*, p 233 ff.   [28] Reiche, vol II, pp 183–4.
[27] Pflugk-Harttung, *Vorgeschichte*, p 293.

was gathering at Quatre Bras and that he would be coming to his assistance in a few hours. As he galloped off, his words were: "At four o'clock, I will be here." [29]

Thurn und Taxis' memoirs mentioned equally simply that, 'The Duke promised to send 20,000 men from his army by 3 o'clock, and after it was agreed to accept battle, he rode back to Quatre Bras.' [30]

Nostitz

At about 1 p.m. the Duke of Wellington arrived, accompanied by General Müffling. A long discussion took place between him and Generals Gneisenau and Grolman in which the Duke repeated his promise of substantial support. At about 3 p.m. [actually around 2 p.m.], the Duke took his leave in order to, as he said, give his troops the necessary orders for their advance. The Field Marshal accompanied him for a distance. I rode with General Müffling. [31]

Grolman

At 1 p.m. the Field Marshal was at the mill of Bussy observing the enemy's movements… It was at this time that the Duke of Wellington came to Prince Blücher to hold their last talks. They agreed on the way in which they would support each other, this being a movement of the Duke's available forces, if not his whole army, via Frasnes towards Gosselies to take the enemy in the flank and rear, and that this movement would have to be accomplished by 4 p.m. that afternoon.

Movements after 5 p.m. would depend on circumstances as the battle developed when a direct intervention would be more advantageous than a distant offensive. The execution of this direct assistance to the Prussian right flank would be left to the Duke to determine according to circumstances and the Duke's judgement.

Meanwhile, the French army was advancing via Fleurus. This at last made the Duke seem to accept that Napoleon was moving with the bulk of his forces against the Prussians. He waited until 1.45 p.m., by which time the French army had fully developed its deployment, and only then did he return to his army.

When the Duke of Wellington made his promise of support, he used the words: "I am convinced that by 2 p.m. I will have so many troops assembled that I can go over to the offensive immediately thereafter."

After this firm commitment, the Prussian side finally made the decision to accept battle. [32]

Reconciling the Different Versions

There are reasons for being cautious about accepting some of these accounts simply as they stand. Müffling's, Dörnberg's, Clausewitz's and Reiche's stories

[29] Clausewitz, p 67.
[30] Thurn und Taxis, p 322.
[31] Nostitz, p 23 f.
[32] Damitz, vol I, pp 117–18.

all appear in their various memoirs or historical accounts, compiled long after the fact, and not based, as far as is known, on any contemporary record they may have kept. Nostitz and Thurn und Taxis wrote their versions drawing on diaries they kept at the time which would tend to make them more reliable.

Müffling's version has to be treated with special care because his account generally tends to be self-important, flavoured with the benefit of hindsight and circumspect when dealing with Müffling's own errors. After all, it was Müffling's job to be aware of everything that was taking place in Wellington's headquarters, a task in which he clearly failed, so he had a motive to be to be sparing with the truth on occasions – as is apparent from his comments on 'the Duke's erroneous calculations' and 'Gneisenau's incorrect assumptions'. As liaison officer between the two headquarters, it was Müffling's duty to point out such matters, but as he did not, it is unlikely that he was aware of them at the time.

Several of the accounts obviously come from Prussians, who might be thought to have an interest in shifting some of the blame for the defeat that followed that day onto the failure of the Duke to live up to his 'promises' of support, but Dörnberg and Thurn und Taxis cannot be accused of being biased in this way. Dörnberg was a Hanoverian and one would expect his sympathies to lie with the British, the protectors of his homeland, and not with the Prussians. As a Bavarian officer, the Prince Thurn und Taxis' interests also lay more with the British than with the Prussians. One would not expect him to take the Prussian side in any dispute, which is another reason for considering this account to be reliable.

However, despite their different viewpoints, all these recollections agree that the meeting discussed how, rather than if, Wellington's army would come and help the Prussians in their battle that day. Reiche, Clausewitz, Nostitz and Thurn und Taxis all agree about 'promises of substantial support' and 'repeated his promise of substantial support', mentioning specific times in the course of the afternoon when this promised help would arrive. Müffling and Dörnberg qualify this slightly with 'so long as I am not attacked myself' and 'I will see what is standing against me' but even from their accounts the general tone of the conversation is clear; Wellington would come to help the Prussians in strength that day.

Grolman takes this a step further by saying that the Prussian commanders had not fully committed themselves to battle until they heard from Wellington at the meeting. Indeed, at that stage, they could quite conceivably have staged a rearguard action with I Army Corps, with II and III Army Corps falling back towards the Gembloux position, where IV Army Corps would arrive the next day. However, this would have left Wellington open to an attack by a substantial part of the French army.

One further account to consider is that of a Prussian artillery officer, Captain Reuter, who commanded 12-pounder Battery No 6 in the I Army Corps Reserve Artillery at Ligny. While the meeting between Wellington and Blücher was in progress, Major-General von Holtzendorf, commander of Blücher's artillery, came up and ordered him to have his number one gun fire a round. 'We were told at the time,' he said, 'that this was a signal to our army corps that the Prince had made up his mind to accept battle.'[33]

Even Fitzroy Somerset's account of the meeting largely agrees with these versions given by the German witnesses,

> The Duke accompanied by his Staff & a small escort of Cavalry rode from Quatre Bras between 11 & 12 o'clock to Blücher's positions. The Marshal was at the Butte St Croix. The Prussian Troops were found in close Column on the Heights in rear of St Amand & Ligny which were occupied & the left of the Prussian Army extended beyond Sombreffe.
>
> The Duke & Blücher saw the French in great force advancing towards the Prussians & the Duke observed to Blücher he would soon be attacked.
>
> The Duke, expecting that our Cavalry, the remainder of the Prince of Orange's Corps, the Guards & Alten's Division would arrive at Quatre Bras about 2 o'clock, told Blücher that he would give him all the support in his power & the Duke gallopped [sic] back to Quatre Bras which he reached about ½ past 2 o'clock.[34]

Wellington and Hardinge

The next eye-witness accounts that should be considered are those of Wellington himself and of Hardinge. Wellington's own recollection was recorded by the Baron de Ros following a conversation with the Duke between 1836 and 1840,

> "I told the Prussian officers, in the presence of Hardinge, that according to my judgement, the exposure of the advanced columns, and, indeed, of the whole army to cannonade, standing as they did so displayed to the aim of the enemy's fire, was not so prudent. The marshy banks of the stream made it out of their power to cross and attack the French, while the latter on the other hand, though they could not attack them, had it in their power to cannonade them and shatter them to pieces, after which they might fall upon them by the bridges at the villages. I said that if I were in Blücher's place with English troops, I should withdraw all the columns I saw scattered about in front, and get more of the troops under shelter of the rising ground. However, they seemed to think they knew best, so I came away very shortly."[35]

Particularly strange here is the comment that the Prussians would not be able to cross the Ligne stream because of its marshy banks which, as they were fighting a defensive battle, they were not likely to want to do, whereas apparently the French would have no problem in crossing the stream by the bridges later on. Furthermore, an examination of the Prussian positions does not support the Duke's claim that the Prussian columns were exposed; those troops deployed in the villages were certainly in cover, and the bulk of the

---

[33] Reuter, p 277. A commentary on this diary together with a translation into English of parts thereof can be found in the *United Service Magazine*, October 1891, in an article entitled 'A Prussian Gunner's Adventures in 1815' by Capt. E. S. May, R.A.

[34] Raglan Papers, A 24–31. [35] As quoted in: Maxwell, vol II, pp 19–20.

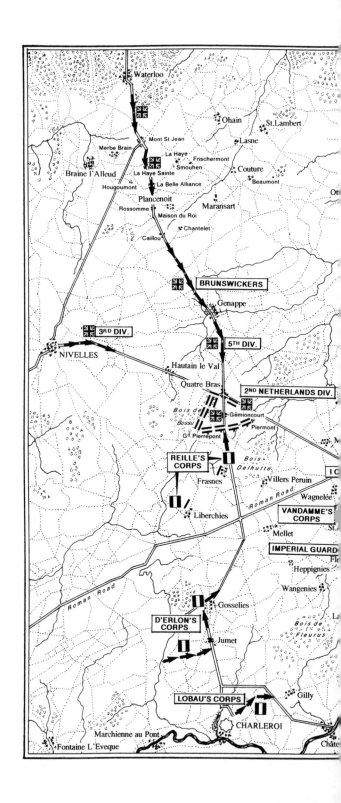

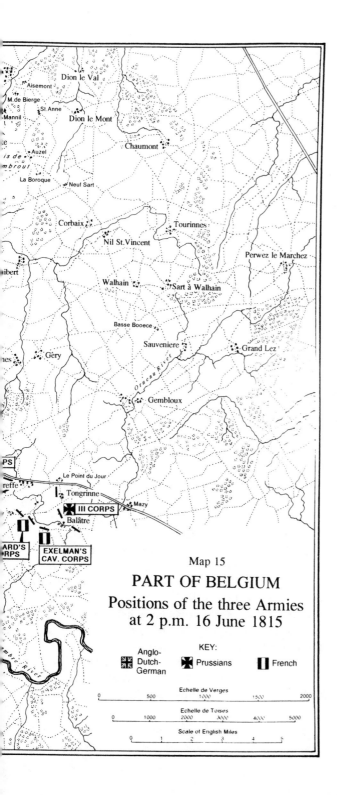

Map 15

PART OF BELGIUM

Positions of the three Armies
at 2 p.m. 16 June 1815

KEY:

Anglo-
Dutch-
German

Prussians

French

Echelle de Verges
0   500   1000   1500   2000

Echelle de Toises
0   1000   2000   3000   4000   5000

Scale of English Miles
0   1   2   3   4   5

reserves were drawn up in dead ground, out of range of the French artillery, and even out of sight of Napoleon, who, having observed the Prussian positions from the vantage point of the Tombe de Ligny, thought for some time, he was facing only one Prussian corps.[36]

Hardinge also made similar comments in a conversation involving the Duke, and the Earl Stanhope, on 26 October 1837. Stanhope recorded the two as saying,

> "When you [Wellington] had examined the Prussian position, I remember you much disapproved of it, and said to me, 'if they fight here, they will be damnably mauled.'" The Duke added, "They were dotted in this way – all their bodies along the slope of a hill, so that no cannon-ball missed its effect upon them."[37]

Again this seems difficult to accept uncritically. Evidently, at no time in the meeting at Brye were Wellington and Hardinge out of earshot of other participants. Their comments must have been made in the presence of witnesses, yet nobody else records having heard any such criticism of the Prussian positions. Indeed, according to the version told to De Ros, the Duke complained to the Prussian officers there, yet none of them recorded such comments; neither did the Hanoverian, nor the Bavarian officer present, and neither did Wellington's military secretary, who gave a detailed account of the Prussian positions and outlined the main point of the discussion. These last three all had good reasons, both personal and political, to have made note of any such comments critical of the Prussian positions. It is also interesting to note that neither Wellington's nor Hardinge's account mention the Duke having promised to support the Prussians that day. As all other witnesses mention this, one wonders why in later conversations, Wellington did not.

Wellington Returns to Quatre Bras

The Duke of Wellington returned to his headquarters certain that his Prussian allies were going to engage a substantial part of Napoleon's army. However, having heard that only three instead of the four army corps expected were going to be available to Blücher, the Duke probably started to become concerned about their ability to hold on for long enough for his own forces to concentrate. It was now clear to Wellington that the arrival of enough of his men to support Blücher was crucial, but he had yet to establish the whereabouts of the remainder of the French army. It is likely that he pondered this point during his ride back to Quatre Bras. When he got there, a substantial French assault on his positions was in progress. Then, and only then, was it clear to Wellington that the French were not going to move around his right, via Mons, and only then did he commit his army unreservedly to support the Prussians, who had already been in action against the French for a day and a half.

---

[36] Charras, vol I, p 184 f.
[37] Stanhope, p 109.

Wellington's German Troops

While Wellington and Blücher were having their discussion at the windmill of Bussy, many of Wellington's German troops were marching with all haste to the front. Most had set off from their concentration points in the early hours of the morning of 16 June. They started to arrive at Quatre Bras some 12 hours later, after an exhausting forced march in the blistering heat of a hot June day, often with little to drink and less to eat. Nevertheless, the Hanoverians and the Brunswickers were thrown into the desperate action at this crucial road junction just as soon as they were available.

The official report on the participation of the Hanoverian troops and King's German Legion described the march of some of these troops,

> The brigade under the command of Colonel Best [4th Hanoverian Brigade] arrived near the battlefield [of Quatre Bras] about 3 p.m., along with the remainder of the troops at that time under the command of Lieutenant-General Picton. It had left Brussels at 3 a.m... [38]

Best's own report then takes up the story,

> At 3 a.m., we marched off, following the 8th British Brigade under the command of Major-General Sir J. Kempt on the cobbled road towards Charleroi. The baggage and ammunition waggons followed under the appropriate escort.
> Arriving in the Forest of Soignes, the brigade was ordered to stop and eat. Hardly an hour had passed when the order to move on and march off was given. Beyond the little town of Genappe, the Brunswick cavalry (hussars and uhlans), led by their duke, caught up with us and passed the column... It was 3 p.m. when the brigade reached this position [at Quatre Bras], and we were the first Hanoverian troops to come under fire.[39]

The official account also described the experiences of the 1st Hanoverian Brigade,

> The 3rd Division under the command of Lieutenant-General C. von Alten, to which this brigade belonged, had concentrated in Soignies on the evening of the 15th. From there, it moved on again at 2 a.m., marching via Braine-le-Comte to Nivelles. At Nivelles, the 2nd Brigade of the King's German Legion was detached, along with the horse battery, to observe the road to Charleroi. The two other brigades of the division, with the foot battery, undertook a forced march of about nine lieues [about 35 km], which it covered in about 15 hours, including the stop at Nivelles, arriving at the battlefield of Quatre Bras about 5 p.m... [40]

The report of the 1st Hanoverian Brigade gave more details,

> At 2 a.m. [on 16 June], the [3rd] Division was ordered to move off, and, after a very difficult march via Braine-le-Comte and Bornival, reached Nivelles

---

[38] Pflugk-Harttung, *Belle Alliance*, pp 9–13.   [40] Pflugk-Harttung, *Belle Alliance*, pp 9–13.
[39] Pflugk-Harttung, *Belle Alliance*, p 19 f.

about 10 a.m. The 2nd Brigade of the King's German Legion was detached towards Charleroi; the 5th British Brigade was to rest at Nivelles, and the 1st Hanoverian Brigade on the road to Quatre Bras.

Hardly had the designated position been reached when the order arrived to move off again immediately and advance along the road to Quatre Bras from where we had, for some considerable time, been hearing heavy cannon fire, and from where crowds of wounded and stragglers, particularly Belgians, had been coming.[41]

The report of Major Müller of the Feldbataillon Bremen described its march to the front as follows,

At 2 a.m., the division marched to Braine-le-Comte where it left the baggage, and went on to Nivelles. At 1 p.m., about half an hour from that place, and on the cobbled road running towards Namur, we halted and rested in a field to the right of the road. Tired out by the oppressive heat and rapid march, several men dropped out, but rejoined the battalion that evening. The order to cook was given. About 2 p.m., cannon and small arms fire could be heard. We could not finish cooking, for at three, the order came to march off as fast as possible, which meant that many of the men left their meat behind, as it was not yet cooked through. Just before that, about 20 Prussian stragglers came along the road, saying they were part of Zieten's Corps.

So the division marched as quickly as it could towards Quatre Bras. On the way there, many wounded, mainly Netherlanders, could be seen being brought back.[42]

The official report of the Feldbataillon Bremen told a similar story,

...it was almost dawn when the Brigade of Generalmajor Graf von Kielmansegge, of which this battalion was part, moved off from Soignies on 16 June... The air was very warm. The march, which was at first very slow, was speeded up, and soon some of the men were dropping out... The division crossed paths with other troops in Nivelles and stopped there for a while... About half an hour from Nivelles, we stopped and set up camp right next to the cobbled road. The stragglers soon caught up with the rearguard. Food was supplied, and we began to cook, but hardly had we started when, at 3 p.m., the British Major-General Sir Colin Halkett, who had ridden on down the road, ordered us to move off quickly. Some soldiers took their half-cooked meat with them, others threw it away, and made do with bread and brandy.[43]

The cavalry, who could at least ride to the front, had life a little easier. Rittmeister Georg von der Decken of the 1st Hussar Regiment of the King's German Legion reported,

...on 16 June at 11 a.m., the regiment, in Tournai, received the order to march off immediately. At 1 p.m., we left Tournai and marched without a rest until

[41] Pflugk-Harttung, *Belle Alliance*, p 15.
[42] Pflugk-Harttung, *Belle Alliance*, p 30.
[43] Pflugk-Harttung, *Belle Alliance*, p 33.

1 a.m., in Braine-le-Comte; here, the regiment fed for two hours, moving off again before dawn.

At noon [on 17 June], the regiment reached the position at Quatre Bras, without having rested or fed.[44]

These various accounts would seem to confirm that only after 2 p.m., when the Duke returned to Quatre Bras from his meeting with Blücher, did his orders for his troops to move there become really urgent. Troops that had left the Brussels area early that morning had considered it appropriate to take a long meal break; now others were forced to leave their partly-cooked dinners behind uneaten. This further confirms that the Duke of Wellington was slow to appreciate the facts of the situation.

[44] Pflugk-Harttung, *Belle Alliance*, p 38.

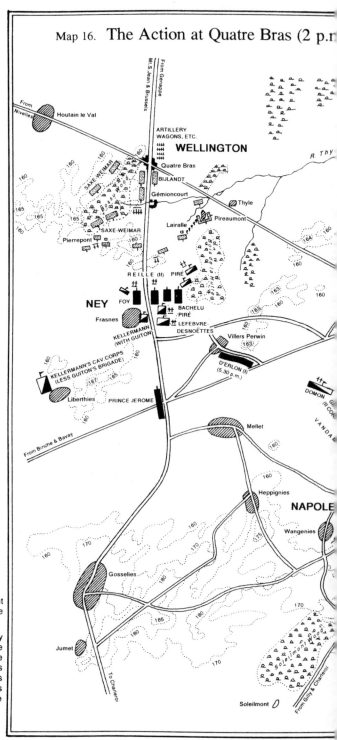

Map 16. The Action at Quatre Bras (2 p.m.)

KEY:

British and Allies

Prussians

French

NOTES:

(a) Only the more important roads and tracks are shown.

(b) Sufficient contours only are inserted to show the shape of the ground; the 160 metre contour is taken as datum-level as no lower contour affects the intervisibility of the two fields.

(c) All heights are in metres.

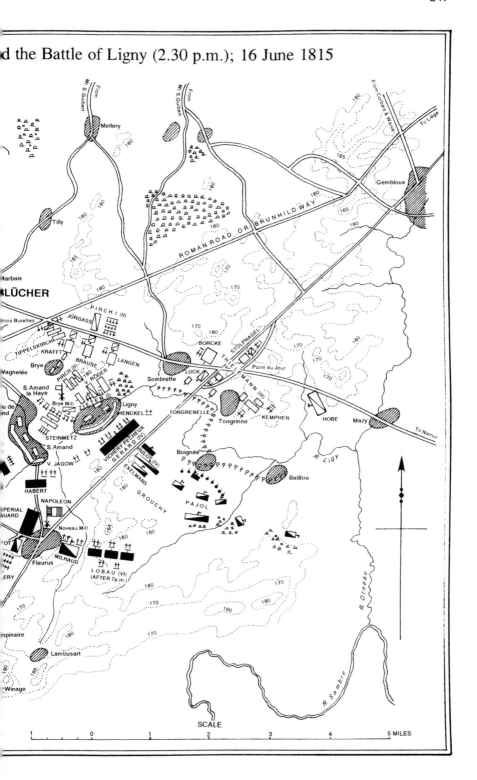

d the Battle of Ligny (2.30 p.m.); 16 June 1815

SCALE

1 0 1 2 3 4 5 MILES

Chapter 13

The Battle of Ligny–Quatre Bras

Ligny–Quatre Bras

As it was the intention of the commanders of the two wings of the Allied forces in the Netherlands to unite their armies to fight a decisive battle against the French invader, the major combats of 16 June 1815 should be regarded as part of a single battle. The Allied failure to accomplish this concentration resulted in Blücher's wing suffering a defeat, and in Wellington's wing, which held its ground that day, being forced to retire as a result of that defeat. Despite having made several promises to the contrary, Wellington only managed to bring part of his forces into action on 16 June. To achieve the desired concentration of their armies, both Blücher and Wellington would have to pull back and select another position. This they accomplished two days later around Mont St Jean, to the south of the village of Waterloo.

The Sombreffe Position

Early in May, as part of the Allied preparations for a possible French invasion, Prussian staff officers had reconnoitred the Sombreffe position. Indeed, Major Graf Groeben had produced a sketch map of it.[1] Thought had been given to deploying two army corps along the line Sombreffe–Balâtre in defensive positions, while the two other corps would seek to outflank the French on their left.[2]

Strategically, Sombreffe was on the road running from Namur, where the Prussian headquarters was originally situated, via Quatre Bras, 13 km away, to Nivelles, the most forward point at which Wellington could be expected to concentrate. Keeping this important lateral link open was vital to allow the two wings of the Allied forces to act in unison against a French invasion. Besides, Bülow's army corps was moving along this road, albeit belatedly, to join with the remainder of the Prussian army.

The terrain around Sombreffe gave a number of advantages to the defence. The undulating countryside contained considerable areas of dead ground in which troops could be hidden. The tall crops, at that time often the height of a man or more, added to the possibilities for concealment. Villages such as St Amand, Ligny, Sombreffe, Tongrinne, Boignée and Balâtre contained a number of stone buildings, which could be used to sustain the defence. The windmill at Bussy and the tall church spires in the defended

---

[1] Weltzien, vol 2, p 147 f and p 172 fn.
[2] Sothen, p 147.

villages were vantage points from which the enemy movements could be observed. This would help in anticipating his attacks and feeding the carefully hidden reserves into the right places at the right time.

The village of Ligny spread over an extent of around 1 km, with its longest axis running from south-west to north-east. It was about 1.3 km away from St Amand and about 800 metres from the next bend in the Ligne brook at Mont Potriaux. From Ligny to Mont Potriaux the brook ran through a marshy meadow which could only be crossed by troops with the greatest difficulty. About half-way between Ligny and Sombreffe, was a wood, the Bois du Loup, which was some 400 to 500 metres across. A line of trees and bushes joined this wood to Ligny.

The villages of St Amand, St Amand la Haye and Wagnelée formed a line running for about 3 km. In front of the centre of St Amand la Haye stood the farmhouse of St Amand le Hameau which consisted of several stout buildings. A sunken road connected it to Wagnelée. The villages each lay in hollows and had ditches and hedges around their perimeters. The walls of the buildings were made of limestone, and were solid enough to offer a good defence. However, most of St Amand and of St Amand la Haye were situated on the western side of the Ligne. Although the south-east end of St Amand was also exposed to the French, taking up a shorter defensive line running directly from St Amand la Haye to the château of Ligny would have meant having to deploy troops in the open, on the slopes leading up to Brye. The roads connecting these villages also assisted the defence.

The village of Brye, covering a front of around 800 metres, was well protected from an attack from the direction of Wagnelée to the west by hedges, undergrowth and buildings running in the direction of St Amand la Haye. The relatively open terrain to the west and south of Wagnelée and St Amand was ideal for a strong counter-attack against the French left flank.

The main vantage point on the battlefield was the windmill of Bussy to the south of Brye, the highest position in the Prussian centre, where Blücher established his headquarters. From there one could not see farther east than Sombreffe whose buildings and trees screened the horizon. To the south and south-west, the valley of the Ligne brook could be observed, as could the far banks and the flat land immediately beyond them. The villages on the far side were also visible. The town of Fleurus and the Charleroi–Namur road marked the limits of vision in that direction. French movements to the south of Fleurus were largely out of sight. Although there would appear to be no record of the Prussians having placed any observers in the upper part of the windmill, it would be surprising if they had not done so.

A second important vantage point was on the heights of Point du Jour east of Sombreffe, where there was a group of houses. In places the view was obscured; to the south and south-west by Tongrinne and Boignée, to the west by Sombreffe, and in a few other sections by the trees along the Ligne brook. This had an effect on the actions of the Prussian III Army Corps that day.

Despite these minor problems with visibility, the sector of the position from Sombreffe to Balâtre, covering communications to Namur and Liège,

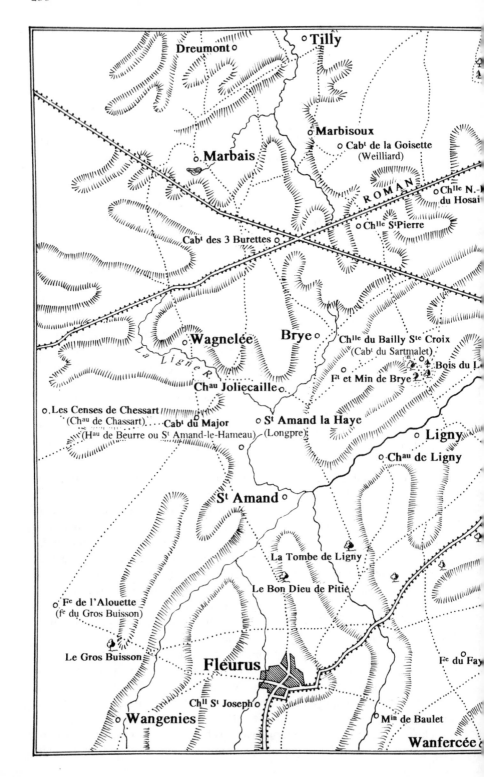

Dreumont o

o **Tilly**

o Marbisoux

o Cabt de la Goisette
(Weilliard)

o **Marbais**

R O M A N

o Chlle N.-
du Hosai

Cabt des 3 Burettes o

o Chlle StPierre

o **Wagnelée**

Brye o

Chlle du Bailly Ste Croix
(Cabt du Sartmalet)

Bois du L

Ft et Min de Brye 2

Chau Joliecaille o

o . Les Censes de Chessart
(Chau de Chassart) . . . .Cabt du Major
(Hau de Beurre ou St Amand-le-Hameau)
o

o St Amand la Haye
(Longpre)

Ligny

o Chau de Ligny

St Amand o

La Tombe de Ligny

Fc de l'Alouette
(fc du Gros Buisson)

Le Bon Dieu de Pitié

Fc du Fay

Le Gros Buisson

Fleurus

o Wangenies

Chll St Joseph o

Min de Baulet

Wanfercée

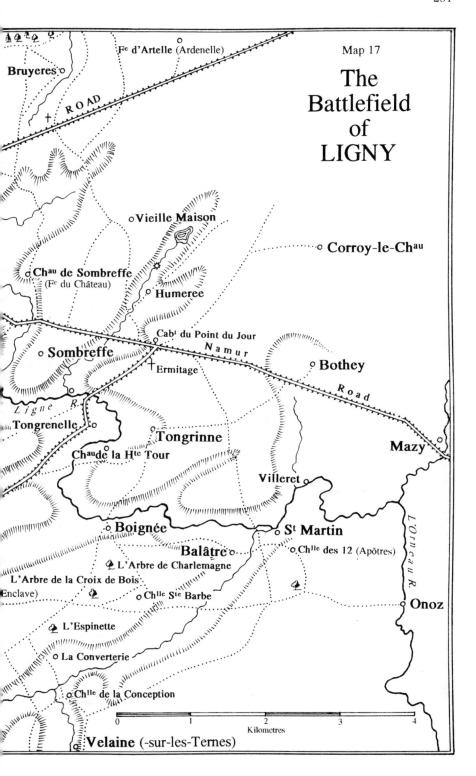

Fᶜ d'Artelle (Ardenelle)

Bruyeres

ROAD

Map 17

The
Battlefield
of
LIGNY

o Vieille Maison

o Corroy-le-Chᵃᵘ

Chᵃᵘ de Sombreffe
(Fᶜ du Château)

o Humeree

Cabᵗ du Point du Jour

Namur

Sombreffe

+ Ermitage

o Bothey

Road

Ligne R.

Tongrenelle

o Tongrinne

Mazy

Chᵃᵘde la Hᵗᵉ Tour

Villeret

L'Orneau R.

o Boignée

Sᵗ Martin

Balâtre

o Chˡˡᵉ des 12 (Apôtres)

L'Arbre de Charlemagne

L'Arbre de la Croix de Bois
Enclave)

o Chˡˡᵉ Sᵗᵉ Barbe

Onoz

L'Espinette

o La Converterie

o Chˡˡᵉ de la Conception

| 0 | 1 | 2 | 3 | 4 |

Kilometres

Velaine (-sur-les-Ternes)

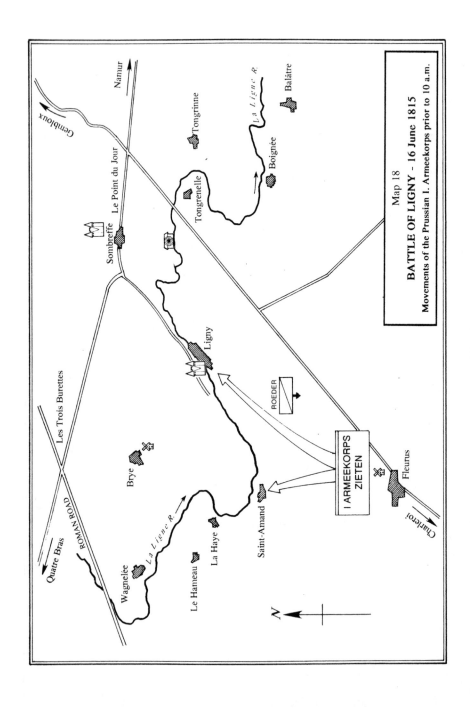

Map 18

BATTLE OF LIGNY - 16 June 1815

Movements of the Prussian I. Armeekorps prior to 10 a.m.

was ideal for a passive defence. Being a metre or so high, the left bank of the Ligne brook was a sufficient barrier to protect defenders from the firepower of the period. The brook itself was only one or two metres wide, but the valley and its marshy terrain presented a formidable obstacle, strengthened and supported by the villages of Tongrinelle, Tongrinne, Boignée and Balâtre.

The major weakness in the Prussian positions was their right flank, which rested precariously in the air, a further indication that support was expected from the direction of Quatre Bras. The open ground here at least gave the Prussians room for local counter-attacks, while III Corps could launch an offensive along its front on the left, although the marshy banks of the Ligne brook would have made the going difficult.

The Prussians chose the villages as their main defensive positions. This was a wise decision because, in addition to the advantages they offered to defence, the relatively poor quality of the Prussian infantry would have been more apparent in an open position. A substantial part of Blücher's forces consisted of raw levies capable of two basic manoeuvres: going forwards in a state of disorder, or going backwards in a state of chaos. Given these options, Blücher needed to exploit the first attribute, while hoping to deal with the second when, and if, it occurred. Young, inexperienced, but enthusiastic Prussian militiamen were more suited to street fighting where the better training of the French would be of less advantage.

The strength of the Prussian position was not confined to the features in the front line. Behind the village of St Amand was a long, gentle slope leading up to Brye. If the French were to seize the village, then they would have to advance uphill, in open terrain, in the face of the Prussian artillery. The assault columns would be bowled over by the round shot, and suffer heavy casualties. The village of Ligny was also in a hollow which rose upwards in the direction of Brye and Sombreffe. Any French breakthrough could be countered by the troops at Brye and the reserves on the Namur road. Were the French to push the Prussians out of both these villages, then the higher ground around Brye was well suited for a rearguard action.

Thus, there were three layers to the Prussian positions. Firstly, the villages of St Amand and Ligny along the front line which were suitable for a determined defence, buying the time needed for Wellington to bring his troops into play. Secondly, the slopes from these villages leading upwards to Brye which would cost the French dear to cross in the face of artillery fire. Finally, there was the village of Brye, which was like the citadel of a fortress, a small but strong place on high ground, suitable for a last line of defence.

Blücher's strategy for the battle was one of aggressive defence. He would use the strong-points on the battlefield to hold up the French, then send his inexperienced troops forward in local counter-attacks to recover any lost positions. These would then be held for as long as possible by fresh troops. These troops, if driven back again, would, in turn, be replaced by fresh troops fed in through another local counter-attack. With this strategy, the Prussian leaders hoped to be able to hold their positions long enough for Wellington to arrive.

254

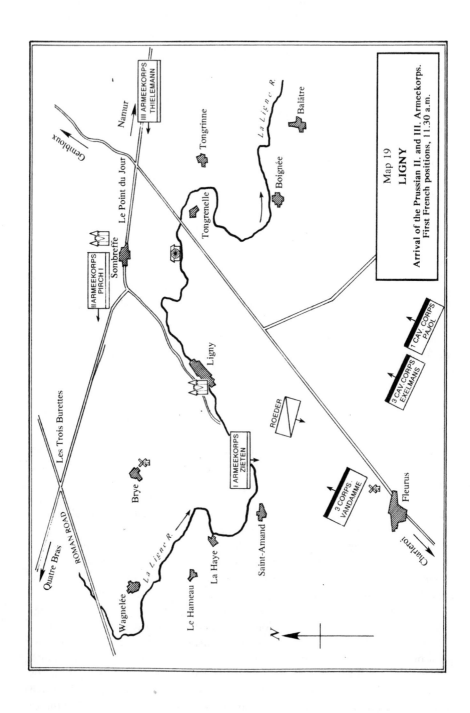

Map 19
LIGNY
Arrival of the Prussian II. and III. Armeekorps.
First French positions, 11.30 a.m.

Napoleon's Intentions

Having forced back Zieten's I Army Corps in the fighting of 15 June, Napoleon considered the Prussian Army to be in the process of withdrawing, with Zieten acting as its rearguard. Before he could turn his attentions against Wellington and move to Brussels, Napoleon would first have to send the Prussians on their way, while ensuring that Wellington could not come to their immediate assistance. The objectives of the previous day had been to seize control of Fleurus and Quatre Bras. These objectives had almost been met, but in the case of Quatre Bras, not quite.

Napoleon thus formed his army into two wings of roughly equal strength. The right wing, under Grouchy, consisting of the III Corps (Vandamme) and IV Corps (Gérard) and the 1st Cavalry Corps (Pajol) and 2nd Cavalry Corps (Exelmans), was to move against the Prussians. The left wing, under Ney, consisting of the I Corps (d'Erlon) and II Corps (Reille), less Girard's 7th Division, the Guard Light Cavalry Division (Lefebvre-Desnoëttes) and the 3rd Cavalry Corps (Kellermann), was to move against Wellington. The Emperor himself kept control of the remainder of the Guard, the VI Corps (Lobau) and the 4th Cavalry Corps (Milhaud). With this reserve, he could move to support either wing, as required.

Napoleon spent the morning of 16 June strengthening his right wing. He brought the Guard up to Fleurus. Girard's division of II Corps was taken away from Ney and placed under Vandamme's command.

That morning, Napoleon issued orders to both Ney and Grouchy, the commanders of the two wings of his army. He informed Ney that he was giving him full control of the 3rd Cavalry Corps, but was taking back the Guard light cavalry to reunite it with the remainder of the Guard. Grouchy, commander of the right wing, was ordered to take the 1st, 2nd and 4th Cavalry Corps to Sombreffe and take up positions there. Vandamme with his III Corps, and Gérard with his IV Corps, were placed under Grouchy's command and likewise ordered to move on Sombreffe, attacking Sombreffe in co-operation should the Prussians show any resistance. The objective that day was to push on as far as Gembloux. Napoleon estimated the Prussian strength around Sombreffe at 40,000 men, little more than a single army corps, and, once he had pushed them back to Gembloux, he intended to swing left with his reserves and hit Wellington next.[3]

Ney was instructed to take I and II Corps together with the 3rd Cavalry Corps and advance on Quatre Bras in the direction of Brussels. He was to keep in contact with Grouchy's wing by detaching a sizeable body of men to Marbais. It was considered likely that the weak Allied force at this intersection would retire in the direction of Nivelles. In this event, Ney was ordered to place one division, supported by cavalry, at Genappe, and move another to Marbais to cover the gap between Sombreffe and Quatre Bras. This latter force was to scout in the direction of Gembloux and Wavre.

The first French columns started to move out of Fleurus to take up their

---

[3] The orders for that morning are reproduced in Delhaize & Aerts, *Waterloo*, pp 348–53.

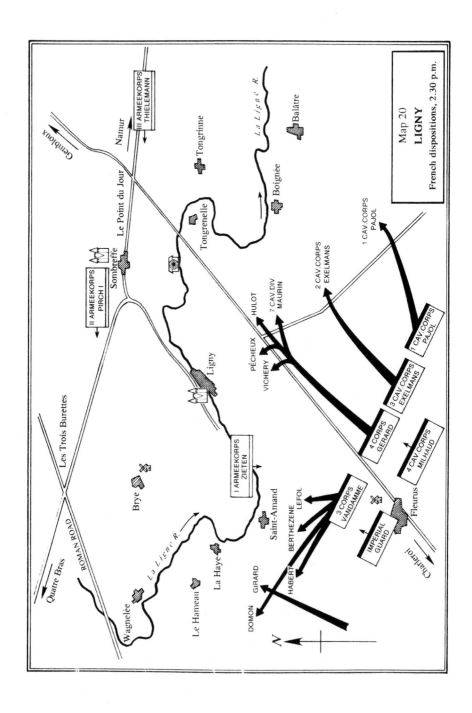

Map 20
LIGNY
French dispositions, 2.30 p.m.

positions at 10 a.m., about the time when the Duke of Wellington first arrived at Quatre Bras. At that early hour, it was clear that the day was going to be hot and stifling. At 11 a.m. Napoleon arrived to inspect the front to loud calls of greeting from his men. The French picket lines exchanged the odd shot with Lützow's 6th Uhlans, the former free corps cavalry recently reorganised as a line regiment. Zieten's artillery above St Amand sent the occasional round of ball into Vandamme's columns. Around noon, Napoleon climbed up the wind-mill of Naveau at Fleurus, from where he observed the Prussian positions. He attached little significance to the reports he had received from Grouchy and Vandamme of a strong Prussian column marching from the direction of Namur to Sombreffe, seeing only Zieten's men drawn up on the slopes leading up to Brye. From this vantage point, he was able to observe the area between St Amand, Brye and Ligny, but any movements behind Ligny in the direction of Sombreffe were obscured from his view.

By 2 p.m. IV Corps had taken up positions for its attack. Gérard had arrived on the battlefield shortly after midday and reconnoitred the Prussian positions with his staff before being charged by the Prussian 6th Uhlans. Beating a hasty retreat, Gérard then went to pay his respects to his Emperor.

The French Positions[4]

The III Corps (Vandamme), supported by Girard's 7th Division drew up to the north of Wangenies, facing north-east towards the Prussian positions in St Amand. Nine squadrons of chasseurs under Domon covered their left flank, deploying out to the Champ de Chassart. Lefol's 8th and Berthezène's 11th Divisions, 11 and eight battalions respectively, were formed in two lines, with Habert's 10th Division of 12 battalions in reserve. Vandamme's right, Lefol's division, reached as far as the chapel of Bon Dieu de Pitié. The artillery, 38 guns, did not arrive until after the beginning of the battle.

Gérard's IV Corps deployed at right angles to the III. It drew up before Ligny facing north-west with Vichery's 13th Division (eight battalions) and Pêcheux's 12th (ten battalions) deployed in two lines north of the Fleurus–Charleroi road, about 1 km from the edge of the village. The divisional and reserve artillery, totalling 24 pieces, was drawn up along a path on the top of a crest about 800 metres from Ligny. There was a gap of about 2 km between Vandamme's right and Gérard's left. This gap was covered by Milhaud's cavalry.

Gérard detached Hulot's 14th Division, six battalions and eight guns, and placed it behind his other divisions, at right angles to them facing north-east along the main road, with Maurin's 7th Cavalry Division, 14 squadrons and six guns, on its flank. Exelmans extended this line of cavalry by drawing up his 31 squadrons of dragoons in two lines along the road from Ligny to Velaine, with a battery of six horse guns on each flank. They faced the Prussian positions in Boignée. Pajol, with the 16 squadrons remaining to him, along with 12 guns and two battalions of infantry detached from Hulot's division, was placed

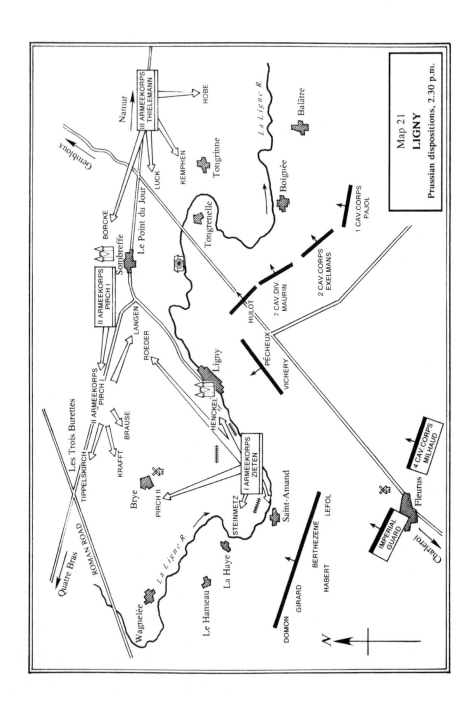

Map 21
LIGNY
Prussian dispositions, 2.30 p.m.

on the far right flank, facing north, covering the road from Fleurus to Onoz.

The Imperial Guard, 23 battalions, 13 squadrons and 96 guns, along with Milhaud's cuirassiers, 24 squadrons and 12 guns, were held in reserve near Fleurus.

The Prussian Deployment[5]

I Army Corps

The I Army Corps (Zieten) started the day around Fleurus, and withdrew slowly to take up positions in and around the villages of Ligny, Brye and St Amand.

The 1st Brigade (Steinmetz) occupied Brye with six companies of infantry, four from F./12th (2nd Brandenburg) Regiment, and two from F./24th Regiment. The two remaining companies of the latter battalion together with the two companies of the Silesian Schützen attached to this brigade were deployed to provide a link between Brye and St Amand. In support behind Brye stood II./1st Westphalian Landwehr Regiment. The remaining six battalions of the brigade, that is the two musketeer battalions each of the Brandenburgers and the 24th Regiment and I. and F./1st Westphalian Landwehr, were placed in support behind St Amand. Steinmetz's men had taken the opportunity of a relatively peaceful morning to rest and recuperate. They had taken much of what they needed the previous night from the hapless inhabitants of Brye and St Amand, and also received supplies that were brought forward to Sombreffe that morning.

Steinmetz instructed his brigade to adopt the following order-of-battle,

1st Line Commander: Major von Blücher (24th Regiment).
Fusilier battalions of the 12th and 24th Regiments and 3rd and 4th Companies of the Silesian Schützen.
2nd Line Commander: Colonel von Hoffmann (Brigade Infantry Commander). The four musketeer battalions of the above regiments, with the 12th Regiment on the right flank.
3rd Line Commander: Major von Hülsen.
1st Westphalian Landwehr Regiment.
Reserves
Horse Battery No. 7 with two squadrons of the 1st Silesian Hussars.
Foot Battery No. 7 was positioned between the 1st and 2nd Lines.[6]

The 2nd Brigade was deployed with its right flank behind the windmill of Bussy at Brye, facing towards St Amand, and with its left flank towards Ligny. The farm near the windmill, which was surrounded by a wall, was occupied by I./6th (1st West Prussian) Infantry Regiment.

The 3rd Brigade occupied the part of St Amand on the eastern bank of the Ligne brook. The main part of the village, which lay on the far bank, was not suited to defence. Likewise, Wagnelée remained unoccupied; the Prussians

---

5 This section is based largely on Weltzien, pp 179–83.
6 Mueller, pp 162–3.

simply did not want to spread their forces too thinly. The forces deployed included the two musketeer battalions of the 29th Regiment, former Berg troops who wore their grey overcoats to conceal their white uniforms, an unpleasant experience in that day's particularly hot sun, and II./3rd Westphalian Landwehr Regiment. The Fusilier Battalions of the 29th and 7th (2nd West Prussian) Regiments were deployed between St Amand and Ligny. In reserve behind Ligny were the remaining four battalions of this brigade: I. and F./2nd Westphalian Landwehr, the two musketeer battalions of the 2nd West Prussians, and the 1st and 2nd Companies of Silesian Schützen.

The 4th Brigade occupied Ligny with four battalions, namely I. and F./19th Line, II. and F./4th Westphalian Landwehr. One of these, the I./19th, occupied the château. The other two battalions from the brigade present that day, II./19th and I./4th Westphalian Landwehr, were placed behind Ligny in support.

The I Army Corps Reserve Cavalry placed five regiments to the rear left of the 2nd Brigade, and deployed one to observe the right flank of the army and to maintain contact with the Netherlands forces. Five batteries of the artillery, totalling 40 guns, were deployed on the heights between St Amand and Ligny; one battery of 12-pounders on the windmill hill near Brye; one battery to the left of Ligny; one battery of horse artillery in support of the 1st Silesian Hussar Regiment on the far right flank; three batteries totalling 24 pieces in reserve behind the 2nd Brigade.

This deployment was completed by 8 a.m. At 11 a.m., the enemy was first sighted in the undergrowth. A column of rising smoke was taken to be a signal for an attack, and shortly thereafter, skirmishers and reconnaissance parties scouted the changed Prussian positions.

II Army Corps

At 1 a.m., from the bivouac in Mazy, Pirch I issued marching orders for his corps,

> At 2 a.m., the Corps is to march off as follows:
> 1) The Reserve Cavalry,
> 2) The Brigades by number, with the surgeons' waggons and pack horses remaining with their battalions,
> 3) The Reserve Artillery with the ammunition waggons.
> The officers allocated to the baggage are to report to Waggonmaster-General Major von Tuchsen in Hannut. The waggons loaded for today, which are also to be used as transport for the wounded, are to deploy from Mazy to the right of the road, as a park, and are to await further orders.[7]

The II Army Corps marched along the cobbled road to Brussels in the direction of Sombreffe, reaching there from about 10 a.m., without a break in the march. Two brigades together with most of the Reserve Artillery and

---

[7] Stawitzky, pp. 46–7.

Cavalry reached Sombreffe around that time, much to the relief of Zieten's men. The remaining two brigades arrived shortly afterwards.

The 5th Brigade was in the lead. After he received Pirch's 1 a.m. orders Tippelskirch gave his men the following order of march,

> The Fusilier Battalion of the 2nd (1st Pomeranian) Regiment.
> The Fusilier Battalion of the 25th Regiment.
> The I. and II. Battalions of the 25th Regiment.
> The I. and II. Battalions of the 5th Westphalian Landwehr Infantry.
> The I. and II. Battalions of the 1st Pomeranian Regiment.
> Artillery Battery No. 10.
> The 3rd Battalion of the 5th Westphalian Landwehr Infantry Regiment.[8]

The 5th Brigade marched through Sombreffe and paraded before Blücher before moving on to the point where the Brussels road met the Roman road. At Trois Burrettes, it halted and reformed, deploying in its usual brigade formation. The vanguard consisted of the F./2nd and F./25th Regiments, followed by the remaining battalions in columns of attack; the first line consisting of four battalions, the second of three. The colour parties of the second line formed up at the intervals in the first line, and half a battalion was deployed to cover each flank. The 6th Brigade drew up to the east of the 5th, just to the south of the Namur road. The 7th Brigade (Brause), tired after its difficult march via Namur, arrived a little later, and took up positions next to the 6th Brigade in front of the II Army Corps Reserve Cavalry and Reserve Artillery. The 8th Brigade, arriving last, drew up south of the Namur road, between Brause's brigade and Sombreffe.

The 5th Brigade was deployed north of Brye, at the junction of the Roman road and the cobbled road to Brussels, and close to the inn aux Trois Burrettes. This brigade was allocated a plentiful supply of artillery. The battalions of the 5th Brigade stacked their arms, resting on the slopes of the heights near Trois Burrettes in the hot sun, making use of the short time available to them before the commencement of battle. About noon, a body of horsemen, Wellington, his staff, companions and escorts, was seen approaching from the direction of Quatre Bras. Most were wearing British uniforms, and some had put their umbrellas up to shade themselves from the heat of the sun. When the Duke passed close to the ranks of the 5th Brigade, he was greeted with cheers. He went on to his meeting with Blücher at the windmill of Bussy.

About 2 p.m. the first shots were heard and dust clouds were seen near Fleurus and St Amand, but to the men of II Army Corps, the French intentions were as yet not clear. Blücher did not expect the first French assault to be against St Amand, but soon had to send the 5th Brigade to Wagnelée to counter the threat coming from Vandamme's III Corps and Girard's division.

In effect II Corps became the battle reserve of I Army Corps. The 5th Brigade, initially deployed to the east of Brye, was later used to occupy the farm at St Amand le Hameau, with its main body being deployed in front of

[8] Stawitzky, p 47.

Wagnelée as a reserve and flank guard. Kraft's 6th Brigade was then moved to between Brye and Ligny in the centre of the position to cover the interval between St Amand and Ligny. The 8th Brigade (Bose) drew up behind the windmill hill, between Brye and the Reserve Cavalry of I Army Corps, as a second line for the 6th Brigade. Of the Reserve Cavalry of II Army Corps, Schulenburg's 3rd Brigade was placed at the disposal of I Corps; Thümen's 1st Brigade was placed near St Amand, to the rear of the right of the artillery deployed between this village and Ligny; Sohr's Brigade was placed behind the gap between Wagnelée and St Amand so as to be able to be used rapidly to contain any breakthrough by the French.

The area between St Amand, Brye and Ligny was thus filled with the troops of two army corps, who were mixed together in such a manner as to make commanding them difficult, let alone any manoeuvring. Blücher's men were left with little choice but to be an anvil suffering several hammer blows. The only hope was that dealing out these blows would wear the French down and hold them up long enough for Wellington to arrive.

III Army Corps

The four brigades, the reserve cavalry and artillery of III Army Corps (Thielemann) began to arrive at noon. The corps occupied the heights east and south-east of Sombreffe from behind the left flank of II Corps. Borcke's 9th Brigade was between Sombreffe and the north side of Mont Potriaux; Kemphen's 10th Brigade occupied the village of Tongrinne, forming the far left flank of the Prussian positions; the 11th Brigade (Luck) was in the centre, west of Point du Jour on the road to Fleurus; and the 12th Brigade (Stülpnagel) to the north of the Point du Jour. A skirmish line was formed from Sombreffe to Boignée, along the edge of the valley of the Ligne brook. Marwitz's 1st Brigade of the corps' reserve cavalry was deployed on the far right flank around Wagnelée, while Lottum's 2nd Brigade was held in reserve at the Point du Jour.

The Netherlanders at Quatre Bras

The Netherlands outposts had fought an engagement with the left wing of Napoleon's forces the previous evening, as we have seen in an earlier chapter. They had done so on their own initiative, choosing not to carry out Wellington's orders to move their entire force on Nivelles. Thanks to Constant Rebeque and Duke Bernhard of Saxe-Weimar, the French had just about been thwarted in their attempt to drive the two Allied armies in the Netherlands apart.

The hamlet of Quatre Bras, part of the commune of Baisy-Thy, consisted of one large farmhouse, an inn and several smaller dwellings along the arms of the cross-roads where the Nivelles–Namur and Brussels–Charleroi roads met. These buildings dominated the undulating countryside nearby. A chain of hills runs north-west to south-east across the Charleroi road about 1.5 km south of Quatre Bras with its high points north and east of Grand-Pierrepont, and north-east of Frasnes. In 1815 a hostelry called the Balcan inn stood where the Charleroi road passed over this line of hills. The slopes north of the Balcan plateau towards Quatre Bras, where much of the coming engagement would be fought, were devoid of trees and undergrowth. The Odomont brook started at Grand-Pierrepont and ran towards the south-west with fields along its banks, down to the farm of Petit-Pierrepont, which was about 600 metres away. The farm of Lairalle stood to the east of the road, towards Pireaumont.

Access to the plateau of Quatre Bras from the south-west could be hindered by defensive positions at the two Pierreponts and the large Bossu wood between them and the Nivelles road. This wood, consisting of tall trees and thick undergrowth, was elongated in shape, narrow at the northern end but widening out considerably at the southern end. Wide footpaths facilitated troop movements.

East of the hamlet of Quatre Bras, the embanked road to Namur formed a natural covered position, with the houses of Pireaumont to the south from where any attacks from the northern edge of the wood of Delhutte (or de la Hutte) could be met. The north end of this wood was less than a kilometre from the Charleroi road, however, and could help cover French movements against the left of the Allied positions.

Between Pireaumont and Quatre Bras, about one kilometre south of the cross-roads at its nearest point, was a valley running at right angles to the Charleroi road. A rivulet ran east in this valley from beside the Charleroi road, forming a pond, the Materne pond, just before joining the Pireaumont river near the Namur road. Next to the Charleroi road, at the head of this valley, stood the large farmhouse of Gemioncourt. This had large towers and walled gardens and orchards offering a strong-point for the defence. The heights, the woods, the tree-lined river banks and the dry stone walls of the various buildings and enclosures all offered good vantage points for skirmish lines.

About 5 a.m., Perponcher deployed the 27th Jager between the farmhouse of Gemioncourt and the pond of Materne, replacing the posts of the III./2nd Nassauers. One company of the 27th spread out to the left of Bijleveld's battery to cover it. Three companies deployed farther to the east, along the north bank of the Pireaumont river, facing the wood of Delhutte. The far left consisted of the remaining two companies of the battalion under Lieutenant-Colonel Grunebosch who drew up his men near the south-west angle of the Materne pond. The 5th Militia Battalion under Lieutenant-Colonel Westenberg was first placed west of the cross-roads at Quatre Bras, then later positioned in a line from the eastern edge of the Bossu wood, over the cobbled road, to a little north-west of Gemioncourt. For the time being, the 8th Battalion was held in reserve north of the buildings at Quatre Bras. When these infantry of the 1st Brigade had arrived, battalions and companies of the 2nd Brigade were sent into the Bossu wood, their skirmishers covering the path along its southern edge. Grunebosch's men threw back several French patrols into the Delhutte woods, but were unable to drive them out of it.

As the II./2nd Nassauers knew the terrain from the combat of the previous evening, two of its companies were sent to reconnoitre, supported by a small detachment of Silesian Hussars who had been cut off from the Prussian Army in the previous day's fighting. They soon clashed with Lefebvre-Desnoëttes' outposts of Guard Lancers. Supported by Bijleveld's guns, the Prussians repulsed the French scouts, but in doing so they lost four troopers and 13 mounts.

The strong measures undertaken by these small Allied units led the French to believe that they were facing a much larger force than they indeed were. Had the French been bold, they could, at this stage of the day, easily have thrown back all the Allied troops before them, captured the vital cross-roads, divided the Allied forces, and made a major contribution to deciding the campaign in their favour. However, Ney erred on the side of caution.

The Prince of Orange arrived at 6 a.m. and inspected the front line, accompanied by Perponcher and Duke Bernhard of Saxe-Weimar. The generals went to the positions held by the Nassauers to observe the situation. Here, they watched French foragers making their cooking fires close by. Behind them, in the tall crops in front of Frasnes, they saw groups of lancers and chasseurs à cheval, but Bachelu's division of infantry was hidden by the buildings and woods.

At 7 a.m. a small body of French troops probed the Netherlanders' positions, but was driven back after a brief exchange of fire. An attempt by two companies of Nassauers to advance towards Frasnes was likewise repelled, as the French had by now brought up artillery support. The morning continued with brief exchanges of fire, probing actions and demonstrations along the line of the front. About noon, the III./2nd Nassauers relieved their 2nd Battalion, which then went for lunch. Clearly, the small Allied forces were not under any appreciable pressure, so when Wellington left to meet Blücher around that time, there was no sign of French intentions to mount an offensive that day.

The Combat at St Amand

The First French Offensive

The French columns moved into their attack positions at 2 p.m. Their right flank formed up opposite Sombreffe, their centre against Ligny, their left against St Amand. The battle began at 2.30 p.m. when Napoleon ordered a signal of three cannon shots to be fired.[9] The III Corps advanced against St Amand, its assault columns preceded by a line of skirmishers, and the band of the 23rd Line playing *La Victoire en Chantant*. Initially, Girard's division stayed behind the III Corps in reserve, but then moved to its left to support the infantry attack on the village which commenced at 3 p.m. Lefol's division moved towards the Prussian positions on the north side of St Amand and at the farmhouse of St Amand le Hameau which were defended by three battalions of the Prussian 3rd Brigade. One of the defenders, from the 29th Regiment, described the scene,

It was between 2 p.m. and 2.30 p.m., when the French attack on the village began. It was carried out with particular audacity by hidden groups of men coming from all sides. It was a truly picturesque view, the red, yellow, green

[9] Houssaye, vol 2, p 167.

plumes and epaulettes of the grenadiers, carabineers and voltigeurs looking like poppies and cornflowers growing in those tall crops. In all places, it came to life with attackers whose sudden appearance was just as frightening to the defenders as their well-aimed shots... [10]

Finding most of St Amand itself unoccupied by the Prussians, the French suffered casualties only from the canister fire of batteries positioned on the heights east of the village. Lefol was leading his division from the front and had a horse killed under him, but kept his men advancing towards the Prussian positions in St Amand la Haye where the French skirmishers soon engaged the skirmish platoons of II./29th Line, and its accompanying volunteer detachment.

A bitter struggle also ensued in St Amand in which both sides suffered heavy casualties. The French had, in the meantime, moved a battery up to the west of St Amand. These guns engaged the II./29th with canister fire. The Prussian battalion had only a sparse hedge for cover, and this was blasted away with the first round from the French. Major von Chevallerie, commander of the battalion, withdrew his skirmishers back to the main body of the battalion and attempted to counter the withering enemy fire with battalion volleys; his men suffered terribly, but managed to prevent the French from advancing any farther. After half an hour, Chevallerie could no longer hold his position, so he led his men back into the cover of St Amand la Haye where they were joined by the skirmishers of the 3rd Westphalian Landwehr under Captain von Wenzel, a former officer of the 29th Regiment.

The I./29th had deployed its skirmishers, under the command of Captain von Bismarck II along the edge of St Amand la Haye. They held their ground when Chevallerie retired. Major von Hymmen, regimental commander of the 29th, then moved two musketeer companies of the 1st Battalion to the edge of the village. The French troops pushing back the II./29th were halted by those two companies and the left wing of Bismarck's skirmishers. Captain von Bismarck described the events in his diary,

> The two battalions [II./29th and II./3rd Westphalian Landwehr] managed to rally to a certain extent in the village, and the combat went on for a good hour during which we held our positions at the edge of the gardens.[11]

On the left of the Prussian positions, there now followed a stationary exchange of fire. After a while, the French attempted several small attacks which were all driven back. The French battery west of St Amand la Haye now shelled St Amand itself, hoping to drive the Prussians out by setting the houses on fire, but was unable to get the buildings to burn.

Vandamme attempted to break this stalemate by committing Girard's division which attacked St Amand la Haye from the west, roughly from the direction of le Hameau. Although the French exposed their left flank with this manoeuvre, the Prussians had no reserves available to take advantage of this.

---

[10] Wellmann, p 85 f.
[11] Wellmann, p 88.

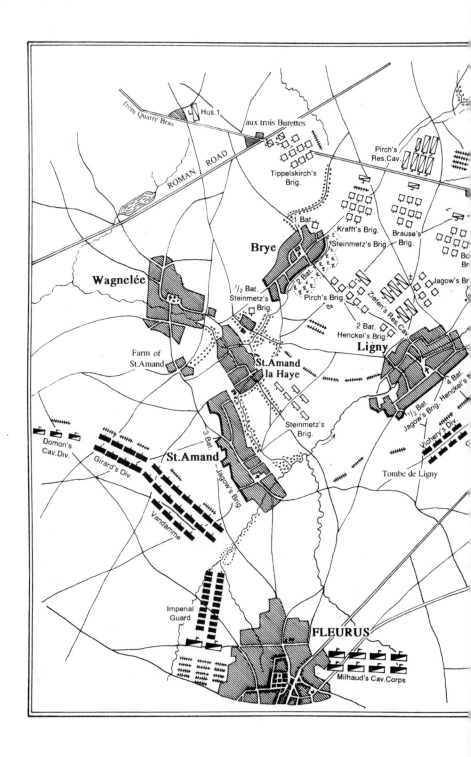

from Quatre Bras

Hus.1

aux trois Burettes

ROMAN ROAD

Tippelskirch's Brig.

Pirch's Res.Cav.

1 Bat.

Krafft's Brig.

Steinmetz's Brig.

Brause's Brig.

Brye

Wagnelée

1/2 Bat. Steinmetz's Brig.

2 Bat.

Pirch's Brig.

Zieten's Res.Cav.

Jagow's Br

Bo Br

2 Bat. Henckel's Brig.

Ligny

Farm of St.Amand

St.Amand la Haye

4 Bat. Henckel's

1/2 Bat. Jagow's Brig.

Vichery's Div.

Domon's Cav.Div.

Girard's Div.

St.Amand

3 Bat. Jagow's Brig.

Steinmetz's Brig.

Tombe de Ligny

Vandamme

Imperial Guard

FLEURUS

Milhaud's Cav.Corps

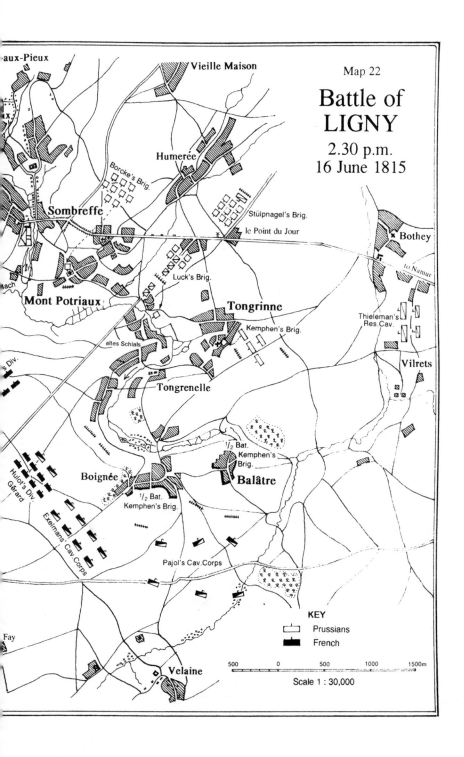

aux-Pieux

Vieille Maison

Humerée

Borcke's Brig.

Sombreffe

Stülpnagel's Brig.

le Point du Jour

Bothey

to Namur

Luck's Brig.

Mont Potriaux

Tongrinne

Thieleman's
Res. Cav.

altes Schlals

Kemphen's Brig.

Vilrets

's Div.

Tongrenelle

¹/₂ Bat.
Kemphen's
Brig.

Hulot's Div.
Gérard

Boignée

Balâtre

¹/₂ Bat.
Kemphen's Brig.

Exelmans Cav. Corps

Pajol's Cav. Corps

Fay

Velaine

Map 22

Battle of
LIGNY
2.30 p.m.
16 June 1815

KEY

Prussians

French

500   0   500   1000   1500m

Scale 1 : 30,000

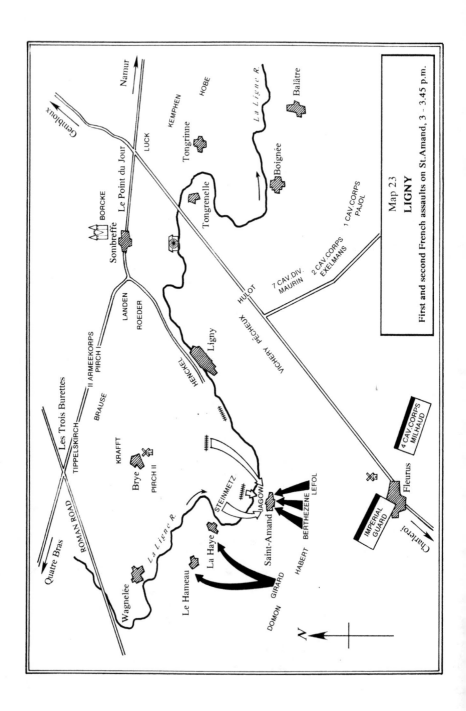

Map 23

LIGNY

First and second French assaults on St. Amand, 3 – 3.45 p.m.

Supported by artillery fire, Girard's men started to force the exhausted Prussians back.

By this stage of the combat, Captain von Webern and Lieutenants von Seydlitz, Hartwig and Goetsch were wounded. Majors von Hymmen and von Chevallerie had their horses shot from under them, and the regimental adjutant was also wounded. The three Prussian battalions defending St Amand la Haye had become tired and were low on ammunition. Though they had held up three French divisions for some time, when the French now pressed home their assault, the Prussians were forced out of their positions and broke under the pressure. Four men of the 8th Company of the 29th, including Vice-Unteroffizier Meyer, a Berg veteran of the Peninsular War, and himself wounded in the arm, fought to rescue Captain von Webern. They dragged him through bushes and down paths, killing two Frenchmen on their way, before they handed him over to the safety of his batman who had a horse ready. Of the four men, only two, Meyer, and Musketeer Schmitz, survived.

Hymmen and Bismarck described the withdrawal in rather more favourable terms, however. Hymmen led the right wing of the I./29th, noting in his report that,

> The groups of soldiers here, and the 2nd Battalion, which had fallen back to this position, were able to concentrate such strong firepower on the advancing enemy that he was forced to hold back until the heavily committed right wing, and the centre gained enough time to withdraw from this part of the village in good order.[12]

Bismarck's account took the story a stage further,

> Finally, the enemy moved a large mass of men towards the entrance of the village, reinforcing his skirmishers at the same time, and thus forced us back. We tried several times to get back into the village, but in vain; partly because we had already suffered heavy losses, partly because we were being fired on in the flank from all directions.[13]

Other Prussian units now tried to block the gap made by the French success. Steinmetz moved the skirmishers of the 12th and 24th Regiments to the north and south of St Amand la Haye to support the retiring troops of the 3rd Brigade. The French attempted to pursue, but were met with canister fire from Foot Battery No. 7, so they fell back to the cover of St Amand.

Captain von Knappe and Captain von Rathenow, leading the skirmish platoons of the musketeer battalions of the 24th Regiment, advanced as far as the Wagnelée brook to the point where it joined the Ligne brook, covering the gap left by the retiring 29th Line. Because of heavy fire from the French troops in Wagnelée, they were unable to advance any farther. Knappe himself was not wounded but his horse was hit five times and still survived. Knappe, already the proud owner of the Iron Cross 1st and 2nd Class, made such a

12 Wellmann, p 88.
13 Wellmann, p 88.

significant contribution to covering St Amand that he received a further commendation that day.[14]

The skirmishers of the 12th and 24th Regiments were next driven off by the French in St Amand la Haye who seemed ready to continue their advance until two battalions of the 12th Regiment attacked them, supported on their left by the 24th Regiment. With drums beating and shouting 'hurrah', they moved forwards in an unusual formation with half of each battalion in line and the other half behind in column. Foot Battery No. 7 supported them with canister fire against the French at the eastern exits of the village. The 12th then pressed home with the bayonet into St Amand la Haye, driving out the French, and re-occupying it.

Elements of Hymmen's 29th Regiment and the II./3rd Westphalian Landwehr moved forward in the wake of this advance, supported by the F./24th and the Silesian Schützen. Hymmen led his men on foot towards St Amand la Haye, where he was wounded. Chevallerie, now also on foot, was struck by a bullet, but his sword-belt buckle protected him from a serious wound.[15] The 24th Regiment also pushed forward to the left and entered St Amand, meeting heavy resistance. Their attack ground to a halt.

The French brought up fresh troops, Vandamme's last division, and recommenced their assault, supported by a heavy bombardment on St Amand. The Prussian losses to the artillery fire were so severe, that they were forced back. Their formations were disrupted by the hedges, ditches and buildings and they fell back in confusion. Captain von Bismarck again described the situation,

> By ourselves, we were unable to make headway and had to fall back again, during which retreat I was almost taken prisoner, as I stayed behind a little too long. Due to the many ditches and hedges in the village, I had to go over a small meadow which was already occupied by the French, about 20 or 30 of them. There was nothing else I could do but ride full tilt through them. None of them was quick enough to hit me, although they all fired.[16]

The last fresh reserves of the 1st Brigade, the inexperienced I. and F./1st Westphalian Landwehr, were committed at this point. Their commander was wounded by the first shot fired at them, however, and the rank and file of the battalions suffered severely under the heavy fire coming from St Amand. They were thrown back. The Fusilier Battalion in particular lost many men.

Meanwhile, Lieutenants Löffler and Müller of the 24th Line did their utmost to rally and reorganise the shattered battalions of their regiment. Löffler was awarded the Iron Cross 1st Class for his efforts, Müller the 2nd Class. Captain von Blankenstein took over command of the 2nd Battalion when its usual commander, Major von Löwenclau, was wounded. Blankenstein later received an Iron Cross 1st Class. Altogether the 24th Regiment lost some 200 men at St Amand.

---

[14] Zychlinski, p 208 f.
[15] Wellmann, p 90.
[16] Wellmann, p 91.

After they were pushed out of the village the regiment was gathered in a hollow hidden by the slope of the higher ground between the Ligne and Wagnelée brooks. Here, they took what cover they could, but the occasional shell or cannon ball, aimed at the Prussian artillery deployed on the height near Brye, fell short, and took its toll. One shell took Lieutenant von Wulffen's head clean off. Major von Laurens, commander of the regiment, and his horse, were blown into the air by another, but both survived, bruised and winded. The 24th sat in this position for about one hour, until 5 p.m. Then it was moved to the point just north-east of Brye where the footpaths from Ligny to Marbisou and from St Amand to Sombreffe met, joining most of the rest of the brigade.[17] The 1st Brigade lost 46 officers and 2,300 men in this action.

The troops from the 3rd Brigade used to support Steinmetz returned to their formation. The official report of the infantry commander of the 3rd Brigade, Colonel von Rüchel-Kleist, praised these three battalions as follows:

> The enemy attacked the village of St Amand forcefully, and, after offering strong resistance, the battalions were forced back by superior numbers. Thanks to the continual arrival of reinforcements, these troops were, however, able to hold on to the village for an appreciable time. Those battalions whose performance stood out most were the two battalions of the 29th Regiment and the 2nd Battalion of the 3rd Westphalian Landwehr.[18]

The Prussian Counter-Attack

Lefol's Division sat tight in St Amand and St Amand la Haye. The Prussians had deployed a number of 12-pounder batteries of heavy artillery against the village, at the upper part of the slope outside it, so any further French advance would have to be uphill, in open terrain and against overwhelming firepower. So long as the Prussian artillery had ammunition to use, the French were not going to advance any farther on this sector of the battlefield.

Blücher ordered Pirch II to advance with his 2nd Brigade and retake St Amand. Meanwhile, Girard had occupied St Amand la Haye from where he could strike any advances on St Amand in the flank, so Pirch II needed to have this threat cleared first. Thus Blücher also ordered Pirch I to send in his 5th Brigade, supported by Sohr's cavalry brigade from II Army Corps (Brandenburg and Pomeranian Hussars, two squadrons of the Neumark Dragoons and Horse Battery No. 6), and Marwitz's 7th and 8th Uhlans from III Army Corps. Major-General von Wahlen-Jürgass, commander of the II Army Corps cavalry, was placed in command of this battle group. The 7th Brigade moved into the positions previously occupied by the 5th, and were ordered to support the advance if necessary.

It was now around 4 p.m. The 2nd Brigade (6th and 28th Regiments, and 2nd Westphalian Landwehr) moved off to attack with the 12th Regiment covering its left flank. The first wave of the assault, consisting of two battalions of

[17] Zychlinski, p 210 ff.
[18] Wellmann, p 91 f.

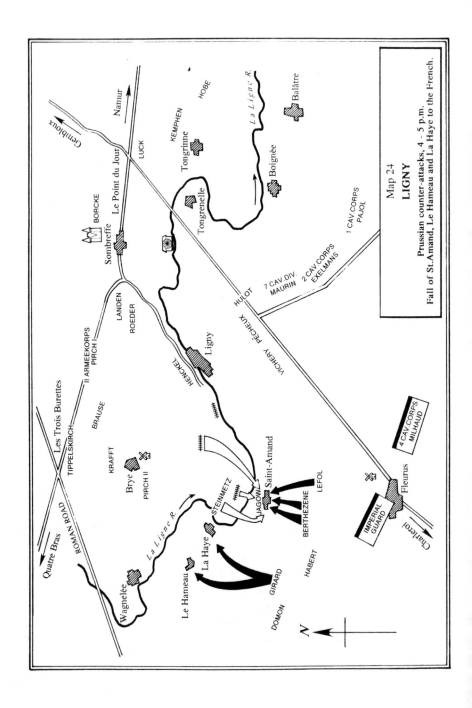

Map 24
LIGNY
Prussian counter-attacks, 4 - 5 p.m.
Fall of St.Amand, Le Hameau and La Haye to the French.

the 28th Regiment and all three of the 2nd Westphalian Landwehr, advanced with fixed bayonets in the face of heavy artillery and small arms fire. The I./28th marched along the sunken road running into St Amand la Haye from the north-east, while the II./28th advanced frontally St Amand with charged arms. Blücher personally led them into the middle of St Amand, driving all before them except for one battalion of French who were well ensconced in a farmhouse at the point where St Amand la Haye joined St Amand. Unable to deploy in the narrow streets, and under continuous heavy fire, the Prussians now suffered severely for their success. Major von Brockhausen, commander of the II./28th, fell, and the crossfire from the French defenders threw the Prussians into a state of confusion.

The officers of the I./28th, seeing that their men could make no more progress, gradually pulled out their companies and tried to restore a semblance of order before throwing their men back into St Amand la Haye. Only Lieutenant Eckstein managed to keep his platoon entirely under control. The II./28th only managed to break into St Amand when the 5th Brigade threatened the French positions with its flanking move through Wagnelée. Musketeers Schürger, Borsbach and Müller of the 5th Company, Musketeer Lass of the 6th, Sergeant Gecke, and Musketeers Schwarz and Erley of the 7th, and Sergeant Bauerhöfer of the 8th particularly distinguished themselves in this action.[19]

Reinforcements were called up from the second line, namely the I./6th Regiment, under Major von Rohr, to attempt to storm the farmhouse. Despite a determined assault, the Prussians were unable to take it, and they fell back, disorganised, to the hedges at the edge of the village to reform. Here, the rallying troops were surprised by French cavalry who threatened to take the battalion's colour. Thanks to an alert colour-bearer, Sergeant Blottner, and a desperate defence by the colour party, the French were cheated of their hoped-for spoils. During the French counter-attack in the area of the farmhouse, General Girard was mortally wounded.[20]

It was now the turn of the II./6th Regiment to move forward. The battalion's skirmish line was ordered to attack with the bayonet, but the French drove it off. All the battalion could now do was to force the French to stay in cover by firing at them. French skirmishers next tried to work their way around the Prussian flank, but Captain von Goddenthow with the 1st Platoon, and Lieutenant von Wranke with the 8th, placed their men behind the hedges and caught the French in a cross-fire, stopping their advance. Captain von Wohlgemuth, with the regiment's fusiliers, was finding it ever more difficult to hold back the growing numbers of French.[21] The 2nd Brigade now had to disengage, and was able to do so and withdraw in good order.

The F./24th Regiment had remained behind the l'Escaille château, just to the north of St Amand la Haye, when the rest of their regiment and brigade had pulled back. At 5 p.m., however, the 9th and 10th Companies under

[19] Neff, pp 27 f.
[20] Conrady, *Sechsten Infanterie-Regiments*, p 245.
[21] Conrady, *Sechsten Infanterie-Regiments*, p 245 f.

Captain Wiegand were ordered to Brye. On the way some of them where wounded by shots fired by men hidden by the tall crops. This may have been friendly fire. At the same time, the 11th and 12th Companies moved to the north of St Amand la Haye where they supported the next assault on St Amand. Wiegand, having already been awarded the Iron Cross 1st and 2nd Class, was commended for his actions that day.[22]

Although the 2nd Brigade had managed to rally after its withdrawal from St Amand, its flank was threatened by a French advance whose columns were covered by a strong line of skirmishers. The direction of the French advance also endangered the Prussian grand battery on the slopes east of St Amand. The I Army Corps cavalry designated to protect this artillery, two squadrons of the 3rd (Brandenburg) Uhlans, and the 1st Kurmark Landwehr Cavalry, charged out of the dead ground where they had been concealed and scattered the French skirmishers before them. Some of these skirmishers fled back to their close-order supports, others tried to take cover in ditches but found no protection there from the long lances of the Prussians. Only the concentrated fire of closed French squares drove back the Brandenburgers. Lieutenant von Thein of the 2nd Squadron was killed in this action, and Lieutenant Tägen of the 3rd received a severe head wound. Uhlan Grosschupf rescued Premier-Lieutenant von Grodzki, whose horse was wounded.[23]

The Action around Wagnelée

The 5th and 7th Brigades from II Army Corps had also come into action as planned to support the 2nd Brigade's efforts. The 5th Brigade had earlier been given orders to, 'Pass through the village of Wagnelée as fast as possible and, on reaching its far side, act according to instructions from General von Jürgass with regard to the actual point of attack.'[24] The Brigade was led by the F./25th under Major von Witzleben, advancing with the F./2nd (1st Pomeranian) Regiment, and closely followed by a first wave under Major von Röbell, which consisted of I. and II./25th and I. and II./5th Westphalian Landwehr, and then the second wave of I. and II./2nd under Major von Cardell.

Tippelskirch, commander of the 5th Brigade, described in his report how the attack began,

> About 4 p.m., when the brigade reached Wagnelée, and had hardly begun to deploy, it was ordered to move rapidly against the village of St Amand [la Haye], which was to be taken by I Corps, to support this attack and to take the enemy in the left flank. This manoeuvre was carried out in such a way that the brigade wheeled to the left, leaving the village of Wagnelée between the centre and right flank, with the wheel consequently going through the village...
>
> With all due haste and order, this attack at first went to plan. The pivot of the wheel was the 3rd [Fusilier] Battalion of the 5th Westphalian Landwehr Regiment under Captain von Caveczinsky.[25]

---

[22] Zychlinski, p 213 ff.
[23] Goltz, p 164 f.

[24] Stawitzky, p 51.
[25] Stawitzky, pp 52–3.

After it had advanced through Wagnelée the 5th Brigade was in a position to threaten the French left flank. The F./2nd Regiment, with its skirmishers led by Captain von Goszicki, engaged a line of French skirmishers about 400 paces south of Wagnelée, throwing them back. Witzleben followed this up with an attack in the direction of the farm of St Amand which drove off two battalions of French.

Major von Röbell attempted to follow up this success by moving with the first wave against St Amand la Haye. However, the manoeuvre was not properly covered by skirmishers, leaving it open to surprise attack, and, to make matters more difficult, the battalions debouching from Wagnelée lost the direction of attack. The main body of the 5th Brigade marched blindly into danger.

Shortly after 4 p.m., the I. and II./25th marched out of Wagnelée through the tall crops. Both battalions were advancing in column and, thanks to the wheeling manoeuvre, now found themselves in the second line of attack, not the first where they had started off. The 1st Battalion tried to move farther right so as to have enough space to deploy, but because of the uneven terrain and tall crops, soon lost sight of the 2nd Battalion, and almost crossed its path. The 2nd Battalion advanced to within 100 paces of the higher ground west of St Amand. The sound of firing could be heard on both flanks, but to the front, everything was quiet. Parts of the 5th Westphalian Landwehr followed them.

Suddenly French troops hidden in the crops only 100 paces to the front of the II./25th Regiment let off two crashing volleys. Despite being hit by this hail of musket balls, the 25th continued to move forward. The 1st Battalion tried to deploy to support the 2nd Battalion, only to find that the distances had been misjudged. Instead the left of the 1st Battalion started to mingle with the right of the 2nd. Major von Helmenstreit, commander of the 1st Battalion had to turn to the right to gain enough room to complete his manoeuvre. His report explained,

> When debouching from Wagnelée, the 2nd Battalion received heavy musket fire from enemy troops about 100 paces distant, which was all the more effective as the battalion had not deployed. However, Major von Seydlitz remained calm under this fire, and had the battalion deploy. The 1st Battalion, led [in this action] by Captain von Machnitzky, which had been moving almost constantly at a trot during this rapid advance, had failed to maintain the distance necessary to deploy, and was thus so restricted by the deployment of the 2nd, that its left flank, instead of being next to the 2nd Battalion, was in front of it, and blocking its line of fire. I thus ordered the battalion to face right, and to march away from the 2nd Battalion.[26]

While the Prussians were sorting out their confused manoeuvres, the French advanced to within 60 paces, their most effective volleys being supported by canister fire from nearby artillery. Despite their problems, the men of the 25th Regiment now started to return fire, only to have the retreating

---

[26] Stawitzky, p 55.

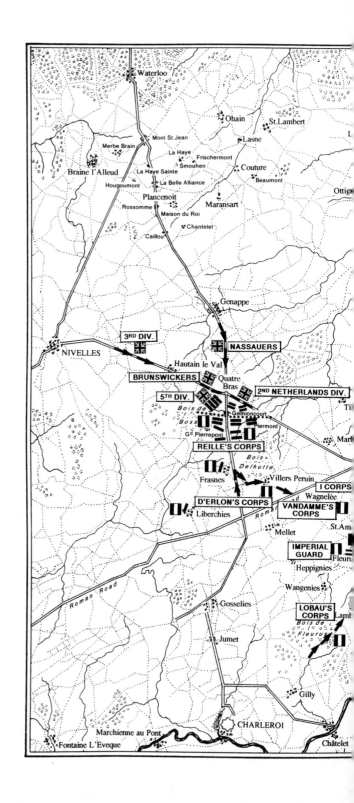

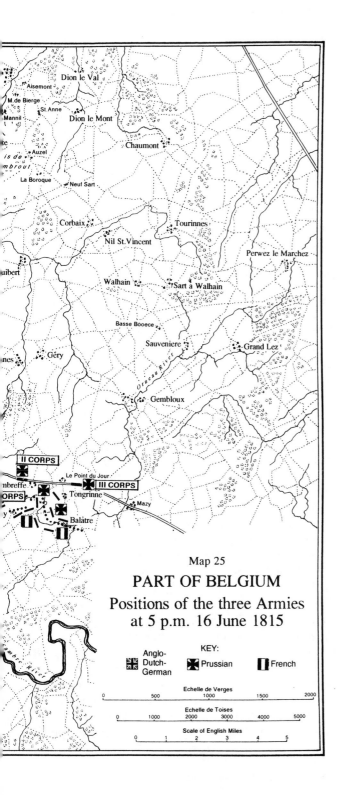

Map 25

PART OF BELGIUM

Positions of the three Armies
at 5 p.m. 16 June 1815

KEY:

Anglo-
Dutch-
German

Prussian

French

Echelle de Verges
0   500   1000   1500   2000

Echelle de Toises
0   1000   2000   3000   4000   5000

Scale of English Miles
0   1   2   3   4   5

skirmishers of 5th Westphalian Landwehr, coming from St Amand le Hameau, break into their lines and force them to stop firing. The Prussian formation dissolved into flight as soon as the French pressed home their advantage.

Major von Röbell, of the 5th Westphalians, men from the Paderborn district, described his rather different view of the incident in detail in his report,

> I ordered Captain von Bülow, commander of the 1st Battalion of the 5th Westphalian Landwehr Regiment, to move to the left, so as to gain enough room to deploy. In doing so, Captain von Bülow encountered the enemy unexpectedly, and, without having deployed, came under heavy canister and shell fire. He fell, and the battalion retreated. The 2nd Battalion of the 5th Westphalian Landwehr Regiment suffered a similar check on the left flank of the first line. A very rapid advance through fields of tall crops in great heat exhausted the men before they even got into the firing line; the officers lost touch with each other in the tall crops and very broken terrain, which itself hindered a rapid deployment of the battalions.[27]

Attempts to re-establish order were not helped when Röbell was severely wounded, and when Major Seydlitz of the II./25th was thrown into a water-filled ditch by his injured horse. The retreating Prussians fell back through Wagnelée which had now been occupied by the volunteer detachment of the 25th, previously guarding the 10th Foot Battery. Lieutenant Luckow, commander of the detachment, was on the point of ordering his men to fall back as well when Major von Helmenstreit of the 1st Battalion came into sight. Luckow asked him for orders, and was told to hold the position. This he did by sending two platoons under Lieutenant Hochstein to the edge of the farm. They remained there until the end of the battle, later being supported by Foot Battery No 10, the latter guarded by a detachment of the 2nd Regiment.

While the two musketeer battalions of the 25th Regiment were in full flight, the vanguard of the 5th Brigade, the F./2nd and F./25th, were continuing their wheeling manoeuvre through St Amand le Hameau and had taken the village without serious opposition. The F./25th then advanced down the poplar-lined road from St Amand le Hameau when it suddenly received a volley of fire from French infantry hidden in the tall crops. Captain von Vietinghoff, commander of the fusiliers, fell wounded, as did the two next most senior officers in the battalion, Captain von Holleben and Premier-Lieutenant von Lüttwitz. Premier-Lieutenant Palm sprang into the breach, coolly leading the battalion in a successful bayonet charge against the French. Seeing a second battalion of French moving up, Palm used the opportunity to fall back on St Amand le Hameau. Lieutenant Pirner, commander of the 10th Company, suffered two bullet wounds, which put him out of action. Lieutenant Richter had his horse shot under him and was also wounded.

Witzleben had the movement stop there, deployed the four skirmish platoons of the battalion, and established a secure point of retreat, which he was able to maintain until the end of the battle. The four skirmish platoons,

---

[27] Stawitzky , pp 56–7.

under Lieutenants Schmidt, Bähr, Schlesike and Ribbeck, held off French cavalry attacks on their positions along the edge of the farm. In one instance, Fusiliers Ellfeld and Häseler, finding themselves cut off by five French troopers, fought them off, standing back to back. Fusilier Heinrich Erfurth, part of Schlesike's platoon, saw French skirmishers about to take two Prussian cannon supporting their position, and helped hold them off long enough for the guns to limber up and depart. Musketeer Kertzer, after receiving a shot to the head, bandaged his wound, and returned to action. Such acts of individual bravery could, however, not hold off such large numbers of French indefinitely. After a determined fight, the Prussians started to fall back on Wagnelée towards the end of the battle.

When Röbell's attack was thrown back in such disorder the second wave of 5th Brigade was just forming up, and part of it was carried away as well. Major von Donap, commander of the I./2nd (1st Pomeranian) Regiment, was wounded at this critical moment, but Captain von Wittke was able to restore order. Then the Pomeranians' two musketeers battalions, led by Cardell and supported by their fusiliers, with Witzleben on the right flank, charged home, taking la Haye at bayonet-point. Heavy losses were suffered, with Major von Reitzenstein, commander of the II./2nd, being wounded. Captain von Korth took command of the 1st Battalion, with Captain von Kleist taking temporary command of the 2nd and Captain von Collignon directing the skirmish action.[28]

Despite this temporary success the attempted flanking attack by the 5th Brigade was a disaster for the Prussians. The shattered remnants of the 25th Regiment and the Westphalian Landwehr had to seek refuge behind the 2nd Regiment and attempt to regroup. However, the fire of Foot Battery No. 10, and the success of the 2nd Regiment's advance did at least deter the French from conducting a pursuit. The broken battalions rallied to the north of Wagnelée.

The Second Prussian Attack

Napoleon now decided to strengthen his offensive by sending a division of the Young Guard to support his left flank. Colbert's brigade of the 1st Cavalry Corps was also sent to join the cavalry on this flank with specific orders to maintain contact with Ney's wing to the west. General Drouot brought over a battery of the Guard Artillery as well.

The Prussians opened a heavy artillery fire on the French columns, causing them to waver. Inspired by this success, the 2nd Brigade moved over to the offensive again and charged into St Amand, chasing the French out at bayonet point. Major Quadt von Hichtenbrock, leading the 28th Regiment, and supported by elements of the 2nd Regiment, gained possession of the church. The I./6th Regiment then tried unsuccessfully to advance beyond the village. French artillery halted this Prussian move, cavalry threatened its flank and the soldiers rapidly retreated. The officers managed to regain control of their men

[28] Mach, p 327 f.

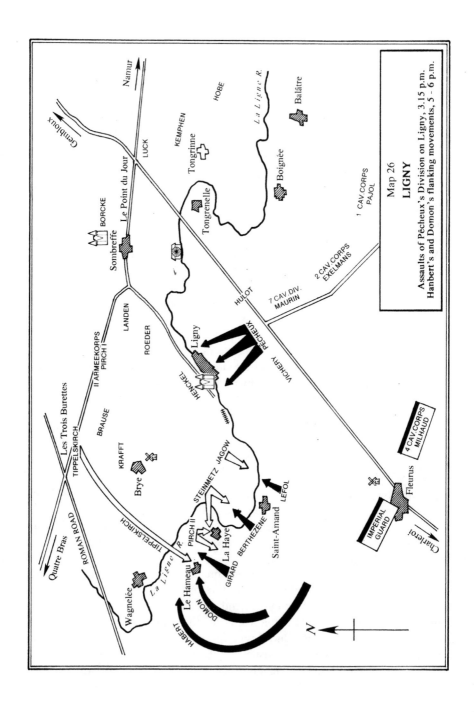

Map 26
LIGNY
Assaults of Pêcheux's Division on Ligny, 3.15 p.m.
Hanbert's and Domon's flanking movements, 5 - 6 p.m.

only with difficulty, and not before their commander, Major von Rohr, was killed. The Prussians fell back to the hedges and walls at the western side of the village, and held their positions.

The position now was that the 6th Regiment was in possession of most of St Amand, with the 2nd Westphalian Landwehr in support, and the 28th holding the village church. The Brandenburg Uhlans and the 1st Kurmark Landwehr Cavalry under Treskow also advanced across the level ground west of the village, the 4th Squadron of the Uhlans pushing back some French cavalry. In that particular action, Colonel von Stutterheim, the commander of the regiment, and Lieutenant Goltz were wounded.[29] On orders from Blücher, Pirch I moved up one of his two remaining cavalry regiments, the Queen's Dragoons, the 4th Kurmark Landwehr Cavalry being kept in reserve. The Queen's Dragoons advanced to the right of the Brandenburg Dragoons.

Both these regiments, having been deployed to protect the Prussian artillery positioned on the slopes above St Amand, had suffered fearfully that day already from French counter-battery fire. Of the Queen's Regiment officers alone, Lieutenant von Stülpnagel was killed by a cannon ball, Premier-Lieutenant von der Groeben had his right leg shattered, Lieutenant Becky had his right eye put out by a shell splinter, while a lump of earth thrown up by an exploding shell struck Lieutenant von Versen with such force that he was knocked unconscious. Major von Streng, the regimental commander, Captain von Raven und von Holleben, and Lieutenants von Versen, Kistmacher and von Mirbach all had horses shot under them, while Major von Schmiterlöw lost two horses this way.[30] Lieutenants von Düringshofen and Meyer of the Brandenburgers were decapitated by cannon balls, and Lieutenant von Beyer died that evening after having his hip smashed by a cannon ball.[31]

More hectic fighting in St Amand followed. In one typical incident the 12-pounder Battery No. 6 became isolated. A troop of French cavalry took the opportunity to try to seize the guns. Fighting back with their ramrods and handspikes, the Prussians drove off their attackers. Lieutenant von Reuter of the battery described the incident,

> Suddenly, on my left flank, along the Ligne brook, I saw an enemy staff officer with about 50 horsemen. While his men moved to attack my position in the rear the officer called out in German, "Surrender, gunners, you are taken prisoner!" With this cry he charged for the gun on our left flank, far in front of his men, and slashed out at limber rider Borchert, killing his horse. The blow was so forceful, that the sabre stuck fast in the saddle, but Borchert jumped off in time. Gunner Sieburg, seizing the opportunity, picked up the trail spike of a 12-pounder, and with the words, "I'll show him how to take prisoners!" hit this officer so hard on his bearskin hat, that he fell from his charger with a smashed head. The riderless horse galloped away into the

---

[29] Goltz, pp 165 f.
[30] Albedyll, vol II, p 308.
[31] Kraatz-Koschlau, p 102.

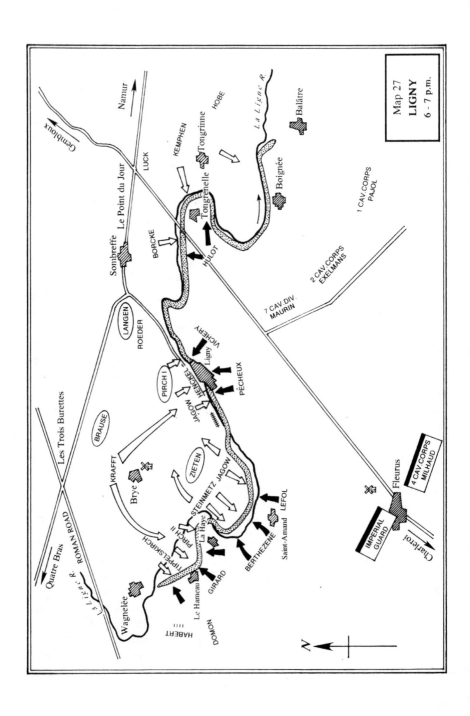

Map 27
LIGNY
6 - 7 p.m.

enemy skirmish line, followed by the 50 enemy horsemen. They lost control of their mounts and rode over their own skirmishers, causing the greatest disorder among them.[32]

The French renewed their assault on St Amand once more, this time attacking the village from three sides. Soon, the battered 2nd Brigade had run out of ammunition. Major von Brockhausen fell from his horse, dead from exhaustion. The Prussians were again driven out of the village, falling back to Brye where they finally got the ammunition they needed. They were not fit to advance again so reinforcements were sent forward from 6th Brigade to retake the important St Amand position while Pirch II reformed his battalions behind Brye. These reinforcements were the F./9th (Colberg) Regiment under Major von Petery, along with all of the 26th Regiment.

The Colberg Fusiliers and the three 26th Regiment battalions moved towards St Amand about 6 p.m. Their skirmish lines entered the village and pushed the French out of the buildings, into the open. Captain von Diest, with the 8th Platoon of the Colberg Fusiliers, linked up with the 26th Regiment, while Petery led the remainder of his men on in company columns. They marched south, through St Amand and then wheeled to the right where they exchanged a number of volleys with the French battalions deployed facing St Amand.[33]

The skirmishers of the F./26th Regiment, under Captain von Liebhaber, reached the gardens to the east of St Amand la Haye. Here, there were just small groups of French. Lieutenant-Colonel von Natzmer led the assault column of the F./26th over the bridge across the brook and towards the main road through the village, foiling preparations by the French to pursue the retiring battalions of the 2nd Brigade. The Prussians, however, met more determined resistance from the French infantry that were established in the solid farm buildings on the far side of the main road. The attack column broke down into battle groups led by officers and sergeants that then set about attacking the French, building by building. Losses were heavy with Natzmer suffering a severe chest wound, and Liebhaber being shot in the thigh.[34]

The 2nd Brigade, having now run out of ammunition, was ordered to fall back on Brye. All that remained here were the two fusilier battalions of the 1st Brigade. These could not hold their positions for long against the continuing French pressure. St Amand and St Amand la Haye again fell to the French.

The Final Prussian Assault

Premier-Lieutenant von Ciriacy, an officer on Pirch I's staff, brought orders for a renewed offensive by 5th Brigade which Jürgass then had implemented. The F./2nd and F./25th Regiments, under Witzleben, advanced on St Amand le Hameau, while I. and II./2nd Regiment and the F./5th Westphalian Landwehr, and one battalion from the 25th Regiment, supported by the fire of Foot Batteries Nos. 10 and 37, assaulted St Amand. Colonel von Thümen

---

[32] MWBl., Beiheft 1890, p 278.
[33] Bagensky, p 236.
[34] Stuckrad, pp 105 f.

284

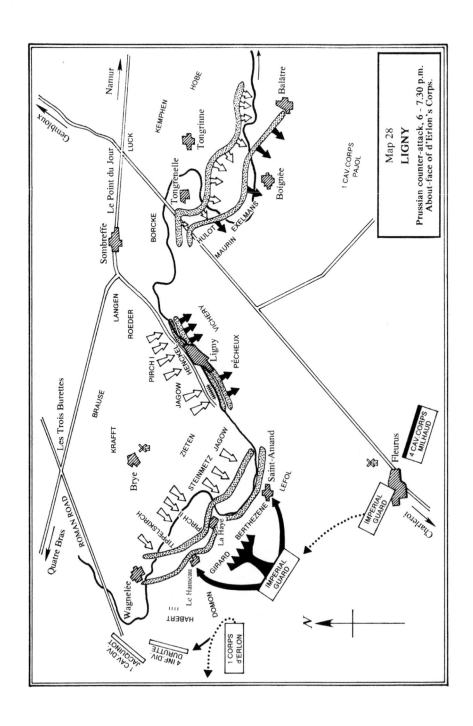

Map 28
LIGNY
Prussian counter-attack, 6 – 7.30 p.m.
About-face of d'Erlon's Corps.

was sent off with the Silesian Uhlans and 11th Hussars to cover the right flank of the 5th Brigade. The 1. and 2./5th Kurmark Landwehr Cavalry were held in reserve.

The French had occupied St Amand la Haye with two battalions which were driven out by the F./2nd and F./25th, with the 11th Hussars covering their flank. The French units in St Amand attempted to recapture la Haye, so there was a vigorous battle between the two villages. St Amand changed hands four times during this fiercely-contested phase but, by about 7 p.m., the F./2nd had run out of ammunition and had to try to hold back the tide of advancing French with its bayonets and musket butts. An eye-witness described the situation,

> The skirmishers of the 2nd Infantry Regiment now spread out in front of the [11th] Hussar Regiment to hold up the enemy who were again moving forwards. As no other troops were available for the purpose, the 11th Hussars did their duty and, despite the heavy losses they were receiving from the fire of the French skirmishers, stood behind our skirmishers. The fighting on this part of the battlefield raged with great violence on both sides. The Prussians continued the struggle with unabated enthusiasm, so much so that hussar troopers rode up to the skirmishers to re-supply them with their own ammunition. Many hussars sacrificed their lives here.[35]

The section of the action fought by the 25th Regiment was equally bitter. The II./25th had rallied after its earlier repulse and was led again by Seydlitz. The battalion skirmishers took the lead followed by the main body in column. Premier-Lieutenant von Bockum led his skirmishers on to the higher ground overlooking Wagnelée and St Amand le Hameau, driving back the French skirmishers. The French battalions there were likewise thrown back by the F./5th Westphalian Landwehr, and the I. and II./2nd Regiment. They were soon joined by the I./25th, which had already lost a quarter of its men so far that day.

A French battalion, moving through the tall crops to reinforce St Amand le Hameau, was spotted because the tops of the French shakos were visible and was therefore taken in the left flank by the I./25th Regiment. Lieutenant Schnelle, commanding the battalion's skirmishers, found himself standing in the crops not far away from a French colour party. His attempt to gain this valued prized resulted in him receiving a severe wound in the thigh. Lieutenant Schmidt, who was close by with his platoon, was shot through the heart. Musketeer Alte of the 4th Company shot the commander of the French skirmishers.

The fighting here became especially frenzied. Neither side took prisoners; instead the wounded were stuck with bayonets and smashed with musket butts. Machnitzky had his 1st Battalion of the 25th deploy into line. The French withdrew, having suffered considerable losses also, as did the exhausted Prussians shortly afterwards. The French did not pursue them. On reaching

---

[35] Eck, p 143.

Wagnelée, the I./25th halted and started to evacuate some of their many wounded to the rear.

The insufferable heat of the day had a dramatic effect on the participants who lost all inhibitions when needing to quench their great thirsts. Friedrich Förster, at that time a lieutenant in the 25th Regiment, wrote, 'I met soldiers on this day whose thirst seemed to be giving them a form of rabies; they were foaming at the mouth and throwing themselves into dirty puddles just to moisten their lips.'[36] Major Graf Henckel von Donnersmarck, commander of the 7th Hussars, mentioned in his memoirs that,

> It was an unbearable heat, and the men were very thirsty. I myself was un-believably thirsty, and saw a militiaman quenching his thirst with his sweaty shako from a puddle of manure. What else could I do? I had him pass me it and took a large mouthful; I can assure you, it did not taste like Hungarian wine.[37]

The French now mounted yet another attack on the weakened 5th Brigade. The situation became increasingly serious for the Prussians. Jürgass called up support from the 7th Brigade which had earlier replaced the 5th on the right flank by the Roman road. Brause, commander of the 7th Brigade, had already deployed the fusilier battalions of the 14th and 22nd Regiments on his left to maintain contact with the 5th Brigade, and the two musketeer battalions of the 14th had already moved towards Brye to get closer to the fighting.

Blücher personally ordered the 14th Regiment into the fray. On hearing of this, Brause also led the F./14th and F./22nd Regiments and I./2nd Elbe Landwehr Regiment into the battle. He had the remaining four battalions of his brigade form up south of the Namur road. Brause first met the F./9th (Colberg) Regiment who had run out of ammunition. He gave it a fresh supply before ordering it back into St Amand with II./14th Regiment. At the same time the I./14th relieved the 2nd Regiment which then withdrew behind Wagnelée where the rest of the 5th Brigade was rallying.

Major von Mirbach led the II./14th into the village, taking it at bayonet-point and repelling a local French counter-attack. Two companies of the battalion held up the French frontally, while the other two companies found their flank, forcing the French back. This success was followed up too vigor-ously, with the battalion pursuing the French out of the village, then suffering a cavalry charge, which forced it to retire back to the cover of the buildings.[38]

The two fusilier battalions of the 7th Brigade were first used to cover Horse Battery No. 5 which had just moved up. The I./2nd Elbe Landwehr marched between the villages of St Amand and la Haye and Jürgass' cavalry. The situation soon demanded that Brause commit more men to these villages. The F./14th Regiment was sent in next, while the Landwehr moved into the gardens. These relatively fresh troops bolstered the defence, and encouraged the Prussians in St Amand to hold on for longer.[39]

---

[36] Stawitzky, p 62 fn.
[37] Henckel von Donnersmarck, p 355.

[38] anon, *Geschichte des 3. Pommerschen Infanterie-Regiments*, p 54 f.
[39] anon, *Infanterie-Regiment Nr. 22*, p 113 f.

Colonel von der Marwitz had also moved up on the right with his cavalry brigade from III Army Corps. He faced a sizeable body of French cavalry with some artillery to his front, but the French were not being particularly active here. French dragoons made one attack which was beaten off by two squadrons of the 7th and 8th Uhlans.[40] An attempt by a regiment of chasseurs à cheval to ride down the skirmishers of the 2nd Regiment was driven back by two squadrons of the 5th Kurmark Landwehr Cavalry.

Marwitz had been also ordered by Jürgass to send out patrols to his right to establish contact with Wellington's army. After all, the hard-pressed Prussians were anxiously awaiting the arrival of the reinforcements promised by Wellington. One of these patrols was led by Sergeant Rosenburg of the 2./8th Uhlans. It eventually returned, bringing with it a French staff officer and his batman, captured in the rear of the French lines, who gave the information that d'Erlon's I Corps was in the vicinity. It was now clear to the Prussians that Wellington was not going to be coming that day.[41]

The Final French Assault

Meanwhile, as will be discussed later in the chapter, the French Imperial Guard was forming up for its final assault on Ligny, the move which would decide the outcome of the battle. The French troops around St Amand included various units of the Imperial Guard required for this attack. As they withdrew to join the attack force their comrades around St Amand accordingly also had to pull back. The Prussians took the withdrawal by the French in this sector as a sign of defeat, so Blücher ordered forward all available battalions of the 8th Brigade, the fusiliers of the 23rd Regiment, and I. and F./3rd Elbe Landwehr. By now, the Prussians had used 39½ battalions in this sector alone.

When Ligny finally fell into French hands and Blücher had no more reserves available, the troops at St Amand were also withdrawn, being quickly followed up by the French, with further clashes taking place. The I./14th Regiment, finding itself attacked on both sides while in a sunken road, faced both ways and drove off the French. Jürgass had the French skirmishers moving out of St Amand charged by the 4./Brandenburg Hussars who threw the French back at first. However, an ever greater number kept coming forward, and in the ensuing close combat, Jürgass himself was shot in the shoulder.

The combat of St Amand petered out by 8.30 p.m. with the remaining Prussian cavalry covering their army's withdrawal. Several attempts by French horsemen to interfere with the retreat were beaten off.

The Combat at Quatre Bras
The Allied Deployment

After a relatively quiet morning on this sector of the battlefield, the French moved forward in force at 2 p.m. The Netherlanders' outposts retired to the farms of Petit and Grand-Pierrepont. The forces available to the Prince of

---

[40] Epner & Braun, pp 8–9.
[41] Förster, p 66.

Orange, who was in command until the Duke of Wellington returned from his meeting with Blücher, were a mere nine battalions, less than 8,000 men, and two batteries of 16 guns in all, with orders to hold this position until reinforcements arrived.

The circumstances certainly did not favour a rapid concentration of the Anglo-Dutch-German army that day. It was a day of blistering heat in which many of the formations the Duke was hoping would be rushing to the front simply had to halt under the afternoon sun or suffer heat stroke. This compounded Wellington's initial delay in getting movement orders to his troops. Then came the chaos at the various choke-points on the line of march. Constant Rebeque and Colonel Abercromby, an officer on Wellington's staff attached to the Prince of Orange's headquarters, met at Nivelles, finding a state of confusion there, as Alten's and Chassé's divisions had arrived at the same time, Chassé from the direction of Mons, Alten from Soignies. Alten's columns had simply cut through Chassé's, forcing the latter to halt his march. His troops rested along the roadside until 1 or 2 p.m., while Alten's exhausted soldiers – some had been on their feet for as many as 15 hours already – continued their march under the hot sun. The noise of battle at Quatre Bras could be heard by all.[42]

The road from Braine-le-Comte to Nivelles was blocked by the baggage of the 3rd British Division. Nobody seemed to be in charge of traffic control, and it was a case of everybody trying to muddle their way through to the front. Much of Wellington's force would not arrive at Quatre Bras until the late evening, when the battle was over.

The front covered by the weak forces under the command of the Prince of Orange was around 3½ km. When the French attacked at 2 p.m., the defenders were in the following positions.[43] The point where the hill crest between Grand-Pierrepont and Pireaumont crossed the Charleroi road was covered by five guns from Bijleveld's battery; two 6-pounders and one howitzer on the eastern side of the cobbled road, one 6-pounder and one howitzer on the western side. The remaining three guns of this battery, under Lieutenant Koopman, were placed near Quatre Bras, covering the road to Namur. Four 6-pounders and two howitzers of Stevenart's foot battery were placed on a hill between the eastern edge of the Bossu wood and Gemioncourt. The remaining two guns of this battery, commanded by Lieutenant Winssinger, were placed on the south-western point of the Bossu wood. All the artillery vehicles were withdrawn to behind Quatre Bras.

The artillery was directly supported by two companies of the III./2nd Nassauers who were deployed in the southern parts of the Bossu wood. The remaining two companies were placed in reserve north of the wood. The 3rd Company of the 27th Jager arrived later to support the artillery.

The main body of the 27th Jager Battalion, under Lieutenant-Colonel Grunebosch, guarded the ground between Gemioncourt and Pireaumont.

---

[42] De Bas & T'Serclaes de Wommersom, vol I, p 462 f.
[43] De Bas & T'Serclaes de Wommersom, vol I, p 479 ff.

Four companies were placed in the front line; one on the hill-crest south-east of Gemioncourt; two on the bridge between the Materne pond and the farm of Lairalle; and one at Pireaumont. The remaining two companies were placed in reserve, directly under Grunebosch's command, at the south-west corner of the Materne pond. This battalion covered a front of around 1 km. The 5th Militia Battalion, under Lieutenant-Colonel Westenberg, deployed one company in the farmhouse of Gemioncourt, with its main body on the hilltop about 150 metres north-west of the farm.

While the III./2nd Nassauers held the south end of the Bossu wood, three more battalions were deployed along the eastern edge of the wood, the I./2nd Nassauers (Saxe-Weimar's 2nd Brigade), 8th Militia (Bijlandt's 1st Brigade), and I./Nassau-Orange (Saxe-Weimar). Detachments from this last battalion also held the farmhouses of Grand and Petit-Pierrepont. The detachment of Nassau volunteers, under Lieutenant Bergmann, covered the far right of the position. Initially, the I./2nd Nassauers deployed two companies outside the wood in skirmish order, but the French Guard Lancers forced them to withdraw to the edge of the wood.

Three further battalions, the II./2nd Nassauers, II./Nassau-Orange Regiment, both from Saxe-Weimar's brigade, and the 7th Militia under Lieutenant-Colonel Singendonck, part of Bijlandt's brigade, were held in reserve at Quatre Bras, but the 7th Militia was soon ordered to enter the Bossu wood. The 7th Line Battalion, under Major van den Sanden, arrived from Nivelles between 2.30 p.m. and 3 p.m. and was placed at first at the sheepfold near Quatre Bras, then pulled back a little to the north. Finally, it too was ordered into the Bossu wood.

Around 2 p.m., strong French forces were seen advancing between the main road and the Delhutte wood. A skirmish line spread out to the left and right of the Balcan inn, opening fire on the farmhouse of Grand-Pierrepont and its defending Nassauers. This action masked the main point of the French assault that was to be on the Allied left and centre. Leaving the main road in a north-easterly direction, Jamin's brigade of Foy's 9th Division with one battery, and the brigades of Husson and Campi of Bachelu's 5th Division, advanced in three columns, side by side, led personally by the corps' commander General Reille. Piré's 2nd Cavalry Division chasseurs à cheval and lancers covered Campi's right. Ney kept Foy's 1st Brigade (Gauthier) in reserve, together with 18 guns stationed on the east of the road and a little south of the Balcan inn. The Guard Light Cavalry, under Lefebvre-Desnoëttes, massed near the main road, on the southern slope of the plateau. Guiton's cuirassier brigade formed up to its left rear in echelon.

By now, Ney had 9,600 infantry, 4,600 cavalry and 34 guns at his disposal. Jérôme's Division, 7,800 men with eight cannon, was passing through Gosselies and would all be in action by about 4 p.m. Three more brigades of Kellermann's cavalry (Picquet, Blancard and Donop; 2,700 sabres and 12 cannon), were also close by and available at Liberchies to the west.

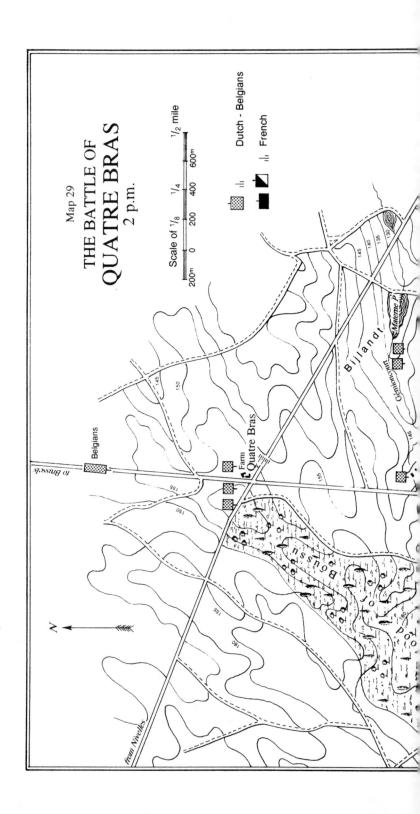

Map 29

THE BATTLE OF
QUATRE BRAS
2 p.m.

Scale of 1/8   1/4   1/2 mile

Dutch - Belgians

French

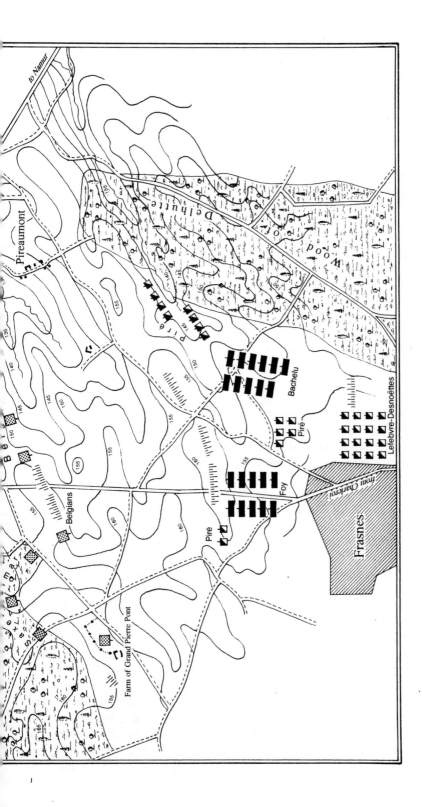

The First French Offensive

As soon as they moved past the farm of Lairalle, Jamin's brigade, led by General Foy, inclined to the north-east and attacked the 27th Jager. Bachelu's two brigades continued to advance north-west towards Pireaumont where they met the other companies of the 27th Jager. After a stiff resistance, the 27th Jager retired towards the Gemioncourt farm. Two companies of the battalion were deployed in the farm's gardens, the remaining companies were stationed to their front and left, 200 paces away.

While this was going on Foy's artillery had unlimbered and opened fire against Bijleveld's and Stevenart's batteries. Bijleveld's battery suffered considerable loss of men and horses to the French fire and was threatened from its left by Foy's columns and Piré's chasseurs whose advance, however, was checked by the marshes in the Lairalle valley. Foy's men moved nearer the Charleroi road where they found more suitable terrain. Stevenart's guns now also took heavy losses from counter-battery fire. The Prince of Orange ordered Captain Stevenart to retire, and Lieutenant Winssinger to move his detachment through the Bossu wood to take Foy's column under fire in support of Bijleveld's battery. Two of Stevenart's guns were pulled back to Quatre Bras so that they could be repaired, and four joined in supplementing Bijleveld's fire. Both Netherlands batteries continued to be hit hard, however.

Meanwhile Gauthier's Brigade was attacking the southern edge of the Bossu wood. The I./Nassau-Orange and the 8th Militia drove back the French a short distance with their fire, before themselves being forced to retire 200 to 300 paces into the wood by a new French advance. Then Duke Bernhard led the volunteers of the I./2nd Nassau and 2 companies of the 7th Militia in a counter-attack which pushed the French back out of the woods at bayonet point again. The Prince of Orange reinforced the Bossu wood with II./Nassau-Orange just before a renewed assault by a still larger body of French troops. These were from Jérôme's division which had marched north out of Frasnes by 4 p.m. Ney sent the division immediately to the Bossu wood, where several battalions quickly deployed into action. The distraction this caused to Saxe-Weimar's attention allowed Gauthier to rally his men and rejoin Foy on the main road.

Faced by four times the number of troops, and running low on ammunition, Duke Bernhard's men fell back slowly and in good order through the wood nearly to the north side and the road to Houtain-le-Val. The III./2nd Nassauers still held the northern end of the wood, however, and from there were able to support the 5th Militia and 27th Jager in the struggle for the Gemioncourt farm which was now also under way.

The young soldiers of Westenberg's 5th Militia had their baptism of fire here, suffering severely from French howitzers. As Jamin's brigade moved in to assault the farm, two companies of the 5th Militia moved forward to support the two companies of the 27th Jager holding the farm gardens. At the same time the four centre companies of the Jager battalion were in the process of withdrawing when Piré's chasseurs struck them, inflicting heavy losses, and scattering many survivors who were only able to rejoin their unit that night. As

Jamin's men closed in Westenberg had to pull back nearly to Quatre Bras.

By now the French had around 17,500 men, 4,700 sabres and 62 guns available. The Netherlanders were in a critical position. They would have had to abandon Quatre Bras if Merlen's Netherlands cavalry, the 5th Light Dragoons and 6th Hussars, had not arrived between 3 p.m. and 3.30 p.m. Shortly after that, eight battalions of British troops under Pack and Kempt from Picton's division marched up from the direction of Genappe. The Netherlanders had just managed to buy the time needed for reinforcements to arrive. Merlen brought 1,000 sabres and two guns with him; Picton's brigades amounted to around 4,600 men with 12 guns.

Merlen's light cavalry deployed to the south of the Namur road, with the 6th Hussars under Colonel Boreel forming the front line, and the 5th Light Dragoons under Lieutenant-Colonel de Mercx in support. The section of the Netherlands horse artillery commanded by Lieutenant van Wassenaar van Sint Pancras positioned itself between the two lines of cavalry. The horses had been saddled since the morning before, and the brigade had already marched nine hours in oppressive heat that day. Both the men and the horses were virtually exhausted, and they really needed a breathing space instead of being committed to action.

The 5th Division Intervenes

Picton's men were moved immediately to a position along the Nivelles–Namur road to the east of Quatre Bras. Even with this reinforcement the Allied left was weak, being menaced by Bachelu's columns around Pireaumont, which were threatening to attack at any moment. Kempt's Brigade, and part of Pack's, formed the front line; some of Best's 4th Hanoverian Brigade (part of 6th Division), who had also just arrived, drew up to their rear, covered by the embankment of the road. Braun's Hanoverian Battery deployed to the right, Rogers' British one on the left of Picton's men. The Allies now had 12,000 men, 600 sabres and 27 cannon at their disposal. The odds were gradually becoming more even.

The sight of reinforcements encouraged the 5th Militia to hang on north of Gemioncourt. They moved forward and stormed the farm at bayonet point, cleared away Jamin's skirmishers from the walls and fields, and then deployed in line to the south of the farm. Some of the French held on in the farm itself, however. Next, the 5th Militia were charged by the Colonel Faudouas' 6th Chasseurs à Cheval. Supported by the fire of Bijleveld's guns, the militiamen gave a volley at close range and beat off the French. A second line of French cavalry suffered a similar fate. A third line, Galbois' 6th Lancers, formed up. The valiant Netherlands militiamen were joined and encouraged by the Prince of Orange.

Next a column of French cavalry and infantry from Jamin's brigade moved east of Gemioncourt. The Prince sent Merlen an order to charge this column, while he reorganised the 5th Militia and 27th Jager to attack its flank. The French were driven off with heavy losses and briefly forced to abandon Gemioncourt.

Colonel Boreel was now ordered to charge General Jamin with his 6th Hussars, but did not fare well. He lost control of his men while they were still deploying, and they were thrown back by a counter-charge from Colonel Simonneau's 1st Chasseurs à Cheval. Pursued by Colonel Jacqueminot's 5th Lancers, they lost one officer and 13 men killed, four officers and 31 men wounded. The French cavalry followed through to Stevenart's and Bijleveld's guns, cutting down many of their crews before hitting the 5th Militia and inflicting more heavy casualties. In these various combats the 27th Jager lost 263 killed and wounded from 751 men, and the 5th Militia 303 killed, wounded and missing from 460 men.

The Prince of Orange was caught up in this rout, but was saved by the speed of his mount. This was also the moment when Wellington returned from his meeting with Blücher at Brye, with his steed also helping to extract him from a similarly precarious position. Fortunately, the fire of the II./Nassau-Orange, supported by British troops, halted the French cavalry. Squadrons from Piré's division then moved up between Pireaumont and the Namur road towards Pack's highlanders. The Scotsmen took cover in the ditches on either side of the road, and their musketry forced the French to turn away. The head of Bachelu's column now appeared. Mercx charged them with his 5th Belgian Light Dragoons, striking the French 6th Chasseurs à Cheval, with a brief hand-to-hand struggle ensuing before Mercx withdrew his men to rally. The French did not pursue. Mercx moved his men back to the sheepfold at Quatre Bras where, being mistaken for Frenchmen, they came under fire from Picton's highlanders.

Allied reinforcements continued to arrive. The remainder of Best's Hanoverians were followed shortly by five of the Brunswick battalions along with their cavalry, their duke at their head. This amounted to nearly 6,000 bayonets and 900 sabres. Best's battalions joined Picton to the south-east of Quatre Bras; the Brunswickers drew up between the Bossu wood and the road to Charleroi.

The Duke of Brunswick, anticipating the next French move, deployed the two Jäger companies of his Vanguard Battalion in the wood of Bossu to his south-west. The appearance of the Jäger was a welcome relief to Saxe-Weimar's Nassauers who had been hard-pressed in the wood by Jérôme's division, and were almost out of ammunition. The grey-clad Brunswick Jäger deployed into groups of four at intervals of six paces, in a ditch near the Gemioncourt brook. Their leader, Captain Berner, had his men place their large, conspicuous hats on the bushes in front of them, which attracted French fire, but caused negligible casualties.[44] The 2nd Light Battalion of Brunswickers, under Major von Brandenstein, was sent towards Pireaumont while the remainder, four battalions of infantry and four squadrons of hussars and uhlans, moved up between the Bossu wood and the Charleroi road.

Ney now decided to launch a determined attack to gain the cross-roads of Quatre Bras. He ordered Bachelu to advance from Pireaumont against the

<hr />

[44] Kortzfleisch, vol II, pp 63–5.

Allied left flank, and Jamin to support him by moving along the eastern side of the Charleroi road. Five batteries of artillery were deployed in support, 16 guns to the east of the Charleroi road, 26 between Pireaumont and the farm of Gemioncourt.

Wellington anticipated what was to come and prepared to meet this assault. Seven of Picton's battalions were drawn up 400 to 500 metres south of Quatre Bras; four of Best's battalions defended the Namur road along with a battalion of the 95th Rifles and Rogers' Battery on their left.

Bachelu's battalions began crossing the brook at Gemioncourt, whose banks were lined with bushes, and were about to reach the northern side when the first line of Picton's men fired a devastating volley at them. This was followed with a bayonet charge against the confused French formations, chasing them away until Piré's cavalry and artillery fire forced the British to fall back. Steady squares of British infantry held off the French cavalry at first, but the square of the 42nd was broken and the 44th was thrown into disorder, the colour of the 44th being fought over.

The Hanoverians were also in the thick of the fighting. Their official report described the action that followed,

> As the enemy advanced on Quatre Bras, the Battalions Lüneburg and Osterode had to deploy in range of enemy cannon fire; the sharpshooters formed a chain of skirmishers in front of the line. The remainder of the brigade followed in the second wave. We advanced thus until the line reached the cobbled road running from Nivelles to Namur, where it stopped and used the ditches along the roadside for its position. The Verden Battalion now linked up with the English brigade which was advancing over the cobbled road on the left flank of the Hanoverians. One of its companies was sent to join the skirmish line…
>
> The enemy's advance was in full swing. His cavalry had just attacked, and ridden through the 42nd Scottish Regiment, which had rushed into action with great boldness. They now reached the skirmish line. This part of the Verden Battalion was not able to fall back quickly enough and was largely ridden down or taken prisoner. The cavalry was on the point of advancing farther over the cobbled road when the two battalions in the ditch fired on them with such effect at close range that they turned around immediately. This way, the breakthrough in the centre was prevented, and fortunately without great loss, and without the remaining battalions of the brigade coming into action.[45]

Best's report outlined his perspective of this episode, describing how Galbois' lancers reached as far as the Namur road, but were unable to break through,

> In front of my brigade on the other side of the cobbled road stood a battalion of the 92nd Highland Scots; they were attacked by a body of cavalry, about two squadrons, mainly of chasseurs à cheval. The brave Scots, who had scrambled into the ditch at the side of the road, let the enemy come close to

45 Pflugk-Harttung, *Belle Alliance*, pp 9–10.

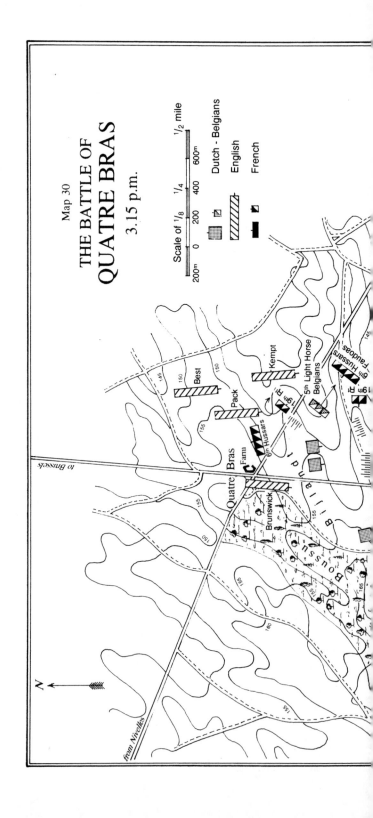

Map 30

THE BATTLE OF
QUATRE BRAS
3.15 p.m.

Scale of ⅛   ¼   ½ mile

200m 0   200   400   600m

Dutch - Belgians

English

French

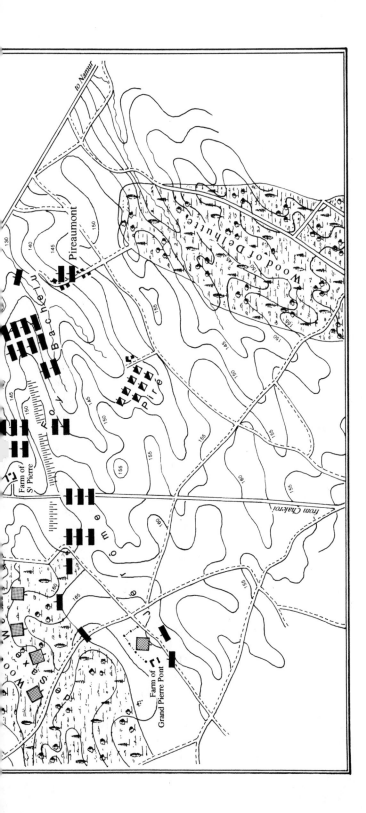

them and then fired so effectively that most of the enemy were killed, and the remainder fled...

About 4 p.m., Lieutenant-General Sir T. Picton ordered one battalion of my brigade into a position to fire at the enemy in such a way [from the ditches along the Namur road]. I gave this order to the Battalion Verden under the command of Major Christian von der Decken. General Picton positioned it himself, and used it to support and extend our line of sharpshooters, with the 1st Company advancing in open order into the skirmish line. Inexperienced in this type of fighting, but full of courage and determined to distinguish itself, part of this company pushed so far forwards that it was cut off by the enemy and taken prisoner. This was Lieutenant von der Horst, Fähnrich Plate and Fähnrich Kotzebue along with several sergeants and 63 men. The captured skirmishers were replaced immediately, and the battalion stood its ground, even though it suffered terribly from the larger number of enemy skirmishers. Lieutenant Waegener of this battalion, and Lieutenant Jenisch, commander of the sharpshooters of the Osterode Battalion, were shot. Major von der Decken gave me the following report of the courageous behaviour of his battalion, particularly the sharpshooters and their leader, Lieutenant Hurtzig:

"Lieutenant Hurtzig was deployed with his sharpshooters, men of the 1st Company, against some enemy skirmishers. The enemy were behind some bushes and trees, pouring deadly fire into our line, which was standing in the open with no cover. Nobody dared to attack this fire-spitting hedge, although troops of all types, English, Scottish and Hanoverians, were standing opposite it. Then Lieutenant Hurtzig ordered his sharpshooters to storm the hedge, with Lieutenant von Hinüber promising to support the attack with part of the 1st company. These two officers then placed themselves at the head of their men, who were at first deterred by the heavy enemy fire. Encouraged by the words of their officers, they charged the hedge, and, with their supports, drove off the enemy. Lieutenant von Hinüber was wounded, later dying of this wound. Although wounded at the commencement of this action, Fähnrich Best of the King's German Legion, who had been posted to these sharp-shooters, courageously led his platoon of sharpshooters into the fire.

"Lieutenant Hurtzig led his men in another attack on the enemy skirmishers and drove them out of their next position, but, so as not to become surrounded, fell back to the first hedge, to which the English and Scots troops, positioned to the left and right, had moved up..." [46]

About 4 p.m. Wellington ordered the Duke of Brunswick to take up a position to the west of the Charleroi road, near Gemioncourt. The French occupied the area to the south of Gemioncourt. The Brunswickers formed up on the north bank of the Gemioncourt brook, the light companies of the Vanguard on their right moving through the Bossu wood to link up with the Jäger. The 1st Line Battalion was led into position by Major Metzner, in column through shell fire. The Life Battalion stood in line at the sheepfold 250 metres south of Quatre Bras. However, because they were threatened by

---

[46] Pflugk-Harttung, *Belle Alliance*, pp 21–2.

French cavalry, they formed square before advancing. By 4.30 p.m., the Brunswickers had taken up their positions. As their left flank was exposed, Pack's 42nd and 44th Foot, partly recovered from the French cavalry attacks, moved up along the road a little. On the left of the Brunswickers, on the Namur road, stood the Lüneburg Landwehr Battalion who had replaced the 92nd Highlanders. Behind the Brunswickers' right, partly covered by a rise in the ground, stood the Brunswick uhlans and hussars. The 2nd and 3rd Line Battalions, under Lieutenant-Colonel von Specht, were held in reserve. The 3rd Line occupied several buildings on the Quatre Bras farm with the 2nd to its right, and a battalion of the 92nd to its left, in the ditch along the roadside.

Ney's response to this movement was to have a battery of 12-pounders unlimber on the path from Gemioncourt to Pierrepont and open fire, along with the batteries already deployed, on the unfortunate Brunswickers. This artillery bombardment was supported by the fire of skirmishers from Foy's division who had moved up to the bushes on the bank of the Gemioncourt brook. Major von Rauschenplat, commander of the Brunswick Vanguard, had his left arm ripped off by a shell splinter. Major von Cramm, commander of the Brunswick Hussars, was fatally wounded. Duke Friedrich Wilhelm, ignored warnings from Major von Wachholtz about his own safety, and stayed on his horse, calmly smoking his pipe to set an example to his young soldiers. The Brunswickers endured this bombardment for the best part of an hour.[47]

The 3rd Division Arrives

This desperate situation was alleviated by the arrival of more troops. Between 5 p.m. and 5.30 p.m., elements of the 3rd British Division started to arrive, including Halkett's and Kielmansegge's brigades, Lloyd's and Cleves' Batteries. The Allied forces now available amounted to 24,000 men with 1,900 sabres and 39 guns. The French were outnumbered, and only had one fresh reserve left, a division of cavalry. Wellington sent Kielmansegge's Hanoverians towards Pireaumont while Halkett's men were placed to the west of Quatre Bras.

Only now was there any artillery available to provide some covering fire to the Brunswickers; Major Lloyd with four 9-pounders moved up to the left of Rauschenplat's companies. Ney responded by deploying two horse batteries from his reserve cavalry, which soon knocked out two of Lloyd's guns and killed a large number of the battery's horses.[48]

Ney then sent in the available parts of the 9th Division under General Foy which advanced between the cobbled road and the wood of Bossu, which was now largely in French hands. The 4th Light, of Jamin's 2nd Brigade, led the assault with one battalion in line and two in column, and accompanied by some artillery. It was followed by the 100th Line and some cavalry support. Gauthier's 1st Brigade, the 92nd and 93rd Line, advanced along the Charleroi road, with Piré's light cavalry to its rear. This force amounted to some ten

---

[47] Kortzfleisch, vol II, pp 66–8.
[48] Kortzfleisch, vol II, p 68.

battalions with 4,700 combatants. There was little the two and a half battalions of Brunswickers could do to stop them, particularly as they were suffering flanking fire from the Bossu wood.

The Vanguard light companies, now being led by Captain von Griesheim, as Captain von Ritterholm was wounded, sought refuge in the wood. The 1st Line Battalion fell back along the road, with the Life Battalion retiring on its eastern flank. The hussars retired along the Nivelles road and the battered remnants of Lloyd's Battery also limbered up and withdrew.

The Duke of Brunswick accompanied his Life Battalion until it came under the cover of the skirmishers of the Lüneburg Landwehr. After having a brief conversation with Colonel Best, the Duke set himself at the head of his Uhlan Squadron, and attacked the French 1st Light Regiment from Jérôme's 6th Division which was now moving up in support of Foy. The fire of this square drove the Brunswickers back in disorder.[49]

The Duke then returned to his Life Battalion who were being attacked by Piré's chasseurs à cheval and lancers, as well as Jérôme's battalions. During this action the Duke of Brunswick was mortally wounded, at the head of his young soldiers, and had to be carried away. The Duke was on his horse about 25 paces in front of the battalion when he came under fire, probably from some of the French lancers. First his horse was struck, and fell, then a second salvo hit the Duke, inflicting the fatal wound. He was rescued by Corporal Kübel and Jäger Rekau of the 1st Company, and Hornist Aue of the 3rd. They carried him to the battalion, using their muskets as a stretcher. Coming under heavy artillery fire here, they took their wounded charge to the Namur road where Major von Wachholtz relieved them.[50]

That night, Colonel Olfermann, until then second-in-command of the Brunswick Corps, wrote the following report to his government,

> ...our much-loved Duke... was hit by a musket ball which smashed through one hand, his abdomen and his liver. This tragic incident occurred about 6 p.m. when His Grace was personally leading two battalions against a strong enemy column which was threatening our entire right flank. Despite being heavily outnumbered, it held back the enemy for a long time, but finally had to fall back on the second line. The last words the Duke spoke before his death were to Major von Wachholtz, and were, "Oh, my dear Wachholtz, where is Olfermann?"[51]

Despite this loss the Allied army was now ready to make an effective riposte. Lieutenant-General Sir Charles Alten, commander of the 3rd Division, in his report to the Duke of Cambridge of 20 June 1815, described the situation,

> Our troops took their positions between Quatre Bras and Sart-Dame[s]-Avelines on the cobbled road to Namur, with the right wing occupying the

---

[49] Kortzfleisch, vol II, pp 68–70.
[50] Kortzfleisch, vol II, p 70.
[51] Pflugk-Harttung, *Belle Alliance*, p 26.

former village, the left the latter. This deployment took place under heavy enemy cannon fire, under which not a single man flinched. The enemy sat tight in a wood to the right of Quatre Bras. This was attacked by our troops, being taken, lost and retaken several times.

Both sides now engaged in a heavy artillery bombardment, and the enemy tried several times to force the left flank, consisting of my division. I sent off the 1st Lüneburg Battalion to drive him again out of the village of Pireaumont, to our fore, which the Brunswick infantry had been forced to leave. Lieutenant-Colonel von Klenke carried out this order with absolute determination, and he was able not only to retake the village, but also to throw the enemy back into a wood the far side of the village, and to repel his subsequent counter-attacks.[52]

The official Hanoverian report added,

They [the remaining troops of the 3rd Division] were ordered to reinforce the left wing of our position and to push back the enemy there. To get to their allocated position, they had to move along the Namur road, passing the front of the entire enemy battle line. Doing so, they were fired on by all the enemy cannon, but their losses were relatively low, as most balls went too high.

An English light battalion and two companies of Brunswick Jäger were the only troops that had until now been available to offer the enemy resistance on the left wing. They had just been attacked with such force, that they had been driven out of the village of Pireaumont and pushed back so far that the enemy skirmishers were able to fire on the head of the column of the 1st Hanoverian Brigade on the road.

The Light [Field] Battalion Lüneburg, which was in the lead, was immediately ordered to deploy for an attack. It carried out this attack with such force that, despite determined resistance, it drove the enemy out of all his positions, not only from the fields and hedges along the road, but also out of the village of Pireaumont and the tip of the wood adjoining it. He only just manage to salvage a battery which he had moved up next to the village. As the resistance stiffened, particularly in the wood, the Battalion Grubenhagen was sent to support the Battalion Lüneburg.[53]

The Quatre Bras report of the 1st Hanoverian Brigade contained the following account,

As we approached Quatre Bras [from Nivelles], the enemy had taken a wood to the right. Thus the brigade was ordered to deploy on both sides of the cobbled road and to send skirmishers against the wood. After we advanced in line, the enemy evacuated the wood. The brigade redeployed into column and moved forwards on the Namur road over the cross-roads at Quatre Bras. At Quatre Bras, we met the Duke of Wellington who had his command post there for the remainder of the day. Shortly before our arrival, the Duke of Brunswick had fallen.

[52] Pflugk-Harttung, *Belle Alliance*, pp 13–14.
[53] Pflugk-Harttung, *Belle Alliance*, pp 10–11.

After passing Quatre Bras, the brigade suffered from heavy artillery fire, and lost many men. The head of the column advanced on the right of the road as far as the village of Pireaumont, where it wheeled, then was ordered to lie down to avoid the enemy artillery fire. The Field Battalion Lüneburg was now to the fore. It was ordered to drive the enemy out of Pireaumont, and carried out this order with such determination that it took the village and would have taken two enemy cannon, which had moved up, in the flank, if it had not been for a Brunswick horn player on our left signalling us to halt. His call was repeated by our buglers, so the two companies which were almost in the rear of the two cannon also halted, and thus the enemy gained enough time to retire. The enemy tried several times to take the village of Pireaumont, but was not successful.[54]

The Second French Offensive

About 6 p.m. the British 5th Brigade, under Major-General Halkett, went into action. Olfermann had rallied the Brunswick 1st Line and Life Battalions and moved up in support. These four battalions had only just reached the fields of tall rye, and the Brunswickers taken up their position in the ditches along the Nivelles road when Ney mounted a last desperate attack.[55] Ney, anticipating the arrival of d'Erlon's I Corps at any moment, threw in the last available battalions of Reille's II Corps.

Alten's report continued,

Then, several enemy columns moved forwards, so I detached the Battalions Grubenhagen, Duke of York and Bremen against them. With artillery support from Captain Cleves, of the [King's German] Legion, the columns were driven back. On my right, enemy cavalry tried, with several charges, to force their way through, but, thanks to the resolute behaviour of my troops, were not successful. In this affair, the Landwehr Battalion Lüneburg under Lieutenant-Colonel von Ramdohr particularly distinguished itself. It let the enemy advance to 30 paces distance before firing a volley that threw back the cavalry with great loss.[56]

Best's report to Alten also described that incident,

I positioned the Lüneburg Battalion along the cobbled road with its right on the gun of the horse battery of the KGL behind a ditch that had been previously occupied by a Scottish regiment. The enemy cavalry made a desperate charge, probably to take the gun. The Lüneburg Battalion remained very calm, not receiving them until they were very close. The fire was so well directed that only a few enemy cavalry survived, several falling only five or six paces from us.[57]

Best's official report gave some more details,

---

[54] Pflugk-Harttung, *Belle Alliance*, pp 15–16.   [56] Pflugk-Harttung, *Belle Alliance*, p 14.

[55] Kortzfleisch, vol II, pp 72–3.   [57] Pflugk-Harttung, *Belle Alliance*, p 18.

Sometime after 5 p.m., a detachment of enemy cavalry (about four squadrons), consisting of cuirassiers, hussars and chasseurs à cheval, was seen forming up to charge, with the apparent intention of taking the gun of the horse artillery of the [King's] German Legion. They came on at full gallop, with a few pieces of horse artillery in reserve, not knowing that our infantry support was not far away; the Lüneburg Battalion had laid down in the ditch along the main road. Meanwhile, our artillery had limbered up to retire to safety.

Just as the enemy came into range, the Lüneburg Battalion stood up and fired from 30 paces with such effect that the larger part of the enemy fell with many of them killed. The rest drew off to the left, to save themselves in a nearby farm, but the British Guardsmen placed there received them with such well-aimed fire that only a few could get away. An enemy cannon was dismounted and fell into our hands.[58]

The French were not yet finished, as the report of the 1st Hanoverian Brigade described,

… [the French] now advanced with stronger columns. Thus the Battalion Lüneburg was reinforced by the Battalion Grubenhagen, two companies of the Duke of York's Battalion in the village of Pireaumont, and two more battalions behind the village in reserve. Thus all attacks were beaten off, and the enemy pursued into a nearby wood. He attempted to support one major attack by sending forward a line of skirmishers to the right of the village towards the road. This resulted in one Jäger company and several sections of the Battalion Bremen being sent against them to attack. This attack was so forceful, that he was thrown back several thousand paces, even abandoning an advantageous position behind ditches and hedges, where the Jäger sat firm, and killed many of the enemy, forcing them to retire over a plain.[59]

Ney had hoped for reinforcements but all that reached him was a messenger with the news that d'Erlon had moved towards Ligny with his entire corps. Realistically this news meant that the day at Quatre Bras could not now be won by the French, as they had too few men available. However, Ney sent off Kellermann's fine cuirassiers, the 8th and 11th Regiments of Guiton's Brigade, in one last desperate charge. Halkett's Brigade was struck by this armoured cavalry. The 69th fired a volley at 30 paces, but lost its king's colour to the French horsemen, and the 33rd was scattered. Piré's lancers and chasseurs followed up, trying in vain to break Halkett's other squares, but the 30th and 73rd remained steady. The French then moved on to attack Pack and Kempt, but with the same lack of success. Instead the French troopers were met with a hail of musket and artillery fire that drove them off. By about 6.45 p.m., the French cavalry attack, and that of the 9th Division had been beaten off. The situation in the Allied centre was saved.[60]

Towards 6.30 p.m., Maitland's 1st Brigade of Guards (about 2,000 men)

[58] Pflugk-Harttung, *Belle Alliance*, pp 22–3.
[59] Pflugk-Harttung, *Belle Alliance*, p 16.
[60] Kortzfleisch, vol II, p 74.

arrived, accompanied by two horse batteries. The infantry were immediately thrown into the Bossu wood, while the artillery took positions to the east of Quatre Bras. The Guards pushed the French back to the edge of the wood, and though they were prevented from going any further by artillery and cavalry, they held the eastern edge of the wood.[61]

The Netherlanders and Nassauers of the 7th Militia, I./Nassau-Orange and II./2nd Nassau, supported by the Brunswick Jäger, took advantage of this advance to occupy ground they had lost earlier. Halkett's brigade pushed forward likewise, supported by two Brunswick line battalions, to the heights to the north of the Gemioncourt brook. The French infantry fell back, though Piré's cavalry moved forward again briefly, forcing the Allies into squares, before they were driven off. At 7 p.m., the remainder of the Brunswick Corps, the 1st and 3rd Light Battalions and the artillery, arrived at Quatre Bras. The reason for their delay does not appear to be on record. These fresh troops were placed in reserve behind their exhausted compatriots.[62]

The Last Moves

More troops, including Kruse's 2,800 Nassauers, arrived for Wellington so that he now had some 30,000 men available to him. This gave Wellington the chance to send in a general attack, supported by his reinforced artillery. Maitland's and Byng's brigades of the 1st Division drew up to attack Jérôme; the 3rd Division advanced along the Charleroi road towards Gemioncourt; the 5th Division continued to engage Bachelu; and the Prince of Orange moved his forces forward finally to eject the French from the Bossu wood.

Night fell, the fighting died down, and Uxbridge's cavalry at last arrived after their forced march. The Allied troops had maintained most of the positions they had held that morning.

The Allied losses amounted to a total of 4,800 men as follows:[63]

British & Hanoverians	2,911 men
Netherlanders	1,073 men
Nassauers	108 men
Brunswickers	708 men

The French lost slightly fewer, 4,140 men

With more troops on their way, Wellington was now in a position to go over to the offensive on 17 June – if Blücher was able to assist him.

The Battle for Ligny

The Prussian Deployment

While the French offensive was commencing at St Amand, a second, much stronger attack force, drawn from IV Corps, marched out of Fleurus. It moved along the main road towards Sombreffe at first, then wheeled to the left in the direction of Ligny, with a substantial line of skirmishers in front. Grouchy's

---

[61] Siborne, H.T., *Waterloo Letters*, p 241 f.
[62] Kortzfleisch, vol II, p 76.
[63] De Bas & T'Serclaes de Wommersom, vol I, p 541.

cavalry moved in support on the right flank of this column, Exelmans' 2nd Corps to the left, Pajol's 1st to the right. Maurin's cavalry division, part of IV Corps, linked up with Exelmans' dragoons.

The I. and II./3rd Kurmark Landwehr Cavalry Regiment, part of the 9th Brigade, who had been covering the road north-east of Fleurus, made a fighting withdrawal to positions behind Mont Potriaux, hotly pursued by French cavalry. Fire from the F./4th Kurmark Landwehr (11th Brigade) close to the bridge near Mont Potriaux, forced the French to desist. The Prussians could now see that a major assault on Ligny was imminent and sent in reinforcements from the 3rd Brigade.

The garrison of Ligny, initially just four battalions of the 4th Brigade, was deployed as follows: the I. and F./19th Regiment on the right, the II. and F./4th Westphalian Landwehr on the left. Captain von Pritzelwitz occupied the château at the south-west end of the village with the skirmish division of I./19th Regiment, later being reinforced by the 9th Company under Captain von Busse. Three platoons of skirmishers were deployed along the walls. Lieutenant von Velten was to defend the west gate, Lieutenant Beyer the east, and Lieutenant von Schickfuss the centre. One platoon of skirmishers under Lieutenant von Kessler was placed behind the hedges. The remainder were drawn up in reserve in the courtyard. The walls were loop-holed, both in and outside the château, and the gates barricaded.

In the part of the village around the château facing the open ground to the south-west, the 1st and 4th Companies placed one platoon behind the hedges along the southern edge of the village, while another was drawn up behind the skirmishers as their support. The 2nd and 3rd Companies were positioned in close order, behind the others, initially on the north bank of the Ligne brook, as a local reserve. The 1st Battalion was led this day by Captain von Freymann, as the usual commander, Major von Courbière, had been injured in a fall from his horse.

To the east, the 10th, 11th and 12th Companies (from the Fusilier Battalion), under the command of Major von Schouler, were drawn up in company columns. Schouler placed his skirmish platoons on the far hedges on the south-east edge of the village, each covering around 100 paces of frontage. The banks of the brook were nearly 2 metres high, so Schouler had his men cut steps into them. The company columns were drawn up along the south road in Ligny, and cut communication paths through the gardens, fences and hedges. The Fusilier Battalion linked up to the east with II./4th Westphalian Landwehr under Major von Rex, and this with the Landwehr's Fusilier Battalion, led by Major von Kuilenstjerna. Major von Groeben was in command in this part of the village. The 10th Company of the 19th Regiment covered the western entrance to the village, while the Landwehr covered the approach to the church.

The II./19th Regiment, under Major von Bünau, stood at the north-east of the village in support of the eastern part, and linked up with III Army Corps. To the right of this battalion was the I./4th Westphalian Landwehr, led by Major von Zastrow. This battle-group was commanded by Major von Stengel.

It was formed in platoon columns and deployed as the brigade reserve to the north of the Ligne brook with the sunken road from Ligny to Sombreffe to its front. However, the skirmishers of the II./19th, under Captain von Glasenapp, were deployed on the far side of the Ligne brook. Glasenapp considered the high corner garden between the sunken roads leading into the north-west end of the village as ideal for the centre of his position, so he sent the four skirmish officers there. As the loss of this point would result in that part of the village becoming untenable, the skirmishers were instructed to fall back on it at any critical moment. The 1st Skirmish Platoon was placed on either side of the sunken road leading to Boignée, behind the hedges and earth walls. The 2nd and 3rd Skirmish Platoons under Lieutenant Eckert occupied the garden itself, while the 4th Platoon occupied a farmhouse next to and slightly to the rear of the garden.[64]

All parts of the village were prepared for the defence with all due haste. Loop holes were cut in the walls, windows removed, doors barricaded, cellars made ready for the defence, and some of the tall crops near the edge of the village cut down. The sunken roads were barricaded with farming equipment.

A grand battery consisting of the foot batteries of the 2nd, 3rd and 4th Brigades and three 12-pounder reserve batteries was positioned on the heights above St Amand and Ligny. Of these 48 guns, 16 were designated to protect the approaches to Ligny.

The First French Offensive

At 2.30 p.m., the French columns could be seen drawing up opposite Ligny along the road from Fleurus to Namur. The French made their first attack on Ligny at 3 p.m. The first attack column moved in on the east of the village. Shortly thereafter, a second column advanced against the centre of the village, and a third to the west end, towards the old château. These attackers were from the divisions of Pêcheux, Vichery and Hulot, some 22 battalions in total. The right-hand column clashed first with Glasenapp's skirmishers. Twice the French skirmishers attempted to expel Glasenapp from the garden, and twice they were beaten off. They attacked with such determination, however, that Stengel had the main body of the II./19th Regiment prepare to move into action from his brigade reserve.[65] The two other French columns fared little better at first. Although supported by a murderous artillery fire, they were driven back to their starting positions beside the line of French guns that had now unlimbered at canister range from Ligny.

Glasenapp's report of the incident began with him discovering the French breaking into his positions,

> I ran to the assembly point as fast as possible. Here, I found my three skirmish platoons confused and in some disorder, so I took the section nearest me and was about to go through a gap in the hedge to enter the garden when I met an enemy sergeant-major who, in German, declared himself to be a deserter.

[64] Leszczynski, p 156 ff.
[65] Leszczynski, p 158.

I had already grasped him by his sword or cartridge box belt and placed the point of my sword at his stomach when he surrendered. On my order, he threw down his musket, which he had been holding up in the air. He was terrified, begging for his life and cursing Napoleon, doing everything that fear causes.

In the garden, I could see no more than 12 enemy soldiers. I took these for deserters as well, and was just about to disarm them when one of these men aimed his musket at me and squeezed the trigger, but, fortunately, had a misfire. I had my men, who had come with me, give fire, and we had hardly killed more than a couple of these men when a strong enemy column, right in front of me, climbed up into the garden. They were carrying a tricolour flag, but I only saw junior officers, and no leader of the column.

I left the garden quickly, ordered my men to take cover in the dry Ligne ditch, and called to Major von Bünau to fire a volley over us. This he did, throwing back the enemy... [66]

Glasenapp's skirmishers followed up, moving as far forward as the sunken road to Tongrinelle, where they received sudden fire from out of the tall crops, suffered heavily losses, and retired in haste.

Major von Bünau, commander of II./19th Regiment, had his battalion, until then in close column, deploy to the left. Bünau was unable to ride his horse because of the rough ground. Instead he dismounted and led his men on foot over the sunken road to Sombreffe up to the Ligne brook, where they halted. The French again pushed forward in column against the skirmishers of the II./19th, driving them back on their close-order supports. Bünau's men fired a volley at the French, who then attempted to deploy to return the fire. While they were doing so Bünau had his battalion fire a second volley and followed it up with a bayonet charge which threw the French back. The Prussians returned to their positions behind the Ligne brook.

While this was going on, the other French columns had also renewed their attacks, trying initially to capture the churchyard at Ligny. Entire battalions were used in skirmish order, causing great difficulties to the Prussian defenders. Hidden by the tall crops, the French were able to get up to the hedges and garden walls and engage the Prussians in close combat. The outnumbered defenders were forced back. However, Major Graf Groeben, chief-of-staff of the Reserve Cavalry of I Army Corps, and other officers managed to rally the men. The Prussians counter-attacked with such vigour that the French had to leave behind two of their cannon. The counter-attack then advanced too far and was driven back in turn by French canister fire. Unfortunately, in this retreat, the Prussians had no means of towing away the captured guns and had to abandon them.

By now, the French had managed to establish a position to the west of Ligny from where they were able to fire into the Prussian flank. Stengel brought his reserve round from the other end of the village to face them. The II./19th Regiment formed line at first, but Bünau had his men break up into smaller groups to take advantage of the terrain. A violent fire-fight took place

[66] Leszczynski, pp 158–9.

until Captain von Chirocz of the 6th Company suddenly gave the order to advance and the entire battalion descended on the French with a loud 'hurrah', throwing them back across the brook. Covered by their artillery, the French reformed and counter-attacked, driving back the Prussians to their starting positions, but were then themselves driven off again in turn. This sequence of events was repeated four times.[67] In the confusion of this battle, the West Prussians and the Westphalian Landwehr mixed together, forming ad hoc battle-groups.

In these combats Stengel's aide, Lieutenant Lange, was wounded, when he led back a group of stragglers from Zastrow's Landwehr. Of the skirmish officers, Lieutenants Eckert, Bauer and von Adlersfeld were also wounded, but both remained in action until they fainted from loss of blood. Zastrow's Landwehr suffered heavily, their commander being severely wounded when his battalion came under canister fire as they chased off their broken attackers.

The French now renewed their frontal attacks on Ligny, while also attempting to gain the flank of the II./19th Regiment with their skirmishers. Their centre column assaulted the entrance to the village leading to the church, while their left column advanced on the western end. The French attacks came and went, and eventually they gained a hold on several positions. As the French pressed into the village a murderous hand-to-hand combat took place in which every house, every room and every cellar was disputed.

In this fighting the 10th Company of the 19th was outflanked, and forced to withdraw, not an easy matter as a pond blocked its retreat. The only available route was along the mill street which was under hostile fire. The company managed to rejoin the 11th and 12th, however, without significant loss. Major Schouler then led the three companies in a counter-attack. This achieved little as the French had forced their way into the village to the east of Landwehr Battalion Rex, capturing the churchyard. By doing so, they outflanked the counter-attack and the three fusilier companies subsequently had to retire across the Ligne brook. Schouler received a significant head wound in this action, but refused to leave his post until the 4th Brigade commander Graf Henckel ordered him to leave. Captain von Borcke replaced him.

The French now controlled a large part of the village of Ligny.

About 4 p.m., the French began their assault on the old château. Lieutenant Kessler soon retired with his skirmish platoon into the courtyard of the château, as he was under fire from the numerous French skirmishers positioned in the hedges around the building. Under the cover of this fire, French sappers attempted to smash down the eastern gate, but Beyer's men shot these dare-devils.

Around 5 p.m., as we have seen, St Amand fell to the French. This meant that they were now able to threaten Ligny from the south-west. A battery was unlimbered 400 paces from the château, and started to shell it, and fire canister against the walls. This enfilading fire affected the whole Ligny position. The French tried to expand their hold on the village, first by bombarding it, then

[67] Leszczynski, pp 159–60.

by sending in small infantry battle-groups while the artillery held its fire.

At 5 p.m. the 1st and 4th Companies of the 19th Regiment had yet to come into action. Only when the French battery started firing against the château did they commence firing as well and, despite the long range, managed to pick off a number of gunners. Later, the French infantry moved against the I./19th's part of Ligny, but were held off. The château was still in Prussian hands at 7 p.m.

The First Prussian Counter-Attack

By about 5 p.m. the village of Ligny with the exception of the château and Freymann's I./19th position was in French hands. Thus, I. and II./7th (2nd West Prussian) Regiment from 3rd Brigade were ordered into Ligny. With a wheel to the left, the 3rd Brigade approached Ligny. Its skirmishers were deployed in the lead to clear the houses and ditches on both sides of the roads from Brye. The two musketeer battalions marched into the village, drums beating and fifes playing, with charged arms and a loud shout of 'hurrah'. Two of the brigade's fusilier battalions, from the 7th and 29th Regiments, moved to the right to cover Foot Batteries Nos. 3 and 8 which were in support.

The 7th Regiment musketeers advanced in column over the meadows towards the village, I./7th down the mill road, II./7th, led personally by the brigade commander General von Jagow, towards the church. The 1st Battalion got as far as the southern edge of the village. The 2nd Battalion passed the unoccupied church before it was hit in the flank by a battalion of French. A second battalion then charged the West Prussians in the other flank. The II./7th fell back in such disorder that it took the I./7th with it. The French failed to follow up with vigour, so the Prussians were able to reform rapidly.[68]

The two battalions reformed into close columns and counter-attacked, forcing their way into the village once again. Their skirmish platoons, under Captain von Witten and Captain von Berg, were detached and sent to storm the churchyard which the French had now occupied. The West Prussians captured their objective, either killing or taking prisoner the French garrison. Both battalions were then preparing to advance south out of the village when they encountered several battalions of French, attacking in close columns. As the Prussians were caught in the narrow streets, and as the French did not have the time to deploy, they both halted to fire as they were. The ensuing exchange of fire lasted half an hour with both sides suffering heavy casualties. The flag pole of the 2nd Battalion was shattered and the colours of both battalions were ripped to pieces by bullets. Captain von Czarnowski, commander of the 1st Battalion, suffered several bullet wounds and died. Many others were killed or wounded.[69]

More Prussian battalions moved into Ligny, including the F./7th and F./29th, as well as other battalions from the 6th and 8th Brigades. In fact, so many troops were sent into the village in short order that the streets became

[68] Lewinski & Brauchitsch, vol I, pp 149–50.
[69] Lewinski & Brauchitsch, vol I, p 150.

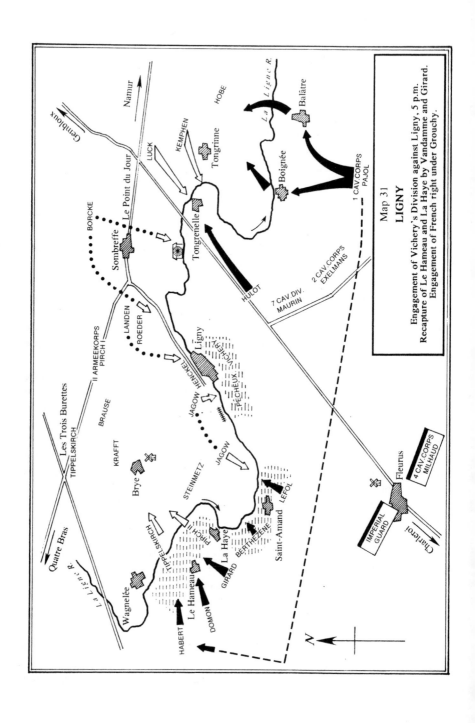

Map 31

LIGNY

Engagement of Vichery's Division against Ligny, 5 p.m.
Recapture of Le Hameau and La Haye by Vandamme and Girard.
Engagement of French right under Grouchy.

overcrowded and control broke down. In the confusion someone said that the French had taken possession of the church spire, so some men started to fire at it. The troops of the II./7th fighting at the edge of the village heard this firing from behind them, and thought they had been surrounded. A salvo of French cannon fire was then enough to break their nerve and make them retreat. Premier-Lieutenant von Bojan attempted to rally the remaining 250 men, which he achieved to an extent, despite taking fire from several directions. Suddenly, a battalion of French from Le Capitaine's 1st Brigade of Vichery's division charged out of a side street. Bojan ordered his men to counter-charge, but the Frenchmen prevailed. They pursued the fleeing Prussians so closely that two Frenchmen attempted to seize the colour of the II./7th which was being carried by Ensign Schulze. Privates Schwenke and Butzki rescued both him and the colour, killing the unfortunate Frenchmen in the process. For their deeds that day, these Prussians were honoured with the Iron Cross, 2nd Class and Russian Order of St George, 5th Class.[70]

Captain Bellmer took the 9th and 10th Companies of the F./29th into Ligny in column after leaving his skirmish platoons behind to protect the artillery batteries. Bellmer's men moved close to the church and engaged some French voltigeurs 100 paces away, in cover behind fences and hedges. Near their position some Westphalian Landwehr were also defending a foot-bridge but were being pushed back. Volleys from the F./29th held this attack off, too. Some French approached the right flank of the fusiliers and called on them to change sides. Evidently, the great heat of that day had led to some of these troops discarding their grey overcoats to reveal their white uniforms and their identity as former Berg troops. Bellmer was shot dead just after having rejected this call. However, Sergeant Schellpeper of the 9th Company spotted the voltigeur who had fired the fatal shot, and returned the compliment the next time the Frenchman raised his head from the cover.

The vicious street fighting continued, being graphically described by one participant,

> In the streets of the village, we fought with clubbed muskets and bayonets. As if overcome by personal hatred, man battled against man. It seemed as if every individual had met his deadliest enemy and rejoiced at the long-awaited opportunity to give expression to this. Pardon was neither asked nor given; the French plunged their bayonets in the chests of those already falling from their wounds; the Prussians swore loudly at their enemies and killed everyone that fell into their hands.[71]

The French now brought up some artillery onto the road by the church. The Berg fusiliers fought tooth and nail to defend Bellmer's body, Lieutenant von Schmeling fighting off two Frenchmen while his fusiliers attempted to drag their former commander away. Schmeling suffered a bayonet wound and was shot in the left arm here. The F./29th were gradually forced back, but not

[70] Lewinski & Brauchitsch, vol I, pp 151–2.
[71] Wellmann, p 99.

before Schmeling suffered two more wounds, one in his abdomen, one in the leg. He was carried away on a limber.[72]

Graf Henckel now ordered a general attack on the southern part of the village. Borcke, with his three fusilier companies of the 19th Regiment, although exhausted by more than two hours of combat, formed a column at the western end of the village, and moved in support of the I. and II./7th. This attack was more successful, reaching the southern edge of the village with such speed that the French gunners there cut the traces and abandoned their guns in haste. However, this success was squandered when the elated Prussians pursued the French out of the village. Again, French troops drawn up in the tall crops were able to surprise the Prussians, driving them off with effective fire at close range. The French followed the broken Prussians back into Ligny, regaining most of their original positions, including the church-yard, which the 7th Regiment had recaptured only a short while earlier.

Schachtmeyer next led his 10th Company of the 19th in a local counter-attack. When a company of French got to about 70 paces from his position, he led 40 or 50 of his men over a wall. From there, they charged the French who continued their advance to within ten paces of the Prussians before falling back in a panic, being chased back over 100 paces.[73]

The Second Prussian Counter-Attack

About 6 p.m., the 6th Brigade went into action. The II./1st Elbe Landwehr was already in Ligny, and four battalions of the brigade in action in St Amand, when General von Krafft was ordered to drive the French out of Ligny with his four remaining battalions, the I. and II./9th (Colberg) Regiment and I. and F./1st Elbe Landwehr. This reinforcement gave the exhausted defenders the impetus to go over to the offensive once again, but this time the Prussians failed to regain the southern parts of the village. By now, many of the buildings in Ligny were in flames, and the surrounding fields were full of wounded.

Krafft's four battalions marched down the slopes from Brye to Ligny under heavy artillery fire. The two musketeer battalions of the Colberg Regiment, under the command of Major von Schmidt, halted briefly just before reaching the village. The skirmish division under Captain von Borcke and Captain von Maltoky and the 80-strong volunteer detachment under Lieutenant von Bagensky, were thrown out in front to begin the attack. The 1st Battalion, under Major von Lukowitz, then advanced down the wide high street, with the 2nd Battalion, under Major von Dorsch, remaining in reserve. The impetus of the first assault drove the French back across the Ligne brook, and the Prussian skirmishers took up positions in the farthest houses.[74]

Krafft only sent in these two battalions at first, keeping his others in reserve. He was soon forced to commit those troops as well when the French brought in their reserves. The battle slowed down; each house had to be attacked and defended individually. The French took a large building which

---

[72] Wellmann, pp 100–1.   [74] Bagensky, p 237.
[73] Leszczynski, p 162.

Jagow and his 7th Regiment unsuccessfully attempted to retake. The French also retook the churchyard where they deployed two cannon. The I./3rd Westphalian Landwehr tried to push them back from there three times but needed to cross a wide ditch over a footbridge first. From there, they would have been able to get to a sunken road which lay on the flank of the church but at every attempt they were met by French reinforcements and repelled.

Borcke led his three companies (F./19th Regiment) across the Ligne brook nine times more, each time being repelled by French counter-attacks. The I./19th held its own in the château, though it was under heavy artillery bombardment. This fire was shattering the very stones of which the château was built, many men being wounded by flying splinters. About 6.30 p.m., the shingle-roofed barn in the château farm went up in flames. The fire was so hot that at 7 p.m. Captain Busse of 9th Company/19th, who commanded this sector, ordered his men, who had also run out of ammunition, to withdraw. The gates from the château were blocked by so much rubble by then, that it would have taken too long to clear them. Instead, the garrison jumped out of the first floor windows, or over the high walls, into the surrounding fields where the 6th Brigade covered their withdrawal.

Blücher now ordered the 8th Brigade to move up gradually to support the 6th Brigade. The 12th Brigade of III Army Corps replaced the 8th at Sombreffe, also throwing out its skirmishers along the Ligne brook. At about 7 p.m. four fresh battalions of the 8th Brigade (I./23rd Regiment and all three battalions of the 21st Regiment) marched into Ligny to relieve the 4th Brigade which had been ordered to fall back to the Bois du Loup to reform. This was a difficult manoeuvre as the 4th Westphalian Landwehr was being pushed back out of Ligny by the French, while the I. and F./19th Regiment had become so mixed up with other troops in Ligny that it took a long time to extricate them. The skirmishers of the I./19th rejoined their unit at 8 p.m. but Busse's men were not able to rejoin their regiment that day at all. Captain von Freymann, commander of the I./19th, described this withdrawal,

> The battalion fell back along the village high street, constantly meeting enemy skirmishers and grenadiers. A cannonball, which tore the arms off two musketeers, threw me off my horse. I would have been taken prisoner but for a charging Prussian Landwehr battalion which gave me the opportunity to join the retreat. I was, however, now separated from the 1st Battalion, but joined up with some Prussian cavalry on the far side of the village. I was knocked unconscious from my horse for a second time by a shell, was carried to Gembloux and rejoined my regiment on the 17th.[75]

The I./23rd, under Major von Buttlar, was ordered to rush to assist the other battalions of the 8th Brigade, and came under heavy artillery fire as it descended the slope into Ligny. Three cannon balls struck the advancing column, one mortally wounding Captain von Sell, a second taking out the entire first file of the colour platoon. Before reaching the village, the battalion

---

[75] Leszczynski, p 165.

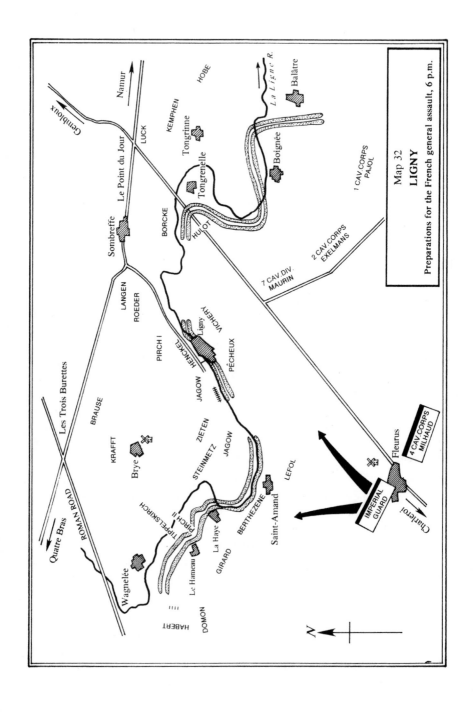

Map 32
LIGNY
Preparations for the French general assault, 6 p.m.

was ordered to drive out the French from the lower part of Ligny. The skirmishers of the I./23rd located a way into the village which appeared to lead to the lower part, but which was already occupied by French soldiers sporting tall bearskins. The French fire was causing the skirmish line to break down when the supports of the 2nd and 3rd Skirmish Platoons charged, forcing back the surprised Frenchmen at bayonet point. The 1st and 4th Skirmish Platoons, taking advantage of the opportunity, rushed to both sides of the entrance, followed by the battalion column. With the drummers beating the charge and the buglers playing it, the battalion made as much noise as possible, trying to give the impression that it was part of a much larger force. The other Prussians in Ligny, inspired by this charge, moved to support the I./23rd. The French were thus forced back, taking cover behind the brook and in the hedges and buildings.[76]

In the course of this bitter fighting, Sergeant Hübner of the skirmishers of the 3rd Company of the 23rd trapped a group of Frenchmen carrying a flag against a hedge. In the subsequent desperate hand-to-hand struggle, the flag was ripped from its pole, Hübner and several of his men stabbed to death, and others wounded. Skirmishers Borst, Kostelnik and Pietreck managed to take away the bands and tassels previously attached to the flag pole.[77]

Buttlar followed up with the 3rd Skirmish Platoon of the 1st and 2nd Companies, and one platoon of the 4th Company, moving along the first path into the village. Captain von Busse was ordered to take his 3rd Company and another platoon from the 4th Company along a second lane to the left, but was unable to shift the French from the buildings there. Busse thus ordered Lieutenant Pruskowsky, with the 1st Skirmish Platoon and the battalion's sappers, to assault the largest farmhouse, while Lieutenant Sörgel attacked along the lane with the 2nd and 4th Skirmish Platoons. Pruskowsky surrounded the building with his skirmishers and gave the sappers covering fire while they smashed down the gates and doors. The Prussians then stormed the building while the French occupants unsuccessfully tried to escape from it by the windows. This action forced the French to retire out of that part of Ligny for a time.[78]

Sörgel covered the lane with the 4th Skirmish Platoon, while the 2nd and 3rd occupied the buildings. The remainder of the men took cover, and there was a short pause in the fighting on this sector of the front. When the French counter-attacked a quarter of an hour later Sörgel fell back on his supports as ordered, but was struck by a bullet and killed. Busse counter-charged the French column, the Prussians getting to within 50 paces of the French before falling back when their captain's horse was shot under him. The Prussians abandoned the buildings they had just captured.[79]

The 21st Regiment staged six assaults without succeeding in clearing its part of the village of the French. The French kept their hold on the part of Ligny on the south bank of the brook, and continued to push their skirmishers

[76] Busse, pp 166–8.
[77] Busse, p 168 fn.
[78] Busse, pp 168–9.
[79] Busse, pp 170–1.

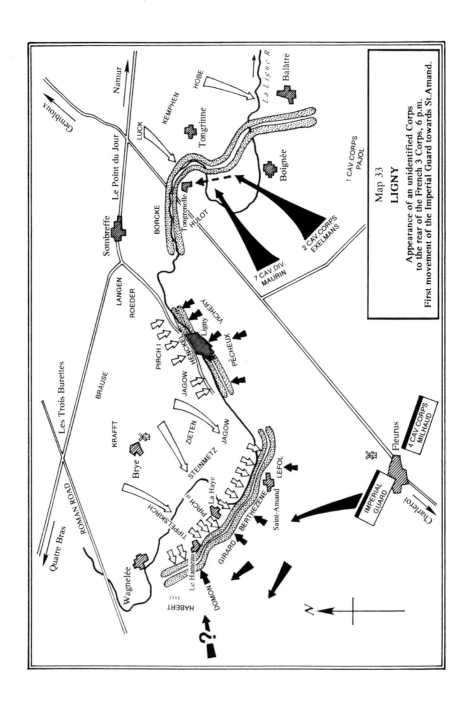

Map 33
LIGNY
Appearance of an unidentified Corps
to the rear of the French 3 Corps, 6 p.m.
First movement of the Imperial Guard towards St. Amand.

over to the Prussian side. The report of Lieutenant-Colonel von Reckow, commander of the 21st Regiment, described the affair,

> The 8th Brigade, of which the regiment allocated to me was part, having been placed in reserve at first, then received the order to follow the 6th Brigade and moved in the direction of the windmill of Bussy. When the Brigade got close to Ligny, and the enemy attack stronger, I immediately noticed that on our left flank, a hill opposite the village of Ligny was not occupied. This was despite the fact that more and more enemy columns were approaching Ligny and the enemy skirmishers had already taken control of the village. I thus asked the brigade [infantry] commander, Colonel von Langen, for permission to take the two [musketeer] battalions of my regiment to occupy this hill on which there was only artillery. I then marched to the left and occupied the hill.
>
> A fearful battle for the village of Ligny now broke out. I immediately sent my skirmishers forward to help to drive the enemy out of the village, and soon moved forwards with the regiment to support them. Our combined forces were, after a murderous combat and with heavy losses, indeed able to drive the enemy from the village. This was, however, not enough; to be master of the position, one would also have to take the heights opposite the village where the enemy had positioned his artillery and deployed his columns of infantry and artillery. As we were too few for that task, we had to restrict ourselves to disputing the village with the enemy.
>
> The regiment stormed the village six times, sometimes in union with other formations, other times quite alone. The enemy counter-attacked six times, but neither side was broken. The men were exhausted and could not advance again, so I saw myself compelled to rally the regiment on the heights behind Ligny, and to allow the men a moment's rest, while the skirmishers were involved in a lively struggle for the village. It was growing dark by now, and the murderous combat in the village did not let up.
>
> Then the enemy received reinforcements and moved forward in force. I advanced in line to delay the enemy with a rapid attack, when suddenly enemy cuirassiers who had moved around Ligny attacked the regiment in the left flank while enemy infantry attacked from the other side.[80]

When Colonel von Langen saw that the battle in the village was getting more difficult, he sent off the I./23rd Regiment and II./3rd Elbe Landwehr in support. He deployed the remainder of his brigade at the Bussy windmill which itself was occupied by the II./23rd Line.

Behind Ligny, the 1st and 4th Brigades attempted to reform. We have seen how some of the 19th Regiment were unable to rejoin the 1st Brigade but most of the remainder were reorganised and provided with fresh ammunition. However, the II./19th had spent much of the day fighting in skirmish order, and its men were totally exhausted when they were ordered to fall back. They had expended their entire supply of ammunition and many had discarded their greatcoats and backpacks because of the heat and the need to crawl

---

[80] Schreiber, p 95.

through gaps in the hedges during the fighting. They fell back as far as Sombreffe before halting to reform. In the confusion of battle the order to assemble at the Bois du Loup was never received. After they had rested at Sombreffe for 15 minutes, a passing staff officer ordered them to Gembloux. The battalion eventually rejoined the regiment at Wavre the next day.

The Prussian defence of Ligny was now on the point of collapse.

The Action at Balâtre and Tongrinne

Fighting on the eastern wing of the position, along the line from Sombreffe to Balâtre, only really started about 6 p.m., and then with only a few troops involved. This fighting began with an exchange of musket fire, with most of the battalions of the Prussian 10th and 11th Brigades then gradually being committed, one after the other, in a battle for the villages here. The villages of Tongrinne and Boignée changed hands several times.

When Colonel von Luck saw the 10th Brigade in action at Tongrinne, he moved the F./4th Kurmark Landwehr to the left, replacing it with the F./3rd Kurmark Landwehr. Shortly after that, he personally led I./4th Kurmark Landwehr to that village. Later, Lieutenant-General von Thielemann sent I./3rd Kurmark Landwehr in support, so, of this brigade, only II./4th Kurmark Landwehr remained uncommitted.

Between 7 p.m. and 8 p.m., as the French withdrew one battery from Tongrinne and depleted their line of cavalry, Thielemann came to believe that the battle of Ligny was going in the Prussians' favour. He thus considered this moment the right one to stage a flanking attack, ordering his cavalry and some of his reserve artillery to move forwards. Major-General von Hobe, the corps' cavalry commander, only had Lottum's 2nd Cavalry Brigade available, since Marwitz's 1st was deployed on the army's right flank. The 2nd Cavalry Brigade had already moved up and deployed behind the 10th Infantry Brigade. Hobe then moved the brigade forwards on the cobbled road towards Fleurus, where Horse Battery No. 19 had unlimbered next to 12-pounder Battery No. 7. They fired on the French but had one gun dismounted by the return fire.

Next, the horse battery rushed along the road to the south-west, followed by two squadrons of the 7th Dragoons, and deployed in a more advanced position, with five guns to the right of the road and two on it, against the same number of French guns. Two more of Hobe's squadrons stayed just east of the bridge across the Ligne, and the other five stayed farther back in reserve. The leading squadron of Prussian dragoons had hardly had the time to deploy, and the artillery to open fire, when two French dragoon regiments, the 5th and 13th, charged and dispersed them. Hobe wanted to come to their aid with the 3./7th Dragoons, but the battery, except for the two guns on the road, had already fallen into French hands, and the Prussian dragoons were pursued at sword point. However, Major-General von Borcke of 9th Brigade, who had been observing this combat, placed his I. and F./1st Kurmark Landwehr behind the hedges and walls along the ditch by the side of the road from where they fired effectively into the flank of the pursuing French cavalry.

Later, the II./1st Kurmark Landwehr moved onto the road.

The F./30th Regiment, also from Borcke's brigade, moved into Tongrinne to support the Fusiliers of the Life Regiment there. The I. and II./30th Regiment under Major von Ditfurth also advanced into the village a little later but the two remaining battalions of the Life Regiment remained in reserve. About 9 p.m. Ditfurth's men were given the order to attack the French on the heights south of the village. Captain von Steinäcker, commander of the skirmishers of the Life Fusiliers, offered to lead these battalions through the unfamiliar terrain in the growing darkness. The columns climbed over a muddy ditch under heavy musket fire, and had to reform after passing this obstacle. The 1st Battalion continued its advance under fire from French skirmishers. The 2nd Battalion followed up 100 paces to its rear, and to the left of the 1st Battalion, marching with its left against another ditch, to cover it from any enemy cavalry charges. The skirmishers of the II./30th under Captain von Veltheim were on the right, seeking to establish contact with the 31st Regiment of 12th Brigade, which was moving up in support.

The I./30th drove the French skirmishing line back on its supports but a volley from these brought the battalion to a halt briefly. Other French skirmishers, hardly visible in the growing darkness, kept popping up and firing into the rear of the battalion, which caused unease. A troop of French dragoons then attacked the rear of the column. There was no time to form square but the 8th Platoon faced about and drove them off. The advance resumed and the first ridge was reached without further problem. At the second, it was a different matter; the French had artillery and infantry drawn up to receive the Prussians. The II./30th moved out to the left then wheeled to the right and endeavoured to gain the flank of the French position, but was counter-charged by French cavalry, and forced to form square. This cavalry was driven off. Next, the French moved forward with both infantry and cavalry against I./30th. This attack, too, was thrown back. As the regiment was in danger of becoming cut off, it was ordered to fall back on the brigade, which itself soon joined the general Prussian retreat from the battlefield.[81]

The 12th Brigade had earlier deployed by Sombreffe and stationed skirmishers along the Ligne brook. The skirmish line had been reinforced by the F./31st Regiment and the F./6th Kurmark Landwehr and was also given the F./5th Kurmark Landwehr Regiment as a reserve. The I. and II./6th Kurmark Landwehr Infantry moved to the right flank, the 3. and 4./6th Kurmark Landwehr Cavalry with two guns from 12-pounder Battery No. 12 to their immediate front, and the 3. and 4./5th Kurmark Landwehr Cavalry farther forward of their front. The remaining four battalions of the brigade stood to the rear of the position.

La Garde au Feu

About 8.30 p.m., a sudden, violent thunderstorm threw the battlefield into darkness. Napoleon knew that his troops had now captured almost all of Ligny

---

[81] Paulitzy & Woedtke, pp 47–55.

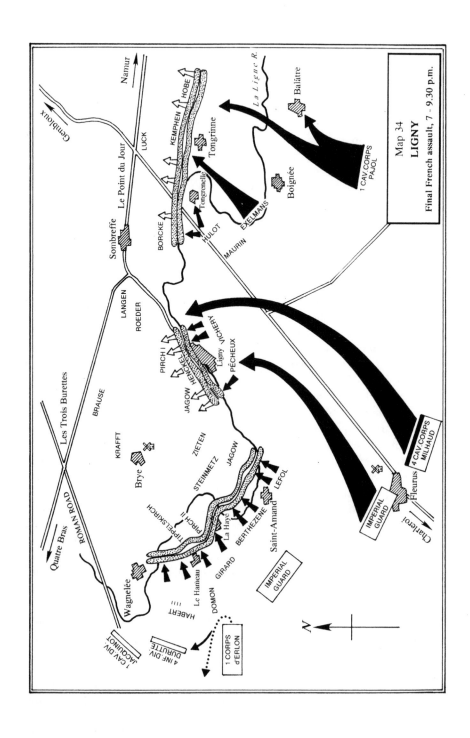

Map 34
LIGNY
Final French assault, 7 – 9.30 p.m.

and chose this dramatic moment to deliver the crucial blow. The Old Guard marched off, followed by the four service squadrons, Delort's and Milhaud's cuirassiers and the Grenadiers à Cheval de la Garde. The first column, consisting of the 2nd, 3rd and 4th Guard Grenadiers moved to the west of the village, the second column, consisting of the 1st Chasseurs and 1st Grenadiers, to the east. Formations of cavalry supported both columns.

The sun had already set when Napoleon's élite troops reached the Prussian lines. The Prussians were exhausted after a long battle and weakened by heavy casualties from the vicious street fighting. They had no reserves left and were no longer able to offer much resistance. Supported by a heavy artillery bombardment, the Imperial Guard made the final, decisive assault on Ligny. Attacking the village from several sides, they put the remaining Prussians to flight.

Still supported by their artillery bombardment, the Guard pressed on. The 21st Regiment attempted to delay the French advance with a quick attack, but was taken in the flank by cavalry. The Colberg Regiment fought off a mass of French horsemen, while Major von Wulffen charged the French foot soldiers with two weak squadrons of the Westphalian Landwehr Cavalry only to be driven off by a volley fired at 20 paces. Foot Battery No. 3, positioned between Brye and the windmill of Bussy, lost one gun to the French cavalry.

The situation in the Prussian centre was now critical, and a desperate measure was needed to stop the army being split in two. Blücher set himself at the head of three regiments of cavalry from I Army Corps, the 6th Uhlans, the 1st West Prussian Dragoons and the 2nd Kurmark Landwehr Cavalry. These regiments had already suffered from the fire of the French batteries and were somewhat weakened. When Lützow's 6th Uhlans charged they were halted by the French fire and Lützow himself was taken prisoner after being trapped under his shot horse. A well-timed flanking attack by French cuirassiers in the Uhlans' right flank threw them back in disorder. The West Prussian Dragoons were likewise taken in the flank, as was the Landwehr Cavalry. All the Prussians were put to flight. Horse Battery No. 2, which was trying to support the attack with fire on the French left flank, was surrounded by French cavalry, but the gunners managed to save their battery by taking it into Brye through an opening in the hedges.

Blücher's Fall

Blücher was in the middle of this chaos. Suddenly, a shot hit his horse and it fell to the ground, trapping the old field marshal underneath it. Nostitz, his ADC, was the only person to notice this in the confusion. As his horse, too, had just been shot, he stayed to protect the Prince. Two more charges of French cavalry passed over the pair before help could arrive. The injured Blücher was carried away from the scene on the horse of Sergeant Schneider of the 2nd Squadron of the 6th Uhlans,[82] a small incident that had lasting implications for European history. The Battle of Waterloo could hardly have been fought and

---

[82] Bothe, p 147.

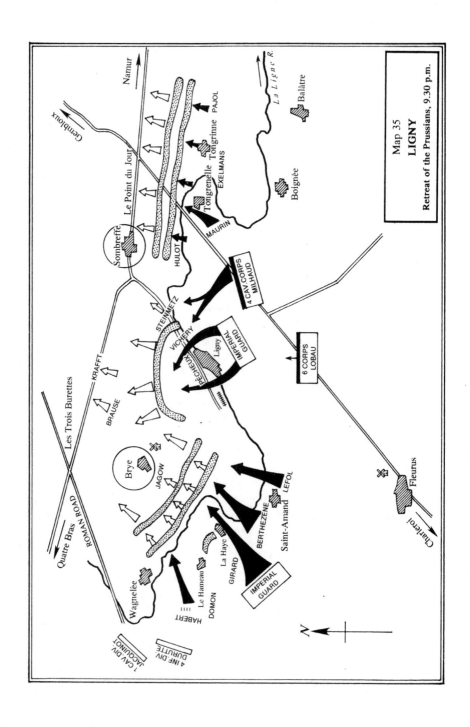

Map 35
LIGNY
Retreat of the Prussians, 9.30 p.m.

won without Blücher's great contribution two days later.

The last remaining Prussian cavalry, the Queen's and Brandenburg Dragoons, and the 4th Kurmark Landwehr Cavalry, led by Major-General von Treskow II, attempted to halt the French advance by making a series of attacks on the French infantry advancing from Ligny and on the cuirassiers. Colonel von Langen, leading II./23rd Regiment from the windmill of Bussy in support of the cavalry, was seriously wounded. This battalion had not got much closer to Ligny when it was surrounded by retreating Prussian cavalry. Holding steady, it prepared to receive the pursuing cuirassiers. The skirmishers of the battalion had already been cut off, yet the French pulled back briefly to reform. The battalion marched on, only to be charged by a regiment of chasseurs à cheval, supported by more columns of French infantry coming out of Ligny itself. Nonetheless the II./23rd held firm, the chasseurs drew back, and the Prussians were able to complete this part of their withdrawal unmolested.[83]

Other Prussian units still had plenty of fight left, too. Captain Gillhausen, hero of the previous day's fighting at Thuin, now led his depleted battalion, the II./1st Westphalian Landwehr which had been in reserve behind Brye, up on to the top of the hill, where it drove off some French cuirassiers pursuing the Prussian infantry. Then it drove off the next line of attacking French cavalry before it successfully repelled three charges by the Guard Cavalry.

At the same time as the French were making their main advance out of Ligny, three regiments of cavalry moved towards Sombreffe. Colonel von Rohr of the 12th Brigade had just marched off with the II./6th Kurmark Landwehr towards Ligny when the French cavalry deployed and advanced towards the right flank of the 12th Brigade. Rohr started to pull his battalion back slowly and ordered the whole brigade back on Sombreffe when the French cavalry charged the entrance to the village, capturing the guns of Foot Battery No. 12. Major von Dorville faced about the last troop of the 6th Kurmark Landwehr Cavalry, and counter-charged the French cavalry in an attempt to halt them. The ensuing combat was so vicious that the lances of the Kurmarkers broke against the metal breast-plates worn by the French cuirassiers. Bringing up infantry in support, the Prussians drove the French from Sombreffe, and recovered one of the captured cannon.

The French cavalry then made a second attempt to advance along the road from Ligny to Sombreffe. The Prussians drove off this attack as well but the withdrawal here soon degenerated into a chaotic retreat. Carl Friccius, commander of the 3rd Westphalian Landwehr, described the scene,

> I took the two battalions in the direction the General [Jagow] had gone, and attempted to link up with the other retiring troops, but had to fight off continuous enemy cavalry charges. The column soon had to go through hedges, over ditches and other obstacles. The enemy pursuit broke off, but all order was lost. Even individual sections could not maintain order in that terrain. Each soldier was on his own, trying to get through the hedges and over

83 Busse, pp 175–6.

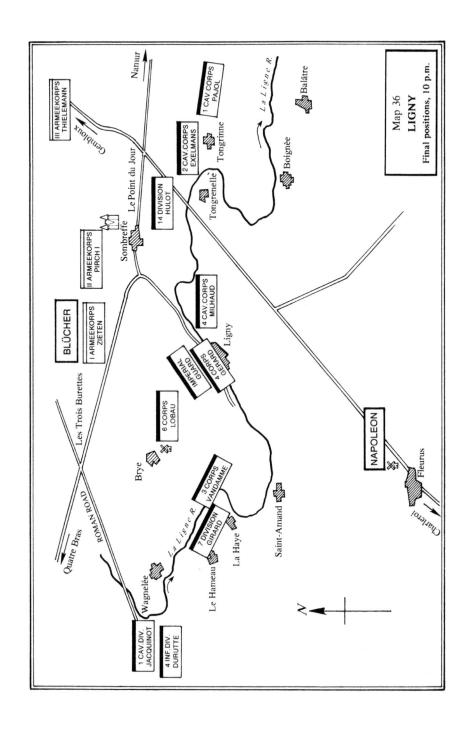

Map 36
LIGNY
Final positions, 10 p.m.

the ditches as quickly as possible. All the parts of the two battalions were soon mixed together. There was no chance to rally the men, because everybody was being carried along in a great stream of humanity...

The retreat went in wild disorder to the village of Tilly, where Prince Blücher spent the night, and where we were ordered to stop. The night was dark, and it was difficult to pass on the order in the chaos and noise. The big column thus moved on... At daybreak, the withdrawal continued in better order to Wavre.[84]

Retreat to Tilly

The command structure of the Prussian army had now broken down. Isolated units of I and II Army Corps were offering limited resistance, but the French were masters of the battlefield around Ligny. Only III Army Corps still able to maintain its positions, although a substantial number of its men deserted, fleeing to Liège and even as far as Aachen.

Zieten's chief-of-staff, Reiche, gave a neat summary of the situation,

> ...at the end of the battle, the village of Brye was still held by troops of I and II Corps, and III Corps remained unaffected in its positions at Sombreffe, while the troops ejected from Ligny, mainly from I and II Corps, had been forced back to the cobbled road running from Nivelles to Namur and, from there, farther back to the old Roman road. As the IV Corps was not going to arrive in time for the battle, it had been sent orders to leave the Orneau valley and Gembloux to its left and to move to the plateau of Artelle.
>
> With the exception of those units that had just come from the combats around Ligny, the troops were in good order, and still capable of fighting. This was not the case for those who had fought around Ligny, but that was to be expected.[85]

It seems from Nostitz's account that the Prussians had not decided on a line of retreat before the battle had started. Blücher's ADC stated,

> I can maintain with utter conviction that neither before nor during the battle were any orders given regarding the direction of any withdrawal that might become necessary. Such orders could not possibly have been given, because they would have depended on the particular circumstances current when such a retreat were ordered.[86]

In the confusion and growing darkness, and with its leader missing, some-body needed to get a hold of the situation before defeat turned into complete disorder and disaster. The Prussians needed to disengage and reform and could only consider offering battle again once they had been joined by Bülow's fresh IV Army Corps. Thus, they would have to link up with Bülow's men who had been ordered to move to the north of Gembloux, on the road leading from Namur to Wavre. The natural line of retreat would therefore be

---

[84] Beitzke, *Hinterlassene Schriften*, p 290 f.
[85] Weltzien, p 200.
[86] Nostitz, p 31.

from Sombreffe north-east to Gembloux. However, such a movement would be away from Wellington's army, and give Napoleon the opportunity of driving home the wedge he was forming between the two wings of the Allied forces.

Instead of taking this route Gneisenau decided instead to move north towards Tilly and Mellery. Various staff officers were sent to block the roads leading to Gembloux and to redirect the retreating Prussian units in the desired direction. Gneisenau did not want to provide his Allies with any reason for withdrawing their army from the Netherlands, and was aware that only by uniting their forces would the Allies be sure of defeating Napoleon. He did not know how the Anglo-Dutch-German Army had fared that day and he might at first have hoped that he would be able to move his forces along the roads leading from Tilly to Genappe, to the rear of Wellington's positions.

However, once the retreat had reached Tilly, many units did not rally but kept going back almost as far as Wavre. Some writers have suggested that it was the intention from the start to go back as far as this. The decisions for the retreat were made at a meeting between Gneisenau and various staff officers and Reiche was the one witness whose account has ever been published. It reads as follows,

> Meanwhile, Gneisenau had taken over after Blücher's accident and ordered the retreat to Tilly. His intention was to maintain contact with the British.
>
> At this moment, I joined Gneisenau on the Roman road where he told me the new direction of the retreat. Although it had been getting dark for some time, I could see clearly from my map that Tilly was not marked on it. As it was probable that other officers were using the same map, which could lead to confusion and uncertainty in this matter, I suggested that instead of taking Tilly as the point of retreat, a town farther along this route which one could take as being on every map should be named. I remarked that even if two points of retreat were named, provided both were in the same direction, that should not cause any confusion. Gneisenau agreed. On my map, I found that Wavre was such a place.
>
> It is not certain, but my suggestion might have been the cause for the retreat going as far as Wavre.[87]

However, when the historian Lettow-Vorbeck examined the record in more detail, referring to documents in the Kriegsarchiv that are now missing, he found a memorandum written by General von Thiele in 1845. In 1815 Thiele had been a colonel on Blücher's staff and, between 10 p.m. and 11 p.m. on 16 June, had brought Thielemann the news of the decision to retreat on Tilly, along with an alternative order to retreat on Gembloux instead, should III Army Corps find the direct route to Tilly blocked by the French.[88] In the event this was the route that Thielemann's corps took. Gneisenau's own

---

[87] Weltzien, p 201.
[88] Lettow-Vorbeck, p 338.

report, written on 20 June 1815, only mentions a movement on Tilly, and not Wavre.[89] Thus, it would appear that the order to fall back as far as Wavre only came later in the night.

The I and II Army Corps were not going to be able to rest that night. Jagow held Brye with three of his battalions (I. and II./Colberg, II./1st Westphalian Landwehr) until 3 a.m. with the rest of his 3rd Brigade still in position on his left, but in a considerable state of disorder. The 1st Brigade had suffered heavily and been pushed back to the Nivelles–Namur road. Pirch II, assisted by the 12-pounder Battery No. 6 and Foot Battery No. 34, managed to restore a certain amount of order to the broken 2nd Brigade battalions leaving the area of St Amand. By midnight all of these units were well on their way to Tilly.

In the confusion of the retreat approximately 8,000 men deserted. These were mainly replacements from the Rhineland and Westphalia, many of them men who had until recently been serving French soldiers. They made off towards Liège and even Aachen before their retreat was brought to a halt.

The retreat was fraught for the rest of the army also. Lieutenant Wedel of the Pomeranian Hussars described his experiences,

That evening, we withdrew without being pursued by the enemy. The mood of the troops was despondent. The rumour spread that Prince Blücher was missing, probably taken prisoner. The retreat happened in great disorder. Nobody knew where we should be going, or at least so it seemed to the subalterns and ordinary soldiers. The paths lined with hedges and ditches, down which the artillery was moving, and which we were to follow, were poor and soon became crowded. There were delays and confusion, which could have had serious consequences if the enemy had fired a few shells at us, and then attacked. However, he did not interfere with us, and order was gradually restored, and the way made free.[90]

Some French units did follow up their victory, though. Lieutenant Hoeken, the second ADC of Lieutenant-Colonel von Röhl, commander of the artillery of II Army Corps, joined one of the regiments of cavalry covering the retreat and described one such incident,

We had been riding forwards at a trot for some time when suddenly we saw a line of enemy cuirassiers about 100 paces to our front. They greeted us with a salvo of carbine fire, and at that moment, our cavalry about turned and rushed away. Although officers and men were screaming for everybody to halt, attempts to stop the flight were in vain, until we all, myself included, got stuck in a swamp... [91]

Hoeken then joined the flood of men moving to Gembloux where he came across an ammunition train of III Army Corps, going with that to Wavre the next day.

[89] GStA, IV HA, Abt. B, 562, p 5.
[90] Wedel, p 250.
[91] Lettow-Vorbeck, p 340 fn.

Reiche, too, described the attempts to restore order and re-direct the retreating men to Tilly,

I now placed Lieutenant von Reisewitz, the General Staff officer accompanying me, at the point of the Roman road where the route to be taken began, and instructed him to have all troops coming to this point take the correct route. Those bodies of troops that had already gone farther down the Roman road, or were on their way to Namur, could not be brought back. This was indeed a bitter blow, but it at least had the advantage of fooling the enemy as to our line of retreat.[92]

Meanwhile, Nostitz was bringing the injured Blücher out of danger but was uncertain where he should be taking his groaning charge. He described his problem,

I thus found myself in a very difficult position concerning the choice of route to take the Prince. I could not ask General Gneisenau or General Grolman as the situation was so dark and confused that trying to find anybody would have been a total waste of effort...

A decision had to be made, so I decided to make towards Wavre, taking the road to Tilly. To my left and right were groups of wounded and men separated from their units, but not one formed body that could have offered the Prince better protection...

We reached the village of Mellery whose inhabitants had deserted it. There was not a single light to be seen. Finally, as we were almost at the far end of the village, I saw the light of a lamp in a window. The Prince had just told me that he could not ride any further and had to get off his horse...

After I had been at my post [guarding Blücher in Mellery] a while, some cavalry troopers rode by. I stopped them and asked them what the situation was. They said they had not seen the enemy, so I said to them the Field Marshal was in this house, gave them his horse to hold and ordered them not to leave the spot until I had returned.

To inform myself of the situation, I rode back in the direction we had just come and met General Steinmetz close to the village. I told him that the Field Marshal was in the village and was suffering so much from his fall that he wanted to stay here. Thus I demanded that he order his infantry escort to guard him. [According to Reiche, these were men of the crack Colberg Regiment under the command of Lieutenant von Somnitz.[93]] The General did so immediately.

I now rushed back to the Prince... By now, several more cavalrymen had gathered in front of the house with our horses; I sent them off in all directions to refute in my name the news that the Prince had been taken prisoner, and tell commanders that the village of Mellery was the place that the Prince would be spending the night. Thanks to this measure, Generals Gneisenau and Grolman joined us before sunrise.

[92] Weltzien, p 201 f.
[93] Weltzien, vol 2, p 203 fn.

We received the expected reports from the various corps and were, early that morning, able to expedite the orders necessary to concentrate the army at Wavre.[94]

Gneisenau had come to Mellery independently of Blücher, and was already in the village when he heard that his commander was also there. Thus, it would seem that it was around Mellery that the Prussian army began to start rallying. In a memorandum written in 1845 Colonel von Wussow, in 1815 a lieutenant on Blücher's staff, reported that he had been ordered by Grolman to ride to the head of the column of retreating troops and to arrange for it to take up a proper marching order. Because of the darkness, the narrow roads and the uncontrollable movement of the troops, Wussow finally reached the head of the column only at daybreak. By then some of the retreating Prussians had reached Lauzelle, just south of Wavre. With the assistance of two other officers, Wussow finally brought the column to a halt by blocking the defile from the wood there. Wussow then sent this report to Grolman,

> I report most humbly to Your Excellency that to bring the troops into a state of relative order, I have made a halt just before the heights of l'Auzel [Lauzelle]. The troops are rallying. As it would perhaps be important to pass the defile of Wavre in good time, I request you most humbly for specific orders to organise either a line of march or to allow the troops to bivouac.[95]

A little later, Wussow received the Grolman's reply, 'I Corps bivouac at Bierges; II Corps at St Anne near Wavre; III Corps at la Bawette; IV Corps at Dion-le-Mont; cannons for repair to Maastricht.'[96]

Prince Thurn und Taxis, the Bavarian representative in Blücher's headquarters, made the following entry in his journal,

> In those circumstances, (about 2 o'clock in the morning of the 17th), the decision was made in Tilly to continue the retreat to Wavre (about four and a half hours farther in the same direction), and to concentrate the four army corps there.[97]

Thus, the choice of Wavre as the point of the retreat would seem to have been made by the ordinary Prussian soldiers voting with their feet, after having been pointed in the general direction by Gneisenau. Only once the retreating Prussians were well on their way back to Wavre, did their higher command decide to concentrate the entire army there.

Order was only restored to the retreating Prussian army around daylight on the 17th, by which time their withdrawal had exposed Wellington's left flank to an attack by the French. Wellington would have no option but to withdraw from Quatre Bras as soon as he found out what had happened.

---

[94] Nostitz, p 31 f.

[95] Lettow-Vorbeck, p 344. He quotes from documents at that time in the Berlin Archives.

[96] Lettow-Vorbeck, p 344. He quotes from documents at that time in the Berlin Archives, mentioning that Grolman's reply was apparently still in Wussow's possession at the time he wrote his memorandum in 1845.

[97] Thurn und Taxis, p 328.

The English historian Charles Chesney summed up the events of the day very neatly,

> Of the tactical faults of Blücher it is not necessary to speak further; and his strategical mistake at the outset, the loss of Bülow by imperfect orders, has been fully noticed before. Of Wellington, viewed individually, it is sufficient to say that his enemy, had matters been properly managed, should have attacked him with 20,000 men more, early in the afternoon; and that he had at dark, thirty hours after the first warning, only present at Quatre Bras three-eighths of his infantry, one-third of his guns, and one-seventh of his cavalry. Truly, in holding his own, the great Englishman owed something that day to fortune.[98]

[98] Chesney, p 129.

Chapter 14

'Mine Enemy' the Prussians

Wellington and his Allies

Before the Congress of Vienna leading Prussian officers viewed Wellington as the great commander who had played a significant role in overthrowing their mutual enemy, Napoleon Bonaparte, and his Empire, but when the Duke became involved in the negotiations after the First Peace this perception began to change. At the Congress of Vienna, Wellington represented his country's interests with great skill and astuteness, outmanoeuvring and out-witting his erstwhile and future ally on several occasions. While some, notably Blücher, continued to regard the Great Duke as an honourable man, others, particularly Gneisenau and Grolman, came to regard him primarily as a politician who would do his utmost to thwart Prussia's ambitions.

We have seen that, at the Congress of Vienna, Britain championed the cause of the smaller German states, and of the Netherlands, against Prussian interests and wishes. This led to a bitter conflict between the victorious Allied powers, almost leading to war between them. Indeed, Britain had gone so far as to sign a secret treaty in January 1815 with the former enemy, France, and with Prussia's traditional enemy, Austria, that aimed at countering Russo-Prussian plans for expansion westwards. By the time the 'Corsican Ogre' landed in France, re-establishing his regime, Wellington had done more than enough to be regarded as a threat to Prussian interests, and as a person who man-ipulated events from behind the scenes. In short, he was no longer considered trustworthy, and his Prussian comrades-in-arms, allies again from March 1815, kept a watchful eye for any behind-the-scenes manoeuvring.

The bickering between Wellington and the Prussians did not end in 1815. There is a record of a series of disputes and at times acrimonious exchanges, between the Duke and the Prussian General Staff, one instance being between General von Grolman and Wellington, which resulted in bitter comments being made in 1836 in the *Militair-Wochenblatt*, the official journal of the Prussian General Staff.[1] In this series of exchanges, Wellington and the Prussians commented critically on the performance and capabilities of each others' armies, particularly during the Waterloo Campaign. The Duke did not regard the Prussians as his friends. In fact, in a letter, dated 8 October 1842, to Major Gurwood, the editor of his *Dispatches*, the Duke described his erstwhile allies as, 'mine enemy'.[2]

---

[1] MWBl, Vol. XXI, No. 22, pp 90–4.
[2] WP 2/93/17.

The Outbreak of Hostilities

Wellington's errors of judgement at the beginning of the campaign have been discussed elsewhere in this work. The reason for his failure to react to the news of the French offensive against the Prussian positions around Charleroi remains, however, a mystery. Although the Duke was well aware of the need for a rapid response to any French moves, he failed to issue orders for his troops to concentrate until early on the evening of 15 June. The intelligence received in Brussels in the days prior to the outbreak of hostilities was so overwhelming there could be little doubt that the French were about to assault the Prussian positions. However, Wellington, unlike his Prussian counterparts, did not react for hours, despite having heard at 7 a.m. on 15 June of the concentration of the French army before Zieten's positions the previous night; despite the news of the outbreak of hostilities received by 9 a.m. on 15 June; and despite having received confirmation of this about 3 p.m. that day. All he did at first was to issue orders between 6 p.m. and 7 p.m. for the concentration, but not the movement of his forces. Only when he heard that night that Blücher was concentrating his entire army, and implementing his part of the Tirlemont agreement, did Wellington finally issue movement orders. Even then these orders were only sent to part of his army and the movements that were set in train did little to support the Prussians directly.

What could explain Wellington's inaction throughout those vital hours? There is certainly some evidence that the Duke was awaiting news from Paris, news that evidently did not arrive. It was possible that the Duke had been deceived by Fouché, the duplicitous French minister of police. As Fouché explained in his memoirs,

> In such a decisive moment, my situation was delicate and difficult; I did not want Napoleon any more, and knew that if he were victorious in this campaign, I would continue to suffer his yoke along with the rest of France, as a victory would prolong his disastrous rule. I had also made commitments to Louis XVIII, which I was not only inclined to keep, but which prudence required me to guarantee. Furthermore, my agents had promised both Metternich and Wellington to move mountains. The generalissimo [i.e. Wellington] required that I at least obtain the plan of campaign for him.
>
> But what were my first thoughts? I thought of what the French people would think, and of the glory of the French army, and of my own honour. I was horrified by the the idea that the word "traitor" would ever appear beside the name of Duke of Otranto [Fouché's title], so I resolved to be pure. However, sides had to be taken; in such circumstances was a statesman to be allowed no resources?
>
> This is what I decided. I had certain knowledge that the unexpected invasion by Napoleon would most likely take place between 16 [June] and, at the latest, 18 [June]. Napoleon wanted to fight a battle with the English army on the 17th, separating it from the Prussians, after having pushed the latter back. He expected to be all the more successful with his plan, as Wellington, on the basis of false information, believed he would be able to put back the commencement of the campaign until 1 July. The success of Napoleon's

undertaking thus depended on surprise. I made my moves accordingly; on the day of Napoleon's departure [from Paris to the front], I sent Madame D. with a message in cipher containing the plan of campaign. At the same time, I laid a number of obstacles at the place she would have to cross the border, so that she could only reach Wellington's headquarters after the event. This accounts for the inexplicable uncertainty of the generalissimo, which has surprised everybody and caused much speculation.[3]

Although Fouché's account is plausible, it seems unlikely that a soldier of Wellington's intellect and experience would rely on a man with Fouché's reputation for double-dealing. The Duke appears neither to have confirmed, nor denied Fouché's story, which was first published in 1842, while Wellington was still alive.

Wellington's lack of action could also be explained by his reputation for caution. Was it the case that, facing history's greatest captain for the first time, the Great Duke hesitated, making no move rather than a false one, until Napoleon's objective was clear? Then there is the fact that Wellington feared a French move against or around his right, cutting him off from the Channel ports and Louis XVIII's government-in-exile in Ghent. In view of the Tirlemont agreement, and the fact that Wellington was very much aware that his army would have to march farther to concentrate than the French would have to march to reach Brussels, then the Duke must have been aware of the potential consequences of a failure to react with all due speed.

At the very least Wellington should have issued orders on the morning of 15 June for his army to concentrate. Thus, when by 3 p.m., it was clear that the French offensive was not merely a bluff, the Duke could have followed these with movement orders. His troops in the vicinity of Brussels could have marched off towards the front that afternoon, perhaps reaching Nivelles by late that night. From there, on 16 June, they could then have moved to counter any French advance via Mons, or to support the Prussians at Fleurus. In such an event, Hill's corps would have been set moving towards Braine-le-Comte on 15 June which would have given him the opportunity of dealing with any threat to the right flank on the 16th, while leaving him the option of moving all or part of his forces to Nivelles and from there to support the Prussians at Sombreffe. Yet Wellington did not make this obvious move, one that would have guarded against both possible threats.

Zieten and the Missing Letters

We have seen that Wellington frequently received information from Zieten, and that there was also a line of communication between Mons and Charleroi, with Wellington having instructed the Netherlanders to keep Zieten informed of any developments. There would seem to have been a good working relationship between Brussels, Charleroi and Mons and it has been shown that Wellington appears to have valued the information Zieten sent him and made every effort to encourage his co-operation. The last report from Zieten

---

[3] Fouché, vol 2, p 341 ff.

contained in Wellington's records is dated 9 June 1815. However, Zieten's records mention later messages sent to and received from Wellington, indicating that the correspondence continued during those vital days from 9 to 15 June. These reports have been referred to in earlier chapters and are summarised in the appendix entitled 'The Missing Letters'.

Around midnight on 14 June, Zieten reported to Wellington the sighting of numerous campfires to his front that confirmed the concentration of French forces already known to be there. This message apparently arrived in Brussels about 7 a.m. on the 15th. This letter may also have contained reference to the Duke's earlier promise, passed on through Colonel von Pfuel, to move to Nivelles in support. What is, however, certain is that in his letter sent from Charleroi to Blücher at 8.15 a.m. on 15 June, Zieten confirmed he had requested Wellington to move there, and mentioned that Wellington had promised him, in response to any French move against Charleroi, to move his army on Nivelles – a promise the Duke did not keep. This letter to Wellington was therefore potentially compromising and is also missing from the Duke's records.

There was further information received by the Prussians from Wellington of which there is no record in the published *Dispatches* or unpublished papers. Müffling certainly sent a letter from Brussels to the Prussian headquarters at 7 p.m. on the 15th. This document, which can still be viewed in the Prussian archives in Berlin, is on British army note-paper, bears a British not a Prussian seal, and is marked 'immediate' and bears three crosses, in the British style for a priority message. Presumably, Müffling wrote it in Wellington's head-quarters, and a British courier carried it. This circumstantial evidence would confirm that Müffling was forwarding information provided by the Duke, or by his staff with Wellington's approval. Between 6 p.m. and 7 p.m. that day, Wellington had issued orders merely for the concentration, and not for the movement of his forces and had not ordered his entire army to Nivelles as the letter stated. The Duke appears to have misled Müffling, who then passed on the incorrect information to his master. It should have been clear to the Duke by then that the French offensive was not a bluff or a feint and that any assurance of support to the Prussians would lead them to continue to concentrate to their right front where they would confront the bulk of the French forces. Without Wellington's promised support there, they would be at a severe disadvantage.

Towards midnight on 15 June, Müffling sent a further report to Blücher indicating that Wellington's army would be concentrated within 12 hours, and that he would have 20,000 men at Quatre Bras by 10 a.m. on 16 June. As Müffling was with Wellington in Brussels, one again assumes that he was passing on information originating from the Duke. All this was consistent, of course, with the report to Blücher written by Müffling on the morning of 15 June which passed on Wellington's order-of-battle and explained how his army could be 'concentrated in a short time'.

Wellington appears therefore to have used Müffling as a conduit for misleading information three times that day. The original documents indicating this were formerly available in the Prussian War Archives. Müffling was Chief of the Prussian General Staff from 1821, and as an author of several historical works on the campaign, had reason and opportunity to study them before writing his autobiography – yet made no mention in his memoirs of these incidents. It would appear that Müffling's memory was selective, perhaps to conceal his own failure to keep Blücher properly informed.

Müffling was not the only source of misinformation. At 6.30 a.m. on 16 June, Major von Brünneck, the staff officer Blücher had sent to establish contact with the Netherlanders at Quatre Bras, reported that the Prince of Orange had told him that most of Wellington's army would be concentrated at Nivelles within three hours. Brünneck would hardly have invented this information and, as the Prince of Orange had just arrived from Brussels where he had been briefed by Wellington, one assumes that he was passing on information from the Duke, information that was incorrect. This view is supported by Constant Rebeque who noted that the Prince told him in a separate conversation that the Duke 'had finally decided to move all his forces to Quatre Bras.'

So by mid-morning of 16 June, the Prussian headquarters had received either directly or indirectly from Wellington, four messages that indicated that his army would be available in force to support the Prussians that day, when they would, as long since agreed with Wellington, be staging a major action in the Sombreffe position.

A Convenient Document

The de Lancey 'Disposition' is a most curious document, as it simply does not make any sense, as will be seen by looking in turn at various of the units in Wellington's army that it discusses.

After Wellington got up at around 5 a.m. on 16 June but before he left Brussels, de Lancey signed an order to Lord Hill to move the 2nd Division to Braine le Comte immediately. The distance to Ath, where this order was sent, was nearly 60 km, so it could not have reached there much before 10 a.m. at the earliest. Yet, apparently, at 7 a.m. de Lancey was writing a 'Disposition' in which the 2nd Division 'had arrived, or were moving on' Braine-le-Comte, when the order for it to do so could not possibly have been delivered, and was 'marching to Nivelles', which it had not yet been ordered to do. In fact, at 7 a.m. the 2nd Division was at Ath, and only received orders to march as far as Enghien at 10 a.m.

Wellington's Reserve included Lambert's and Best's brigades of the 6th Division. Lambert's brigade was based in Ghent and was not ordered to the front until the evening of 16 June. As Wellington had not issued any movement orders to it, he must have known its real position. As Best's brigade was marching south behind the 5th Division that morning the Duke can hardly have been ignorant of its whereabouts either.

Uxbridge's cavalry had first been ordered to assemble at Ninove, then in the 'after orders' of the 15th instructed to go to Enghien. On the morning of 16 June de Lancey sent a further instruction to move to Braine-le-Comte. This order was received about 6 a.m. The distance from Ninove to Braine is around

25 km. By 7 a.m. the cavalry had accordingly left Ninove but had not even got as far as Enghien. It was certainly not 'at Braine' at 7 a.m. as the 'Disposition' claimed, nor was it marching to Nivelles and Quatre Bras at that time. De Lancey must have know where he sent the orders, how long it would take for them to get there, and how long it would be before these troops could arrive.

The Brunswick Corps spent the night of 15/16 June bivouacked to the north of Brussels, between there and Vilvoorde. It had a good 40 km to cover that day, marching along the same road as Picton's 5th Division. The whole of the Brunswick Corps could hardly be expected at Quatre Bras until evening and it was certainly not 'beyond Waterloo' as De Lancey apparently claimed at 7 a.m.

The Nassau Brigade did not move off until 9 a.m. on 16 June.[4] They too were only beyond Brussels at the time de Lancey was apparently claiming they were 'beyond Waterloo', and arrived at Quatre Bras at 8 p.m., after the fighting had finished. Again, Wellington had instructed de Lancey to send the Nassauers their marching orders. Both must have known where they were, and when they were going to arrive.

The question that arises after this comparative analysis of the 'Disposition' with the real situation, and with both de Lancey's and Wellington's knowledge of the current positions of their forces, is why did de Lancey compose a document that was for the most part fictional and why did he then, apparently, present it to his commander, who was also versed in the actual situation? There is no logical reason for de Lancey to have written this document at 7 a.m. on 15 June, and equally, there is no logical reason why Wellington would have based his Frasnes letter on it.

Furthermore, as it has been established that Wellington only started issuing orders for parts of his army to move to Quatre Bras from around 11 a.m. on 16 June, how could de Lancey possibly have entered this information in a 'Disposition' written at 7 a.m. that day? Clearly the 'Disposition' was written after the event, and probably after de Lancey's mortal wounding at Waterloo on the 18th.

The Frasnes Letter

This document remains the most damning piece of evidence in support of the theory that the Duke of Wellington deliberately misled his ally into fighting the battle at Ligny. Having issued several sets of orders to his troops in the hours before writing this letter at 10.30 a.m., Wellington had a good idea of where his men were and of when they were likely to be available at the front. It is difficult to argue that he merely slipped up when he told Blücher, for example, that Hill was as far forward as Braine-le-Comte. What other intention could Wellington have had in presenting such misleading information to Blücher, than to ensure that the Prussians would make a stand at Ligny to buy the time needed by the Duke to make up for his errors of judgement the previous day? And the Frasnes letter is another of those documents of which

4 Lettow-Vorbeck, p 523.

The 'Frasnes Letter'
A Comparison between the Letter and Reality

Unit	Position according to letter	Position in reality	Proximity to Prussians
Prince of Orange's Corps	One division at Frasnes	2nd (Netherlands) Division at Frasnes	In contact with Prussians
	One division at Quatre Bras	1st (British) Division marching to Braine-le-Comte	Out of contact with Prussians
Reserve	Between Waterloo and Genappe	5th Division at Waterloo awaiting orders	Seen by Müffling
		6th Division between Ghent and Asse	Out of contact with Prussians
Cavalry	Nivelles by midday	Between Ninove and Enghien, too far from Nivelles	Out of contact with the Prussians
Hill's Corps	Braine-le-Comte	2nd Division between Ath and Enghien	Out of contact with the Prussians
		4th Division between Oudenaarde and Enghien	Out of contact with the Prussians

In the Frasnes Letter, all the positions given by Wellington of troops in contact with the Prussians are correct, while the positions of the troops out of contact with the Prussians are incorrect, and these troops are given as much closer to the Prussian positions than in fact they were.

---

no copy survives in Wellington's records. Some of the discrepancies in the Frasnes letter are noted below, but for a complete comparison of its content with the actual positions of Wellington's troops, see the table above.

According to the 'orders' sent on the 15th, the 4th Division, part of Hill's corps, was to collect at Grammont and Oudenaarde, and the 'after orders' were for it to move from those positions to Enghien. These messages, travelling up to 70 km, would have taken a good five hours to arrive. The first orders would have arrived about midnight, the 'after orders' about three hours later. Assuming it set out at daybreak on 16 June, the 4th Division would have arrived at Enghien, a distance of 40 km, about ten hours later, that is, about 2 p.m., and at Braine-le-Comte about 5 p.m. The de Lancey Disposition is in fact correct on this point, but this part at least of Hill's Corps was not 'at Braine-le-Comte' at 10.30 as the Frasnes letter claimed and was not going to be there until early evening. Both de Lancey and Wellington knew this before the Frasnes letter was written, yet that is not what the Field Marshal was told.

On the morning of 16 June, when Wellington rode to Quatre Bras, he passed the actual positions of the 5th Division, part of the Reserve, resting near to the village of Waterloo, where he had ordered them the previous evening. After he rode on to Quatre Bras and established what the situation was there, he ordered 5th Division to Quatre Bras. This order was issued at more or less the same time the Duke wrote the Frasnes letter. Yet he told Blücher that Picton's men, whom he had seen a short while before, were much nearer the front than they actually were. Could that possibly have been an error?

Lambert's brigade from the Reserve would certainly not 'arrive at midday' as we have seen. Best's brigade of Hanoverian militia was also part of the Reserve and would be available for action that day. The Duke gave Blücher accurate information on this brigade's positions but the difference may have been that Müffling and others had also seen Best on the way to the front that morning. The 2nd and 3rd Netherlands Divisions were the closest to the Prussians and Wellington could count on them already being in contact with the Prussians. Wellington's statement to Blücher on the positions of these two Netherlands divisions was correct. The 1st Netherlands Division, around Zottegem, was not in contact with the Prussians, and was not where Wellington claimed to Blücher it was.

The 'Frasnes Letter' and de Lancey 'Disposition' A Comparison

Unit	Sub-Unit	'Frasnes Letter'	'Disposition'
Prince of Orange's Corps	2nd (Netherlands) Division	Frasnes	Nivelles & Quatre Bras
Prince of Orange's Corps	1st (British) Division	Quatre Bras	Braine-le-Comte, marching to Nivelles & Quatre Bras
Reserve	5th Division	Between Waterloo & Genappe	Beyond Waterloo, marching to Genappe
Cavalry		Nivelles by midday	Braine-le-Comte, marching to Nivelles & Quatre Bras
Hill' Corps	2nd Division	Braine-le-Comte	Braine-le-Comte, marching to Nivelles
Hill's Corps	4th Division	Braine-le-Comte	Oudenaarde, marching to Braine-le-Comte

Although these two documents correspond on a number of points of information, they do not correspond on all.

On the whole, the 'Disposition' presents the concentration of Wellington's army as much more advanced than it actually was, to the extent that it supports the Duke's misleading letter to Blücher. Like the 'Disposition', the positions of the army indicated in the Frasnes letter are only correct in part. The positions given of the troops nearest the Prussians, or seen by a Prussian officer, are correct, whereas the positions of the troops not in

The de Lancey 'Disposition' and the
'Memorandum on the Battle of Waterloo'.

Unit	'Disposition' (positions as at 7 a.m., 15 June)	'Memorandum'
Reserve	Beyond Waterloo marching to Genappe	Arrived at Quatre Bras (between 1 and 3 p.m.)
1st Division	Braine-le-Comte, marching to Nivelles and Quatre Bras	Arrived at Quatre Bras (not long after 3 p.m.)
Cavalry	Braine-le-Comte, marching to Nivelles and Quatre Bras	Arrived at Quatre Bras (not long after 3 p.m.)

The troop positions given by Wellington in his 'Memorandum' of 1842 are entirely consistent with the positions and movements as given in the 'Disposition', yet a number of these are consistently incorrect. The 'Disposition' was not at hand when Wellington's *Dispatches* were first published in 1838, yet was found by 1847 when it was published in that edition of the *Dispatches*, and supported the erroneous statements made by the Duke in 1842.

direct contact with the Prussians are incorrect. Most misleading was the claim that Hill and his corps were already at Braine-le-Comte when they would only be able to concentrate there the next day. If Blücher had been told the truth he might have reconsidered the possibility he had earlier rejected of fighting only a rearguard action at Ligny that day.

Wellington's collected dispatches, correspondence, and memoranda were first published in the 12-volume series, which started to appear in 1837. The Waterloo volume of the first edition of the *Dispatches* was published in 1838. It did not contain a copy of the de Lancey Disposition. In 1842, the Duke wrote his 'Memorandum on the Battle of Waterloo', which contained comments on Clausewitz's criticisms of aspects of his handling of the campaign. In the 'Memorandum', written after Wellington had consulted his recently published *Dispatches*,[5] the Duke not only insisted that he first heard of the commencement of hostilities at 3 p.m. on 15 June, but also made various claims about the positions of his troops. These claims included, 'the two armies were united about mid-day of the 16th of June... These troops, forming the reserve, were now joined [by 3 p.m.] by those of the 1st division of infantry, and the cavalry... '[6]

These claims were not correct, though they correspond with the positions given in the 'Disposition'. Two years later in the first edition of his history of the campaign, William Siborne followed the line given by the Duke on various points (see, for instance, Siborne, *History*, [first edition], p 76, 'It was between three and four o'clock in the afternoon of the 15th that the Duke of

5 Stafford, p 235 f.
6 WSD, vol X, p 525.

Wellington received information of the advance of the French Army'). Over the ensuing years, Siborne corresponded with Major von Gerwien of the Prussian General Staff, who brought a number of errors to his attention. These letters can be found in the 'Waterloo Correspondence'.[7] The documentary evidence provided by the Prussian General Staff led Siborne to change his opinion on a number of issues, changes that appeared in the third edition of his history published in 1848 (e.g. p 36: 'His [Zieten's] report to the Duke of Wellington arrived in Brussels at 9 o'clock in the morning). Siborne evidently came to prefer the Prussian version of certain events to that given by the Duke of Wellington.

In the meantime, in 1847, a second edition of the Waterloo volume of Wellington's *Dispatches* had been published. This contained the de Lancey Disposition, a document that now supported the misleading statements in the Duke's 'Memorandum'. De Lancey had met a soldier's death a week after Waterloo and there was no wish to challenge his reputation; if he had made errors in his 'Disposition', then nobody would make an issue of this.

But did de Lancey write it? The 'Disposition' is merely attributed to him. The version printed in the 1847 edition of the *Dispatches* is neither signed nor written by de Lancey personally, but was apparently provided by de Lacy Evans, a major attached to Ponsonby's 2nd Cavalry Brigade. Evans, unlike de Lancey, was still alive at the time it was first published, but no original handwritten version is extant. The 'Disposition' now exists only in the printed form and the historian Major-General Robinson, writing in 1910, mentioned that when he examined the Wellington Papers, he too was unable to locate the original even then.[8] A comparison with other examples of Evans' handwriting of 1815 and of 1847 thus cannot be made. Thus, one cannot be certain that Evans did actually copy it, but as is clear from above, the 'Disposition' is such nonsense it is most unlikely to have been written by de Lancey at 7 a.m. on 16 June 1815.

What is also a mystery is when and why Evans apparently made a copy of this document. It seems unlikely, first of all, that he made his copy contemporaneously. Evans was an 'extra aide-de-camp' to Ponsonby and the headquarters of Ponsonby's brigade was in Ghent. Ponsonby was at the Duchess of Richmond's ball on 15 June but Evans does not seem to have attended or at least he was not on the guest list.[9] If Evans was in Brussels, but not at the ball, it would be unlikely that, as an officer not attached to the headquarters, he would have been given the task of writing out a document for de Lancey. In addition Ponsonby is known to have left Brussels to return to his headquarters in the early hours of that morning and if Evans, his ADC, had been in town, at the ball or not, then it is likely that he would have departed along with his commander before the 'Disposition' was supposedly written.

All the more strange is that the contents of the 'Disposition', as apparently copied by Evans, conflict with Evans' own report on the Battle of Waterloo as

---

[7] BL, Add MS 34,708, fols 263–74.
[8] *Journal of the Royal United Service Institution*, vol LIV, January to June 1910, p 590 fn.
[9] De Bas, *Prins Frederik* , vol III, pp 1176–8.

given to Major-General Sir George Murray. The pertinent section of this report mentioned that, 'On the 16th [June] were fought the Sanguinary Battles of Ligny and Quatre Bras. In both cases, the Enemy possessed a vast numerical superiority. The 4th Prussian Corps being yet absent, as was the whole of the British Cavalry, besides a large Portion of Artillery and Infantry.'[10] If he did not know of the 'Disposition' at the time it was composed why would he later have copied and signed a document that conflicted with the facts as he knew them?

The evidence therefore suggests that neither de Lancey nor de Lacy Evans had anything to do with this document. It was apparently not available when the first edition of Wellington's *Dispatches* was published in 1838 but then conveniently appeared, and then only in the printed form, in 1847, over 30 years after de Lancey's death, shortly after the Duke had written his misleading statements on certain events in the Waterloo Campaign, which the 'Disposition' supported.

Wellington's Headquarters Papers

It is generally believed that certain parts of Wellington's headquarters papers went missing when de Lancey was wounded at the Battle of Waterloo on 18 June 1815. De Lancey's wound was severe, his condition worsened, and he died a week later in the village of Waterloo. For most of that time, however, he had all his wits about him, was coherent and lucid, received several high-ranking visitors, and was tended by his wife.[11] The story of the 'missing headquarters papers' would appear to have originated with Major John Gurwood, editor of Wellington's *Dispatches*, who wrote in a footnote in Volume XII of the 1838 edition that, 'The original instructions issued to Colonel De Lancey [i.e. those on which he based the orders issued on 15 June] were lost with that officer's papers.'[12] If one is to accept this comment, it would seem that at no time, as he lingered, did the QMG's thoughts once turn to the important set of confidential military documents for which he was responsible, and that nobody else, particularly visitors such as Wellington and Scovell, nor anybody else in the Duke's headquarters, took the trouble of locating them. The fact that a copy of, for instance, de Lancey's orders drafted in the early hours of 13 June 1815 can be found in Lowe's papers supports the contention that they did indeed survive the QMG's demise, going missing at a later date.[13]

More direct evidence that they did survive is found in a letter Gurwood wrote dated 23 March 1838 to William Siborne, author of the famous *History* of the campaign,

> ...the orders of movement &c, from the registers of the QMG's dept... of course were never mislaid, even at the unfortunate moment of Col Delancey's death. I should think that Col Frith might give you some hint where these are to be found.[14]

[10] NLS, Ad MS 46.9.19, fol 111.
[11] Ward, *A Week at Waterloo in 1815*, p 68 ff.
[12] WD, vol XII, p 474, fn.
[13] BL Add MS 20,192, fols 270–1.
[14] BL Add MS 34,706 fols 460–1.

It is unclear who Colonel Frith was but an officer of this name certainly appears to have existed. The *Army List* of 1838 mentions a Lieutenant-Colonel John Warton Frith as being an officer of the 58th Foot and this may have been the same person as the Captain John Frith, noted as being attached to the Bourbon Regiment in the 1815 *Army List*.

Gurwood's conflicting statements were written within a short space of time. Gurwood happened to be editing the 1815 volume of the *Dispatches* in the early part of 1838, so one would expect him to be aware of the whereabouts of relevant papers. On 5 February 1838, for example he wrote to John Murray, the publisher of the work, to tell him he expected the manuscript would be ready by July.[15] Thus, it would seem that between March and July that year, the QMG's papers went missing, and that somehow de Lancey, dead since 1815, was once again claimed to have played a part, just as he appeared to have done with the 'Disposition' discussed above. The Duke of Wellington collaborated closely with Major Gurwood in the production of the *Dispatches*.

My attempts to locate the 1815 letter-books of Lieutenant-Colonel Scovell, Wellington's head of military communication, have also been unsuccessful. These letter-books would contain not only a list of the correspondence coming into and leaving Wellington's headquarters, but also a brief outline of each message's contents. However, certain of Scovell's private papers can be found in the Public Record Office in London. These papers indicate that news of the outbreak of hostilities on 15 June had reached Wellington's headquarters much earlier than the Duke claimed in his report to Bathurst of 19 June 1815. Unlike de Lancey, Scovell survived the Battle of Waterloo, and indeed outlived Wellington, dying in 1861 at the age of 87. Thus, the cause of his letter-books being mislaid was not as a result of any confusion created by a mortal wound.

What adds to the mystery surrounding the Headquarters Papers is that while the QMG's registers are missing, and the military letter-books cannot be located, the 'General Orders' for the period did not go missing. Indeed, they were published in 1837. The 'General Orders' covered mundane matters relating to the daily running of the army, from 'Accompts (Military)' to 'Wounded'. There was nothing that could have been used as evidence for or against the Prussian accusations against Wellington. The Adjutant-General's letter-books, in which the 'General Orders' are listed, have likewise survived, and can be found with the collection of Wellington Papers at the University of Southampton.[16] These, too, contain nothing that might compromise the Duke.

Sight of the missing documents would settle once and for all the issue of what Wellington did or did not hear from Zieten, what he did or did not write to the Prussians, and when he first heard of the outbreak of hostilities, and above all either confirm or refute the suggestion that he deliberately deceived his ally. Moreover, if these letter-books did indeed confirm that the Duke

---

[15] Records of John Murray (Publishers) Ltd., London.
[16] WP 9/5/2 contains the entries for June 1815.

received Zieten's despatch of 4.45 a.m. at 9 a.m. on 15 June, then that would contradict Wellington's official report to Bathurst written on the 19th, which claimed that the news arrived only that evening. In turn this would have forced the Duke to explain why he waited until 6 p.m. before even beginning to react.

The Meeting at Brye

There is a certain inconsistency in the accounts of this important meeting. Both Wellington's and Hardinge's most detailed accounts appear only in second-hand reports of conversations they supposedly had years later. Neither account mentions the substance of the meeting at Brye, namely, in what manner the Duke was going to support the Prussians that day. While most witnesses speak of Wellington's promised support, the Duke and his liaison officer evidently only recorded implications that Blücher was a poor tactician and unwise in accepting battle at Ligny. However, at Tirlemont as far back as 3 May 1815, Wellington and Blücher had agreed that, in the event of a French offensive in this direction, the Prussians would fight a holding action with part of their army in this position. Why then was it that, years later, the Duke started complaining that the position he agreed the Prussians would take up was poorly chosen?

What Hardinge and Wellington actually said to each other at the meeting would have been spoken in the presence not only of the Prussian leaders, but also of a Hanoverian and a Bavarian officer, as well as the Duke's military secretary, Fitzroy Somerset. Each of these produced his own written account, presumably more carefully considered than any casual conversation the Duke may have had 20 or more years later. Not one of those three non-Prussians mentioned a conversation even vaguely similar to what Hardinge and Wellington described. So where and when did the conversation, in which the Prussian positions were apparently criticised, take place?

We also know that Wellington did not make such criticisms of the Prussian positions at several very good opportunities to do so. When Wellington wrote his 'Memorandum' in 1842 it was specifically produced against a background of friction with the Prussians, and particularly with Clausewitz and Grolman.[17] Yet in the 'Memorandum' Wellington made no critical comments of the Prussian positions. In his letter of 28 January 1845 to J.W. Croker, Secretary of the Admiralty from 1809 to 1830, Wellington related, 'I reached the Prussian army; was at their head-quarters; stayed there a considerable time; saw the army formed; the commencement of the battle; and returned to join my own army assembled and assembling at Quatre Bras.'[18] Once again there is no criticism of the Prussian positions.

Some of the accounts that tell of Wellington criticising the Prussians are also suspect. The recollection of the Baron de Ros, quoted in Chapter 12 and

---

[17] See MWBl, vol XX, 1836, pp 90–4. Here, Grolman complained bitterly about certain comments recently made to Parliament by Wellington on the Prussian Army. This was one of several acrimonious exchanges.

[18] Jennings, vol III, p 175.

published in Maxwell's *Life of Wellington* in 1900, ends with the claim that Wellington could observe the Battle of Ligny through his glass from Quatre Bras, which is quite impossible as the distance is several kilometres and there are hills in the way. If de Ros' account of the conversation is accurate, the Duke was clearly telling him tall stories, so how reliable were his comments on the Prussian positions? And if de Ros' account is inaccurate regarding this final comment, can it be trusted at all?

The final report of Wellington criticising the Prussian deployment dates from 25 September 1851, shortly before the old Duke died. These comments were apparently made during a conversation with the Earl of Ellesmere. Wellington supposedly said,

> "It is true that I went to the Moulin de Bry[e] and saw the Prussian army formed to receive battle. My observation was, 'We each of us know our own army best! I should not have formed mine in this defensive position as yours is. I should have held them further back, and would have thus protected them from the effect of the French artillery.' Gneisenau made me an angry answer – I believe, that the Prussians liked to see the enemy!" [19]

It is interesting to note that in the same work, there is a copy of notes made by Wellington on the article on Waterloo submitted by Ellesmere to the *Quarterly Review* in 1845.[20] Here, the Duke made no criticisms of the Prussian positions at Ligny, even though he made mention of the meeting at Brye. In addition Müffling's record on this point is entirely specific, 'The Duke examined the measures taken and appeared to be satisfied with them.'

The view from the French side would support the contention that the Prussian positions were, in fact, sound. While the meeting at Brye was taking place, Napoleon had been reconnoitring the Prussian positions. Shortly after, at 2 p.m., he had Marshal Soult, his chief-of-staff, send the following message to Marshal Ney, 'The Emperor has charged me to inform you that the enemy has assembled one corps of troops between Sombreffe and Brye, and that at 2.30 p.m., Marshal Grouchy will attack them with the III and IV Corps.'[21]

In later accounts Napoleon and his apologists tried to deny this error[22] but the truth is that the Prussian position at Ligny was so well chosen, and their troops so well deployed in the dead ground, in tall crops and in villages, that even having reviewed their positions from the vantage point of the Tombe de Ligny, Napoleon failed to observe two of the three corps there. This is a clear indication of exactly how well chosen the Prussian positions were, and how much value should be placed on Wellington's alleged comments.

It would now be useful to consider what might have been going through the Duke's mind during the meeting at Brye. His concerns from the previous night about the situation at Quatre Bras must have given way that morning to a sense of relief when he observed the lack of French activity at the vital cross-roads. At Brye, he could clearly see the substantial force of French soldiery

---

[19] Stafford, p 186.
[20] Stafford, p 191 ff.
[21] Charras, *Histoire*, vol I, p 184 f.

[22] See for instance, Gourgaud, *Campagne de dix-huit cent quinze*, p 55.

gathered before Blücher, but was probably wondering where the remainder of Napoleon's army might be. If it was not at Fleurus, and not at Quatre Bras, then was it in the process of marching around his right flank and cutting him off from the Channel ports? Until the Duke had established what the rest of Napoleon's forces were doing on 16 June, it would make sense according to this assessment to order only a small part of his army to Quatre Bras, just enough men to secure his line of communications with the Prussians. The rest could be left at points from where they could move quickly south-westwards, if required, to counter the feared French move. Only when the Duke returned to Quatre Bras later that afternoon did the whereabouts of the French troops, until then unaccounted for, become apparent.

Deploying to Quatre Bras

We have seen that, up to the time when he left Brussels for the front on the morning of 16 June, Wellington had yet to order a single unit to go to Quatre Bras that day. The Reserve in Brussels had been ordered to march 'to the point where the road to Nivelles separates', that is to Mont St Jean. Only Picton's 5th British Division was ordered to go to Quatre Bras on the morning of 16 June, and then not until nearly midday.

As for other units, an examination of various records shows that the 1st Division was ordered to Braine-le-Comte at 10 p.m. on 15 June. Arriving there at 9 a.m. the next day, it awaited orders, which either did not arrive, or were not sent. Later, it marched to Nivelles on its own initiative, and at 3 p.m. at last received orders to march to Quatre Bras.[23] The 3rd Division was only ordered to march to Nivelles,[24] but marched on Quatre Bras once it had reached this destination, so one assumes that such orders were issued once it got there. No other unit appears to have been ordered to Quatre Bras until the afternoon of 16 June, that is, after the fighting had started.

The Prince of Orange's statement that, about midnight on 15/16 June, Wellington had decided to 'move all his forces to Quatre Bras' is thus questionable. That may indeed have been what Wellington told the Prince, but this statement conflicts with the Duke's actions. Uxbridge, too, only appears to have been sent orders to move on Quatre Bras after 4 p.m. on 16 June, although Wellington possibly told Dörnberg otherwise. What is more likely is that the Duke hedged his bets, fearing a move against his right, via Mons, and ordered the bulk of his forces on Enghien, Braine-le-Comte and Nivelles, from where they could counter such a threat. It would seem that the Duke made a firm commitment to bring most of his forces to Quatre Bras only after fighting began there on the afternoon of 16 June, around the time he returned from his meeting with the Prussians at Brye, when the first serious French attack on Quatre Bras finally made their strategy clear to him.

During the meeting at Brye, Wellington had repeated his promises to the Prussians to come to their aid that day with a substantial force even, according

---

[23] Hamilton, pp 15–16.
[24] Lettow-Vorbeck, p 522.

to one witness, with 20,000 men. This was the same number he had told Müffling at midnight that he would have at Quatre Bras by 10 a.m. that day. But at the time of the meeting at Brye, only the 2nd Netherlands Division of about 7,500 men was present at Quatre Bras, and all that had been ordered to reinforce them there was the 5th British Division, not much more than 7,000 men more. Taking off any troops needed to hold this important road junction, Wellington could hardly have had half of the promised number of men available for any flanking move. That was, of course, not what the Duke had told his allies.

Why did Blücher fight at Ligny?

Given an accurate account of the situation by Wellington, it was possible that Blücher might have staged only a rearguard action at Ligny with his I Army Corps, ordering the II and III Army Corps to move to the Gembloux position to be joined there by IV Army Corps, and so concentrating the entire Prussian Army for battle on 17 June. In such circumstances, Napoleon would have been able to switch the emphasis of his attack from the Prussians to Wellington, whose scattered forces he could easily have overrun, possibly reaching the gates of Brussels by the evening of 16 June. Clearly, if Wellington had informed Blücher of how behind-hand his concentration was, then he risked the defeat of the Anglo-Dutch army.

Wellington thus had two choices before him on the morning of 16 June. He could inform Blücher of the facts, admitting his error, and asking, or even begging, the Prussians to make a determined stand at Ligny, allowing his forces to concentrate for battle on 17 June. Alternatively, Wellington could try to bluff his way through the situation, hoping the Prussians could hang on in the Sombreffe position long enough for sufficient of his forces to arrive to play a significant role in that day's battle. After all, on the morning of 16 June, when Wellington wrote the misleading Frasnes letter to Blücher, there was no significant French activity at Quatre Bras – so though he had fewer men than he was promising Blücher he would have available, Wellington might have believed that he would still be able to stage a flanking attack on the French at Ligny. Even 10,000 men taking Vandamme's Corps in the flank might well have been a heavy enough blow to decide the day there, or failing that, at least to establish a stalemate that day, allowing both Bülow and the remainder of the Anglo-Dutch-German forces to arrive the next day.

However, when the French moved larger forces against Quatre Bras in the afternoon of 16 June, that possibility disappeared. Despite that, helped greatly by the French blunders, the Duke held his positions at Quatre Bras, and would have been able to go over to the offensive on 17 June, had the Prussians managed to hold their positions for just an hour or two more the previous evening. There had been a good chance that Wellington's bluff might have succeeded, but it did not.

With Blücher's determination to defeat the French, and his admiration for Wellington, it would have been quite likely that, told the truth by the Duke, the Prince would have made every effort to assist his respected ally, and fought the battle of Ligny in such circumstances. As the French historian Général Gaspard Gourgaud put it,

> If Blücher were to have only two battalions available, he would have used these to support the English army, while one could take it for granted that Wellington would not attack the French army in support of Blücher until he had concentrated his entire army.[25]

However, by being frank with his ally, then Wellington would have lost face, and would have had to admit that all the previous information on his movements he had sent to Blücher via Müffling and others, was false. By the time of the meeting with Blücher at Brye, the Duke had committed himself to this duplicitous course of action, so there was no going back now.

The Retreat to Tilly and Wavre

After the defeat of the Prussian forces at Ligny, Gneisenau, commanding the Prussian troops in Blücher's continued absence, had every intention of maintaining contact with the wing of the Allied forces led by the Duke of Wellington. First he had the road leading eastwards to Namur closed off, then he attempted to rally his men at Tilly, close to the battlefield of Ligny, from where he could either have moved the next day to support the Anglo-Dutch-German army, should it have maintained its positions at Quatre Bras, or, if it had not, to the north and towards reinforcements. However, control over the retreating Prussian troops could not be restored in the course of that night, and was only re-established when their straggling columns had gone much farther, almost to Wavre, contrary to what Gneisenau had wished. Significantly, Gneisenau had done his utmost to ensure that his Prussians did not retreat eastward to Liège or Gembloux, but in a direction that would allow close contact with their allies to be maintained. Gneisenau's decision made it possible for the Prussians to intervene in the Battle of Waterloo in decisive force. It was one of the most crucial decisions of the campaign.

Allied Losses

By the end of the fighting on 16 June, the Allies had lost around 25,000 men. Of these, almost 90 per cent were Germans – Prussians, Hanoverians, Brunswickers and Nassauers. Fewer than 10 per cent were British and the remainder were Netherlanders. The lion's share of the fighting had fallen on the Prussian Army, particularly on Zieten's I Corps, which alone lost nearly 40 per cent of its strength, dead, wounded and missing. The three Prussian corps engaged on 15 and 16 June had lost an average of 22 per cent.of their strength The relatively small number of British troops who had participated in the fighting on those days suffered a similar percentage of losses. The other German contingents and the Netherlanders suffered proportionately fewer. A more detailed breakdown of these figures can be found in the tables on the next two pages.

---

[25] Gourgaud, pp 42–3.

Casualty Charts for 15 and 16 June 1815

Prussian Army of the Lower Rhine

Unit	Starting Strength	Killed	Wounded	Missing	Total	% age of unit
I Army Corps						
1st Brigade	9,071	241	700	1,439	2,380	26%
2nd Brigade	8,018	937	2,222	1,393	4,552	56%
3rd Brigade	7,146	195	716	1,572	2,483	34%
4th Brigade	4,900	642	525	1,401	2,568	52%
Reserve Cavalry	2,175	112	218	297	627	28%
Reserve Artillery	1,223	25	67	9	101	8%
Total	32,533	2,152	4,448	6,111	12,711	39%
II Army Corps						
5th Brigade	7,153	264	1,034	601	1,899	26%
6th Brigade	6,762	575	627	323	1,525	22%
7th Brigade	6,403	30	171	182	383	5%
8th Brigade	6,548	148	719	420	1,287	19%
Reserve Cavalry	4,471	61	199	110	370	8%
Reserve Artillery	1,501	27	51	192	270	17%
Total	32,838	1,105	2,801	1,828	5,734	17%
III Army Corps	25,318	341	1,332	426	2,099	8%
Grand Total	90,689	3,598	8,581	8,365	20,544	22%

The artillery lost a total of 21 cannon.

These included: 2 from 12-pounder Battery No. 4, damaged in action
1 from 12-pounder Battery No. 6
2 from 12-pounder Battery No. 8, damaged in action
1 from 12-pounder Battery, No. not recorded
1 from Foot Battery No. 3
2 from Foot Battery No. 4
1 from Foot Battery No. 12. (howitzer)
6 from Horse Battery No. 14
5 from Horse Battery No. 19

Based on Plotho, p 116.

Wellington's and Blücher's Performance

The most fundamental error made on the Allied side up to the evening of 16 June was the Duke of Wellington's initial judgement that the French offensive on 15 June was a bluff, and that he need not react to it. This mistake led to the Prussian Army suffering a significant check at the Battle of Ligny on 16 June. A second potentially grave error was that made by Wellington when his orders to the Prince of Orange would have allowed the French to separate the two wings of the Allied forces in the Low Countries – if they had been implemented. Fortunately for him, Wellington had subordinates of the calibre

Casualty Charts for 15 and 16 June 1815[1]

The Anglo-Dutch-German Army

Unit	Starting Strength	Killed	Wounded	Missing	Total	% age of unit
German Troops						
Brunswickers[2]	5,537	99	487	210	796	14%
Hanoverians	5,771[3]	?	?	?	388[4]	7%
Total	14,188	?	?	?	1,184	8%
British Troops[5]						
1st Brigade	1,997	43	491	0	514	26%
2nd Brigade	2,064	0	7	0	7	0%
5th Brigade	2,254	62	249	14	325	14%
8th Brigade	2,471	68	522	0	590	24%
9th Brigade	2,173	107	727	17	851	39%
Total	10,959	280	1996	31	2,287	21%
Netherlands & Nassau Troops[6]						
2nd Division	8,177	117	482	290	889	11%
2nd Cavalry Brigade	1,082	51	120	0	171	16%
Total	9,259	168	602	290	1060	11%

Total Allied Casualties

Contingent	Losses	% age of total
Prussians	20,544	82%
Other German troops	1,184	5%
British	2,287	9%
Netherlanders (including Nassauers)	1,060	4%
Total	25,075	100%

[1] Based mainly on Plotho, p 116.
[2] Taken from Kortzfleisch, vol 2, p 81.
[3] Based on Siborne, *History*, pp 531 ff.
[4] *Die Königlich Deutsche Legion und das Hannoversche Corps bei Waterloo*, p 13.
[5] Based on Siborne, *History*, p 555.
[6] Based on De Bas & T'Serclaes de Wommersom, vol III.

of Constant Rebeque and Duke Bernhard who used their initiative and disobeyed their master.

A further serious error made by Wellington was his misjudgement of the situation at Quatre Bras on the morning of 16 June. Surely his long experience in the Peninsula should have told him that it was possible that the French army, often inactive in the morning, was resting, foraging and feeding, after their strenuous marches and combats the day before, before fighting in the afternoon. Yet he appears to have considered their lack of activity rather as another indication that they were moving around his right flank.

Thus far, Wellington had failed to react to the outbreak of hostilities until too late, and failed to appreciate the French intentions and react correctly. Failures in Prussian generalship were also to blame for the defeat at Ligny, however, especially the faulty staff work that meant that one quarter of their army was not available for that day's combat. Moreover, had the Prussians dealt with the Saxon issue with greater sensitivity in the months leading up to the campaign, then a further 14,000 troops might have been at their disposal on 16 June. The result of all these deficiencies was that the Allies suffered a major setback, in which over 90 per cent of the casualties were suffered by Britain's allies, almost entirely by German soldiers.

Prussian Accusations against Wellington

From the outset, the Prussian high command regarded Wellington's failure to support them on 16 June with suspicion, and, over the coming weeks, senior Prussian officers were to comment on the matter to various people. Their consistent accusations contrast with Wellington's casual comments some years later, which also appear to have altered with time and circumstances. Blücher's official report on Ligny sent to his king on 17 June noted, for example,

> Likewise, the Duke of Wellington's army, despite promises and expectations, was not concentrated enough to operate against the enemy effectively... This is the result of an engagement that could have ended in a complete victory had either IV Corps, or the Duke of Wellington, as was agreed, joined the battle.[26]

Blücher also wrote to Major-General von Dobschütz, Prussian Military Governor of the Central Rhine, in a similar vein, stating clearly that, 'Wellington was supposed to be ready at 10 a.m. [on 16 June] at Quatre Bras to march to our aid.'[27]

The Field Marshal's report to royal headquarters also commented,

> The Duke of Wellington and myself had agreed that the army against which the main attack was made, would stay in defence, while that against which the feint was made, would go over to the offensive.[28]

Gneisenau's personal report of the battle, written at midday on 17 June, noted,

> On the morning of 16 June, the Duke of Wellington promised to be at Quatre Bras with 20,000 men, his cavalry in Nivelles... why the Duke of Wellington's concentration happened so late and in such low numbers remains to be clarified by both sides.[29]

In a further letter Gneisenau also wrote,

---

[26] Ollech, p 162; Lehmann, p 284.
[27] Lehmann, p 284.

[28] Lehmann, p 284.
[29] Lettow-Vorbeck, pp 526–527.

After I Army Corps had fought such a long action on 15 June, we received written assurances from the Duke of Wellington that, if the enemy were to attack us, he would attack the enemy's rear; he expected such assurances from us if he were to be attacked... [30]

In a letter dated 6 August 1815 to Alexander Gibsone, Consul in Danzig, Gneisenau repeated this opinion,

The misfortune we suffered on 16 [June] was because the Duke of W[elling-ton] was not able to concentrate his army. He had agreed time and again, including on 15 June in some detail, that he would do so within 12 hours and had concurred with us that whichever of the two armies the enemy would attack, the other would fall on his rear. But the Duke could not accomplish the concentration of his army, apparently due to errors in his calculations of time and distance. [31]

One wonders if Gneisenau had, by then, had the opportunity of raising the issue with Wellington, and if the Duke had offered him such an explanation for his failure to keep his promises.

Even Blücher's good opinion of the Duke wavered eventually. In a letter to Gneisenau dated 5 September 1815 he wrote,

Wellington's conduct was not always good, for if we had supported him on 18 [June] as he had us on 16 [June], then Fouché could not have named him the saviour of France. [32]

It would seem as if the old Field Marshal had finally realised that his earlier trust in the Great Duke had been misplaced.

The historian examining Wellington's activities on 16 June is therefore inevitably confronted by a number of questionable documents and statements, a 'Disposition' that cannot be genuine, accounts of several occasions on which the Duke made promises of support to the Prussians he knew he could not or would not keep, three claims that he had already moved his army on Quatre Bras when he had yet to decide to do so, a letter in which Wellington knowingly misled Blücher, a 'Memorandum' that contains false statements, documents which are missing from the record, and two accounts of a meeting that vary so significantly from those of the majority of its participants, that one has to wonder if it is really the same meeting that is being discussed. The weight of all this evidence indicates that the Duke of Wellington, in pursuit of personal aims, did indeed deliberately mislead his Prussian allies into fighting a battle at Ligny on 16 June 1815 in unfavourable circumstances and in the knowledge that he could not offer adequate assistance, and that subsequent to this, he endeavoured to mislead future students of the campaign by falsifying parts of the record.

---

[30] Lehmann, p 284 f. [32] Delbrück, p 660.
[31] Delbrück, p 659.

Appendices

Timetable of Events on 15 June 1815

Time	Place	Event
02.30	Thuin	Pajol moved up towards Prussian positions.
		Comment: The French offensive was about to begin.
03.00	Thuin	Reille's and d'Erlon's corps followed in support
04.00	Thuin	French artillery opened fire.
04.00	Charleroi	Zieten got out of bed.
04.45	Charleroi	Zieten sent messages to Blücher and Wellington. That to Blücher arrived by 08.30, that to Wellington by 09.00.
		Comment: As Zieten's message to Blücher mentioned the French offensive beginning at 04.30, the messages must have been written shortly thereafter.
04.45?	Fontaine l'Evêque	Steinmetz reported the outbreak of hostilities to Merlen. The report arrived at 08.00.
08.00	St Symphorien	Arnauld arrived at Merlen's headquarters with news of commencement of hostilities. Forwarded to Mons where it arrived at 09.30.
08.00	Charleroi	French assault began.
08.00?	St Symphorien	Merlen sent report of the outbreak of hostilities to Braine-le-Comte, where it arrived about 11.00.
08.15	Charleroi	Zieten reported to Blücher that the French assault on Charleroi was beginning.
08.30	Namur	Zieten's message arrived in Blücher's headquarters.
		Comment: Blücher ordered the concentration of his army.
09.00	Brussels	Zieten's message arrived in Wellington's HQ.
		Comment: Wellington did not react.
09.00	Namur	Blücher replied to Zieten, informing him that he had already ordered the concentration of the rest of his army.
09.30	Mons	News of the French offensive arrived from St. Symphorien. Forwarded to Braine-le-Comte where it arrived about midday.
10.30	Mons	Behr sent the news direct to the Prince of Orange in Brussels, where it arrived about 15.00.
11.00	Charleroi	Zieten reported its fall to Blücher and Müffling. The message arrived in Brussels about 15.00.
11.00	Haine-la-Pierre	Chassé reported to Braine-le-Comte that the Prussians had evacuated Binche.
11.30	Namur	Blücher informed Bülow of the outbreak of war.
12.00	Namur	Blücher sent report of his actions to Müffling in Brussels. This message arrived about 17.00.
12.00	Braine-le-Comte	Dörnberg's message arrived. It was not forwarded to Brussels.

13.30	Fleurus?	Zieten reported his withdrawal to Fleurus. The message arrived that evening.
14.00	Braine-le-Comte	Berkeley forwarded Dörnberg's message to Brussels, where it arrived about 18.00.
15.00	Brussels	Behr's report to Prince of Orange arrived.
15.00	Brussels	Zieten's report to Müffling arrived.
15.00	Braine-le-Comte	Constant Rebeque issued deployment orders to Perponcher and Collaert.
18.00	Brussels	Berkeley's message arrived.
18.00-19.00	Brussels	Wellington issued his orders.
	Comment:	These were largely orders for concentration and not movement.
19.00	Brussels	Müffling sent report of Wellington's actions so far.
21.00	Quatre Bras	Prince Bernhard of Saxe-Weimar reported the current situation to Perponcher in Nivelles.
21.30?	Sombreffe	Gneisenau sent report to Zieten updating him on the movements that day.
22.00?	Brussels	Report from Blücher arrived with news of his intention to concentrate his army at the front the next day.
22.00	Brussels	Wellington issued his 'after orders'.
22.00	Sombreffe	Blücher sent report of day's events to Imperial Headquarters in Heidelberg which arrived on 19 June.
22.15	Braine-le-Comte	Constant Rebeque issued deployment orders to Perponcher at Nivelles.
22.30	Braine-le-Comte	Constant Rebeque sent on urgent report of French breakthrough at Quatre Bras which arrived in Brussels about midnight.
23.30	Sombreffe	Blücher sent report on day's events to King of Prussia.
24.00	Brussels	Webster arrived with news of French advance to Quatre Bras.

Messages 15–16 June 1815

Time sent	Place of origin	From	Subject	Sent to	Destination	Arrived
00.00?	Charleroi	Zieten	French camp fires	Wellington	Brussels	07.00
04.45	Charleroi	Zieten	Outbreak of hostilities	Blücher	Namur	08.30
04.45	Charleroi	Zieten	Outbreak of hostilities	Wellington	Brussels	09.00
04.45?	Fontaine l'Evêque	Steinmetz	Outbreak of hostilities	Merlen	St Symphorien	08.00
08.00	St Symphorien	Merlen	Outbreak of hostilities	Dörnberg	Mons	09.30
08.00?	St Symphorien	Merlen	Outbreak of hostilities	Constant Rebeque	Braine-le-Comte	11.00
08.15	Charleroi	Zieten	I Army Corps falling back	Blücher	Namur	?
09.00	Namur	Blücher	Prussian army moving to front	Zieten	Charleroi	?
09.30	Mons	Dörnberg	Outbreak of hostilities	Berkeley	Braine-le-Comte	12.00
10.30	Mons	Behr	Outbreak of hostilities	Prince of Orange	Brussels	15.00
11.00	Haine-La-Pierre	Chassé	Prussians evacuated Binche	Constant Rebeque	Braine-le-Comte	14.30
11.00	Charleroi	Zieten	Fall of Charleroi	Müffling	Brussels	15.00
11.00	Charleroi	Zieten	Fall of Charleroi	Blücher	Namur	16.00?
11.00	Namur	Blücher	HQ moving to Sombreffe	Zieten	Charleroi	?
11.30	Namur	Blücher	Movement orders	Bülow	Hannut	?
12.00	Braine-le-Comte	Constant Rebeque	Forwarded Behr's message to Prince of Orange	Prince of Orange	Brussels	15.00
12.00	Namur	Blücher	Situation report	Müffling	Brussels	17.00
13.30	Gilly	Zieten	I Army Corps falling back on Fleurus	Blücher	Namur or Sombreffe	16.30?
14.00	Braine-le-Comte	Berkeley	Outbreak of hostilities	Wellington	Brussels	18.00
15.00	Braine-le-Comte	Constant Rebeque	Deployment orders	Perponcher	Nivelles	?
15.00	Braine-le-Comte	Constant Rebeque	Deployment orders	Collaert	Boussoit-sur-Haine	?

Time sent	Place of origin	From	Subject	Sent to	Destination	Arrived
7.00?	Sombreffe?	Blücher	Prussians concentrating at Sombreffe	Müffling	Brussels	22.00?
18.00	Brussels	Prince of Orange	Army to assemble at 04.00 on 16 June	Constant Rebeque	Braine-le-Comte	21.00
18.00-19.00	Brussels	Wellington	Orders to begin concentration of army	various	various	various
19.00	Brussels	Müffling	Situation report	Blücher	Sombreffe	24.00
20.00?	Mons	Dörnberg	No French at Mons, all moved on Charleroi	Wellington	Brussels	23.30?
21.00	Quatre Bras	Prince Bernhard	Situation report	Perponcher	Nivelles	?
21.30?	Sombreffe	Gneisenau	Situation report	Zieten	Fleurus	?
22.00	Sombreffe	Blücher	Outbreak of hostilities and situation report	Schwarzenberg	Heidelberg	19 June
22.00	Brussels	Wellington	After orders to his army	various	various	various
22.15	Braine-le-Comte	Constant Rebeque	Deployment orders	Perponcher	Nivelles	?
22.30	Braine-le-Comte	Constant Rebeque	French broken through to Quatre Bras	Prince of Orange	Brussels	after midnight
23.30	Sombreffe	Blücher	Outbreak of hostilities and situation report	Friedrich Wilhelm III Berlin		?
23.30	Braine-le-Comte	Constant Rebeque	Deployment orders	Collaert	Boussoit-sur-Haine	?
23.30	Braine-le-Comte	Constant Rebeque	Movement orders	Chassé	Beaume	?
00.15	Braine-le-Comte	Constant Rebeque	Movement orders	Perponcher	Nivelles	01.30

All messages referred to in this table are discussed, and usually quoted, as well as being footnoted, often for both the time of arrival and despatch, in the relevant chapters earlier in the book.

Wellington's Headquarters Papers

Papers	Person Responsible	Contents	Comments	Location
Adjutant-General's Letter Books	Col. Sir John Elley	Correspondence relating to the daily running of the army.	Not compromising, Present	University of Southampton, WP9/5/1 and WP9/5/2.
QMG's Registers	Col. Sir Wm. de Lancey	Lists all orders issued by Wellington to his troops.	Potentially compromising, Missing	Held by Col. Frith in March 1838? Missing by July 1838.
Military Letter Books	Lt.-Col. Sir George Scovell	Contains copies of all incoming and outgoing correspondence.	Potentially compromising, Missing	Whereabouts unknown.
General Orders	Duke of Wellington	Orders relating to the daily running of the army.	Not compromising, Present	Published in 1837.

Thus, of the important headquarters papers, those that were potentially compromising to Wellington are missing. The QMG's registers disappeared in mysterious circumstances during the editorial process of the 1815 volume of the *Dispatches*, while Scovell's Letter Books are missing, and there appears to be no explanation for this. Those papers available are not compromising.

A Comparison of the de Lancey 'Disposition' with the actual situation

Formation	Where it was 'at or marching to at 7 a.m.', according to the 'Disposition'.	Where it really was at 7 a.m. and had been ordered to march to.	Where it was 'ordered to proceed to at 7a.m.'	What orders it really received by 7 a.m., and when it marched off to those places given in the 'Disposition'.
1st Division	Braine-le-Comte	Between Enghien and Braine-le-Comte, marching to Braine.	Nivelles and Quatre Bras	Arrived at Braine by 9 a.m. where it received no further orders. Waited there until noon, then marched to Nivelles on its own initiative. Arriving there at 3 p.m., it received orders to march to Quatre Bras.
2nd Division	Braine-le-Comte	Ath. Orders to march from Ath to Enghien not received until 10 a.m. Orders to move to Braine were issued the morning of 16 June.	Nivelles	No orders received by 7 a.m. Orders to march on Nivelles issued on the morning of 16 June, some time after 7 a.m., possibly 9 a.m., possibly first that evening. Marched to Nivelles on 17 June.
3rd Division	Nivelles	Marched from Braine to Nivelles, arriving there 9.30 a.m.	Quatre Bras	As there are no orders to move to Quatre Bras on record, and as those issued on the morning of 16 June are on record, the assumption is that 3rd Division was moved on Quatre Bras once it arrived at Nivelles.

Formation	Where it was 'at or marching to at 7 a.m.', according to the 'Disposition'.	Where it really was at 7 a.m. and had been ordered to march to.	Where it was 'ordered to proceed to at 7a.m.'	What orders it really received by 7 a.m., and when it marched off to those places given in the 'Disposition'.
4th Division	Oudenaarde	Ordered to move from Grammont and Oudenaarde to Enghien. It then marched on to Braine where it arrived late that night.	Braine-le-Comte	There is no record of orders to march to Braine being issued to the 4th Division, although Hill, the Corps commander, was ordered to move to Braine on the morning of 16 June. Orders to march to Nivelles were issued on 16 June.
5th Division	Beyond Waterloo	Ordered to march to Waterloo at the Duchess of Richmond's Ball. It was not 'beyond Waterloo' by 7 a.m.	Genappe	There is no record of orders to march to Genappe being issued to the 5th Division. It reached Quatre Bras at 2 p.m.
6th Division (Lambert's Brigade)	Asse	Asse. Apparently no orders were issued to it on 15 June. At least, there are none on record.	Genappe and Quatre Bras	On the evening of 16 June, this brigade was ordered to march from Asse to Genappe on 17 June.
4th Hanoverian Brigade	Beyond Waterloo	Still in Brussels area, marching south, but not yet 'beyond Waterloo'.	Genappe and Quatre Bras	There is no record of such orders having been issued to this brigade, but it arrived at Genappe about 1 p.m., and was at Quatre Bras by 3.30 p.m.
5th Hanoverian Brigade	Hal	Hal. No marching orders had been issued by 7a.m.	Genappe and Quatre Bras	At 11 a.m., it was ordered to march to Waterloo.

Formation	Where it was 'at or marching to at 7 a.m.', according to the 'Disposition'.	Where it really was at 7 a.m. and had been ordered to march to.	Where it was 'ordered to proceed to at 7a.m.'	What orders it really received by 7 a.m., and when it marched off to those places given in the 'Disposition'.
2nd Division & 3rd Division Army of the Low Countries		2nd Division was at Quatre Bras. 3rd Division was marching to Nivelles.	At Nivelles and Quatre Bras	Both divisions had been ordered to concentrate at Nivelles, but 2nd Division ignored the orders. 3rd Division remained at Nivelles and did not move to Quatre Bras.
1st Division & Indian Brigade, Army of the Low Countries	Zottegem	Zottegem	Enghien	The orders issued that morning to march to Enghien did not arrive until 1.30 p.m. Arrived at Enghien 5 a.m. on 17th.
Dörnberg's Brigade, Cumberland Hussars	Beyond Waterloo	Between Vilvoorde and Brussels.	Genappe and Quatre Bras	There are no such orders on record. These troops arrived at Genappe about midday, but only some of them were sent to Quatre Bras.
Rest of the cavalry	Braine-le-Comte	Between Ninove and Enghien.	Nivelles and Quatre Bras	Ordered to march on Braine. Orders to march to Quatre Bras were first issued there at 4 p.m.
Brunswick Corps	Beyond Waterloo	Laeken, north of Brussels.	Genappe	There are no such orders on record. This Corps passed Genappe between 1 and 2 p.m.
Nassauers	Beyond Waterloo	On the Louvain road. There are no marching orders on record.	Genappe	There are no such orders on record. They reached Quatre Bras late that evening, thus passing Genappe that afternoon.

Where the Anglo-Dutch-German Forces Really Were[1]

Formation (Commander)	Position on 15 June	Orders received	After Orders received	Started off 16 June at	Arrived Time	Arrived Place	Sources
I Corps Prince of Orange	Braine-le-Comte (headquarters)	10.30 p.m.					De Bas & T'Serclaes de Wommersom
1st Division (Cooke)	Enghien (headquarters)	Morning of 15 June, ordered to assemble at Ath	1.30 a.m., 16 June, ordered to move from Enghien to Braine-le-Comte	2 a.m.			Hamilton
2nd & 3rd 1st Guards	Enghien	8 p.m.	1.30 a.m.	4 a.m. from Hove	9 a.m. 3 p.m.	Braine-le-Comte Nivelles	Hamilton
2nd Coldstream Guards	Enghien	?	?		4 p.m.	Quatre Bras	Marker
2nd/3rd Guards	Enghien	?	?		4 p.m.	Quatre Bras	Marker
3rd Division (Alten)	Soignies (headquarters)	Evening	?	?	?	Quatre Bras	Schwertfeger
2nd/30th Foot	Around Soignies			2 a.m.	After 5 p.m.	Quatre Bras	Cannon, Bannatyne
33rd Foot	Soignies	2 a.m.		2 a.m. ?	2 p.m. ?	Nivelles Quatre Bras	Lee
2nd/69th Foot							Not available
2nd/73rd Foot		Evening 4 p.m., marched to Soignies, arriving 6 p.m.	Left there midnight, marched until 8 a.m.	? 3 p.m.		Quatre Bras Quatre Bras	Cannon Morris
2nd Brigade KGL	Ecaussinnes	Daybreak, 16th		Daybreak 2 a.m.	Midnight	Quatre Bras	Schwertfeger
1st Hanoverian Brigade	Between Mons	3 p.m., 15 June			10 a.m.	Nivelles	Belle Alliance

Formation (Commander)	Position on 15 June	Orders received	After Orders received	Started off 16 June at	Arrived Time	Place	Sources
2nd Dutch-Belgian Division (Perponcher)	Nivelles (headquarters)	In action at Quatre Bras, evening 15 June					De Bas & T'Serclaes de Wommersom
3rd Dutch-Belgian Division (Chassé)	Rœulx (headquarters)	Left in reserve at Nivelles					
II Corps (Hill)	Ath						
2nd Division (Clinton)	Ath (headquarters)						
1st/52nd Foot	Ellignies-Sainte-Anne	10 a.m., 16 June		10.20 a.m.	12 p.m. / 7 a.m. (17th)	Braine-le-Comte / Nivelles	Leeke / Moore Smith
1st/71st Foot	Ath, Tournai	Morning, 16 June			Late that night	Nivelles	Cannon
2nd/ & 3rd/95th Foot							Not available
1st Brigade KGL							Not available
3rd Hanoverian Brigade							Not available
4th Division (Colville)	Oudenaarde (headquarters)	6 a.m., 16 June			17 June	Braine-le-Comte	Colville
3rd/14th Foot	Acren	that night	that night	Next morning	Long after dark 17 June	Braine-le-Comte / Nivelles	Albemarle
1st/23rd Foot	Grammont	15 June			Evening of 17 June	Braine l'Alleud	Cannon
51st Foot	Grammont			8 a.m.	Night 17 June	Braine-le-Comte / Nivelles	Wylly, Wheater, Wheeler
2nd/35th Foot							Not available

Formation (Commander)	Position on 15 June	Orders received	After Orders received	Started off 16 June at Daybreak	Arrived Time	Arrived Place	Sources
1st/54th Foot[2]	Courtrai	Late on 15 June		Daybreak	?	Enghien	Atkinson
2nd/59th Foot*							Not available
1st/91st Foot					17 June	Braine-le-Comte	Goff
6th Hanoverian Brigade							Not available
1st Dutch-Belgian Division (Stedman)	Between Grammont and Ghent	2 p.m., 16 June, ordered to concentrate at Zottegem and march on Enghien		5 p.m.	3–4 a.m., 17 June	Enghien	De Bas & T'Serclaes de Wommersom
Indian Brigade (Anthing)	Bambrugge (headquarters)						Not available
Reserve (Wellington)	Brussels (headquarters)						
5th Division (Picton)	In and around Brussels	7 p.m.		'in the night time'	2 p.m.	Quatre Bras	USJ, 1841, Pt II.
1st/28th Foot	Brussels	Ordered at 10 p.m. to assemble at midnight at Palace Royale		4 a.m.	2.30 p.m.	Quatre Bras	Brodigan
1st/32nd Foot	Brussels	Late on 15 June		2 a.m.	3 p.m.	Quatre Bras	Swiney
1st/79th Foot	Brussels	10 p.m.		4 a.m.	Before 2.45 p.m.	Quatre Bras	Jameson
1st/95th Rifles	Brussels		11 p.m. / 11 p.m.	Morning Daylight	3 p.m.	Quatre Bras / Quatre Bras	Costello Verner
3rd/1st Foot	Brussels		Night of 15 June		'soon after midday'	Quatre Bras	Cannon
1st/42nd Foot	Brussels	Night of 15 June		4 a.m.	?	Quatre Bras	Cannon
2nd/44th Foot	Brussels	Evening of 15 June		Daylight	2.30 p.m.	Quatre Bras	Carter
1st/92nd Foot	Brussels	Evening of 15 June		Sunrise	2.30 p.m.	Quatre Bras	Cannon Gardyne

Formation (Commander)	Position on 15 June	Orders received	After Orders received	Started off 16 June at	Arrived Time	Arrived Place	Sources
5th Hanoverian Brigade		Night of 15 June, assembled at Hal		Noon	6 p.m. / 11 p.m.	Waterloo / Genappes	Vorgeschichte, 307
6th Division (Cole)	In and around Brussels						
1st/4th Foot	Brussels	Late on 15 June		Late 15 June?	Did not arrive on 16 June		Cowper
1st/27th Foot	Ghent	?	?	Marched for Brussels	Did not arrive on 16 June		Regimental Historical Records Committee
1st/40th Foot	Ghent	5 a.m. on 16 June		Shortly after 5 a.m.	?	Direction Brussels	Smythies
2nd/81st Foot	Brussels	? To be ready to march at 4 a.m. on 16 June		Remained in Brussels on guard duty			Rogers
4th Hanoverian Brigade	Brussels	?	?	3 a.m.	3 p.m.	Quatre Bras	Schwertfeger
Brunswick Corps	In and around Brussels	11 p.m.		'early'	'after 10 or 11 hours'	Quatre Bras	Belle-Alliance
Nassau Contingent	In and around Brussels	11 p.m.	1.30 a.m., 16 June	9 a.m. without 3rd Batt	8 p.m.	Quatre Bras	Vorgeschichte, 305 f.
Reserve Cavalry (Uxbridge)	Grammont and Ninove	By 11.45 p.m., 15 June	4.30-6 a.m., 16 June		Night	Quatre Bras	Paget Papers / De Bas & T'Serclaes de Wommersom
1st & 2nd Life Guards	Meerbeck & Ninove	Early on 16 June		6 a.m.	Night	Quatre Bras	Cannon
Royal Horse Guards		Morning of 16 June			Night	Between Quatre Bras and Genappe	Packe

Formation (Commander)	Position on 15 June	Orders received	After Orders received	Started off 16 June at	Arrived Time	Place	Sources
1st Dragoon Guards		3 a.m.		9 a.m.	4 p.m. 8 p.m.	Braine-le-Comte Quatre Bras	Mann
1st (Royal) Dragoons	Between Brussels and Ghent	1.45 a.m., 16 June	5 a.m.	6 a.m.	11 p.m.	Quatre Bras	Ainslie WSD, x, 481 Cannon
2nd Dragoons	Between Brussels and Ghent	Just after midnight. 1.45 a.m. 16 June		Daybreak ? Before day	Evening After dark After dusk	Quatre Bras Quatre Bras Quatre Bras	Cannon Almack WSD, x, 481
6th Dragoons		1.45 a.m., 16 June		4 a.m.	Little before midnight	Quatre Bras	Cannon WSD, x, 481
1st KGL Light Dragoons							Not available
2nd KGL Light Dragoons							Not available
23rd Light Dragoons							Not available
11th Light Dragoons	Eine near Oudenaarde		'early hour'		6-7 p.m.	Quatre Bras	Cannon
12th Light Dragoons				Morning	Sunset	Quatre Bras	Cannon
16th Light Dragoons				5 a.m.	? afternoon	Quatre Bras	Tomkinson
2nd KGL Hussars							Not available
7th Hussars		At the Duchess of Richmond's Ball		? a.m.	'too late'	Quatre Bras	Barrett
15th Hussars				Daybreak	Evening	Quatre Bras	Cannon
6th Brigade (Vivian)	Sint-Maria-Lierde	Daybreak, i.e. about 4 a.m.		5 a.m.	'too late' Close of day	Quatre Bras Quatre Bras	Vivian Memoirs; Murray Papers, NAM 7406-35-2
1st KGL Hussars	Tournai	11 a.m.		1 p.m.	Noon, 17th	Quatre Bras	Belle-Alliance

Formation (Commander)	Position on 15 June	Orders received	After Orders received	Started off 16 June at	Arrived Time	Arrived Place	Sources
10th Hussars	Oultre, Voorde	After midnight		Shortly after midnight	9 p.m.	Quatre Bras	Cannon, Liddell
18th Hussars			4.30 a.m, 16 June		4 p.m. 'too late'	Braine-le-Comte	Malet
3rd KGL Hussars							Not available
13th Light Dragoons	Kester, Herfelingen, Pepingen, Bogaarden, Heikruis		3–4 a.m., 16 June. Ordered to Enghien, then via Braine-le-Comte to Nivelles. Then to Quatre Bras.	11 p.m.		Quatre Bras	Barrett
Prince Regent's Hussars							Not available
Bremen-Verden Hussars	Valenciennes, Quesnoy	Morning, 16 June		Evening to Lens	Night of 17 June	Hal via Enghien	Vorgeschichte, 308
Dutch-Belgian Heavy Cavalry	Rœulx						De Bas & T'Serclaes de Wommersom
1st Dutch-Belgian Light Cavalry	Havré						De Bas & T'Serclaes de Wommersom
2nd Dutch-Belgian Light Cavalry	St Symphorien						De Bas & T'Serclaes de Wommersom

1 Based on the relevant sections of WD, vol XII and Siborne.
2 Wellington ordered this regiment before nightfall to march at daybreak on 17 June to Nivelles.

The 'Missing Letters'

Correspondence to and from the Duke of Wellington, 14–16 June 1815

Time/Date	To/From	Contents	Comments	Status	Source
09.30, 14 June	From: Dörnberg	Report from front	Not compromising, from own troops	Present	WSD, X, 476
?, 14 June	To: Duc de Feltre	Armaments for the Royalists	Not compromising, to friendly government	Present	WD, XII, 463 ff
?, 14 June	To: Prince of Orange	Preparations at Ath	Not compromising, to friendly government	Present	WD XII, 465 f
?, 14 June	To: Metternich	Supplies for Austrian Army	Not compromising, to friendly government	Present	WD, XII, 466 ff
15.00, 14 June	From: Dörnberg	Report from front	Not compromising, from own troops	Present	WSD, X, 477 f
22.00, 14 June	From: Hardinge	Report from Prussian headquarters	Not compromising, from own troops	Present	WSD, X, 476
?, 14 June	From: Castlereagh	Report from London	Not compromising, from own government	Present	WSD, X, 477
?, 14 June	To: Zieten	Promise of support	Compromising, to rival government	**Missing**	GStA, Rep 92, A 48 fol 32
00.00, 15 June	From: Zieten	Report from front	Compromising, from rival government	**Missing**	Gleig
04.45, 15 June	From: Zieten	Report from front	Compromising, from rival government	**Missing**	Hafner
09.30, 15 June	From: Dörnberg	Report from front	Not compromising, from own troops	Present	WSD, X, 481
?, 15 June	From: Dalrymple	Report from Milan	Not compromising, from own government	Present	WSD, X, 479
13.00, 15 June	To: Clinton	Renumbering divisions	Not compromising, to own army	Present	WD, XII, 469 f
?, 15 June	From: Dillon	Intelligence from Paris	Not compromising, from own government	Present	WSD, X, 479
14.00, 15 June	From: Berkeley	Report from front	Not compromising, from own troops	Present	WSD, X, 480

Time/Date	To/From	Contents	Comments	Status	Source
?, 15 June	To: Czar of Russia	Plans for invasion of France	Not compromising, to friendly government	Present	WD, XII, 470 ff
?, 15 June	From: Brook Taylor	Report from Stuttgart	Not compromising, from own government	Present	WSD, X, 478 f
17.00, 15 June	From: Prince of Orange	Report from front	Not compromising, from friendly government	Present	WSD, X, 475
18.00–19.00, 15 June	To: own army	Orders to concentrate	Not compromising, to own troops	Present	WD, XII, 472 f
21.30, 15 June	To: Duc de Berri	News of outbreak of hostilities	Not compromising, to friendly government	Present	WD, XII, 473
22.00, 15 June	To: Duc de Feltre	News of outbreak of hostilities	Not compromising in this context, vaguely worded, but potentially compromising when taken in context, to friendly government	Present	WD, XII, 473 f
22.00, 15 June	To: own army	'after orders'	Not compromising, to own troops	Present	WD, XII, 474
evening, 15 June	To: Gneisenau	Promise of support	Compromising, to rival government	**Missing**	Delbrück, 659
early, 16 June	To: Hill	movement order	Not compromising, to own troops	Present	WD, XII, 474
morning, 16 June	To: Hill	further movement order	Not compromising, to own troops	Present	WD, XII, 474
07.00, 16 June	From: de Lancey	'Disposition'	Not compromising, from own army. Supports misleading statements made in 1842.	**Missing at first (in 1838) Found before 1847**	WSD, X, 496
? 09.00, 16 June	To: Hill	further movement order	Not compromising, to own troops	Present	WD, XII, 475
morning, 16 June	To: Reserve Artillery	movement order	Not compromising, to own troops	Present	WD, XII, 475
morning, 16 June	To: Lambert	movement order	Not compromising, to own troops	Present	WD, XII, 475
10.30, 16 June	To: Blücher	'Frasnes letter'	Compromising, to rival commander	**Missing**	Ollech

It is interesting to note there is a pattern to the documents missing from Wellington's records; potentially compromising documents to or from the Prussians are simply not there, while the documents from or to friendly sources are present.

Timetable of Events on 16 June 1815

Time	Place	Event
00.00?	Brussels	Lt. Webster arrives at the Duchess of Richmond's ball with message that the French have broken through to Quatre Bras.
		Comment: *This timing is approximate and based on the sequence of events.*
00.00–01.00	Brussels	Wellington instructs his officers to leave the ball one by one and return to their posts.
00.15	Braine-le-Comte	Constant Rebeque issues movement orders to Perponcher.
03.00	Brussels	Wellington retires to bed.
04.00–05.00	Brussels	Dörnberg wakes Wellington.
05.00–07.00	Brussels	Wellington sends orders to Hill.
		Comment: *The timing is supposition, but the message was written before Wellington left Brussels.*
05.00	Brussels	Wellington starts his ride to the front.
07.00–09.00	Waterloo	Wellington meets Dörnberg.
		Comment: *The timing is supposition based on Wellington needing two hours to ride 20 km.*
10.00	Quatre Bras	Wellington arrives at Quatre Bras.
10.30	Frasnes	Wellington writes to Blücher.
12.00–12.30?	Frasnes	Wellington leaves to ride to Brye.
		Comment: *The timing is supposition. The distance between the two points is approximately 12 km.*
13.00	Brye	Wellington arrives.
13.30–14.00	Brye	Wellington leaves to return to Quatre Bras.
		Comment: *Reiche says 13.30. It may have been a little later.*
14.30	Ligny	Battle starts. French attack St Amand.
14.30	Quatre Bras	Battle starts.
15.00	Ligny	First French assault on Ligny.
15.00	Quatre Bras	5th Division arrives.
16.00	Ligny	Prussians counter-attack at St Amand.
16.00	Ligny	Prussians move against Wagnelée.
16.00	Ligny	French storm Ligny château.
17.00	Quatre Bras	3rd Division arrives.
17.00	Ligny	Prussians counter-attack at Ligny.
18.00	Quatre Bras	Second French offensive starts.
18.30	Ligny	Final Prussian assault on St Amand.
19.00	Ligny	Prussian III Army Corps moves into action at Balâtre and Tongrinne.
20.00	Ligny	Final French assault on St Amand.
20.00	Quatre Bras	Last fighting.
20.30	Ligny	Final French assault.

Speeds at which bodies of troops marched.

The speeds at which various formations of troops were considered able to march were roughly as given in the table below:

Strength and composition of marching column	Good roads, favourable conditions	Average roads and conditions	Poor roads and conditions	Very unfavourable conditions
1 Infantry Battalion or 1 Foot Battery	3.75 km/h	2.8 km/h	2.25 km/h	1.9 km/h
1 Cavalry Regiment or 1 Horse Battery	4.5 km/h	3.75 km/h	2.8 km/h	2.25 km/h
1 large Supply or Artillery Train	2.8 km/h	2.25 km/h	1.4 km/h	1.1 km/h
1 Infantry Division (Prussian Brigade)	3.2 km/h	2.5 km/h	2.0 km/h	1.6 km/h
1 Cavalry Division with its Artillery	3.75 km/h	2.8 km/h	2.25 km/h	1.9 km/h
1 Infantry Corps	2.6 km/h	2.0 km/h	1.6 km/h	1.25 km/h
1 Cavalry Corps	3.0 km/h	2.2 km/h	1.7 km/h	1.4 km/h

The figures given are approximate, and the average rates to be expected. They are based on the principle that the larger the formation, and the more difficult the conditions, the slower the rate. 'Very unfavourable conditions' includes when in a combat situation, in extreme weather conditions, such as very hot weather, a storm where the rain or snow is blowing directly into the marchers' faces, when marching on a icy surface, etc

Based on Boehn, p 295.

Orders of Battle

Prussian Army – 15 and 16 June 1815[1]

(a key to abbreviations used in this order of battle appears on p 373)

Commander in Chief	*Generalfeldmarschall Fürst Blücher von Wahlstatt*		
Chief-of-staff	*GL Graf von Gneisenau*		
General Staff	GM von Grolmann		
	OB von Pfuel		
	OBL von Witzleben		
	Maj von Lützow		
	Kap von Vigny		
Adjutants	Maj von Weyrach		
	Maj von Brünneck		
	Maj Graf von Nostitz		
	Kap Sprenger		
Artillery	GM von Holtzendorff		
	(replaced after 16th June by OBL von Röhl, II Corps)		

I. Armeekorps	*GL von Zieten*		
Chief-of-staff	OBL von Reiche		
Artillery	OBL Lehmann		

1. Brigade	*GM von Steinmetz*		
12. (2. Brandenburgisches) IR		(3 battalions)	2,027 men
24. IR		(3 battalions)	2,340 men
1. Westfälisches LIR		(3 battalions)	2,403 men
3. & 4. Komp. Schlesisches Schützen-Bataillon			315 men
1. Schlesisches HR		(3 squadrons)	454 men
6pf. FB Nr. 7			145 men
RB Nr. 7			151 men

2. Brigade	*GM von Pirch II*		
6. (1. Westpreussisches) IR		(3 battalions)	2,375 men
28. IR		(3 battalions)	2,189 men
2. Westfälisches LIR		(3 battalions)	2169 men
6pf. FB Nr. 3			143 men

3. Brigade	*GM von Jagow*		
7. (2. Westpreussisches) IR		(3 battalions)	2,117 men
29. IR		(3 battalions)	2,154 men
3. Westfälisches LIR		(3 battalions)	1979 men
1. & 2. Komp. Schlesische Schützen-Bataillon			316 men
6pf. FB Nr. 8			141 men

4. Brigade	*GM Graf Henckel von Donnersmarck*		
13. IR		(detached)	
19. IR		(3 battalions)	1,783 men
4. Westfälisches LIR		(3 battalions)	2184 men
6pf. FB Nr. 15			139 men

Reserve-Kavallerie	*GL von Roeder*		
Staff:	Maj Graf von der Groeben		
I. Brigade	*GM von Tresckow* II		
Brandenburgisches DR Nr. 5		(4 squadrons)	585 men
I. Westpreussisches DR Nr. 2		(3 squadrons)	393 men
Brandenburgisches UR Nr. 3		(3 squadrons)	403 men
RB Nr. 2			145 men
2. Brigade	OBL von Lützow		
6. UR		(3 squadrons)	362 men
I. Kurmärkisches LKR		(3 squadrons)	179 men
2. Kurmärkisches LKR		(4 squadrons)	247 men
Westfälisches LKR		(4 squadrons)	551 men
Reserve-Artillerie	Maj von Rentzell		
12pf. FB Nr. 2			162 men
12pf. FB Nr. 6			172 men
6pf. FB Nr. I			107 men
RB Nr. 10			124 men
7pf. HB Nr. I			151 men

II. Armeekorps — *GM von Pirch* I

Chief-of-staff	OB Aster		
Artillery	OBL von Röhl		
5. Brigade	*GM von Tippelskirch*		
2. (I. Pommersches) IR		(3 battalions)	2,323 men
25. IR		(3 battalions)	2,002 men
5. Westfälisches LIR		(3 battalions)	2,062 men
6pf. FB Nr. 10			111 men
6. Brigade	*GM von Krafft*		
9. (Kolbergsches) IR		(3 battalions)	2,377 men
26. IR		(3 battalions)	1,646 men
I. Elb-LIR		(3 battalions)	2,196 men
6pf. FB Nr. 5			115 men
7. Brigade	*GM von Brause*		
14. IR		(3 battalions)	2,225 men
22. IR		(3 battalions)	1,816 men
2. Elb-LIR		(3 battalions)	2,196 men
6pf. FB Nr. 34			116 men
8. Brigade	*GM von Bose*		
21. IR		(3 battalions)	2,217 men
23. IR		(3 battalions)	1,547 men
3. Elb-LIR		(3 battalions)	2,196 men
6pf. FB Nr. 12			112 men
Reserve-Kavallerie	*GM von Wahlen-Jürgass*		
I. Brigade	OB von Thümen		
DR Königin Nr. I		(4 squadrons)	515 men
Neumärkisches DR Nr. 6		(4 squadrons)	390 men
Schlesisches UR Nr. 2		(4 squadrons)	419 men
RB Nr. 6			128 men

2. *Brigade* OBL von Sohr

Brandenburgisches HR Nr. 3	(4 squadrons)	473 men
Pommersches HR Nr. 5	(4 squadrons)	473 men
11. HR		375 men

(1. & 2. Esk. attached to 5. Brigade, 3. & 4. Esk. to 6. Brigade)

3. *Brigade* OB Graf von der Schulenburg

4. Kurmärkisches LKR	(6 squadrons)	435 men
5. Kurmärkisches LKR	(4 squadrons)	388 men
Elb-LKR		473 men

(1. & 3. Esk. attached to 7. Brigade, 2. & 4. Esk. to 8. Brigade)

Reserve-Artillerie Maj Lehmann

12pf. FB Nr. 4	192 men
12pf. FB Nr. 8	171 men
6pf. FB Nr. 37	102 men
RB Nr. 5	114 men
RB Nr. 14	121 men

III. Armeekorps *GL Freiherr von Thielemann*

Chief-of-staff OB von Clausewitz

9. Brigade *GM von Borcke*

8. (Leib-) IR	(3 battalions)	2,184 men
30. IR	(3 battalions)	2,170 men
1. Kurmärkisches LIR	(3 battalions)	1,903 men
3. Kurmärkisches LKR	(1. & 2. Esk.)	171 men
6pf. FB Nr. 18		129 men

10. Brigade *OB von Kemphen*

20. IR	(detached)	
27. IR	(3 battalions)	1,952 men
2.Kurmärkisches LIR	(3 battalions)	1,894 men
3.Kurmärkisches LKR	(3. & 4. Esk.)	171 men
6pf. FB Nr. 35		113 men

11. Brigade *OB von Luck*

32. IR	(not formed)	
3. Kurmärkisches LIR	(3 battalions)	2,054 men
4. Kurmärkisches LIR	(3 battalions)	1,987 men
6. Kurmärkisches LKR	(1. & 2. Esk.)	160 men

12. Brigade *OB von Stülpnagel*

31. IR	(3 battalions)	2,269 men
5. Kurmärkisches LIR	(3 battalions)	1,885 men
6. Kurmärkisches LIR	(3 battalions)	1,885 men
6. Kurmärkisches LKR	(3. & 4. Esk.)	160 men

Reserve-Kavallerie *GM von Hobe*

1. *Brigade* OB von der Marwitz

7. UR	(3 squadrons)	322 men
8. UR	(4 squadrons)	527 men

2. *Brigade*	OB Graf von Lottum		
7. DR		(3 squadrons)	330 men
9. HR		(3 squadrons)	375 men
5. UR		(3 squadrons)	370 men
RB Nr. 20			114 men
Reserve-Artillerie	Maj von Grevenitz		
12pf. FB Nr. 7			172 men
RB Nr. 18			125 men
RB Nr. 19			122 men

Abbreviations

The following abbreviations are used throughout this order-of-battle:

C-in-C	Commander-in-Chief	
GL	Generallieutenant	Lieutenant-General
GM	Generalmajor	Major-General
OB	Oberst	Colonel
OBL	Oberstlieutenant	Lieutenant-Colonel
Maj	Major	Major
Kap	Kapitain	Captain of infantry or artillery
IR	Infanterie-Regiment	Regiment of Foot
LIR	Landwehr-Infanterie-Regiment	Regiment of Foot Militia
LKR	Landwehr-Kavallerie-Regiment	Regiment of Horse Militia
HR	Husaren-Regiment	Regiment of Hussars
DR	Dragoner-Regiment	Regiment of Dragoons
UR	Ulanen-Regiment	Regiment of Lancers
FB	Fussbatterie	Foot Battery
HB	Haubitzebatterie	Howitzer Battery
RB	reitende Batterie	Horse Battery
Esk	Eskadron	Squadron
Komp	Kompagnie	Company
6pf.	6 pfündige	6-pounder
7pf.	7 pfündige	7-pounder
10pf.	10 pfündige	10-pounder
12pf.	12 pfündige	12-pounder

Each artillery battery had an establishment of eight guns distributed as follows:

6-pounder foot and horse batteries	six 6-pounders, two 7-pounder howitzers
12-pounder foot batteries	six 12-pounders, two 10-pounder howitzers
howitzer batteries	eight 7-pounder howitzers

---

[1] As at 12 June 1815. Based on Lettow-Vorbeck, *Napoleons Untergang 1815*, pp 469 ff.

French Army, Ligny, 16 June 1815

Commander in Chief	**S.M. l'Empereur Napoléon**
Aides de camp	Duc de Plaisance, Comte Drouot, Comte Corbineau, Comte Flahaut, Comte Dejean, Baron Bernard, Comte de la Bédoyère
Officier d'ordonnance	Colonel Gourgaud
Grand quartier général	
Major général	*le maréchal Soult, duc de Dalmatie*
Chef d'état-major général	LG Comte Bailly de Monthion
Chargé du service des prisonniers de guerre	le maréchal de camp baron Dentzel

La Garde Impériale

Aide-major général	*LG Comte Drouot*
Commandant l'infanterie	LG Comte Friant
Commandant en second	Comte Morand
Commandant l'artillerie et les marins	Baron Desvaux de Saint-Maurice
Commandant le génie	Baron Haxo
Commandant la jeune garde	Comte Duhesme

Vieille garde (infanterie)

1er Division	*LG Comte Roguet*		
1er grenadiers à pied	Baron Petit	(2 battalions)	1,006 men
2e grenadiers à pied	Baron Christiani	(2 battalions)	1,063 men
3e grenadiers à pied	Poret de Morvan	(2 battalions)	1,146 men
4e grenadiers à pied	Harlet	(1 battalion)	503 men
2e Division	*LG Comte Michel*		
1er chasseurs à pied	Comte Cambronne	(2 battalions)	1,271 men
2e chasseurs à pied	Baron Pelet	(2 battalions)	1,031 men
3e chasseurs à pied	Mallet	(2 battalions)	1,028 men
4e chasseurs à pied	Henrion	(2 battalions)	1,041 men

Jeune garde (infanterie)

1re Brigade	Chartran		
1er voltigeurs		(2 battalions)	1,188 men
1er tirailleurs	Trappier de Malcolm	(2 battalions)	935 men
2e Brigade	Guye		
3e voltigeurs	Hurel	(2 battalions)	1083 men
3e tirailleurs	Pailhès	(2 battalions)	960 men

Cavalerie lègere	*at Quatre Bras*		
Cavalerie de réserve	Baron Guyot		
Grenadiers à cheval	Dubois	(6 squadrons)	796 men
Dragons	Hoffmayer	(7 squadrons)	816 men
Artillerie à pied	Lallemand 9 coys	(72 guns)	702 men
Artillerie à cheval	Duchand 4 coys	(24 guns)	380 men

1er Corps d'Armee
marching between Quatre Bras and Ligny

2e Corps d'Armee

at *Quatre Bras, except:*

7e Division d'Infanterie

LG Baron Girard

I re Brigade — Baron Devilliers

I I e léger	Sébastiani	(2 battalions)	913 men
82e de ligne	Matis	(I battalion)	550 men

2e Brigade — Baron Piat

I2e léger	Mouttet	(3 battalions)	1,141 men
4e de ligne	Foullain	(2 battalions)	1,157 men
2e Artillerie à pied, 3e comp.		(8 guns)	180 men

3e Corps d'Armee

LG Comte Vandamme

Chef d'État-Major	LG Comte Guilleminot
Sous-chef	Trezel
Commandant l'artillerie	Doguereau
Commandant le génie	Nempde

8e Division d'Infanterie

Baron Lefol

I re Brigade — Billard

I5e léger	Brice	(3 battalions)	1,676 men
23e de ligne	Baron Vernier	(3 battalions)	1,152 men

2e Brigade — Baron Corsin

37e de ligne	Fortier	(3 battalions)	1,117 men
64e de ligne	Dubalen	(2 battalions)	891 men
6e Artillerie à pied, 7e comp.		(8 guns)	187 men

I0e Division d'Infanterie

Baron Habert

I re Brigade — Baron Gengoult

34e de ligne	Mouton	(3 battalions)	1,384 men
88e de ligne	Baillon	(3 battalions)	1,265 men

2e Brigade — Dupeyroux

22e de ligne	Fantin des Odoards	(3 battalions)	1,406 men
70e de ligne	Baron Maury	(2 battalions)	909 men
2e étranger (Suisses)	Stoffel	(I battalion)	386 men
2e Artillerie à pied, 18e comp.		(8 guns)	89 men

I I e Division d'Infanterie

LG Baron Berthezène

I re Brigade — Baron Dufour

I2e de ligne	Baron Beaudinot	(2 battalions)	1,171 men
56e de ligne	Delahaye	(2 battalions)	1,234 men

2e Brigade — Baron Lagarde

33e de ligne	Baron Maire	(2 battalions)	1,097 men
86e de ligne	Pelicier	(2 battalions)	870 men
2e Artillerie à pied, 17e comp.		(8 guns)	96 men

3e Division de Cavalerie

Baron Domon

I re Brigade — Baron Dommanget

4e chasseurs à cheval	Desmichels	(3 squadrons)	306 men
9e chasseurs à cheval	Dukermont	(3 squadrons)	337 men

2e Brigade — Baron Vinot

I2e chasseurs à cheval	Grouchy	(3 squadrons)	289 men
2e artillerie à cheval, 4e comp.		(6 guns)	74 men

Artillerie de Réserve

2e artillerie à pied, I re comp.		(4 guns)	95 men
2e artillerie à pied, 19e comp.		(4 guns)	97 men

4e Corps d'Armee — LG Comte Gérard

Chef d'État-Major Général	Saint-Rémy		
Sous-Chef	Simon Lorière		
Commandant l'artillerie	Baron Baltus		
Commandant le génie	Valazé		

12e Division d'Infanterie — Baron Pêcheux

1re Brigade	Rome		
30e de ligne	Ramand	(3 battalions)	1,399 men
96e de ligne	Gougeon	(3 battalions)	1,387 men
2e Brigade	Schaeffer		
63e de ligne	Laurède	(3 battalions)	1,214 men
6e léger	Gemeau	(1 battalion)	591 men
5e artillerie à pied, 2e comp.		(8 guns)	98 men

13e Division d'Infanterie — Baron Vichery

1re Brigade	Le Capitaine		
59e de ligne	Chevalier Laurain	(2 battalions)	1,015 men
76e de ligne	Condamy	(2 battalions)	1,014 men
2e Brigade	Desprez		
48e de ligne	Péraldi	(2 battalions)	834 men
69e de ligne	Hervé	(2 battalions)	1,077 men
5e artillerie à pied, 1re comp.		(8 guns)	97 men

14e Division d'Infanterie — Hulot

1re Brigade	Hulst		
9e léger	Baume	(2 battalions)	1,215 men
111e de ligne	Baron Sausset	(2 battalions)	1,035 men
2e Brigade	Toussaint		
44e de ligne	Paolini	(2 battalions)	934 men
50e de ligne	Lavigne	(2 battalions)	874 men
5e artillerie à pied, one comp.		(8 guns)	80 men

7e Division de Cavalerie légère — LG Maurin

1re Brigade	Vallin		
6e hussards	Prince de Savois-Carignan	(3 squadrons)	387 men
8e chasseurs à cheval	Schneit	(3 squadrons)	371 men
2e Brigade	Berruyer		
6e dragons	Mugnier	(4 squadrons)	488 men
16e dragons	Fortin	(4 squadrons)	326 men
3e artillerie à cheval, 3e comp.		(6 guns)	162 men
Artillerie de Réserve			
5e artillerie à pied, one comp.		(8 guns)	200 men

6e Corps d'Armee — did not participate

Reserve de Cavalerie — le maréchal Comte de Grouchy

Chef d'État-Major	Baron Le Sénécal		

1er Corps de Cavalerie — LG Comte Pajol

Chef d'État-Major	Picard		

4e Division de Cavalerie — Baron Soult

1re Brigade	Baron Houssin de Saint-Laurent		
1er hussards	Clary	(4 squadrons)	486 men

4e hussards	Blot	(4 squadrons)	346 men
2e *Brigade*	Baron Ameil		
5e hussards	Baron Liégeard	(4 battalions)	399 men
1er artillerie à cheval, 1re comp.		(6 guns)	70 men
5e Division de Cavalerie	*Baron Subervie*		
1re Brigade	Comte A. Colbert		
1er lanciers	Jacquinot	(4 squadrons)	375 men
2e lanciers	Sourd	(4 squadrons)	379 men
2e *Brigade*	Merlin		
11e chasseurs à cheval	Baron Nicolas	(4 squadrons)	336 men
1er artillerie à cheval, 3e comp.		(6 guns)	74 men
2e Corps de Cavalerie	*LG Comte Exelmans*		
Chef d'État-Major	Feroussat		
9e Division de Cavalerie	*Baron Strolz*		
1re Brigade	Baron Burthe		
5e dragons	Canevas St-Amand	(4 squadrons)	465 men
13e dragons	Saviot	(4 squadrons)	389 men
2e *Brigade*	Baron Vincent		
15e dragons	Chaillot	(4 squadrons)	381 men
20e dragons	Briqueville	(4 squadrons)	316 men
1er artillerie à cheval, 4e comp.		(6 guns)	55 men
10e Division de Cavalerie	*Baron Chastel*		
1re Brigade	Baron Bonnemains		
4e dragons	Bouquerot des Essarts	(4 squadrons)	530 men
12e dragons	Bureaux de Pusy	(4 squadrons)	510 men
2e *Brigade*	Berton		
14e dragons	Séguier	(4 squadrons)	339 men
17e dragons	Labiffe	(3 squadrons)	287 men
4e artillerie à cheval, 4e comp.		(6 guns)	60 men
4e Corps de Cavalerie	*Comte Milhaud*		
Chef d'État-Major:	Baron Chasseriau		
13e Division de Cavalerie	Comte Wathier Saint-Alphonse		
1re Brigade	Dubois		
1er cuirassiers	Comte Ordener	(4 squadrons)	411 men
4e cuirassiers	Habert	(3 squadrons)	278 men
2e *Brigade*	Baron Travers		
7e cuirassiers	Richardot	(2 squadrons)	151 men
12e cuirassiers	Thurot	(2 squadrons)	226 men
1er artillerie à cheval, 5e comp.		(6 guns)	75 men
14e Division de Cavalerie	*Baron Delort*		
1re Brigade	Baron Farine		
5e cuirassiers	Gobert	(3 squadrons)	380 men
10e cuirassiers	Lahuberdière	(3 squadrons)	309 men
2e *Brigade*	Baron Vial		
6e cuirassiers	Martin	(4 squadrons)	474 men
9e cuirassiers	Bigarne	(3 squadrons)	327 men
3e artillerie à cheval, 4e comp.		(6 guns)	70 men

French Army, Quatre Bras, 16 June 1815

Commander in Chief	*le maréchal Ney, Prince de la Moskowa*		
2e Corps d'Armee	***LG Comte Reille***		
Chef d'État-Major	LG. Baron P. Lacroix		
Sous-chef	Lecouturier		
Commandant d'artillerie:	Baron Pelletier		
Commandant le génie	Baron de Richemont		
5e Division d'Infanterie	*Baron Bachelu*		
Ire Brigade	Baron Husson		
2e léger	Maigrot	(3 battalions)	1,713 men
61e de ligne	Baron Bouge	(2 battalions)	858 men
2e Brigade	Campi		
72e de ligne	Thibault	(2 battalions)	975 men
108e de ligne	Higonet	(3 battalions)	1,401 men
9e Artillerie à pied, 18e comp.	Deshaulles	(8 guns)	191 men
Ier Génie, Ier comp. du Ier bataillon			87 men
6e Division d'Infanterie	*LG Jérôme Bonaparte*		
Ire Brigade	Baron Baudin		
Ier léger	de Cubières	(3 battalions)	1,888 men
3e de ligne	Baron Vautrin	(2 battalions)	1,143 men
2e Brigade	Baron Soye		
Ier de ligne	Chevalier Cornebize	(3 battalions)	1,795 men
2e de ligne	Trippe	(3 battalions)	1,795 men
2e Artillerie à pied, 2e comp.	Meunier	(8 guns)	200 men
Ier Génie, 2e comp. du Ier bataillon			86 men
7e Division d'Infanterie	*at Ligny*		
9e Division d'Infanterie	*Foy*		
Ire Brigade	Gauthier		
92e de ligne	Tissot	(2 battalions)	1,068 men
93e de ligne	Massot	(3 battalions)	1,486 men
2e Brigade	Vicomte J.B. Jamin		
100e de ligne	Braun	(3 battalions)	1,118 men
4e léger	Peyris	(3 battalions)	1,636 men
6e Artillerie à pied, Ier comp.	Tacon	(8 guns)	187 men
Ier Génie, 4e comp. du Ier bataillon			86 men
2e Division de Cavalerie	*Marquis de Piré*		
Ire Brigade	Baron Hubert		
Ier Chasseurs à Cheval	Simonneau	(4 squadrons)	485 men
6e Chasseurs à Cheval	de Faudoas	(4 squadrons)	560 men
2e Brigade	Wathiez		
5e lanciers	Baron Jacqueminot	(3 squadrons)	412 men
6e lanciers	Galbois	(4 squadrons)	405 men
4e Artillerie à cheval, 2e comp.	Gronnier	(6 guns)	163 men

Réserve d'Artillerie
2e Artillerie à pied, 7e comp.   (8 guns)   180 men

3e Corps de Cavalerie   *LG Kellermann, comte de Valmy*
Chef d'État-Major   Tancarville

11e Division de Cavalerie   *Baron l'Héritier*
1re Brigade   Baron Picquet
2e Dragons   Planzeaux   (4 squadrons)   543 men
7e Dragons   Léopold   (4 squadrons)   475 men
2e Brigade   Baron Guiton
8e Cuirassiers   Garavaque   (3 squadrons)   421 men
11e Cuirassiers   Courtier   (2 battalions)   304 men
2e Artillerie à cheval, 3e comp.   de Marcillac   (6 guns)
75 men

12e Division de Cavalerie   *Roussel d'Hurbal*
1re Brigade   Baron Blancard
1er carabineers   Rogé   (3 squadrons)   403 men
2e carabineers   Beugnat   (3 squadrons)   380 men
2e Brigade   Baron Donop
2e cuirassiers   Grandjean   (2 squadrons)   292 men
3e cuirassiers   Lacroix   (4 squadrons)   427 men
2e artillerie à cheval, 2e comp.   (6 guns)   78 men

Division de Cavalerie Légère de la Garde Impériale
                         Comte Lefebvre-Desnoëttes
Chasseurs à cheval   Baron F. Lallemand   (7 squadrons)   1,197 men
Lanciers: E. Colbert   (6 squadrons)   880 men
                                              (4 'Red', 2 'Polish')

Unless otherwise noted, all divisions are commanded by a général de division, all brigades by a général de brigade. LG = Lieutenant-Général

Based on Delhaize & Aerts, pp 76 ff.

Anglo-Dutch-German Army, Quatre-Bras, 16 June 1815

I Corps	HRH The Prince of Orange	
1st (British) Division	*Major-General Sir George Cooke*	
1st (British) Brigade	Major-General Sir Peregrine Maitland	
2/1st Regiment of Foot Guards		976 men
3/1st Regiment of Foot Guards		1,021 men
2nd (British) Brigade	Major-General Sir John Byng	
2/Coldstream Regiment of Foot Guards		1,003 men
2/3rd Regiment of Foot Guards		1,061 men
Artillery	Lt.-Col. S.G. Adye	
Sandham's Battery, RA,	(5 9-pdrs, 1 howitzer)	390 men
Kuhlmann's Battery, KGL	(5 6-pdrs, 1 howitzer)	220 men
3rd (British) Division	*Lt.-General Sir Charles Alten*	
5th (British) Brigade	Major-General Sir Colin Halkett	
2/30th (Cambridgeshire) Regiment of Foot		615 men
33rd (1st Yorkshire [West Riding]) Regiment of Foot		561 men
2/69th (South Lincolnshire) Regiment of Foot		516 men
2/73rd (Highland) Regiment of Foot		562 men
2nd KGL Brigade	not present.	
1st (Hanoverian) Brigade	Major-General Count Kielmansegge	
Bremen Field Battalion		512 men
Verden Field Battalion		533 men
York Field Battalion		607 men
Lüneburg Field Battalion		595 men
Grubenhagen Field Battalion		621 men
Feldjäger-Korps		321 men
Artillery	Lt.-Col. J.S. Williamson	
Lloyd's Battery, RA	(5 9-pdrs, 1 howitzer)	390 men
Cleeves' Battery, RA	(5 9-pdrs, 1 howitzer)	86 men
2nd (Netherlands) Division	*Lt.-General Baron de Perponcher-Sedlnitzky*	
Chief-of-Staff	Col. Baron P.-H. van Zuylen van Nyevelt	
1st Brigade	Major-General Count van Bijlandt	
7th (Belgian) Line Regiment		678 men
27th (Dutch) Jager Battalion		786 men
5th Militia Battalion		460 men
7th Militia Battalion		651 men
8th Militia Battalion		543 men
Horse Battery Bijleveld	(8 6-pdrs)	104 men
2nd Brigade	Major-General Duke Bernhard of Saxe-Weimar	
I./2nd Nassau Regiment		895 men
II./2nd Nassau Regiment		857 men
III./2nd Nassau Regiment		871 men
I. Nassau-Orange Regiment		865 men

II. Nassau-Orange Regiment		666 men
Nassau Freiwillige Jäger Detachment, (1 company)		172 men
Stevenart's Battery	(8 6-pdrs)	116 men

2nd (Netherlands) Cavalry Brigade Major-General Baron J.-B. van Merlen

6th Dutch-Belgian Hussar Regiment		610 men
5th Belgian Light Dragoon Regiment		421 men
Horse Battery van Pittius	(4 6-pdrs)	66 men

Reserve

5th (British) Division *Lt.-General Sir Thomas Picton*

8th Brigade Major-General Sir James Kempt

1/28th (North Gloucestershire) Regiment of Foot	557 men
1/32nd (Cornwall) Regiment of Foot	662 men
1/79 (Cameron Highlanders) Regiment of Foot	703 men
1/95th (Rifles) Regiment of Foot	549 men

9th Brigade Major-General Sir Denis Pack

3/1st (Royal) Regiment of Foot	604 men
1/42nd (Royal Highland) Regiment of Foot	526 men
2/44th (East Essex) Regiment of Foot	455 men
1/92nd (Highland) Regiment of Foot	588 men

5th (Hanoverian) Brigade not present

Artillery Major Heisse

Rogers Battery, RA	(5 9-pdrs, 1 howitzer)	260 men
Braun (Hanoverian)	(5 9-pdrs, 1 howitzer)	233 men

6th (British) Division *Lt.-General Hon. Sir Lowry Cole*

10th (British) Brigade not present

4th (Hanoverian) Brigade Colonel Carl Best

Verden Landwehr Battalion	621 men
Lüneburg Landwehr Battalion	624 men
Osterode Landwehr Battalion	677 men
Münden Landwehr Battalion	660 men

Brunswick Contingent *Herzog Friedrich Wilhelm*

Avantgarden-Bataillon	672 men
Husaren-Regiment	690 men
Ulanen-Eskadron	232 men

Leichte Brigade Oberstlieutenant von Buttlar

Leib Bataillon	672 men
1. leichtes Bataillon	672 men
2. leichtes Bataillon	672 men
3. leichtes Bataillon	672 men

Linien-Brigade Oberstlieutenant von Specht

1. Linien-Bataillon	672 men
2. Linien-Bataillon	672 men
3. Linien-Bataillon	672 men

Artillery Major Mahn

Reitende Batterie	(8 6-pdrs)	216 men
Fussbatterie	(8 6-pdrs)	294 men

Nassau Contingent	Generalmajor von Kruse	
1st Nassau Regiment	Oberst von Steuben	
I Battalion		933 men
II Battalion		933 men
Landwehr Battalion		930 men

Based on Siborne, *History*, p 531 ff, and De Bas & T'Serclaes de Wommersom, vol III, p 94 ff.

Bibliography

Manuscript Sources

Manuscript	Accession Mark	Location
Aberdeen Manuscript	Add MS 43,252	British Library, London
Bathurst's Papers	Add MS 38,261	British Library, London
Castlereagh Papers	D3030	Public Record Office of Northern Ireland, Belfast
Castlereagh Papers	FO 92	Public Record Office, London
Cathcart Papers		Private collection
Colville Papers	NRA(S) 39	Private collection
Constant Rebeque, Journal of	Coll 66	Algemeen Rijksarchief, The Hague
De Lacy Evans' Papers	Ad MS 46.9.19	National Library of Scotland
Gneisenau Papers	Rep 92	Geheimes Staatsarchiv Preussischer Kulturbesitz, Berlin
Gurwood's Papers	30/26/41-44	Public Record Office, London
Hill's Military Correspondence	MS 61	Dorset Record Office, Dorchester
Hill's Papers	Add MS 35,062	British Library, London
Lowe's Papers	Add MSS 20,114 & 20,192	British Library, London
Murray's Papers	7406-35	National Army Museum, London
Records of John Murray (Publishers) Ltd.		London
Oldfield Manuscript	7403-147	National Army Museum, London
Paget Papers (Uxbridge)	644/A/21	Private collection
Raglan Papers (Fitzroy Somerset)		Gwent County Record Office
Scovell Papers	WO 37 / 12	Public Record Office, London
Somerset-Croker's Papers	Add MS 41,124	British Library, London
Vandeleur's Papers	TCD MS 4022a	Trinity College, Dublin
Vivian's Private Papers	7709-6	National Army Museum, London
Waterloo Correspondence	Add MSS 34,703-34,708	British Library, London
Waterloo Papers	Add MS 19,590	British Library, London
Wellington Papers	WP, various	Hartley Library, University of Southampton

Printed Sources

anon, *Allgemeine Deutsche Biographie*, Zehnter Band, Leipzig, 1879

anon, *British and Foreign State Papers*, 3 vols, London 1831–1841

anon, *Die Königlich Deutsche Legion und das Hannoversche Corps bei Waterloo*, Hanover, 1865 anon, *Exerzir-Reglement für die Infanterie der Königlich Preussischen Armee*, Berlin 1812

anon, *Geschichte des 1. Oberschlesischen Infanterie-Regiments Nr. 22*, Berlin, 1884

anon, *Geschichte des 3. Pommerschen Infanterie-Regiments (Nr. 14) während der Kriegsjahre 1813, 14 und 15*, Bromberg, 1860

anon, *Life of Field-Marshal Lord Raglan*, London, 1855

anon, 'Operations of the Fifth or Picton's Division in the Campaign of Waterloo', *United Service Journal*, Part II, London, 1841

anon, *The Royal Inniskilling Fusiliers*, London, 1928

anon, 'Waterloo by a Private Soldier', *United Service Journal*, Part I, London, 1831

Aa, A. J. van der, *Biographisch Woordenboek der Nederlanden*, Harlem, 1855

Ainslie, General de, *Historical record of the First or the Royal Regiment of Dragoons*, London, 1887

Albedyll, Georg von, *Geschichte des Kürassier-Regiments Königin (Pommersches) Nr. 2.*, II. Theil, Berlin, 1904

Albemarle, George Thomas, Earl of, *Fifty Years of My Life*, Vol. II, London, 1876

Almack, Edward, *The History of the Second Dragoons 'Royal Scots Greys'*, London, 1908

Angeberg, Comte d' (ed), *Le congrès de Vienne et les traités de 1815*, 4 vols, Paris, 1864

Ardenne, Armand von, *Bergische Lanziers - Westfälische Husaren Nr. 11*, Berlin, 1877

Atkinson, C. T., *The Dorsetshire Regiment*, Oxford, 1947

Bagensky, Karl von, *Geschichte des 9ten Infanterie-Regiments genannt Colbergsches*, Berlin, 1842

Bannatyne, Lieut.-Col. Neil, *History of the Thirtieth Regiment*, London, 1923

Barrett, C. R. B., *The 7th (Queen's Own) Hussars*, Vol. I, London, 1914

Barrett, C. R. B., *History of the XIII Hussars*, Edinburgh & London, 1911

Beitzke, Dr. H., *Hinterlassene Schriften des Dr. Carl Friccius*, Berlin, 1866

Boehn, Hubert von, *Generalstabsgeschäfte*, Potsdam, 1862

Bothe, Heinrich, *Geschichte des Thüringischen Ulanen-Regiments Nr. 6*, Berlin, 1865

Botzenhart, Erich; Hubatsch, Walther; Thielen, Peter (eds), *Freiherr vom Stein: Briefe und amtliche Schriften*, 10 vols., Stuttgart, 1957–1974

Brett-James, Anthony (ed), *Edward Costello, The Peninsular and Waterloo Campaigns*, London, 1967

Brodigan, Lieut.-Col. F., *Historical Records of the Twenty-Eighth North Gloucestershire Regiment*, London, 1884

Busse, Max von, *Geschichte des Königlich Preussischen Dreiundzwanzigsten Infanterie-Regiments*, Görlitz, 1859

Cannon, Richard, *Historical Record of the XXX Regiment*, London, 1887

Cannon, Richard, *Historical Record of the Eleventh or The Prince Albert's Own Regiment of Hussars*, London, 1843

Cannon, Richard, *Historical Record of the Fifteenth Hussars*, London, 1841

Cannon, Richard, *Historical Record of the First or Royal Regiment of Foot*, London, 1837

Cannon, Richard, *Historical Record of the Forty-Second of Foot*, London, 1845

Cannon, Richard, *Historical Record of the Life Guards*, London, 1837

Cannon, Richard, *Historical Record of the Royal Regiment of Scots Dragoons*, London, 1840

Cannon, Richard, *Historical Record of the Seventy-First Regiment*, London, 1852

Cannon, Richard, *Historical Record of the Seventy-Third Regiment*, London, 1851

Cannon, Richard, *Historical Record of the Sixth, or Inniskilling Regiment of Dragoons*, London, 1847

Cannon, Richard, *Historical Record of the Thirteenth Regiment of Light Dragoons*, London, 1842

Cannon, Richard, *Historical Record of the Twelfth or The Prince of Wales's Royal Regiment of Lancers*, London, 1842

Cannon, Richard, *Historical Record of the Twenty-Third Regiment of Foot*, London, 1844

Carter, Thomas, *Historical Record of the Forty-Fourth*, London, 1864

Chandler, David, *Campaigns of Napoleon*, New York and London, 1966

Charras, Jean Baptiste Adolphe, *Histoire de la campagne de 1815. Waterloo*, Paris, 1869

Chalfont, Lord, (ed), *Waterloo – Battle of Three Armies*, London, 1979

Chesney, Col. Charles C., R.E., *Waterloo Lectures: A Study of the Campaign of 1815*, London, 1907. Reprinted London, 1997

Clausewitz, Carl von, *Der Feldzug von 1815 in Frankreich*, Berlin, 1835

Colenbrander, Herman Theodor (ed), *Gedenkstukken der algemeene Geschiedenis van Nederland van 1740 tot 1840*, 22 vols, the Hague, 1905–22

Conrady, Emil von, *Geschichte des Königlich Preussischen Sechsten Infanterie-Regiments*, Glogau, 1857

Conrady, Emil von, *Leben und Wirkung von Carl von Grolman*, II. Theil, Berlin, 1895

Cowper, Col. L. I., *The King's Own*, Vol II, Oxford, 1939

Dalton, Charles, *Waterloo Roll Call*, London, 1890. Reprinted London, 1971

Damitz, Carl von, *Geschichte des Feldzuges von 1815 in den Niederlanden und Frankreich*, 2 vols., Berlin, Posen & Bromberg, 1837-38

De Bas, F., *Prins Frederik der Nederlanden en zijn tijd*, derde deel, IIde stuk, Schiedam, 1904

De Bas & T'Serclaes de Wommersom, *La campagne de 1815 aux pays-bas*, 3 vols, Brussels, 1908

Delbrück, Hans, *Das Leben des Feldmarschalls Grafen Neithardt von Gneisenau*, 4. Band, Berlin, 1880

Delbrück, Hans, 'Einiges zum Feldzuge von 1815', *Zeitschrift für Preussische Geschichte und Landeskunde*, 14. Jahrgang, Berlin, 1877

Delhaize, Jules, & Aerts, Winand, *Études Relatives à la Campagne de 1815 en Belgique*, Vol 1, Brussels, 1915

Dudley Ward, C. H., *A Romance of the Nineteenth Century*, London, 1923

Dziengel, Johann David von, *Geschichte des Königlich Preussischen Zweiten Ulanen-Regiments*, Potsdam, 1858

Eck, von, *Geschichte des 2. Westfälischen Husaren-Regiments Nr.11*, Mainz, 1893

Edmonds, Br.-General Sir James E., 'Wellington's Staff at Waterloo', *Journal of the Society of Army Historical Research*, vol XII, London, 1933

Epner & Braun, *Geschichte des Ulanen-Regiments Grossherzog Friedrich von Baden*

(Rheinisches) Nr. 7, Berlin, 1909

Fleischman, Theo & Aerts, Winand, *Bruxelles pendant la bataille de Waterloo*, Brussels, 1956

Förster, *Geschichte des Königlich Preussischen Ulanen-Regiments Graf zu Dohna (Ostpreussisches) Nr. 8*, Berlin, 1890

Fouché, Joseph, *Mémoires de Joseph Fouché, duc d'Otrante*, 2 vols, Paris, 1824

Fraser, Sir Wm., *Words on Wellington*, London, 1889

Gleig, Mary E. (ed), *Personal Reminiscences of the Duke of Wellington*, Edinburgh & London, 1904

Gleig, Rev. G. R., *History of the Life of Arthur Duke of Wellington*, Vol II, London, 1858

Goff, G. L., *Historical Records of the 91st Argyllshire Highlanders*, London, 1891

Goltz, Georg Friedrich Gottlob, *Geschichte des Königlich Preussischen dritten Ulanen-Regiments*, Fürstemwalde, 1841

Gourgaud, Gaspard, *La campagne de dix-huit cent quinze*, Paris, 1818

Granville, Castalia Countess, *Lord Granville Leveson Gower*, London, 1916

Greenhill Gardyne, Lieut.-Col. C., *The Life of a Regiment*, Edinburgh, 1901

Griewank, Karl, *Der Wiener Kongress und die Neuordnung Europas 1814/15*, Leipzig, 1942,

Gronow, R.H., *Reminiscences and Recollections*, London, 1889. New edition London, 1964

Grosser Generalstab, *Das Preussische Heer in den Jahren 1814 und 1815*, Berlin, 1914

Grosser Generalstab, *Das Preussische Heer im Jahre 1812*, Berlin, 1912

Gurwood, John (ed), *Dispatches of Field Marshal The Duke of Wellington*, 12 vols, London, 1837–1839

Hafner, Dietrich, 'Hans Carl Ernst Graf von Zieten', *Militärisches*, Heft I: January 1896, Leipzig

Hamilton, Lieut.-General Sir F. W., *The Origin and History of the First or Grenadier Guards*, Vol III, London, 1874

Hay, Capt. Wm., *Reminiscences 1808–1815 under Wellington*, London, 1901

Henckel von Donnersmarck, Graf, *Erinnerungen aus meinem Leben*, Zerbst, 1846

Hofmann, General von, *Zur Geschichte des Feldzuges von 1815*, Berlin, 1851

Houssaye, Henry, *1815*, 3 vols, Paris, 1914,

Hudleston, F. J., *Warriors in Undress*, London, 1925

Isenbart, Wilhelm, *Geschichte des Herzoglich Nassauischen 2. Regiments*, Berlin, 1891

Jackson, Basil, *Notes and Reminiscences of a Staff Officer*, London, 1903

Jameson, Capt. Robert, *Historical Record of the Seventy-Ninth Regiment of Foot*, Edinburgh & London, 1863

Jennings, Louis J., *The Correspondence and Diaries of John Wilson Croker*, 3 vols, London, 1885

Jonnet, V., 'Das "Constantsche" Tagebuch und die Vorgeschichte der Schlacht bei Belle-Alliance', *Jahrbücher für die deutsche Armee und Marine*, July–December 1908, Berlin

Kincaid, Capt. J., *Adventures in the Rifle Brigade, in the Peninsula, France, and the Netherlands, from 1809 to 1815*, London, 1830. Reprinted London, 1929

Klüber, Johann Ludwig, *Acten des Wiener Congresses in den Jahren 1814 und 1815*,

8 vols, Erlangen, 1815–1819

Klüber, Johann Ludwig, *Übersicht der diplomatischen Verhandlungen des Wiener Congresses*, 3 vols, Frankfurt am Main, 1816

Kolb, Richard, *Unter Nassaus Fahnen*, Wiesbaden, 1904

Kortzfleisch, Gustav von, *Geschichte des Herzoglich Braunschweigischen Infanterie-Regiments*, 2. Band, Brunswick, 1898

Kraatz-Koschlau, M. T. von, *Geschichte des 1. Brandenburgischen Dragoner-Regiments Nr.2*, Berlin, 1878

Kraehe, Enno, 'Wellington and the Reconstruction of the Allied Armies during the Hundred Days', *International Historical Review*, vol XI, No 1, February 1989

Kraehe, Enno, *Metternich's German Policy*, vol II, *The Congress of Vienna 1814–1815*, Princeton, 1983

Leach, *Rough Sketches of the Life of an Old Soldier*, London, 1831

Lee, Albert, *History of the Thirty-third Foot*, London, 1922

Lehmann, Max, 'Zur Geschichte des Jahres 1815', *Historische Zeitschrift*, Munich, 1877

Lettow-Vorbeck, Generalmajor von, *Napoleons Untergang 1815*, Berlin, 1904

Leszczynski, Rudolf von, *50 Jahre Geschichte des Königlich Preussischen 2. Posenschen Infanterie-Regiments Nr. 19*, Luxembourg, 1863

Lewinski & Brauchitsch, *Geschichte des Grenadier-Regiments König Wilhelm I. (2. Westpreussischen) Nr. 7*, Glogau, 1897

Liddell, Col. R. S., *The Memoirs of the Tenth Royal Hussars*, London, 1891

Liddell Hart, Capt. B. H. (ed), *The Letters of Private Wheeler 1809–1828*, London, 1951

Mach, A. von, *Geschichte des Königlich Preussischen Zweiten Infanterie- genannt Königs-Regiments*, Berlin, Posen and Bromberg, 1843

Malet, Col. Harold, *The Historical Memoirs of the XVIIIth Hussars*, London, 1907

Malet, M. Albert, *Louis XVIII et les Cent-Jours à Gand*, Paris, 1902

Mann, Michael, *And They Rode On*, London, 1984

Marker, R. J., *The Record of the Coldstream Guards 1650–1918, Part I 1650–1907*, London, 1923

Maurice, Major-General Sir F., *The History of the Scots Guards*, London, 1934

Maxwell, Rowan, *Life of Wellington*, 2 vols, London, 1899

May, Capt. E. S., R.A., 'A Prussian Gunner's Adventures in 1815', *United Service Magazine*, London, October 1891

Mayer, Hauptmann, *Geschichte des Hamburgischen Contingents*, Hamburg, 1874

McGrigor, Sir James, *Autobiography and Services*, London, 1861,

Moore Smith, G. C., *The Life of John Colborne, Field-Marshal Lord Seaton*, London, 1903

Müller, Dr Paul, 'Wellingtons Schuld an der Niederlage bei Ligny', *Jahrbücher für die deutsche Armee und Marine*, Berlin, 1908

Mueller, Hugo von, *Geschichte des Grenadier-Regiments Prinz Carl von Preussen (2. Brandenburgisches) Nr 12*, Berlin, 1875

Müffling, Freiherr Friedrich Carl Ferdinand von, *Aus meinem Leben*, Berlin, 1851. Translated as *From My Life, together with Memoirs of the Campaign of 1813 and 1814*, London, 1853; reprinted London, 1997

Neff, Wilhelm, *Geschichte des Infanterie-Regiments von Goeben (2.Rheinischen) Nr. 28*, Berlin, 1890

Neumann, Léopold, *Recueil des traités et conventions conclus par l'Autriche*, 5 vols, Leipzig, 1855–1859

Nostitz, Graf von, 'Das Tagebuch des Generals der Kavallerie Grafen von Nostitz'. II. Theil, *Kriegsgeschichtliche Einzelschriften*, Heft 6, Berlin, 1885

Ollech, General von, *Geschichte des Feldzuges von 1815*, Berlin, 1876

Otto, Felix von, *Geschichte des 2. Schlesischen Jäger-Bataillons Nr. 6*, Berlin, 1902

Packe, Edmund, *An Historical Record of the Royal Regiment of Horse Guards*, London, 1847

Paulitzy & Woedtke, *Geschichte des 4. Rheinischen Infanterie-Regiments Nr. 30*, Berlin, 1884

Petersdorff, *General Johann Adolph Freiherr von Thielemann*, Leipzig, 1894)

Pflugk-Harttung, Julius von, *Belle Alliance*, Berlin, 1915

Pflugk-Harttung, Julius von, 'Berichterstattung an Wellington vor der Schlacht bei Ligny', *Historisches Jahrbuch*, XXIV. Band, Munich, 1903

Pflugk-Harttung, Julius von, 'Über die Ausrüstung der Norddeutschen Heere 1815', *Beiheft zum Militär-Wochenblatt*, 8. Heft, Berlin, 1911

Pflugk-Harttung, Julius von, 'Die Aufzeichnungen des Generals Ferdinand von Stosch über Gneisenau', *Beiheft zum Militär-Wochenblatt*, 11. Heft, Berlin, 1910

Pflugk-Harttung, Julius von, 'Die Gegensätze zwischen England und Preussen wegen der Bundestruppen 1815', *Forschungen zur Brandenburgischen und Preussischen Geschichte*, 24. Band, Leipzig, 1911

Pflugk-Harttung, Julius von, *Das Preussische Heer und die Norddeutschen Bundestruppen*, Gotha, 1911

Pflugk-Harttung, Julius von, 'Die Vorgeschichte der Schlacht bei Quatre-Bras', *Neue Militärische Blätter*, 60. Band, Berlin, 1902

Pflugk-Harttung, Julius von, 'Der Verrat im Kriege 1815', *Jahrbücher für die deutsche Armee und Marine*, No. 382, Berlin, July 1903

Pflugk-Harttung, Julius von, 'Die Verhandlung Wellingtons und Blüchers auf der Windmühle bei Brye (16. Juni 1815)', *Historisches Jahrbuch*, XXIII. Band, Munich, 1902

Pflugk-Harttung, Julius von, *Vorgeschichte der Schlacht bei Belle-Alliance. Wellington*, Berlin, 1903

Pflugk-Harttung, Julius von, 'Zu Blüchers Brief an den König von Preussen vom 17. Juni 1815', *Jahrbücher für die deutsche Armee und Marine*, Berlin, 1904

Pflugk-Harttung, Julius von, 'Archivalische Beiträge zur Geschichte des Feldzuges 1815 (16. bis 24. Juni 1815)', *Jahrbücher für die deutsche Armee und Marine*, Berlin, July–December 1906

Pflugk-Harttung, Julius von, 'Die Schlacht bei Ligny', *Die Armee: Zeitschrift der Kriegswissenschaft für Offiziere aller Waffen des stehenden Heeres und des Beurlaubtenstandes*, Nr. 2 + 3, Berlin, 1902.

Plotho, Carl von, *Der Krieg des verbündeten Europa gegen Frankreich im Jahre 1815*, Berlin, 1818

Poten, B. von, 'Des Königs Deutsche Legion 1803 bis 1816', *Beiheft zum Militär-Wochenblatt*, 11. Heft, Berlin 1905

Priesdorff, Kurt von, *Soldatisches Führertum*, Hamburg, no date given

Ravenstein, Heinrich, *Historische Darstellung der wichtigsten Ereignisse des Königlich-Preussischen Zweiten Kürassier-Regiments*, Berlin, Posen & Bromberg, 1827

Reeve, Henry (ed), *The Greville Memoirs*, London, 1874

Renouard, C., *Das Norddeutsche Bundes-Korps im Feldzuge von 1815*, Hanover, 1865

Reuter, E. von, 'Erinnerungen eines Preussischen Artillerieoffiziers aus den Jahren 1798 bis 1815', *Beiheft zum Militär-Wochenblatt*, Berlin, 1890

Robinson, Major-General, 'Waterloo and the De Lancey Memorandum', *Journal of the Royal United Service Institution*, vol LIV, January to June 1910, London

Ropes, John Codman, *The Campaign of Waterloo – A Military History*, New York, 1906.

Rössler, Alfred von, *Geschichte des Königlich Preussischen 1. Nassauischen Infanterie-Regiments Nr. 87*, Berlin, 1882

Rössler, Philip von, *Die Geschichte der Herzoglich Nassauischen Truppen*, Wiesbaden, 1863

Rogers, S., *Historical Record of the Eighty-First Regiment*, Gibraltar, 1872

Sabine, Major-General Edward (ed), *Letters of Colonel Sir Augustus Simon Frazer*, London, 1859

Schirmer, Friedrich, 'Die hannoverschen Neuformationen 1813/15', *Zeitschrift für Heereskunde*, Berlin, 1931

Schirmer, Friedrich, 'Die Landwehr im Rahmen der Armee des Königreichs Hannover (1814/20)', *Zeitschrift für Heereskunde*, Hamburg, 1957

Schreiber, Gustav, *Geschichte des Infanterie-Regiments von Borcke (4. Pommerschen) Nr. 21*, Berlin, 1889

Schwartz, Karl, *Leben des Generals Carl von Clausewitz*, Berlin, 1878

Schwertfeger, Bernhard, *Geschichte der Königlich Deutschen Legion 1803–1816*, 2 vols, Hanover and Leipzig, 1907

Scriba, von, 'Einige allgemeine Bemerkungen über den Feldzug im Jahre 1815 und besonders über die Schlachten von les Quatre Bras und Waterloo', *Internationale Revue über die gesamten Armee und Marine*, Berlin, 1892

Selby, John (ed), *Thomas Morris: the Napoleonic Wars*, London, 1967

Sherwig, John M., *Guineas and Gunpowder*, Cambridge, MA, 1969

Siborne, H. T., *Waterloo Letters*, London, 1891. Reprinted London, 1993

Siborne, Wm., *History of the war in France and Belgium, 1815*, London, 1848. Reprinted London, 1990, 1995

Sichart, A. & R., *Geschichte der Königlich-Hannoverschen Armee*, 5. Band, Hanover & Leipzig, 1898

Sidney, Rev. Edwin, *The Life of Lord Hill*, London, 1845

Smythies, Capt. R. H. Raymond, *Historical Records of the 40th (2nd Somersetshire) Regiment*, Devonport, 1894

Sothen, Hauptmann von, 'Zur Schlacht bei Ligny', *Beiheft zum Militär-Wochenblatt*, 4. Heft, Berlin, 1898

Stafford, Alice Countess of (ed), *Personal Reminiscences of the Duke of Wellington by Francis the first Earl of Ellesmere*, London, 1904

Stanhope, Philip Henry, 5th Earl, *Notes of Conversations with the Duke of Wellington, 1831–1851*, London, 1888

Starklof, R., *Das Leben des Herzogs Bernhard von Sachsen-Weimar*, 2. Band, Gotha, 1866

Stawitzky, E. H. Ludwig, *Geschichte des Königlich Preussischen 25ten Infanterie-Regiments*, Koblenz, 1857

Stephen, Leslie, & Lee, Sidney (eds), *Dictionary of National Biography*, Oxford, 1921–2

Stuckrad, Bruno von, *Geschichte des 1. Madgeburgischen Infanterie-Regiments Nr. 26*, Berlin, 1888

Swiney, Col. G. C., *Historical Records of the 32nd (Cornwall) Light Infantry*, London, 1893

Swinton, J. R., *A Sketch of the Life of Georgiana, Lady de Ros*, London, 1893

Thurn und Taxis, Prinz August von, *Aus drei Feldzügen 1812 bis 1815*, Leipzig, 1912

Tomkinson, W., *The Diary of a Cavalry Officer*, London, 1894. Reprinted London, 1971

Unger, W. von, *Blücher*, 2. Band, Berlin, 1908

Unger, W. von, *Gneisenau*, Berlin, 1914

Vane, Charles Wm., *Correspondence, Despatches and Other Papers of Viscount Castlereagh*, Vol IX & X, London, 1852

Verner, Lieut.-Col. W., *A British Rifle Man*, London, 1899

Vivian, Claud, *First Baron Hussey – A Memoir*, London, 1897

Wachholtz, Freiherr Ludwig von, *Geschichte des Herzoglich Braunschweigschen Armee-Corps*, Brunswick, 1816

Wagner, *Plane der Schlachte und Treffen*, 4. Heft, Berlin, 1825

Ward, Major B. R. (ed), *A Week at Waterloo in 1815*, London, 1906

Webster, C. K. , *British Diplomacy 1813-1815*, London, 1921

Webster, C. K., *The Congress of Vienna 1814-1815*, London, 1918

Webster, Sir Charles, *The Foreign Policy of Castlereagh*, 2 vols, London, 1963

Wedel, Carl Anton Wilhelm Graf von, *Geschichte eines Offiziers*, Berlin, 1897

Wellington, 2nd Duke, *Supplementary Despatches, Correspondence, and Memoranda of Field Marshal Arthur Duke of Wellington*, 16 vols, London, 1857-72

Wellmann, Richard, *Geschichte des Infanterie-Regiments von Horn (3tes Rheinisches) No 29*, Trier, 1894

Weltzien, Karl von (ed), *Memoiren des königlich preussischen Generals der Infanterie Ludwig von Reiche*, 2. Theil, Leipzig, 1857

Wheater, W., *A Record of the Services of the Fifty-First*, London, 1870

Wüppermann, W. E. A., *De vorming van het Nederlandsche Leger*, Breda, 1900

Wylly, Col. H. C., *History of the King's Own Yorkshire Light Infantry*, Vol I, London, 1926

Young, Julian Charles, *A Memoir of Charles Mayne Young*, London, 1871

Zezschwitz, General von, *Aktenmässige Darstellung der königlich preussischen Decimation des seinem Eide treu gebliebenen Sächsischen Heeres im Jahre 1815*, Leipzig & Grimma, 1850

Zychlinski, Franz von, *Geschichte des 24. Infanterie-Regiments*, 1. Theil, Berlin, 1854

Index

Aachen 64, 85, 88, 90, 93, 103, 104, 188, 325, 327
Aberdeen, Earl of 29
Alexander, Czar of Russia 105, 108, 195
Anglo-Dutch-German Army
Staff 138
Contingents
Brunswick 45, 77–80, 109, 121, 210, 212, 229, 243, 294, 299, 300, 302, 304, 336
Hanoverian 74–7, 86, 106, 109, 121, 210, 212, 228, 243, 302, 303
King's German Legion 42, 46, 109, 121, 243, 298, 302, 303
Nassau 42, 44, 45, 46, 47, 48, 80–2, 109, 121, 304, 336
Netherlanders 97, 108
Corps
II Corps 157, 229, 233, 333
Reserve 212, 213, 223, 233, 335, 337
Divisions
1st British 210, 212, 213, 228, 232, 239, 304, 345
2nd British 210, 212, 228, 229, 335
3rd British 210, 212, 213, 228, 232, 239, 243, 288, 299, 300, 301, 304, 345
4th British 210, 212, 213, 228, 337
5th British 197, 198, 210, 212, 213, 215, 216, 223, 228, 232, 234, 292, 304, 336, 338, 346
6th British 213, 228, 229, 335
1st Netherlands 212, 229, 338
2nd Netherlands 126, 200, 208, 210, 217, 224, 229, 338, 346
3rd Netherlands 126, 150, 199, 210, 217, 229, 338
Netherlands Cavalry 125
Brigades
1st British (Guards) 303
5th British 244, 302
8th British 243
2nd KGL 243, 244
1st Hanoverian 243, 244, 301, 303

4th Hanoverian 243, 293
Cavalry Regiments
1st Hussars 209
7th Hussars 228
9th Light Dragoons 208, 215
10th Hussars 197
Infantry Regiments
1st Foot Guards 196
11th Foot 138
30th Foot 303
33rd Foot 303
42nd Highlanders 295, 299
44th Foot 295, 299
69th Foot 303
73rd Foot 20, 303
81st Foot 210
92nd Highlanders 295, 299
95th Rifles 223, 295
Regiment Nassau-Orange 46, 80, 81, 200, 206, 289, 292, 304
1st Nassau Regiment 47, 80, 81, 289
2nd Nassau Infantry Regiment 47, 80, 81, 200, 201, 203, 206, 263, 264, 288, 289, 292, 294, 304
Antwerp 31, 84, 89, 93, 97, 187, 234
Auerstedt, Battle of 21, 24, 55, 61
Avesnes 107, 131, 136, 152, 153, 154, 155, 159, 179

Bachelu, Lt-General 203, 206, 264, 289, 292, 293, 294, 295, 304
Balâtre 248, 253
Bathurst, Lord 88, 104, 343
Beaumont 154, 156, 157, 159, 160, 161, 169, 179
Behr, Major-General 137, 148, 151, 154, 196
Berkeley, Lt-Colonel 196, 199, 210, 212
Bernhard of Saxe-Weimar, Prince 47, 82, 200, 201, 206, 262, 264, 289, 292, 294, 349
Berthezène, Lt-General 257
Blücher von Wahlstadt, Feldmarschall Prince 22, 28, 41, 45, 49, 50, 51, 52,

53, 60, 61, 62, 65, 100, 101, 102, 112, 116, 117, 118, 122, 123, 126, 127, 131, 134, 138, 139, 146, 147, 153, 154, 155, 157, 159, 161, 170, 187, 188, 189, 190, 192, 193, 194, 196, 207, 210, 212, 213, 218, 219, 221, 222, 224, 232, 233, 234, 235, 236, 239, 243, 245, 248, 249, 253, 264, 271, 281, 288, 294, 304, 321, 325, 326, 328, 329, 330, 331, 334, 335, 336, 338, 339, 345, 346, 347, 348, 350, 351

Boignée 248, 253, 257

Bonaparte, Jérôme 77, 154, 155, 170, 289, 292, 294, 300, 304

Bonaparte, Napoleon 27, 29, 37, 39, 49, 51, 61, 77, 84, 85, 86, 87, 89, 90, 91, 92, 93, 94, 96, 98, 103, 104, 106, 107, 108, 112, 113, 116, 122, 124, 125, 135, 136, 140, 141, 146, 149, 151, 152, 153, 154, 156, 157, 159, 160, 161, 165, 168, 172, 182, 189, 192, 196, 198, 209, 216, 234, 242, 255, 257, 264, 321, 331, 333, 344, 345

Borstell, Generallieutenant von 25, 50, 52, 85, 90, 104, 118

Bossu wood 203, 288, 289, 298, 304

Bourmont, Lt-General 170

Boyen, Generalmajor von 61, 69, 89, 119

Braine-le-Comte 95, 97, 113, 123, 125, 137, 156, 192, 195, 196, 199, 206, 207, 213, 215, 216, 217, 228, 232, 243, 244, 245, 288, 333, 335, 336, 337, 339, 345

British Army *see* Anglo-Dutch-German Army

Brockhausen, Carl Christian von 89, 121

Brunswick Corps *see* Anglo-Dutch-German Army, *Contingents*

Brunswick, Friedrich Wilhelm, Duke of 77, 79, 294, 298, 299, 300, 301

Brussels 92, 93, 94, 96, 97, 98, 103, 104, 112, 113, 137, 139, 142, 143, 146, 147, 150, 153, 154, 157, 159, 160, 161, 174, 190, 192, 194, 196, 197, 198, 200, 201, 209, 212, 213, 215, 216, 223, 225, 228, 234, 245,

255, 260, 261, 333, 334, 335, 337, 340

Brye 219, 220, 233, 234, 235, 236, 249, 257, 259, 260, 261, 262, 283, 294, 321, 325, 343, 344, 345, 347

Bülow von Dennewitz, General Graf 25, 31, 62, 100, 102, 187, 188, 189, 190, 218, 219, 220, 248, 325, 330

Bussy windmill 220, 234, 248, 249, 261, 334

Castlereagh, Viscount 19, 29, 30, 31, 32, 33, 36, 41, 42, 103, 104, 105

Cathcart, Viscount 29, 33, 42

Charleroi 109, 118, 127, 131, 142, 143, 146, 149, 155, 156, 160, 161, 164, 165, 168, 169, 174, 176, 182, 186, 188, 189, 190, 194, 197, 199, 200, 203, 206, 213, 215, 216, 217, 218, 235, 243, 249, 257, 263, 288, 292, 294, 295, 298, 299, 304, 332, 333, 334

Chassé, Lt-General Baron de 150, 199, 207, 208, 217, 288

Chaumont, Treaty of 30, 39

Clancarty, Lord 33, 53, 105, 106, 117

Clausewitz, Oberst Carl von 25, 60, 100, 151, 155, 194, 235, 236, 237, 238, 339, 343

Collaert, Lt-General Baron de 125, 148, 150, 154, 207, 208, 217

Congress of Vienna 20, 24, 32, 33, 36, 39, 89

Constant Rebeque, General Baron de 22, 23, 89, 125, 126, 138, 150, 151, 156, 199, 200, 201, 206, 207, 210, 217, 224, 262, 288, 335, 349

D'Erlon, Lt-General 148, 160, 164, 165, 169, 255, 287, 302, 303

De Lancey, Colonel Sir William Howe 19, 138, 153, 228, 229, 232, 335, 336, 337, 341, 342

De Lancey 'Disposition' 228–9, 232, 335–6, 337

Delhutte wood 263, 289

Delort, Lt-General 168, 321

Dennewitz, Battle of 25

Domon, Lt-General 161, 168, 174, 217, 257

Dörnberg, Generalmajor von 52, 77, 95, 119, 137, 140, 142, 146, 148, 149,

150, 151, 152, 153, 154, 156, 157, 159, 192, 195, 210, 212, 215, 224, 225, 229, 232, 233, 234, 237, 238
Duhesme, Lt-General 177

Elba 23, 27, 39, 84
Enghien 192, 196, 210, 213, 225, 229, 335, 336, 337, 345
Erfurt, Siege of 21, 23
Exelmans, Lt-General 255, 305

Feltre, Duc de 147, 152, 193, 197
Fitzroy Somerset, Lt-Colonel 138, 196, 223, 232, 234, 239, 343
Fleurus 21, 115, 116, 118, 119, 174, 176, 179, 180, 185, 186, 188, 189, 198, 199, 206, 217, 218, 237, 255, 257, 261, 262, 304, 305, 333, 345
Fouché, Joseph 136, 332, 333
Foy, Lt-General 289, 292, 299, 300
Franz I, Emperor of Austria 28
Frasnes 190, 192, 200, 201, 203, 210, 217, 225, 232, 237, 264
'Frasnes Letter' 232–3, 336–41, 346
French Army
  Composition of 99
  Imperial Guard 125, 141, 147, 149, 151, 153, 154, 160, 161, 164, 165, 168, 172, 177, 183, 184, 189, 192, 198, 201, 203, 206, 217, 255, 264, 279, 287, 289, 321, 323
  Reserve Cavalry 160, 168, 217
  Army Corps
  I Corps 156, 160, 164, 165, 168, 189, 255, 302
  II Corps 154, 160, 164, 165, 168, 170, 179, 217, 255, 302
  III Corps 151, 160, 161, 164, 165, 168, 217, 255, 257, 261, 264, 344
  IV Corps 151, 160, 161, 168, 218, 255, 257, 304, 305, 344
  VI Corps 160, 164, 168, 217, 255
  Cavalry Corps
  1st Cavalry Corps 161, 174, 176, 218, 305
  2nd Cavalry Corps 182, 218, 305
  3rd Cavalry Corps 218
  4th Cavalry Corps 165, 218
  Divisions
  see name of commander

Friedrich August, King of Saxony 48, 49, 51, 54, 55
Friedrich Wilhelm III, King of Prussia 28, 56, 60, 87, 91, 99, 100, 101, 120, 191

Gembloux 189, 219, 221, 255, 325, 326, 327, 347
Gemioncourt 203, 206, 263, 288, 292, 293, 298, 304
Genappe 82, 198, 200, 201, 223, 229, 243, 326, 335
Gérard, Lt-General 160, 165, 168, 170, 255, 257
German Army
  III Federal Army Corps 25, 90
  V Federal Army Corps 46, 47, 48
  North German Federal Army Corps 46, 49, 50, 102, 151, 154
German Legion (formerly Russo-German Legion) 59, 65, 68, 74
Ghigny, Major-General Baron de 125, 200
Gillhausen, Kapitain von 135, 170, 171, 177, 178, 179, 323
Gilly 176, 180, 182, 185, 217
Girard, Lt-General 179, 217, 255, 257, 261, 264, 265, 269
Gneisenau, Generallieutenant Graf Neidhardt von 21, 23, 28, 49, 54, 60, 61, 62, 84, 100, 102, 103, 104, 105, 107, 113, 117, 119, 120, 121, 137, 138, 151, 152, 156, 157, 159, 187, 188, 218, 219, 220, 221, 234, 235, 236, 237, 326, 328, 329, 331, 344, 347, 350, 351
Gosselies 172, 176, 177, 178, 179, 182, 199, 217, 236, 237, 289
Grand Pierrepont 206, 262, 263
Grant, Lt-Colonel Colquhoun 138
Grolman, General Carl von 24, 51, 60, 62, 65, 100, 139, 188, 221, 235, 237, 238, 328, 329, 331, 343
Grossgörschen, Battle of 24, 61
Grouchy, Marshal 154, 164, 169, 182, 217, 255, 304, 344

Habert, Lt-General 257
Hannut 187, 188, 189, 198, 218, 220, 221, 260

Hanseatic Contingent 82–3
Hardenberg, Prince 28, 31, 32, 33, 36, 53, 56, 89, 117
Hardinge, Lt-Colonel Sir Henry 19, 104, 120, 122, 138, 142, 146, 148, 151, 157, 235, 239, 242, 343
Henckel von Donnersmarck, Generalmajor Graf 99, 312
Hill, Lt-General Lord 98, 156, 212, 232, 233, 333, 335, 336, 339
Hofmann, Oberst von 127, 173, 174
Hulot, Lt-General 257, 306

Jackson, Lt. Basil 194
Jagow, Generalmajor von 90, 176, 185, 313, 323
Jena, Battle of 21, 25, 48, 55, 160
Jérôme see Bonaparte, Jérôme
Jürgass, Generalmajor von Wahlen-271, 283, 286, 287

Kalckreuth, Feldmarschall von 100, 101
Kellermann, Lt-General 255, 289, 303
KGL see Anglo-Dutch-German Army, Contingents, King's German Legion
King's German Legion see Anglo-Dutch-German Army, Contingents
Kleist von Nollendorf, General Graf 39, 40, 47, 55, 57, 58, 62, 69, 84, 85, 86, 88, 89, 90, 91, 92, 93, 95, 96, 98, 99, 100, 101, 102, 151, 154
Knesebeck, Generallieutenant von der 33, 40, 42, 43, 91, 100, 101, 151
Kolberg, Siege of 21, 23

Lefebvre-Desnoëttes, Lt-General 177, 203, 255, 264, 289
Lefol, Lt-General 257, 265, 271
Leipzig, Battle of 27, 28, 47, 49, 50, 61
Liège 19, 50, 51, 64, 82, 85, 88, 89, 91, 96, 104, 117, 218, 219, 325, 327, 347
Ligne Brook 187, 220, 239, 259, 262
Ligny 64, 161, 185, 215, 220, 239, 248, 249, 253, 257, 259, 260, 262, 264, 271, 287, 303, 304–25, 336, 339, 341, 343, 344

Lille 89, 90, 91, 93, 94, 112, 137, 146, 151, 152, 156
Lobau, Lt-General 160, 164, 168, 255
Louis XVIII, King of France 87, 88, 89, 90, 92, 192, 332, 333
Lowe, Sir Hudson 84, 88, 92, 93, 94, 97, 98, 341
Lützow, Oberstlieutenant von 130, 176, 180, 257, 321
Lützow's Freikorps 59, 67, 83, 178
Luxembourg 32, 85, 87, 88, 89, 101, 107

Mainz 32, 33, 39, 43, 44, 46, 47, 87, 101
Marschall, Freiherr von 40, 44, 47
Maubeuge 125, 126, 127, 137, 143, 146, 147, 149, 151, 152, 153, 154, 155, 156, 157, 164
Maurin, Lt-General 257
Mellery 326, 328, 329
Merlen, Major-General Baron van 125, 137, 154, 155, 156, 157, 159, 195, 196, 199, 200, 292
Metternich, Prince 28, 29, 33, 36, 54, 332
Milhaud, Lt-General 255, 321
Mons 52, 72, 83, 87, 93, 109, 112, 113, 125, 137, 140, 141, 146, 149, 156, 157, 161, 164, 195, 196, 198, 199, 215, 234, 242, 288, 333
Mont St Jean 207, 224, 248, 345
Müffling, Generalmajor von 54, 90, 91, 92, 95, 96, 97, 121, 122, 137, 140, 141, 146, 149, 157, 192, 193, 195, 196, 197, 198, 199, 212, 213, 215, 223, 232, 233, 234, 237, 238, 334, 335, 338, 344, 346, 347
Münster, Graf 28, 32, 33, 45, 56

Namur 51, 82, 87, 93, 94, 97, 103, 116, 117, 118, 119, 123, 131, 139, 143, 147, 148, 152, 154, 155, 157, 160, 165, 172, 187, 188, 196, 197, 198, 206, 218, 220, 225, 235, 248, 249, 261, 293, 325, 347
Napoleon see Bonaparte, Napoleon
Nassau Contingent see Anglo-Dutch-German Army, Contingents

Ney, Marshal 255, 292, 299, 302, 344
Nivelles 82, 95, 97, 109, 112, 123,
  126, 159, 192, 193, 200, 201, 207,
  208, 212, 213, 215, 216, 217, 224,
  225, 228, 232, 236, 243, 244, 262,
  288, 293, 301, 325, 333, 334, 345, 350
Nostitz, Graf von 54, 62, 117, 221,
  233, 235, 238, 321, 325, 328

Orange, Prince of 21, 31, 32, 48, 72,
  84, 85, 88, 89, 91, 92, 93, 95, 96, 97,
  98, 105, 112, 113, 117, 137, 147, 148,
  150, 152, 154, 156, 157, 195, 196,
  200, 207, 209, 210, 212, 215, 216,
  224, 225, 232, 236, 264, 288, 292,
  293, 294, 304, 335, 345, 348
Ostend 98

Pajol, Lt-General 161, 165, 168, 169,
  174, 176, 305
Paris, Peace of 30
Pêcheux, Lt-General 257, 306
Perponcher-Sedlnitzky, Lt-General
  48, 82, 150, 179, 200, 206, 207, 208,
  217, 223, 263
Picton, Lt-General Sir Thomas 197,
  215, 216, 223, 243, 298, 336, 345
Pirch I, Generalmajor von 25, 99, 118,
  219, 260, 261, 281, 286
Pirch II, Generalmajor von 126, 127,
  171, 172, 173, 180, 182, 185, 271, 283
Piré, Lt-General 217, 289, 292, 299,
  300
Pireaumont 263, 288, 289, 294, 299,
  301, 302
Plancenoit 25
Prince of Orange see Orange, Prince
  of
Prussian Army
  Cavalry 64
  Landwehr 59, 64, 66, 67
  1812 Reglement 65, 66, 77
  General Staff 62–3
  Army of the Lower Rhine 63, 102,
    103, 155
  Army Corps
    I Army Corps 24, 63, 64, 85, 115,
      116, 118, 126, 127, 134, 142, 176,
      186, 187, 188, 190, 218, 220, 238,
      255, 259, 261, 273, 307, 321, 325,
      327, 329, 346, 347, 351
    II Army Corps 25, 50, 52, 63, 64,
      85, 90, 118, 153, 155, 187, 188,
      189, 190, 198, 218, 219, 220, 238,
      260, 261, 262, 271, 325, 327, 329,
      346
    III Army Corps 50, 52, 63, 64, 65,
      85, 90, 118, 119, 151, 153, 187,
      188, 190, 198, 218, 219, 220,
      235, 238, 249, 253, 262, 271,
      287, 305, 313, 325, 326, 327,
      329, 346
    IV Army Corps 63, 64, 118, 119,
      187, 188, 190, 198, 218, 220, 221,
      222, 234, 238, 325, 329, 341, 350
    V Army Corps 63
    VI Army Corps 63
    VII Army Corps (Reserve Corps)
      63
  Brigades
    1st Brigade 115, 116, 118, 126, 127,
      129, 131, 132, 170, 171, 173, 176,
      177, 179, 182, 185, 186, 220, 259,
      270, 271, 306, 317, 327
    2nd Brigade 67, 115, 116, 118, 126,
      130, 134, 170, 171, 172, 176, 177,
      180, 182, 185, 186, 196, 199, 200,
      259, 260, 271, 273, 274, 286, 287,
      306
    3rd Brigade 115, 127, 170, 176,
      185, 186, 220, 259, 264, 269, 271,
      306, 327
    4th Brigade 115, 170, 186, 220,
      260, 305, 317
    5th Brigade 261, 271, 273, 274,
      275, 278, 279, 286
    6th Brigade 261, 262, 309, 313
    7th Brigade 91, 261, 271, 274, 286
    8th Brigade 218, 261, 262, 287,
      309, 313, 317
    9th Brigade 262, 318
    10th Brigade 262, 317
    11th Brigade 262, 305, 317
    12th Brigade 262, 271, 313, 319,
      323
  Infantry Regiments
    2nd Regiment 67, 261, 274, 275,
      278, 279, 283, 285

6th Regiment (1st West Prussian) 67, 131, 134, 172, 173, 180, 182, 183, 185, 259, 271, 273, 279

7th Regiment (2nd West Prussian) 67, 185, 186, 260, 309, 311, 312, 313

8th Regiment (Life) 67, 319

9th Regiment 67, 283, 312, 321, 327

12th Regiment (2nd Brandenburg) 67, 132, 178, 179, 259, 269, 270

14th Regiment 67, 286, 287

19th Regiment 67, 170, 260, 305, 306, 307, 308, 309, 312, 313, 317

21st Regiment 67, 313, 315, 317, 321

22nd Regiment 67, 218, 286

23rd Regiment 67, 287, 313, 315, 317, 323

24th Regiment 67, 134, 259, 269, 270, 271, 273

25th Regiment 67, 218, 261, 274, 275, 278, 279, 283, 285, 286

26th Regiment 67, 68, 283

27th Regiment 67, 68

28th Regiment 67, 134, 170, 172, 174, 180, 182, 183, 184, 186, 271, 273, 279

29th Regiment 67, 176, 177, 178, 185, 260, 264, 265, 269, 270, 271, 309, 311

30th Regiment 67, 319

31st Regiment 67, 68, 312

Silesian Schützen 130, 134, 179, 185, 259, 260

Landwehr Infantry Regiments

1st Elbe Landwehr Infantry 312

2nd Elbe Landwehr Infantry 286

3rd Elbe Landwehr Infantry 287, 317

1st Kurmark Landwehr Infantry 319

3rd Kurmark Landwehr Infantry 318

4th Kurmark Landwehr Infantry 305, 318

5th Kurmark Landwehr Infantry 319

6th Kurmark Landwehr Infantry 319, 323

1st Westphalian Landwehr Infantry 134, 169, 171, 174, 178, 259, 270, 323

2nd Westphalian Landwehr Infantry 134, 170, 172, 180, 185, 260, 271, 273, 281

3rd Westphalian Landwehr Infantry 260, 265, 270, 271, 313, 323

4th Westphalian Landwehr Infantry 260, 305, 313

5th Westphalian Landwehr Infantry 261, 274, 275, 278, 283, 285

Cavalry Regiments

1st Dragoons (Queen's) 281, 323

2nd Dragoons (1st West Prussian) 134, 172, 184, 321

5th Dragoons (Brandenburg) 185, 281, 323

6th Dragoons (Neumark) 155, 271

7th Dragoons 318

3rd Hussars (Brandenburg) 271, 287

4th Hussars (1st Silesian) 129, 132, 178, 179, 180, 224, 259, 260, 263

5th Hussars (Pomeranian) 218, 271, 327

11th Hussars 285

2nd Uhlans (Silesian) 189, 285

3rd Uhlans (Brandenburg) 274, 281

6th Uhlans 68, 176, 177, 178, 180, 257, 321

7th Uhlans 271, 287

8th Uhlans 271, 287

Landwehr Cavalry Regiments

1st Kurmark Landwehr Cavalry 274, 281

2nd Kurmark Landwehr Cavalry 321

3rd Kurmark Landwehr Cavalry 305

4th Kurmark Landwehr Cavalry 323

5th Kurmark Landwehr Cavalry 285, 287, 319

6th Kurmark Landwehr Cavalry 319, 323

Westphalian Landwehr Cavalry Regiment 180

Artillery batteries
  12-pounder Battery No. 6 238
  12-pounder Battery No. 7 318
  12-pounder Battery No. 12 319
  Foot Battery No. 3 134
  Foot Battery No. 7 130, 134, 259,
    269, 270
  Foot Battery No. 8 309
  Foot Battery No. 10 261, 278
  Foot Battery No. 12 323
  Foot Battery No. 34 327
  Foot Battery No. 37 286
  Horse Battery No. 2 185
  Horse Battery No. 5 286
  Horse Battery No. 7 130, 134, 180,
    259
  Horse Battery No. 19 318
Prusso-Hessian Treaty of 4 May 1815
  58

Quatre Bras 22, 48, 82, 109, 123, 159,
  179, 192, 200, 201, 203, 207, 208,
  212, 213, 215, 216, 217, 221, 223,
  224, 229, 232, 233, 234, 236, 237,
  239, 242, 243, 244, 245, 248, 253,
  255, 257, 261, 262–4, 287–304, 329,
  330, 334, 337, 338, 341, 343, 344,
  345, 346, 349, 351

Rebeque *see* Constant Rebeque
Reiche, Oberstlieutenant von 187,
  218, 235, 236, 237, 238, 325, 326, 328
Reille, Lt-General 148, 153, 155, 160,
  164, 165, 168, 169, 255, 302
Richmond, Duchess of, Ball given by
  215, 216, 340
Roeder, Generalmajor von 91, 92, 93,
  95, 103, 176, 185
Russo-German Legion *see* German
  Legion
Ryssel, General 50, 51

Sambre River 107, 130, 154, 156, 160,
  165, 168, 169, 171, 172, 174, 185,
  190, 196, 197, 212
Saxon Contingent 44, 48, 52, 109, 117
Saxony 36, 37, 101, 350
Scharnhorst 60, 61
Schwarzenberg, Prince 40, 42, 87,
  107, 108, 123, 189

Scovell, Lt-Colonel 138, 194, 341, 342
Soignes, Forest of 223, 243
Sombreffe 123, 187, 188, 190, 191,
  195, 196, 198, 213, 216, 218, 219,
  220, 221, 234, 239, 248, 249, 255,
  257, 260, 261, 262, 264, 304, 323,
  325, 326, 333, 346
Somerset *see* Fitzroy Somerset
Soult, Marshal 153, 157, 161, 344
St Amand 179, 180, 220, 235, 239,
  248, 249, 253, 257, 259, 260, 261,
  262, 264–74, 279–87, 304, 306, 308,
  327
Stein, Baron vom 61
Steinmetz, Generalmajor von 90, 126,
  131, 132, 134, 137, 154, 155, 159,
  171, 172, 173, 174, 178, 179, 182,
  185, 195, 199, 219, 259, 269, 271, 328
Stewart, Lt-General Lord Charles 19,
  29, 33, 45, 100, 108, 138, 189
Stuart, Sir Charles 86, 89, 95, 104

Talleyrand, Prince 33, 36
Thielemann, Generallieutenant von
  49, 50, 104, 153, 219, 262, 326
Thümen, Oberst von 262, 283
Thurn und Taxis, Prince August 235,
  236, 237, 238, 329
Tilly, Retreat to 325–30, 347
Tirlemont, Conference of 52, 54, 79,
  116, 117, 127, 161, 189, 190, 333, 343
Tombe de Ligny 186
Tongrenelle 253
Tongrinne 248, 253, 262
Treaty of 3 January 1815 104
Trip, Major-General Baron 125, 150

Uxbridge, Lt-General Lord 114, 154,
  210, 212, 225, 228, 304, 335, 345

Vandamme, Lt-General 148, 151,
  155, 160, 161, 164, 165, 168, 169,
  182, 257, 261, 265, 346
Vendée, uprising 122, 142, 146, 147,
  148, 150, 192
Vichery, Lt-General 257, 306, 311
Vienna, Congress of *see* Congress of
  Vienna
Vivian, Sir Hussey 209

Wagnée 177
Wagnelée 249, 259, 261, 262, 274–9, 286
War of the Bavarian Succession, 1778–9 25
Wars of Liberation, 1813–15 23, 24, 25, 27, 49, 59, 64, 100
Waterloo 194, 216, 217, 223, 224, 228, 248, 321, 336, 337, 341, 344
Wavre 255, 325, 326, 327, 329, 347
Webster, Lt. 208, 215, 216, 217
Wellesley, Arthur see Wellington, Duke of
Wellington, Duke of 19, 20, 23, 31, 33, 36, 40, 41, 42, 45, 46, 47, 48, 51, 52, 53, 54, 57, 58, 71, 77, 79, 80, 82, 83, 93, 94, 98, 100, 102, 103, 104, 105, 106, 107, 108, 109, 112, 113, 116, 117, 118, 120, 121, 122, 123, 126, 127, 134, 136, 137, 138, 139, 140, 142, 143, 146, 147, 148, 150, 151, 152, 153, 154, 156, 157, 159, 161, 187, 189, 190, 192, 193, 194, 195, 197, 199, 200, 207, 209, 210, 212, 213, 215, 216, 217, 221, 222, 223, 224, 225, 229, 232, 233, 234, 235, 236, 237, 238, 239, 242, 243, 245, 248, 253, 257, 261, 262, 264, 287, 288, 294, 295, 298, 299, 301, 304, 326, 329, 330, 331, 332, 333, 334, 335, 336, 337, 338, 339, 340, 342, 343, 344, 346, 347, 348, 349, 350, 351

Westphalia 36, 55, 68, 74, 77, 79, 86, 327
Wilhelm, Kurfürst of Hessen-Kassel 55, 56, 57, 58, 119
Willem I, King of the United Netherlands (formerly the Prince Sovereign) 20, 23, 46, 84, 88, 94, 95, 96, 98, 120, 121, 123

Yorck, General von 62, 100

Zastrow, Generallieutenant von 56, 57, 58, 200, 201, 203, 206
Zezschwitz, Oberst von 50, 52, 54
Zieten, Generalmajor von 85, 89, 90, 91, 96, 97, 99, 103, 104, 109, 112, 115, 116, 117, 118, 127, 131, 134, 137, 142, 143, 146, 148, 149, 151, 152, 154, 155, 157, 159, 161, 169, 170, 171, 172, 173, 182, 183, 185, 186, 187, 188, 190, 192, 193, 194, 196, 197, 198, 206, 209, 212, 219, 220, 221, 244, 255, 259, 261, 325, 332, 333, 334, 342, 343, 347